# A TRIBE APART

# A
# TRIBE
# APART

### A JOURNEY INTO THE HEART OF AMERICAN ADOLESCENCE

## PATRICIA HERSCH

FAWCETT COLUMBINE
*The Ballantine Publishing Group • New York*

http://www.randomhouse.com

Library of Congress Cataloging-in-Publication Data
Hersch, Patricia.
    A tribe apart : a journey into the heart of American adolescence /
Patricia Hersch.—1st ed.
        p.   cm.
    ISBN 0-449-90767-8 (alk. paper)
    1. Teenagers—United States.   I. Title.
HQ796.H43   1998                                                   97-42945
305.235'0973—dc21

Designed by Ruth Kolbert

Manufactured in the United States of America

First Edition: April 1998
10  9  8  7  6  5  4  3  2  1

For Jay, my partner in making dreams come true.

# CONTENTS

PART III
## MAKING SENSE

# A TRIBE APART

# *Alone*

*T*he figure of his mom in the doorway of their townhouse fades in the rearview mirror as seventeen-year-old Jonathan Tompkins pulls out of the parking lot in his Volkswagen Rabbit. He tries to erase from his mind the image of the worry in her eyes as she hugged him goodbye, still clutching one of the two loaves of his favorite raisin-walnut bread she had purchased fresh that morning. At first he was annoyed with her for offering the bread at all. He is supposed to be fasting the next several days. But she was just trying to be a good mom. He is glad he compromised and took one loaf. He is going on a Vision Quest, a solitary four-day rite of passage.

The idea of going on a Vision Quest began to blossom last winter when his mom gave him **The Vision,** *by Tom Brown Jr., a book describing the Native American learnings and self-knowledge Brown gained on his own solitary forays into the wilderness. The book resonated inside Jonathan. Since the summer after eighth grade, when he spent a month backpacking in the Bighorn wilderness with the National Outdoor Leadership School in Wyoming, Jonathan had sought refuge in the outdoors. To Jonathan, the wilderness is less scary than the halls of his high school. In the wilderness, the challenges are clear. You survive by knowledge of nature and your wits. In high school, the rules of the game are always changing and reality is a slippery slope.*

*The hour-and-a-half drive from his home in Reston, Virginia, to the George Washington National Forest is a familiar one. Usually he feels tension melt away as he travels through the rich farmland and old homes steeped in Civil War history just beyond Reston. But today he is nervous. He struggles to maintain his determination. In the space of twenty-four hours he's gone from day camp counselor leading ten-year-olds in song to lonely spiritual wanderer, from a regular seventeen-year-old suburban teen who loves to hang out with his friends, go kayaking, and listen to Grateful Dead albums to an initiate upon an ancient pathway to manhood. He reminds himself this is his choice.*

*When he gets to the forest, he pulls his car into the tiny parking area at the base of the trail. "As I closed the car door it was the strangest feeling," Jonathan recalls. "I looked at the car door and knew in four days I'd be back after sitting in the woods by myself, and it would be the same 1984 Volkswagen Rabbit but I might be different."*

*He gathers his belongings, takes a deep breath, and walks around the gate that marks the footpath heading north toward Signal Knob. The path is narrow and rocky, and it winds upward along the edge of the mountain. The summer has been dry, and dust blows around him with every step.*

*As the late afternoon sun casts dancing shadows through the trees, the cicadas burst into song. Their constant whir is the only sound besides his footsteps as he hikes toward his destination. He passes no other hikers along the way.*

*Aware that the days are already getting shorter, he picks up his pace in order to set up camp before dark. Where has summer gone? he wonders. On this late August day, the earth whispers of the change of seasons.*

*His senior year. He can hardly believe it. The last year at home. It is scary and exciting. Mostly it is agitating. There is so much pressure building as the school year approaches. It's like the last chance to get things right.*

*After approximately two miles, Jonathan comes to an area of low green grasses that offers a clear view of Signal Knob. He decides to turn off the marked trail and go directly up the mountain. A sudden charge of confidence surges in him as he leaves the dirt path and starts his trek through the grass. He remembers how, at day camp, the other counselors affectionately nicknamed him "Mancub" or "Mowgli" from the movie* Jungle Book. *He is Mancub darting through the grasses. He is Mancub, king of the mountains, friend of all living things.*

*The grasses give way to brush, and after a while boulders replace the brush. Playfulness is overcome by the challenge of the terrain. Jonathan works his way dexterously up the rocky ledges, gripping tightly with his fingers and camping boots to protect his uncovered legs. The concentration required takes his mind off everything until he reaches the crest, about three quarters of a mile from the trail. At 2,220 feet, the top of the mountain, dotted with chestnut oaks and mountain laurel, offers a spectacular view of the Shenandoah Valley, a long ribbon of lush green farmland edged by the Allegheny Mountains on the far side. But he doesn't notice. It is 7 P.M., and Jonathan Tompkins is scared and lonely.*

*Keep busy, he tells himself. He goes about the tasks of establishing a campsite. He sets up his tent along the ridge; he will leave it standing during his Vision Quest as an emergency retreat. He unpacks his supplies and collects firewood. After he builds a fire, he cooks a "lousy meal of gummy pasta and lumpy cheese" and drinks his first quart of water. He thinks it unfortunate that he can't provide a decent final meal for himself. It's only 8:30 and he wishes like hell that he were tired. Eager to soothe himself, he reaches for his native drum, holds it between his knees, and begins with a soft stroke across the top, a hard hit or two, and then, with eyes closed, lets the rhythm develop.*

*In his crowd of friends, native drumming had caught on during the past spring. His buddy Bill carried a drum in his car and Jonathan got hooked playing it along with Grateful Dead tapes while they drove. Then Alan and Joan bought theirs, and they'd all gather in the local park and improvise rhythms. Sometimes they'd read their own poetry to the beat. Jonathan loved his drum, which he'd purchased during the summer. He kept it on the coffee table in his living room at home and often, when he was alone, he would beat his drum and find himself expressing feelings in rhythm and song that he'd have had trouble speaking directly.*

*Finally, exhausted from the physical and mental stress of the day,* he spreads his blanket and stretches out his six-foot frame, resting his head on folded arms. Inhaling the sweet smell of wild berries, gazing at a sky filled with stars, he knows it is right to be here. In minutes, he falls asleep.

Up early the next morning, his first thought is, Okay, get your stuff. Let's go do this thing. He skips breakfast as a way of officially beginning his Vision Quest and does a quick search for a secluded site. The idea is simple: the place must be enclosed to discourage looking around and to force looking inward. In five minutes he sees a location that will work. A big dead tree had fallen over, its weathered limbs creating a tangled enclave obscuring the surrounding area. Jonathan works his way inside among the rotting branches and finds a spot where he can sit. He spreads out his blanket and places the remaining gallon of water beside it. Within arm's reach, he stacks his clothes, his bread, and his drum. Then he sits down on the blanket thinking he is filled with all the wrong feelings: instead of peacefulness he feels himself hateful, restless, and trapped. Maybe this is a terrible idea. Maybe he should go backpacking instead.

He hears some noise in the bushes that captures his attention. Four small brown-and-white chickadees fly out and perch on one of the dead branches about ten feet from where he sits. They come closer and look at him. "I'm thinking, maybe I don't ever want to leave here because the birds are part of this place and now I am part of this place too."

That feeling lasts about ten minutes. The birds fly away and the day drags on endlessly. He rails at the sun's intensity. He watches ants walk across his legs. He hates ants. But he can't kill them. He's supposed to be communing with nature and must respect all creatures of the earth as one. The flies buzzing around his head are maddening. For fourteen hours, he squirms and shifts his position a million times. This first day, Jonathan is aware only of the interminable march of time and his own incredible boredom and discomfort. The feel of the rocks under his slim body—how they jut and poke and irritate. The stupefying heat. The biggest moment of the day is at sunset when he decides to eat a quarter of the bread.

He's not sure what makes the difference, the small amount of food or the coming repose of night, but suddenly his mood improves. He gets a "great feeling of everything being fine: everything being wonderful." Brown, in his book, writes about having faith in the process, in the supernatural, in creation and in yourself. Jonathan feels a pang of inadequacy. He certainly does not have a grasp of complete faith. He is an unsure visitor in every domain of his life. But if he waits, maybe if he just waits, the answers, the feelings will come. When darkness at last descends, and the stars once again fill the sky, he feels soothed. The first day is ending and he has survived. He smiles and plays his drum and sings about his friends and about the world he has left behind.

The morning of the second day, he wakes up to the sound of the birds. He decides to take the second quarter of bread and slice it in half and have one piece for breakfast and one for dinner. Leaning back awkwardly against the branches, he tries to eat slowly even though he is ravenously hungry. He sips the warm water from his jug carefully, remembering that he must conserve enough for three days. The same chickadees land on the branch before him as he eats. He swears they are checking him out.

He runs his hand along the smooth bark of the dead tree. He feels the rocks hitting his thighs below, the radiant energy of the sun unrelenting in a cloudless sky. He hears the gentle swoosh of a light breeze, a symphony of chirping birds, the buzzing of flies, his own breath. He feels discomfort through every fiber of his being. He isn't a good enough friend. He is too hung up on his own insecurities and doesn't pay enough attention to the unspoken feelings of his friends. He doesn't show them how important they are to him. It's his senior year and he will be leaving Andy, Alan, Bill, and Joan. They will scatter and it will never be the same. And, oh God, the worst of all, only one more year at home with his parents. The pain is so great he moans aloud and literally writhes in agony, facing this fact fully for the first time.

He thinks of the years he has wasted with his mom and dad. "When you're in seventh, eighth, ninth, even tenth grade, you don't want to be seen with your parents, and I thought about how horrible that must have been. I kept seeing their faces and thinking of all the mean things I've done to them. Like my mom is taking courses at Georgetown, and she got accepted into the honors program last year. I acted like it was no big deal. I didn't acknowledge it was special for her when she was so proud of herself. I could have been nicer." He considers how fragile everything is with his parents and with life in general, "how delicate the balance is for what makes us happy, what we all hang on to, what keeps us going."

The call of a bird brings him back. Then the quiet. It is so still in nature. Nothing seems to be happening and yet everything is happening. Never has Jonathan felt so grateful for the coming of night and the peace of sleep.

It is fear he wakes up with at daybreak on the third day. Fear of the pain he felt the day before, fear of not being able to change things with his parents, and his friends. Fear of having spent forty-eight hours in total isolation and achieving none of the light of understanding he craves. As he slowly nibbles his ration of bread, he thinks about leaving. "Each day I thought maybe I should leave to-day because of some reason. But I was reluctant to leave before the four days because I was afraid that if some kind of process was happening to me, what if I stopped it halfway?"

The third day is as interminable as the previous two. Hour after hour, he squirms and shifts his position. He feels parched and light-headed, alternately starved and sick to his stomach. He goes over and over all the things he has done wrong in his life. Again and again he berates himself for not being more sensitive to those he cares about. But on the third night, something amazing happens. The shroud of pain and failure engulfing him lifts with the rising of the stars. This is what he has been waiting for: a flash of insight coming from his heart and spreading like a healing balm on his burdened soul.

Self-knowledge. Awareness. Empathy for the lives of those around him. Belief in his capacity to change. These are the bounty of the third night. He is more aware of his role in the lives of his parents and friends. He will be more sensitive. He cringes with remorse remembering how his mom wanted to go to the circus last year and his immediate reaction had been, " 'Give me a break.' I think I was afraid we would look funny, the two of us." He vows to improve. He picks up his drum and sings songs of hope and love to those people he misses so much. He sings of how he will return soon, a better person.

When he awakens the fourth morning, he knows he has slept late because the sun is already high in the sky. Thank goodness it is his *last day. Actually, he still isn't sure about this. He has counted about a hundred times trying to figure out the earliest he can leave. He thinks maybe four sunrises and four sunsets equals four days, but in the end decides that the fifth sunrise marks the end of four full twenty-four-hour days.*

*This final day he tries to concentrate on eking out the last bit of wisdom so he can return home strong and confident. But it is hard. He mostly lies around. He is scared that his parents are getting old and will be dying soon and that he has not been a good enough son. He is worried that he will get back and be unable to keep his resolve.*

*The fifth morning greets him with brilliant blue skies, a day when the earth sparkles. He swears it is one of the most beautiful days he has ever seen. But the elation he feels is masked by the utter fatigue and weakness of his body. He gathers his belongings, takes the last sips of water berating himself for not bringing enough to keep himself hydrated, and works his way through the maze of branches. He loads his backpack and goes to gather up his tent. He pauses to take one last look at the tangled tree, which now holds his secrets. Then he trudges out. At the juncture of the trail, the level ground is a welcome sight. He straightens up and begins to realize that he actually accomplished what he set out to do, that maybe it really was some-thing for a regular kid like himself to have spent these days alone in contemplation.*

*Venturing out on his own, sustained by a single loaf of bread, Jonathan Tompkins came down from the mountain different in ways he would not yet understand. When he got home, he never shared the details of his journey into the wilderness and into himself with his friends or his family. There was no time to process the experience. He left the next morning with his mom to look at colleges. School started a few days after he returned. One thing changed for certain: when the Big Apple Circus came to Reston that October, Jonathan Tompkins took his mom.*

# INTRODUCTION

I t is 6:40 in the morning, dark and cold. As I run through the well-manicured streets of Reston, Virginia, the town is awakening. I pass a street where a school bus is parked, its engine running to warm it. Although it doesn't leave for a few minutes, the kids are beginning to gather. Like a yellow clubhouse on wheels, the bus beckons with its warm, lit interior. The youngsters walk singly and in pairs, some speaking softly, but mostly they are quiet, the haze of sleep marking their slow, plodding steps. Although I am acquainted with many of the neighborhood kids, I can't make out their faces in the lingering darkness of this early October morning. Darkness descends so quickly in fall, shrouding these teens, one month into the school year, in a blanket of anonymity. Out here Jonathan Tompkins is just another vague presence, not the vital and passionate outdoorsman or the generous son. Out here the vivacious cheerleader, the class clown, the depressed freshman, the worried senior are hidden from view, part of an anonymous gaggle of teens, their rumble of low voices and soft giggles creating an undertone to the beginning of the day. They stand in shadows as I run past, small groups on corners, looking like statues forming a tableau of adolescence outlined by the slowly rising sun. The scene is the same on street corners all across this suburban community outside of Washington, D.C. The gathering of schoolchildren starts with those headed for the high school and the middle school, to be repeated later as the buses retrace their routes to pick up the elementary school kids. Soon the schools will fill up and the neighborhoods will empty out, people sorted and shifted from place to place, reordering the community from one of families to a culture of children.

All over the country the pattern is the same, the gathering up of young people, the leaving of adults to separate worlds, not to be brought together again until evening. Briefcases, diaper bags, and backpacks, the totems of modern society, are lined up ready to grab as family members dash outside with a fleeting hope that they are adequately prepared for the day. Front doors open and shut, families disperse, rush, rush, rushing to get going, to get there—wherever—on time. Nobody stands at the door and waves at anybody else—everybody is on the run. By 8:30 A.M., neighborhoods stand still and silent, hollow monuments to family life.

Around 3:00 in the afternoon in Reston, the middle and high school buses return, and at streets with inviting suburban names like Ambleside Court, Deep Run Lane, and Steeplechase, approximately three thousand adolescents hop off, fling their backpacks over their shoulders, and meander toward home, sometimes alone, sometimes with friends. Keys in hand, they open doors all over the community. Then the doors shut. It's their world now. With the exception of a few lone outposts where adults await their return, nobody's home but the kids.

Day after day, month after month, year after year, I run past the kids waiting for the buses to Langston Hughes Middle School and South Lakes High School, a changing group of individuals, the same scene—a vague mass of kids growing up in a world that rushes past them until one of them steps out of the shadows and demands attention by doing something extraordinarily wonderful or troubling, outrageous or awful. The rest of the time, especially for the average, everyday kid who goes along not making waves, the grown-up world doesn't pay much attention. Adults, burned out by the years of day care arrangements, are happy the kids are old enough to be on their own. Besides, most believe adolescents prefer being left alone. In the calm, everybody just goes about his or her life.

I run past them. Over time, I've passed one or another of my three sons, who have grown up here. Out there on the corner, even my own children fall into the shadows as they join their peers in another world before my eyes. They have stepped inside the adolescent community, a perplexing place where kids these days are growing up among themselves, out of the range of adult vision. I run past the bus several times as it goes from stop to stop, and I am aware of how distant they seem, how separate. I wonder why and whether anybody else cares.

Nobody is paying much attention to individual adolescents, but everyone is hysterical about the aggregate. Just utter the word "adolescents," and all anybody talks about are problems. Like the darkening skies of an impending summer storm, study after study points to problems and inadequacies in today's kids. As early as 1989, *Turning Points: Preparing American Youth for the Twenty-first Century*, the groundbreaking report of the Carnegie Council on Adolescent Development, warned that "by age 15, substantial numbers of American youth are at risk of reaching adulthood unable to meet adequately the requirements of the workplace, the commitments of relationships in families and with friends, and the responsibilities of participation in a democratic society. These youth are among the estimated 7 million young people—one in four adolescents—who are extremely vulnerable to multiple high risk behaviors and school failure. Another 7 million may be at moderate risk. . . ." In other words, *half* of all America's adolescents are at some risk for serious problems like substance abuse; early, unprotected sexual intercourse; dangerous accident-prone lifestyles; delinquent behavior; and dropping out of school. The report concluded that today's children are susceptible to "a vortex of new risks . . . almost unknown to their parents or grandparents."

For *The Troubled Journey*, a report issued in 1990 by the Minnesota-based Search Institute, approximately 50,000 youths from sixth through twelfth grade in mostly small midwestern communities were surveyed, and only one in ten met a set of criteria for "optimal healthy development." Even more troubling, the trends from sixth to twelfth grade go downhill. And these are kids in what we would consider the best American communities—small, midwestern, with more than 80 percent of families intact. By 1996, the sample had stretched to include more than 250,000 students in more than 460 rural, urban, and suburban communities, and nothing had improved. Peter L. Benson, president of the Search Institute, recently concluded that "America has forgotten how to raise healthy kids."

All parents feel an ominous sense—like distant rumbles of thunder moving closer and closer—that even their child could be caught in the deluge of adolescent dysfunction sweeping the nation, manifesting itself in everything from drugs, sex, and underachievement to depression, suicide, and crime. Most threatening is the news that risky behaviors are beginning at younger and younger ages. In 1991, the University of Michigan's "Monitoring the Future" study, which looks at trends in adolescent drug, cigarette, and alcohol use, added eighth graders to its samples. Now the researchers are considering going down to seventh graders.

Such statistics haunted me as a parent and a journalist for years. In 1990, I began clipping stories on adolescence from *The New York Times* and *The Washington Post* and watched a phenomenon occur: the stories went from covering *those kids* wilding in Central Park, shooting each other in the inner city, failing in ghetto schools, being shipped off to psychiatric hospitals in suburbia, to stories that reported on *all our kids*. Occasional pieces multiplied to a constant onslaught of alarmist tales on how badly adolescents are doing, until today one can hardly separate the nation's problems from the problems of our adolescents. In 1989, the American Medical Association's new department of adolescent health announced a "Healthy Youth by the Year 2000" project, joining legions of other groups putting adolescence under the microscope of statistical surveys and policy recommendations. By 1991, the Centers for Disease Control had begun issuing biennial reports on risky behaviors. My bookcases overflowed with studies, reports, and other publications on adolescents. My clip file outgrew a large file cabinet, and one sad day I decided not to clip every single report of another teen shooting because such stories simply overran all other coverage.

Over the years, the tone of discourse on adolescents has become shrill and frightened. Increasingly desperate attempts to understand and know them fragment them into pieces of behavior that are "good" or "bad." They are labeled and classified like so many phyla in the animal kingdom, by how they look and how they act. Theories abound on how to manage them, fix them, and improve them, as if they were products off an assembly line: just tinker with the educational system, manipulate the drug messages, impose citywide curfews, make more rules, write contracts, build more detention centers, be tough. Maybe if we just tell adolescents to say no, no, no to everything we disapprove of, maybe then they will be okay. But the piecemeal attempts to mend, motivate, or rescue them obscure the larger reality: *We don't know them.*

America's own adolescents have become strangers. They are a tribe apart, remote, mysterious, vaguely threatening. The tribal notion is so commonplace that it is hard to know whether it derives from the kids or from adults, but the result is that somewhere in the transition from twelve to thirteen, our nation's children slip into a netherworld of adolescence that too often becomes a self-fulfilling prophecy of estrangement. The individual child feels lost to a world of teens, viewed mostly in the aggregate, notorious for what they do wrong, judged for their inadequacies, known by labels and statistics that frighten and put off adults.

For years I had been writing stories about adolescents, but like most journalists, I wrote about the dramatic—street kids, kids in detention, in psychiatric hospitals, gay and lesbian teens—and the worrisome—sex, drinking, and issues of trust. At the same time, I was raising my own adolescents, who I found to be exasperating, challenging, and totally fascinating when they weren't testing every parenting skill I had. I was discovering with my children that the intuitive, organic methods of child raising my husband and I had always felt so comfortable with were often inadequate with adolescents who traveled in a world unlike the one we grew up in.

I knew something was askew, things didn't make sense. In a community like mine, few kids are in Real Trouble. There are incidents that parents blow off as an isolated adolescent adventure, an occasional annoying vandalism or fistfight, a rare shocking crime or accidental death or suicide. Mostly adults grumble about grades, parties, friends, curfews—the usual. The underage drinking, the occasional stashes of pot, the coed sleepovers have somehow become part of the normal aggravations for today's parents, or perhaps part of parents' strong denial that their child's life could include such activities. Yet always just beneath the surface is cold fear of what terrible things can happen to any teen.

It is a conundrum: by all indications a substantial portion of kids we know must be participating in seriously unhealthy behaviors; yet, in most communities outside inner cities, the kids we see appear remarkably like the adolescents we remember from our own childhoods. The ordinary everyday adolescents we see at high school football games, at back-to-school nights, the kids hanging out at the local shopping centers, the ones who load our car at the grocery store, the sitters for the children down the street, the counselors at day camp, the athletes and the cheerleaders and the kids in third-period English class don't seem like "those kinds of kids." Styles change, music changes, but the shadow of a mustache on a thirteen-year-old boy, the rough-and-tumble pickup basketball games, the groups of giggling girls, the lingering kisses of young lovers, the Homecoming celebration, the prom, graduation, all look similar to what we recall. There is a confounding lack of congruence between what adults see and what we are told is true. What constitutes a "normal" adolescence in today's world may or may not be camouflaged by appearances.

I needed to explore this lack of congruence further. Perhaps the way we experience kids in traditional settings may not be a true indicator of the whole fabric of their lives. I knew in my gut that the statistics didn't mean we had a generation of "bad kids" but rather that the fabric of adolescence itself has changed. Researchers tend to zero in on one vector or another, but the changing experience that eludes hard data is the richest. This was the great unexplored wilderness. Something was happening in the shadows that had transformed the experience of growing up. I had to find out what. Whatever constituted "normal adolescence" for "regular kids" today had been eclipsed by the emphasis on the sensational. There was a huge gap in the knowledge so necessary not only for parents, but also for society. If the statistics were true, we needed to understand better how the sensational issues might play out in a young person's day-to-day life. But not just the problems: we needed a sense of the whole kid. There was only one place to go for the answers—the kids themselves. Six years ago, I decided to become an explorer, to enter into their tribe and discover the nature of adolescent life from the inside. If "regular" adolescence had been lost in the shadows, I wanted to yank it into the sunlight.

Reston, my home for over twenty years, seemed a good laboratory for my study. More than simply a pleasant suburb eighteen miles west of Washington, D.C., Reston is a so-called New Town, a planned community, set in the Virginia countryside, with pathways and pools, tennis courts and village shopping centers, and a European-style new downtown built for people, with cafés and a skating rink. It is a place founded for families to mature—from its tot lots to its playing fields, from its fast-food places to its gourmet restaurants. Its visionary founder, Robert E. Simon, told a reporter over thirty years ago that his goal was "to create neighborhoods where people can be born, married, rear their kids and grow old." In a postwar world where neighborhood and community had been ravaged by social change, Simon was reinventing the American Dream. But even better: Reston was a place philosophically based on racial and ethnic integration, far ahead of its time in supporting cultural diversity. Child care was part of the master plan before ground was broken in 1963.

The adolescents of Reston are surrounded by an environment that at least superficially appears nurturing. Many, like my sons, have grown up here from preschool through high school. My sons' memories include the sweet innocent moments of feeding the ducks at Lake Anne, camp overnights in the yet-undeveloped woods, shared recollections of teachers all three have had in schools all three have attended. Their pediatricians are here, the pathways on which they have ridden their bicycles, the streets where they learned to drive. Their dad and I chose Reston because it was a pioneering community, incorporating time-honored American values of neighborhood and home. Our families of origin might be in distant places, but our children would have firm roots.

Just as the American Dream is ragged around the edges, the idealistic community of Reston is no utopia. Although essentially middle-class, it has always accommodated a portion of affluent Fairfax County's low-income housing, and there have been racial and cultural clashes. In 1987, the plan stretched to include a shelter for the homeless. Like everywhere else in America these days, Reston worries about its youth. There have been forums and symposiums, pressure for more lit basketball courts. As in other communities, the middle and high schools have a full-time police officer. There have been signs of gang graffiti on the pathways and schools have increased their vigilance. Kids are often shooed away from parks and from "loitering" in the Town Center. Even in a place like Reston that supports a multiplicity of community clubs and organizations and has a deep tradition of volunteering and an annual community celebration, even in such a place adolescents often lack firm mooring. And like everywhere else in America, between 8 A.M. and 6 P.M., Reston is a working town, and its neighborhoods house the community of kids.

Jonathan Tompkins is one of them. I met him in the most ordinary way. When he was a junior, I spoke to his English class about teens and music—a favorite topic of mine—and was struck by his wry sense of humor and his quiet but intensely thoughtful remarks. That might have been the end of it except that Joan, another youngster I was interviewing and a good friend of his, suggested one summer day that I interview Jonathan "because he is really cool. He thinks a lot about life, he's kind, likes the Grateful Dead, and is really an environmental kind of guy." Sounded interesting, and besides, I liked to follow up on the kids' suggestions. On the designated Saturday in August, he arrived promptly at noon, tall, slender, and deeply tanned, dressed in shorts, a pale yellow T-shirt, and Birkenstocks, eager to talk. We hit it off at once. What a delightful surprise to find he only had an hour and a half to spend with me because he was setting out on a Vision Quest. I was excited. I could not have imagined a more appropriate beginning for my book. When he returned and had time to share his experience, in a single recollection he revealed what is at the heart of every adolescent. Adolescence is a journey, a search for self in every dimension of being. It is about dreams, fears, and hopes, as much as about hormones, SAT scores, and fashion. It is about endless possibilities as well as dead ends. It is searching, testing, experimentation. It is growth: it is undeniable that the young person at any one point in time will be different one year later—different physically, intellectually, emotionally, and experientially.

But for him, this amazing epiphany just happened to be where he was going after our first interview. He could have as easily been going to 7-Eleven for a Slurpee, or for a swim at the local pool. Jonathan never thought about the bravery, steadfastness, and commitment that it took to go off into the mountains to contemplate his life. All he could think of was how inadequate he felt, how scary it was to face his parents' aging, his upcoming departure for college, and especially himself. His mother, like parents everywhere must do, took a leap of faith letting him go, knowing she could only prepare her child partially for the journey away from home, persuading him to take just the proverbial half loaf along. Rather than feeling good that she had gotten him to take something to sustain him when he had wanted nothing at all, she only wished she had been able to give him more. When Jonathan Tompkins ventured into the unknown, his experience laid bare the essential drama of adolescence.

Yet I might have never heard the story. The serendipity of my speaking to Jonathan that particular afternoon only underscored how

much of the real lives of adolescents we must be missing. The fact
that he never told anybody about his quest in detail made me wonder how many other things about our adolescents are secret: not just
things on the sly that parents torment themselves about, but meaningful issues, ways of expressing themselves, struggles—the things
at the heart of who they are.

Like Jonathan, all adolescents are ultimately alone in their search
for identity whether at the top of a mountain or in a crowded room,
flopped on their bed listening to music alone or strolling the mall in a
pack. It cannot be forgotten that the self-conscious journey inevitably also occurs *in a context*. Today's teens have grown up in the
midst of enormous social changes that have shaped, reshaped, distorted, and sometimes decimated the basic parameters for healthy
development. They have grown up with parents who are still seeking
answers about what it means to be an adult man or woman. They
have lived in families that seldom coincide with the old ideal, and in a
culture where the traditional wisdom of how to raise children has
been replaced by a kind of daily improvisation as parents try to fit
child rearing into their busy lives. At a time when adolescents need
to emulate role models, the adults around them are moving targets.
Nobody seems to know what is "normal" anymore.

Jonathan's Vision Quest was also a tangible and dramatic example
of the intensity of the search for self-identity that propels adolescents along different pathways. He instinctively knew that he needed
time away for introspection and chose an ancient rite of passage. By
contrast, few youngsters today seek confirmation of their changing
status on a mountaintop. There are few community-sanctioned moments or formalized thresholds that mark steps on the road toward
adulthood. Teen life is out of sync. For too many kids a first date,
confirmation, a bar mitzvah, or even high school graduation is a side
trip on a jagged path to growing up. What is the meaning of a
driver's license or turning eighteen when so many kids have already
assumed grown-up responsibilities for cooking, shopping, cleaning,
self-care, and care of siblings for years when they might have preferred playing? What is the meaning of their venturing out from
home when the older generation is already gone? Sometimes, as a
reaction to the confusion, today's kids would just as likely herald in
"adulthood" with a beer or a bong.

Their rites of passage—ways to find meaning and a prescribed place in the adult community—are understandably out of whack when the old pathways are inadequate to assuring success in the adult world due to economics and a changing workplace. Youngsters have lost more than secure families and adult interaction: they grow up in a world that lacks consistency and structure. There are no magic formulas to financial security, job stability, marital harmony. Technology and the media create a world without boundaries. For adolescents there is available a dizzying array of lifestyle choices, at the same time that home and community fail to provide a balancing sense of security.

The changing contexts rob development of its coherency. Like a handful of pebbles tossed in a raging stream, young people today, as well as many adults around them, seem rushed along in currents out of their control, often ending up in completely unexpected places. Sometimes the experience is positive, as it was in Jonathan's journey, but too often these days the results can be negative, irreversible, even deadly. The main problems for today's adolescents are found not in the now-discredited Sturm und Drang model of adolescent rebellion against adult society, but rather in the search for identity in an amorphous and unpredictable environment.

A clear picture of adolescents, of even our own children, eludes us—not necessarily because they are rebelling, or avoiding or evading us. *It is because we aren't there.* Not just parents, but any adults. American society has left its children behind as the cost of progress in the workplace. This isn't about working parents, right or wrong, but an issue for society to set its priorities and to pay attention to its young in the same way it pays attention to its income. The sad truth is American society has yet to work out how to give quality care to its babies during the workday. In late 1997, as this book goes to press, the Clinton administration is launching yet another day care initiative citing an "urgent need for safe affordable child care," according to *The New York Times.* We've been hearing the same thing since the seventies when women started working in record numbers and little has changed. Meanwhile adolescents are growing up with no adults around, a deficit of attention, and no discussion about whether it matters at all.

The most stunning change for adolescents today is their aloneness. The adolescents of the nineties are more isolated and more unsupervised than other generations. It used to be that kids sneaked time away from adults. The proverbial kisses stolen in the backseat of a car, or the forbidden cigarette smoked behind the garage, bestowed a grown-up thrill of getting away with the forbidden. The real excitement was in not getting caught by a watchful (or nosy) neighbor who'd call Mom. Today Mom is at work. Neighbors are often strangers. Relatives live in distant places. This changes everything. It changes access to a bed, a liquor cabinet, a car. The kids have all the responsibility for making decisions, often in a void, or they create an ersatz family with their buddies and let them decide. These days youngsters can easily do more good or bad without other people knowing about it.

Time alone creates its own context, its own imperatives. The aloneness of today's adolescents changes the essential nature of the journey. "In all societies since the beginning of time, adolescents have learned to become adults by observing, imitating and interacting with grown-ups around them," write Mihaly Csikzentmihalyi and Reed Larson in *Being Adolescent*. "It is therefore startling how little time [modern] teenagers spend in the company of adults." In their study, Csikzentmihalyi and Larson found that adolescents spent only 4.8 percent of their time with their parents and only 2 percent with adults who were not their parents.

Not only have adults become separated from their own children, says sociologist Dale Blyth, of the Search Institute, "Even more importantly, they have gotten separated from the other children in the community. As that happens you have less and less people who might see something to be concerned about, to talk about, and less ability to act collectively to do something about it." It is a problem not just for families but for communities when the generations get so separated. The effects go beyond issues of rules and discipline to the idea exchanges between generations that do not occur, the conversations not held, the guidance and role modeling not taking place, the wisdom and traditions no longer filtering down inevitably. How can kids imitate and learn from adults if they never talk to them? How can they form the connections to trust adult wisdom if there is inadequate contact? How can they decide what to accept and reject from the previous generation when exposure is limited? The generational threads that used to weave their way into the fabric of growing up are missing. "It is a much bigger transformation than women in the workplace. That is like the last step," says social historian

Sarah Larson. "The first step is that no matter what their economic class, people used to live in houses full of people. If they were wealthy or middle-class they had servants. If poor, they had relatives or boarders. Nuclear families did not live in separate households or spaces separated from their families or neighbors. In the twentieth century, not only are children alone, but everybody is alone."

According to *A Matter of Time: Risk and Opportunity in the Nonschool Hours*, a 1992 report published by the Carnegie Council on Adolescent Development, about 40 percent of adolescents' waking hours are spent in "discretionary activities—not committed to other activities [such as eating, school, homework, chores, or working for pay]." Many young people "spend virtually all of their discretionary time without companionship or supervision by responsible adults." If eating, homework and chores are done without adults present, over half of adolescents' time could easily be spent on their own. Their aloneness gives this generation unequaled freedom of determination in many areas of their lives. As one sixteen-year-old girl explains it, "You basically have a life of your own."

In the vacuum where traditional behavioral expectations for young people used to exist, in the silence of empty homes and neighborhoods, young people have built their own community. The adolescent community is a creation by default, an amorphous grouping of young people that constitutes the world in which adolescents spend their time. Their dependence on each other fulfills the universal human longing for community, and inadvertently cements the notion of a tribe apart. More than a group of peers, it becomes in isolation a society with its own values, ethics, rules, worldview, rites of passage, worries, joys, and momentum. It becomes teacher, adviser, entertainer, challenger, nurturer, inspirer, and sometimes destroyer.

Teens, of course, have always loved to hang out with each other, but the changing circumstances in American life over the past several decades have increasingly transformed this perennial adolescent pastime into a force with a power of its own. From the bobby soxers to the hippies, American teens found a way to make a separate statement of who they were. The sheer size of the baby boom generation, however, brought adolescent culture front and center as a separate entity whose music, style, and voices of defiance demanded attention. A subject of intense national fascination and vexation, the source of immense parental frustration, the sixties kids—most parents of today's teens—were written about, talked about, worried about as a defiant horde, an army of youth, and the tribal notion was here to stay. Never mind that most teens were not protesting, smoking pot, or wearing long hair and beads. It felt that way. The media cemented the image. And unlike teens of previous generations, who did most of their breaking of rules quietly behind their parents' backs, the sixties kids perfected "in your face," leaving their children—today's generation—with a double challenge: how to do more than what they imagine their parents did, and how to get their parents' attention when their parents are not home to achieve the satisfactions of "in your face."

The "generation gap" was a rallying cry in the sixties. The term became a shorthand for the radically different ways in which the young and the old—at the time "anyone over thirty"—saw the world. It was a declaration of separateness. But this separateness paradoxically required that each generation have knowledge of the other's point of view in order to criticize it. From the point of view of the kids, it was their parents' Vietnam War that was hated, their parents' materialism, their parents' racism, their parents' sexism. Without the acknowledged values of the mainstream culture, there could be no counterculture—that was the fun, that fueled the angst. The older generation sent the young to college in record numbers, creating youthful troops for demonstrations that flaunted distrust and hatred of the establishment. "Us versus Them" required the active engagement of Them. It was a period of intense interaction between age groups. Baby boomers became a national obsession, and the attention was gratifying. Today's kids often feel invisible. Often they have to act out to get any attention at all.

The sixties kids wanted freedom and space. Parents didn't think it was such a great idea. The adults in the sixties, to their children's disgust, wanted rules and control. So today's parents think the adolescent desire for space is part of the natural order of growing up. They extend to their own children the privilege of being left alone.

The sixties cemented in the public imagination the idea that treating teens as a tribe apart is right and proper. So now when teens act in ways we are not entirely comfortable with, we are not sure whether we should intercede or not. The issue for adults is not necessarily one of neglect but more often of simply wanting to do the right thing—which may be letting teens "do their own thing." How much space do kids need? How much should adults intrude? Parents who grew up in the sixties find such issues confusing.

Look at the anguish and debate over whether to talk about parental marijuana use in the sixties to today's teens. Should we tell or not? Similarly, we rallied around the notion of free love and now aren't so sure about teens having sex. Everything is open to debate and unfortunately there isn't time, consensus, or perhaps will to figure it out. So the issues are thrown back at the kids.

In the nineties, the generation gap is a gaping hole that severs the continuity of generations. The new generation gap has nothing to do with social change, with intellectual questioning or opposition to causes. Instead it arises from a new social reality. Today's kids have an abundance of that "space" the sixties kids coveted, enough to do their "own thing" with great regularity. Their dramatic separation from the adult world is rarely considered as a phenomenon in its own right, yet it may be the key to that life in the shadows. It creates a milieu for growing up that adults categorically cannot understand because their absence causes it. It transforms the environment for all kids—even for the small number who may actually have parents or another adult at home or in the neighborhood. But how? And is it a state of affairs worth changing? That is the central curiosity of this book.

My idea was simple. A lone adult wanderer, I would enter into the adolescent world, get to know it on its own terms, and tell representative stories of growing up from the points of view of eight kids. My sample would not only be selected to illustrate the whole spectrum of adolescence from seventh through twelfth grade. The study would stretch over a period of several years, from 1992 through 1995, with updates to the present, 1997, to get a sense of development and maturation.

Getting inside took some time. I started in the schools. My task was to identify kids in the "mainstream," whatever that meant these days. Get past the sensational, the purple-haired, ring-in-the-nose, deadbeat, threatening, exceptional grab-your-senses kinds of kids and seek out the "regular" kids who appeared balanced, willing to work, relatively well behaved, and respectful. I sought the kinds of kids who adult readers would look at and immediately recall somebody they once knew in junior high or high school.

But first it made sense to backtrack to where, experientially, adolescence really begins, in the leap from elementary to middle school, which typically occurs in sixth grade. I went to Forest Edge Elementary School in the spring of 1992 to observe the impending change, to experience firsthand the preparation and transition to middle school, to see and hear the students process the meaning of middle school, and to physically experience their move in the fall. The students would teach me the way it looked, smelled, sounded, and felt to leave where they were.

These sixth-graders and I all started classes together in the fall. They went to seventh grade, and I filled my days with visits to all the grades from seventh through twelfth at Langston Hughes Middle School and South Lakes High School. I went to school all day long for a year, regularly attending classes in which I could volunteer my time and skills as a working journalist/author. The classes knew I was working on a book, but the agreement with the school system was that I would not formally interview in school. That was fine with me. What I wanted was to get in touch with the rhythms of school, to regularly experience kids' lives on the inside, to see, as the kids say, "what's up." By the time my book was finished, I had gone to classes, assemblies, events; had witnessed crises, celebrations, and the ordinary flow of several school years. I observed boring classes and exciting classes, and many run-of-the-mill classes. Sometimes I took over classes, led discussions, shared my craft. But mostly I was a fly on the wall and that was my intention. As the research progressed, I continued to go to school, though less frequently, and to follow specifically the subjects of my book in their school experience. For three full years and more, I always returned to school—even up to the present, with my youngest son—to keep grounded in the most structured part of each adolescent's day.

As that first semester came to a close, I had assembled a list of students to interview, "regular kids," about sixty. I knew nothing about them except what I observed in school, and the only private exchanges we had were when I asked whether they would be willing to be interviewed. Since I was dealing with minors, before we spoke I needed parental approval. After the initial contact was made and the parents had an opportunity to talk to me, they were asked to sign a permission form that gave me unfettered access to their child, no questions asked about what I found out. I was forthright with the parents: undoubtedly I would discover things that they might be interested in knowing. But the point was to find out the true nature of adolescence and unless there was a pact of confidentiality between their youngster and myself, I would never gain enough trust to learn the truth. Obviously, I am a parent too, so if I came upon something dangerous, I would not ignore it. There was a measure of protection because as a matter of policy I would be changing names in the book, although not the details of lives. Based on my knowledge of my own children's adolescence, parents could rest easier knowing that the lengthy process of writing and publishing a book virtually assured that their youngsters would have matured and moved on from where they were during my research, thereby tempering any shocking information that might come out. The parents were trailblazers in their own right. They cared enough about the larger purpose of this book to trust me with the truths of their kids' lives—stories they would not know until publication.

Over a period of approximately six months, I interviewed all the kids in the initial group, and gradually selected eight whose responses form the substance of this book. These eight I interviewed again and again over a period of three years, and occasionally right until publication. They were selected to cover the gamut of grades from middle school through high school, so the reader would be left with both a sense of the maturing that occurs during the time frame of the book and also the texture of distinct ages and stages within. I also considered gender, ethnicity, and family status. Four of the youngsters come from intact families, two from single parent families (one living with the father, one living with the mother), and two live in a stepfamily. I knew the parents of some of the kids already; others I never met except through phone contact or a nod hello at the door. The differences had mostly to do with ages and the relationship the kids had with their folks—the younger the child, the more likely I would be to interact with the parents. When I knew the parents, sometimes it gave me a check on facts and a window on differences between the parents' and the child's view of a situation. I also knew some of the kids before working on the book, but I came to know them differently when I was an author and not just a "Reston Mom." Even when I wasn't formally at work on the project, my path and the paths of the kids often crossed, since we all live in the same community. It gave a depth and breadth I would never have achieved if I'd had to travel to other places. I was in Reston twenty-four hours a day, so the chances of my seeing something new and interesting were much higher. It also meant I could never really put the book aside, because I was immersed in it totally.

The book is organized to bring readers on the journey I took. In Part One, "Stepping Inside," the world of school from the kids' perspective is explored and the main characters are introduced, with their stories revealed around school issues. In Part Two, "Making Contact," a different focus of each youngster's life is exposed as that youngster related it to me. Whether through school, social life, sports, or family, the individuality of each young person and what he or she was grappling with at that moment is recounted. In Part Three, "Making Sense," the action continues with a rare look inside the adolescent minds making sense of their lives. Like the leaves of an artichoke peeled away, each part brings readers closer to the heart of the growing-up experience of each character.

The story of each character is chronological, but the overall book is only loosely so. All the stories in each part take place between 1992 and 1995, with the epilogue bringing the evolution up to the present. The chapters, however, in that time frame are not necessarily sequential except within the story of each character. Most studies of adolescents are written with an eye on "appropriate age and stage development." But adolescence is a sloppy thing. A kid can be easily part little child and part adult; two kids the same age can act like they are years apart. That is why I have included three youngsters the same age in the book and don't lay out adolescence year by year but rather character by character. The pace of their lives varies, the dramatic and mundane elements are woven in different proportions. There are no neat progressions in adolescent life any more than there are in adult life.

In the end, I didn't just select my eight main characters. They also chose me. All of them understood this would be a long-term commitment, and they would be enlightening a large audience with their stories. They were willing to invest in the project. Readers will join Chris Hughes as their leader into middle school after sharing the end of his sixth-grade year. What a window he provides on the leap into adolescence from childhood! I chose him because he was such a little boy in the best sense of the term, an innocent as he made the move. His fears about being stuck in a locker, taking showers, were so reminiscent of everybody's memories of seventh grade that I knew he would reveal in bold relief the differences for this generation. At the same time I started middle school with Chris, I met Jessica Jones in eighth grade. She intrigued me with her spirited intelligence and outspokenness during a year in which there had been so much fury about Carol Gilligan's studies of how young adolescent girls lose their self-esteem.* Charles Sutter, the perennial class leader, and Brendon Lamont and Courtney Smith, the new Joe and Sally Highschool, were all freshmen when I started. Actually, Courtney plopped into the sample when I was interviewing her sister Ann. She sat with us at their house, started talking, and didn't stop. She was so lively and open, so nonstop descriptive of freshman life that I was instantly won over, especially when she revealed her crush on Brendon. The contrast between her and her sister was also intriguing. I had met Ann in my daily visits to the journalism class. I liked her nononsense attitude and determination and also was amused by the old-fashioned way she was always complaining about her mom. Joan Garcia was in both journalism and creative writing, so I saw her a lot. I was drawn to her gentleness and sincerity, and her born-again-hippie style. Jonathan was the oldest. Not only did he represent the senior's dilemmas with what feel like the first big life decisions, but I also admit to finding in his serious way of always trying to figure things out a link to the high school girl I used to be.

So much is written about adolescents *not* communicating; this is a book of communication. These life stories would never have come to the fore through calculated interviews in antiseptic settings. The depth of revelation is a product of mutual caring and conversations between my main characters and me that took place in an atmosphere of mutual respect in many settings over a long period of time. From my first tentative, worried steps into their world to a situation where we spoke freely about their lives, I was involved in relating honestly, openly, and effectively with adolescents, and they related back. The rich texture of their lives as they explained themselves is a testament to the ability of this age group to communicate. But communication does not come easily or through gimmicks. It took time, attention, and a willingness to face my own discomfort and vulnerabilities. Maybe my process can be helpful to others trying to connect better with adolescents. In this spirit I have written brief explanations at the beginnings of the sections describing how my approach worked and the evolution of the conversations over time.

This book is the first report from the homefront: the "regular" adolescents of Reston, Virginia, laid open their lives and their hearts

*Meeting at the Crossroads: Women's Psychology and Girls' Development, by Lyn Mikel Brown and Carol Gilligan (Harvard University Press, 1992).

to speak for the great unknown mass of their counterparts across the country. These are their stories—unique yet together creating a portrait of contemporary adolescence for many kids in America today. They lead and we walk beside them, watching, listening to them telling us what's going on, what matters and how it all works. We discover them as they discover themselves.

The evolving story, the research that could take me in unknown directions at any time depending on the suggestions of my main characters, placed me squarely in the dynamics of their lives. Sometimes I felt the same emotional vulnerability they did because I was deeply involved in the unfolding of their lives and because those emotions of adolescence are so close to the surface in the adults most of us become. I found their stories charged with a kinetic energy that got my heart racing, brought me to tears, filled me with joy, reminded me of my youth, made me want to make it easier for them, filled me with the anticipation of what would happen next.

Rather than walking as an adult reporter observing a foreign terrain and trying to describe it as it appears, I ventured inside the minds, hearts, and actions of these young people and viewed it through their eyes. It is easy to judge the risks and the sensible paths from an adult perspective, but this does not lead us to an intimate understanding of what young people face and have to navigate on a day-to-day basis. What the kids think is important and what adults do may be entirely different. This is why I carefully avoided interacting with parents, interviewing teachers and other adults, contacting researchers, and reading studies for most of the process. I needed to be able to immerse myself in the adolescent way of seeing. When I didn't understand something, I asked the kids, because it was their explanation I was after. Only when my interviews were done did I go back and read the studies, and talk to adults. But only as a backdrop or perspective. I trusted the kids and was unafraid of displaying my adult ignorance. As a result, they did an excellent job of deciphering themselves.

This book strives to make adolescence whole again. "I'm not who I seem on the outside," one girl said in challenge. It was as direct a plea as I've heard to seek the truth about who adolescents are. As I approached them, there was pathos: "Why would you want to talk to me? I'm not a drug addict; I'm not an alcoholic. I'm just a regular kid." There was satisfaction: In a thank you note for a graduation gift, one girl wrote, "Thank you for taking the time to realize that all kids aren't committing a crime or having babies. You have made me realize that my accomplishments are worthwhile. It is kind of nice to hear words of encouragement from people other than my family." There was joy: "Mrs. Hersch, want to talk?"

We talked and talked. We talked in cars, in fast-food restaurants, in their homes, in parks, at malls, at football games, in the halls at school, in my office, on the phone, at the all-night track meet (at 2:30 in the morning). Most of the kids were never tentative but dove right in, eager to share what mattered to them. They learned quickly that they could tell me anything—they could even use profanity if it was appropriate to the story. I wasn't there to judge, although sometimes I couldn't help but give advice or my opinion, and, in fact, sometimes they solicited my input. After all, I am a mother. All the youngsters were polite and respectful. They also watched out for me, making sure I got safe passage in their world.

There was a plea to be heard and to be understood that led to the great unfolding of stories. Their stories reflect an unspoken yearning for a congruence most have never known—not because they come from parents who don't care, schools that don't care, or a community that doesn't value them, but rather because there hasn't been time for adults to lead them through the process of growing up.

I was particularly struck by how deeply all the youngsters I spoke to struggled with important issues. It took time to get them to open up, but it was amazing what could be learned if one was willing to sit and listen. They guided me and I in turn share with you. They have much to teach us. We need to hear adolescents, and not when we are shouting at them or when they are shouting at us. They need to be heard when sitting face to face with someone who is interested in them as individuals.

We spend so much time telling young children "You are special, you are unique," but somehow when kids reach adolescence we treat them as an undifferentiated mutant blob. The young people within these pages are special and courageous.

This book reveals adolescent life in process—the good, the bad, the frightening, the inspiring. The point is not simply that good kids can be bad, or that the school system needs fixing, but rather that labels so easily planted on teens obscure their more interesting reality. In fact, one of the most powerful themes exposed through the simple act of taking the time really to know these kids is that they hold enormous potential. Sometimes they have the internal fortitude to use it, other times it languishes unappreciated or becomes twisted into negative uses.

The book's focus on regular kids will reveal that what is ordinary everyday life for them is far different from what we know and much more complex and profound than we had ever imagined—the ordinary becomes an extraordinary tale of growing up today. At the heart of the paradox of adolescence is that much of what we worry about they take in stride as normal. That's why applying our standards to them does not often get at the truth. While adults tend to judge an act, a grade, a particular attitude, the fact is that kids are for the most part trying to do the best they can. By joining them in their world, we can see where we might be needed. We might also learn why adults seem to be having a hard time getting through.

As for the kids whose lives make up this book, knowing them has been an incomparable experience. Their commitment to me both in time and in openness made my vision a reality. With their help, new worlds opened up, and their honesty about the varied aspects of their lives revealed perhaps for the first time the reality of growing up today. Their unfolding lives both connect with the part of us that remembers and transport us to a place that is as remote and foreign to our experience as Jonathan's wilderness.

"The teenager has been classified as a remote being," wrote Jonathan in his private journal. "There is an unspeakable distance between youth and the grown-up world." But kids and grown-ups do not have to be strangers. Aloneness makes adolescents a tribe apart. This book, created through conversations with adolescents, reaches across that gulf and begins to bridge the distance. One kid at a time.

# STEPPING

# INSIDE

*M*y first morning of school, I was scared. I had no idea what would result, who would be my subjects of study. Suddenly it didn't matter that I'd been writing about adolescent issues for years. This was different. I felt like a kid myself, nervous, wondering if I'd fit in, be able to pull it off. I wasn't even sure what to wear—a professional-looking pants suit, blue jeans like the kids, something arty like a writer. I decided on chinos and a black T-shirt with funky jewelry—a combination of all three. I grabbed my briefcase and ran out the door, afraid to be late my first day.

I walked into Langston Hughes Middle School along with busloads of students. Entering the doors, I was assaulted by a wall of sound and activity. It was madness: kids whizzing past me, teachers helplessly trying to slow them down, noisy caverns between the lockers bellowing with voices. I spent the morning going to classes, my map of the school clutched in my hand as I struggled to get to the rooms on time.

At lunchtime I switched to South Lakes High School. What a relief to be out in the fresh air walking from one school to the other! The break was too short. Inside South Lakes the inhabitants were larger, the male voices deeper—all making me feel smaller. I got hopelessly lost trying to find my way around. It was bigger and even more confusing than Hughes.

For a few weeks I was overwhelmed. This wasn't a mere classroom visit or parent-teacher meeting like I was used to—stay for a short period of time and leave. Waking up and going to school for an entire school day, day after day, was exhausting. Like an explorer from the courts of Europe entering the wilds of the New World, I experienced culture shock. My head swam in the swarms of young people, the mass of color, style, activity, noise, posturing, movement in so many directions that it often made me want to flee to the solitary quiet and control of my office. Even in an orderly classroom or assembly, the variety of kids and styles, the buzz of adolescent energy felt impossible to grab, let alone decipher and explain. I had to learn to be patient, to suffer the self-consciousness and isolation, to resist the urge to run and bond with the adults. I tried to focus on the individuals in the throng that swirled around me each day. I was in the middle of a story not yet revealed. I had to stick it out believing that eventually my vision would clear and I would be able to really see and connect with this alien world.

So it went for weeks. Each day I would check in at the school main office and pick up the requisite Visitor sticker. I might as well have been wearing a cap that said "I'm an Outsider. Stare at me!" I didn't work in the schools, I seemed to be everywhere rather than in one place, so both teachers and kids wanted to know what I was doing there all the time. It was so uncomfortable at the beginning. I purposely had no game plan. I wanted my direction to emerge from the situation.

Sometimes kids would ask me what I was doing there but then they wouldn't hang around for a long explanation. Kids I already knew might say hi but not stop and talk. As stupid as it sounds, I'd feel a little hurt. But I was a stranger in the middle of the adolescent tribe. I knew it would take time to earn their respect. By the time the final bell rang those first days, I would have the most splitting headache. Sometimes, especially that first month, I wished I could be back at Forest Edge Elementary School where I had begun my research the spring before. There I was received warmly, I knew my place. Now I was sounding like a brand-new seventh grader myself.

I was also uncomfortable finding myself revisiting my own feelings about school, emotions that seldom surface in my usual role as a mother at a PTA meeting or Open House. I had to deal with those old sensations of feeling caged in middle school, the rawness of everything about it. In the high school I found myself wanting to share my old excitement about learning, which too often seemed absent. Sometimes I just wanted to put down my head and doze in classes so boring and even stupid that I couldn't keep my eyes open. I tried taking a pop quiz with the kids and recalled the same cold fear of being unprepared. I found myself resentful of the way some teachers treated their students with disrespect. I became mesmerized all over again with the way school clocks always jump backwards before moving forward.

Little by little things changed. I took over classes and talked about writing. The kids perked up. Most kids found it hard to believe that I was willing to take so much time with them. They began to understand that my constant presence was me learning about them, not making judgments. One told another I was an okay person. They could talk to me and I'd listen. We started on neutral ground, talking about school.

In Part One I am observer, stepping inside their world with an idea and an intention that would hinge on relationships that as yet did not exist. Chapters 1 through 6 are a combination of what I saw and what my newly identified characters said about it. I didn't know the kids well, nor did they know me. We were getting acquainted. They liked my asking them to talk about school from their perspective. What matters to them, bothers them, and touches them are often surprising. I observed the visceral fears Chris and his classmates had about middle school, and Jessica's total annoyance with it. Brendon, Courtney, and Charles's unique experiences of the same grade quickly separated the horde of students into individuals. The ethics seminar Jonathan attended not only highlighted this generation's view of ethics but also illustrated the reverberations of his Vision Quest in his daily life. Ann and Joan's relationship to the school paper and to each other hinted at much bigger stories about their lives that I was still in the dark about. Their experiences in journalism class also revealed the magic chemistry of a good teacher in kids' lives.

Certain aspects of school struck me too. I was amazed at the significance of the leap from sixth to seventh grade, how out-of-sync middle school seemed to be with early adolescent needs. My three high school freshmen revealed the emptiness of old traditions and the power of the new adolescent subculture. I was struck by the newspaper as an expression of today's adolescent world and the insights it could give into their spin on the big issues.

This first part of the book begins the journey into the world of today's kids by stepping inside the schools, domains designed by and theoretically under the control of adults for the education of a nation's children. Inside, they are interactive arenas where education often takes second place to the personal dramas of growing up played out against the backdrop of all the issues of modern society.

The saga begins in sixth grade.

# On the Brink

In a cozy rambler set on a heavily treed lot on a quiet cul de sac, an alarm clock rings and eleven-year-old Chris Hughes rolls out of bed almost fully dressed. It is a trick he came up with the year before to save time. He showers at night and puts on his shirt and underwear for the next day. If it were cold, he'd put his pants on too. The hardest part is keeping his head straight on the pillow when he lies down so that his hair won't dry weirdly. If it does, he has to wet it under the faucet in the morning. His father thinks this is hilarious and teases him when he comes in to kiss him good night. In fact, his father gives him a hard time about his crew cut. But Chris has grown up hating his naturally curly hair. As soon as he had a choice, he'd had those curls shorn and now he watches for the little turning over of the ends that means it is time for a new buzz cut.

Chris is a no-nonsense young man. He does his homework right after he comes home from school. He makes sure his mom or dad signs any forms from school immediately. He packs his backpack at night and lays it on the floor by his bed. In the morning, his mom always has the same lunch, packed in a brown paper bag, waiting on the kitchen table: smooth peanut butter and grape jelly on wheat bread, a boxed drink, a small bag of raisins, and dessert. He likes things that way. Dependable.

Seven-thirty, right on the button, he walks through the kitchen door wearing his favorite short-sleeved Buffalo Bills T-shirt (which, in the style of the season, hangs down to his knees), gray sweatpants, white Reebok pump basketball shoes worn permanently untied (although, unlike many kids, he actually leaves the laces in them) over scrunched white tube socks. Short-sleeved shirts worn year-round are de rigueur for a fashionable sixth-grade boy, and Chris has a collection reflecting all the major sports. He stops to pet the dogs now jumping up and down to get his attention, and absentmindedly hugs his mom good morning. She's in her usual seat with her customary cup of coffee. Most days he likes this private time with his mom after his brother Jim has left for high school. It is a comforting routine even when they hardly talk. But not today.

He'd like to tell his mom he isn't hungry, but then he'd have to hear the breakfast-is-the-most-important-meal-of-the-day lecture. So he rummages through the cereal cabinet and spreads the thinnest possible layer of Crispy Wheats and Raisins in the bottom of his bowl, splashes in some milk, pours himself a glass of orange juice, and sits down at the table hardly paying any attention to his favorite morning rituals: watching G.I. Joe cartoons and reading the sports section of *The Washington Post*.

His blue eyes stare into space as he pushes his cereal around. He thinks he has a stomachache, he tells his mom. She knows what this is about: today his sixth-grade class is visiting Langston Hughes Middle School.

It's just a visit, he tells himself. It isn't like he is going to stay there. But who's he kidding? The Real Thing—seventh grade—will happen soon enough.

He just realized the other day that he's spent his whole life at Forest Edge Elementary. He could walk around it in his sleep he'd been there so long. The teachers are nice, and recess is always fun.

It is the best being in sixth grade. You have all the power. He can look at the little kids and realize how grown-up he's become. Chris, a "school patrol" since fourth grade, is now a "bus patrol," which is "the coolest because you can sort of arrest people" if they don't follow the rules. In fact, with his friends Brad, Tony, Jeff, Gene, and a few others all volunteering for this position, there are almost as many enforcement officials on Chris's bus as riders. He has a great bunch of friends, most of whom he's known forever. Even if they aren't in each other's classes each year, they always get together at lunch and on the playground. They are wildly competitive in the classroom and on the playing field, all striving for excellence. They have challenged each other in soccer, football, and basketball since they were little boys. They try to write longer stories than each other, get more As, win more awards, but all in good humor. They've competed on Atari, Nintendo, and now Sega Genesis. That's how long they've been friends. Chris looks forward to meeting new people— but what if he gets into classes without any of his old buddies?

The panic is rising. He has been told tales of Sevey-Bip Day, a one-day free-for-all in which the eighth graders hit the seventh graders at will in a sort of middle school initiation rite. Seventh graders he knows this year have already been giving ominous warnings. His mom tries to reassure him that the event will be forbidden by the school administration. But parents don't know what happens in the school. The kids do it, he has heard, when teachers are not looking.

His teachers keep making a big deal about how his class is the first to have "middle school" within the elementary school. The sixth graders have been moved to an isolated corner of Forest Edge so that they feel a bit separate from the younger kids. It's set up in three homerooms, and the classes move among the teachers for science, social studies, math, and language arts. Volunteers have come into the school to allow the students brief forays into electives like photography, computers, and creative writing, although this part fizzled when not enough volunteers could be found. Forest Edge, like schools everywhere, has found that the always dependable stream of volunteers has slowed to a trickle as most parents work, and other demands take precedence.

Chris doesn't know it, but his class represents the leading edge of a nationwide movement to restructure the education of early adolescents, which was first outlined in *Turning Points*, the study by the Carnegie Council for Adolescent Development. The idea is that a team of teachers, teaching their specific subjects, will have shared responsibility for a group of youngsters, and that this will allow ongoing communication among the teachers, collaborative teaching projects, and a community feeling that has been missing in anonymous junior high schools. "Junior high" is out and "middle school" is in, in recognition that early adolescence is a particularly vulnerable time for developing at-risk behaviors, and that youngsters need greater support and nurturing than junior high schools traditionally have given them.

Chris's class was one of the first in Fairfax County to institute the

change that will combine sixth through eighth grades in separate
middle schools over a period of several years. The principal of Forest
Edge, Frank Bensinger, is impressed. "We found that with the middle
school model, discipline went down a ton," he says. "It made an incredible difference because in sixth grade, kids' eyes are beginning to
open up. They are beginning to look at that movement out of the
neighborhood as a grown-up thing. There was an elevation of self-
esteem—'We are not being looked at as little kids'—and the school
was recognizing that. The adults knew they were only changing
classes in a tiny little sixth-grade area, but that little piece made the
kids feel bigger. We decided to let them all go to lunch at the same
time and you would have thought we set them free!"

Yeah, yeah, yeah, thinks Chris. He'd heard the middle school spiel.
It was definitely cool at Forest Edge. But who are they kidding? Next
year is Big Time.

At 8:15, Chris leaves his house to wait for the bus. It is so dumb to
have to ride to school when he lives less than a quarter mile away. In
fact, for most of his years at Forest Edge he walked. Reston, designed
with pedestrians in mind, links each elementary school to the surrounding neighborhood by a labyrinth of paths and underpasses that
keep walkers off the main intersections. On the way to Forest Edge,
Chris used to stroll along a small creek and through a wooded area
adjacent to the school. A kid could daydream on such walks, crunch
leaves in the fall, stomp footprints in the snow, watch bugs. If your
best friend lived nearby, you could share morning secrets. Often big
brothers and sisters were seen with younger siblings in tow. Now
only those across the street from the school walk daily, and for the
rest, the battalion of county school buses, the vans from child care
centers, and a growing fleet of parents' minivans safely deliver the
children of Reston to their respective schools. This is one of the subtle changes eroding this family-oriented community. The buses for
elementary school kids living less than one mile from the school had
been added because of some "incidents"—nothing horrible, but definitely frightening for young children intimidated by older kids out
earlier from the middle and high schools, or by strangers on paths in
the mornings. The official explanation was that it was just as easy for
buses traveling back to school to pick up more kids.

When his brothers were little, Chris's mom and dad thought
nothing about their walking to school alone. Not only did it give the
boys a great feeling of being on their own, but it also harkened back

to the parents' memories of growing up—the walk to school, the bike ride to the candy store, an afternoon movie alone with friends. In those times, there was a cadence to the process of growing up, a socially agreed-upon sequence of age-appropriate behaviors that have now been replaced by a developmental free-for-all with great unsupervised leaps of freedom counterpoised with tight new restraints.

In a jolting generational flip-flop, the fabric of growing up has been altered. It is no longer a matter of parents recalling, "When I was your age . . ." Instead, a compressed history is lived out within one set of siblings, where one brother shakes his head in disbelief at the changes affecting the life of another only a few years younger. Not that Chris and his peers recognize anything different. This is, after all, their "normal" world. They take for granted the scene of young teens smoking and drinking in the woods after school. They shrug with an air of resignation when they hear that the weekly movies shown at neighborhood pools in the summer are canceled because of rowdy behavior by teens. They do not seem to notice that the underpass near school, once decorated by Chris's older brother's day camp group with brightly colored dinosaur murals, is now desecrated with gang graffiti. Above the words I LOVE JEN D. are spray-painted X-PLICIT CRIPZ and SUCK MY DICK.

Chris remembers his brothers having lots of friends around, but accepts the fact that even though his mom and dad work at home, he cannot easily go to many of his friends' houses after school because they are alone, and they can't come to his house because they must care for younger siblings. The heady freedom to play in groups after school is now curtailed as parents tell their latchkey kids to stay inside until they come home from work. So even though Chris can go outside to play, even though his folks could drive him anywhere, he often gets stuck alone in front of the television, just as his friends are glued to theirs.

The school has changed too, as have many others in Fairfax County. Forest Edge is fighting for funds as Fairfax County becomes increasingly the home of families without children. Such voters make the passage of school bonds more difficult, precisely at the same time that more immigrants, often with large families, are moving into the area. The D.C. suburbs have always been cosmopolitan, easily incorporating many cultures. But the immigration stream is less from the educated middle class and more from the poor fleeing areas affected by war and political turmoil, people who have received little or no

schooling in their native lands. Between 1987 and the present, the
English as a Second Language program has more than doubled to ac-
commodate immigrants from over 150 countries representing 75
languages.

Forest Edge, built in 1969 as a school on the leading edge of innovation, illustrates the wild swings of educational theory within a
brief span of a generation: the elementary school lives of the Hughes
children. Oldest brother Mark began kindergarten in 1976 in a setting of open classrooms; Jim barely got there and the walls went back
up; and by the time Chris arrived in 1985, there was a hard-line return to basic, more traditional education. In Mark and Jim's days,
there were no "Drug Free Zone" signs, no visitor passes, no permanent necklace IDs for personnel, no walkie talkies. "Self-esteem" was
the buzzword, not "literacy testing."

Things are tougher at school for Chris and his peers. Yet at the
same time a hard line is instituted on elevating standards to compete
in the age of technology, the school faces erosion from within—
frustrated teachers who are not compensated adequately, overworked
parents who lack time to be involved in their children's education,
and a host of cultural problems now played out in the classroom. By
Chris's sixth-grade year, Forest Edge had become a school of 57 percent ESL students—a proportion taxing the efforts of classroom teachers and special services in a time of decreasing funds. All this in what
is considered one of the nation's finest school systems.

As the bright red front doors of the school swing open on this
cool, gray March morning in 1992, the feeling is sunny. The high-
pitched sounds of children's voices fill the air. There are hugs and
kisses from parents in jogging suits and business suits who drop
their youngsters at the door. Mr. Bensinger is there to dispense kind
personal words to students. A comforting throwback, he is everyone's favorite principal, portly and bespectacled, in rumpled suit and
tie slightly askew. A genuinely warm smile lifts his whisk-broom
mustache. In a testament to how schoolchildren are part of their parents' commuter society, a "Kiss and Ride" sign directs parents to the
spot for dropping off their kids. This being a year or two before
teacher molestation hit the media, the teachers of Forest Edge often
give a hug or squeeze hello, something needed and always appreciated by the children.

Inside the school the walls are lined everywhere with art, poetry,
and other student work—a colorful, explosive celebration of the

unique expression of each child. Now Black History Month has been joined by celebration of Hispanic, Asian, and Indian cultures, highlighted by an International Celebration devoted to the cuisine and culture of the international community. A brightly colored mural along the main hall shows children of many races and nationalities, a reminder that the children are part of a global village. The melting pot has new meaning for this generation; their life stories, woven with war, famine, injustice, loss, separate them, yet merge them in new ways. The schools are where it is happening, and Chris and his friends are at the vanguard of multicultural harmony, looking like a Benetton advertisement with an Anglo, a biracial American, a Vietnamese, a Chinese, an African American, an African, and a Latino bonded closely. The beauty of these friendships is the naturalness of boys growing up together sharing more similarities than differences, so that race becomes essentially irrelevant. But the change within just a few years is striking.

The morning routines continue. There is a long line at the school store, right before the morning bell rings, with youngsters buying "cool pencils" of football teams, graphic designs in metallic and fluorescent colors, as well as other supplies. Children scurry into the cafeteria to hang out with friends before classes begin.

But none of this matters to Chris and the other sixth graders as they await the moment when they will board the waiting buses to Langston Hughes. Even though it is only March, today they begin their journey to the future.

Mary Frances Musgrave, director of guidance at Langston Hughes, is waiting for the Forest Edge students as the buses pull up. Dressed impeccably in a two-piece pink knit suit, she is a tall, soft-spoken woman with a smile that puts everybody immediately at ease. There is something comforting about her conservative pastel look that conjures up visions of *Leave It to Beaver*, familiar to the kids through reruns. Her blond hair, soft white skin, and clear-rimmed glasses complete the fifties look. She greets the students warmly, as she will welcome, over the next two weeks, the students of the other six elementary schools in Reston that feed into Hughes.

The usually boisterous sixth graders walk quietly, almost deferentially, as they file into the Little Theater, a small windowless auditorium with carpeted steps that serve as bleacher seats. A half hour ago they felt big and grown-up, but now sitting in this gigantic strange school they feel like ants. As they filed in there were snickers among the seventh and eighth graders near the door—just loud enough so the teachers didn't hear the sixth graders being called "the Little People."

The welcomes and introductions over, Musgrave gets right to the first Big Question on everybody's mind: "In P.E. classes showers are not required. If you want to take one, there are six private stalls with curtains. Don't give a second thought to people staring at you. There are only four minutes between activities and when the bell rings, everyone is in a hurry." A hundred tense faces begin to relax.

More information than can possibly be processed is delivered in rapid-fire order: School begins at 7:30 A.M. and ends at 2:30 P.M. There are seven periods. Kids are organized in teams of about 125 students who share English, social studies, science, and math teachers, resource teachers, and a counselor. They can choose two electives per semester, like art, journalism, creative writing, chorus, or band. The audience begins to squirm and whisper.

Then the bell rings for change of periods. They can't see anything in this windowless room, but the noise is incredible. Approximately 1,100 adolescents—the entire school—simultaneously erupt from their classrooms and burst forth with crashing, slamming, banging, rushing, laughing sounds, a rolling river of noise that washes around them everywhere. Then, when the bell rings for the next class, it ceases abruptly. Wow. That is something, Chris thinks to himself.

Picking up after the disruption, Musgrave tells them there are twelve hundred lockers in the main lobby of the school, and they will each be assigned their own. The audience gasps at the number. Musgrave looks at them with exaggerated seriousness and tells them they must "never tell anybody their locker combination. Not even your parents." It is as if the importance of lockers and secrecy cannot be emphasized enough. There has been a lot of stealing, she is sorry to say. You must make sure you tuck your entire jacket into the locker so nobody can pull it out. Don't ever bring anything valuable to school.

"Every nine weeks we have locker clean-outs," Musgrave goes on. "You're allowed to tape pictures on your locker, get a mirror, make it uniquely yours—as long as there is nothing with drug or alcohol connotations." This is noted by the sixth graders, who are still proud to wear their "Just Say No" club shirts and who have been indoctrinated with antidrug messages for years. She informs them there will be a locker dropped off in their school in June so they can practice opening the lock, and encourages them to practice with a combination lock over the summer. And then a final ominous note: The lockers assigned to them are theirs and the adults of the school "won't search them without a good reason."

The locker etiquette is interesting but not the main thing on everybody's mind. When a panel of seventh graders, formerly Forest Edge students, comes in to answer questions, the very first is predictable: "Has anyone ever been locked in a locker?" Musgrave turns the question over to a young man who lets his listeners know that it is impossible, "because there is a shelf and no seventh grader is that small." But then he points out, much to the chagrin of teachers, that kids have sometimes been stuffed in trash cans by other kids.

The sixth graders come to life when able to chat with their peers, now veterans of this mysterious place. They find out: "Art is cool because you are allowed to eat stuff and listen to music." "Innovations and Inventions" (which their parents knew as shop) and "Teen Living" (which parents knew as home economics) are also good choices, because "You can make neat things and talk to friends." They are warned they have no time to hang out between classes and "mousse their hair," that they need to develop strategies so they don't need to return to their lockers between every period. If they are late too often, they can get detention or even fail a class. One girl says, "When I first came to this school I thought I would die because the rules were so strict," but you get used to them. They learn that the acronym for in-school suspension is TLC (Temporary Learning Center, a small room where you sit with a monitor and do your work); that detention is the next worst thing and can take place during lunch or after school; and expulsion is being thrown out of school for "really being bad, like having a weapon or something." There is no place to "skip" except the bathroom. These are all new dimensions of school entirely—skipping, detention, fights, stuffing students in trash cans. It is as if some mysterious evil comes over regular kids, something bad happens to you in middle school. But nobody asks about this. Finally, someone brings up showers again. The answer is unequivocal: "Nobody is embarrassed about PE because nobody ever takes showers."

They finally get a tour of the school, which Musgrave had described as "the capital beltway." Built on one floor with classrooms in a circle, with the hub shared by lockers smack in the middle, a gymnasium on one side, and the media/resource center on the other, it is

totally confusing. The sixth graders are so overwhelmed that they
are either stunned or slaphappy. They wander in and out of classrooms with what seem like thousands of Big Kids all staring and joking at their expense in a wildly complicated maze of hallways that go
around and around.

Orientation is disorienting. For sixth graders used to their little
nurturing world, where they enjoyed seniority for several years,
Hughes feels big, anonymous, and confusing and hints of dangers.
When asked what he remembered from this event, Chris recalled: "I
noticed the gym. That's what I liked. It had a rubber floor and everybody started jumping up and down. I noticed the locker rooms were
pretty dirty." The rest was overload.

Spring is filled with thoughts of endings and the meaning of next
year. After spring break, teachers notice a change, an increase in "attitude," a growing interest in the opposite sex, but especially an exuberance and boisterousness that becomes harder to contain. There are
wildly competitive kick ball tournaments during recess. One day in
early June, Mrs. Downes's room serves as a portrait of early adolescence: one table is surrounded by three boys and three girls—two
of the girls sitting provocatively with their legs crossed, and the
boys casually macho—all absorbed in conversation and giggles. In the
middle of the room, several boys and girls concentrate on wiring a
working bell. Others combine in same-sex groups, drawing, talking,
or playing board games. At the mirror hung in a corner of the room,
Chris, Gene, and his friend Mike are making faces and trying to outdo
each other in ugly mugs. The beauty of the classroom setup is that it
offers the youngsters a variety of comfortable places to be themselves.

The pace picks up as the school year comes closer to an end. Class
selections are made for next year. Plans are worked out for an end-
of-year celebration. The kids, hard to contain, have developed, according to their teachers, "a short-timers' attitude."

In early June, Langston Hughes principal Ed Thacker comes for a
visit, bringing an actual locker. In a final testament to elementary
school, the youngsters sit on the floor and in small chairs in the
school library to listen to him. Much is reiteration of the spring visit
to Hughes, only this time Chris gets up the courage to ask his question: "Even though you say we can't get stuck in a locker, if we were
to, how would we get out?" He is simply told it won't happen—
which does not make him very happy.

The kids are informed there will be no Sevey-Bip Day, that their lockers are their "home away from home" and if they forget their locker combination their second-period teacher will have it. Mr. Thacker emphasizes that it is "okay to get good grades" and they should not be scared of anything because there are always receptive adults to help them. But the same unsettling message comes through again when he relays the three cardinal rules for keeping safe and out of trouble in middle school:

1. Control your hands (keep them to yourself);
2. Control your feet—no running, no tripping, and get to class on time;
3. Control your mouth—don't say "ugly things," because they just feed the rumor mill.

This talk is foreign and unsettling to kids like Chris and his friends, who have gone through elementary school competing for excellence. It is not lost on them that this authority figure, the principal of their new school, feels it necessary to tell them it is okay to get good grades, and that they need to control themselves. "It's like in elementary school you are special but in middle school, you'd better behave," says Chris. Again, it registers in the minds of the listeners that there are dangers ahead, not only around them but *in* them.

Finally, in a confusing about-face, a quick change of tone that will plague the world of adolescents from hence forward, Thacker warmly concludes: "You are not going to be Forest Edge Eagles anymore. You are going to be Hughes Panthers for a few years." There is silence as this sinks in. Then smiles all around.

This seventh-grade business has unleashed a roller coaster of emotions in the sixth graders. A sense of big changes impending has them excited, confused, and scared. They share class schedules with friends, hoping to have a buddy to share the adventure. They wonder if they will be on the same bus route, if they will still be friends if on different teams. They are less worried about the routine of changing classes because of the "middle school" within Forest Edge this year. They have learned what it is like to experience different teaching styles. But what is clear is that their academic confidence doesn't touch the notion that changing schools symbolizes the true beginning of adolescence: "Like when you are in elementary school people think you are a kid. But when you get to seventh grade they think you are an adolescent," says one boy.

Back in their classrooms, the sixth graders are invited to speak openly about how they imagine seventh grade. In a written survey the week before, the question "In seventh grade I will ..." had elicited a consistent reply among over one hundred kids: "feel like I'm growing up," "be a young adult," "feel more like a teenager," "have more privileges." They grasp for the words to explain the meaning: they imagine feeling more pressure, more responsibility as life and school get more serious. In the peer setting they worry about having "less power," as Chris's friend Jeff explains, "because we're the smaller bunch and they are the bigger bunch." But they also see a quantum leap in freedom represented by getting to choose their electives, deciding to stay after school if they want and taking the late bus home, going to their locker or not, deciding their own bedtimes, staying out with friends as late as they want to. In their minds, these choices are all equivalent.

The girls seem to have a great deal to say on social life. "Seventh graders should get to go places without their parents. If their parents say they are too young, we just say they should trust us." That's right, says this girl's friend. "They should see how it goes the first time and if the kids are irresponsible or something happens, then maybe they have to wait until eighth grade." The girls think they should be able to go to the mall, to 7-Eleven, to fast-food restaurants within walking distance, to the Reston Town Center, to movies, to parties. All the kids, well versed in Just Say No programs, are aware that parties harbor the potential dangers of alcohol, drugs, and fights, but nobody has much to say about that.

The boys seem much more interested in potential trouble and protection: "There is only one thing I'm scared of if you stay out all by yourself until late or with your friends, some older kids at the mall might start messing with you and you won't know what to do and what if your friends all run away?" This unleashes a barrage of stories about times these kids have been scared even early in the evening by older groups hanging out. There is a darkness they are fighting to illuminate in the recesses of their young minds, a darkness almost unthinkable in this pleasant suburb. It's a mixture of what they see on TV, what they experience, and how they extrapolate their lessons.

"If you are staying out late at night, I think you should be allowed to have protection if you need it. Not Mace. I know Mace works but you might be so scared you wouldn't use it," says an eleven-year-old boy with big brown eyes and long bangs that he keeps brushing off his face. "When you are in high school, I think you should be able to buy a gun." His classmates get into a huge argument among themselves about whether this is a good idea—but if they get a gun, they should have an Uzi or a Glock, not a Saturday Night Special. As they continue arguing about ammunition, a soft-spoken boy interjects his thoughts: "I think you have a point but I think that maybe you shouldn't have a gun but a little knife for protection because teenagers might get out of control." His classmates clap. The teachers stand around listening, stunned at what they are hearing.

A week later at the farewell bagel breakfast all is forgotten. An army of parents has worked together to create an elegant, embracing celebration of this important passage in their children's lives. There are real white tablecloths, balloons, programs, commemorative place cards, and loving, proud parents all around—serving, smiling, hugging, and taking pictures. An original song-and-piano medley, "Memories of Forest Edge," is played. There are a few speeches. Chris is called up for a host of awards, and finally his diploma. His parents take "a million pictures," and to his chagrin, his mom cries. She isn't the only one. Tearful parents freeze-frame the moment of innocence and togetherness. Everything wonderful about the school and the community surrounds these children at this moment and everybody knows from this point forward it will be more complicated.

The next night is the official sixth-grade party at a nearby community center with an Olympic-sized pool. Chris makes his parents promise to drop him off and not stay, and his mom has to practically beg for permission to come and watch for a few minutes toward the end. It is a scene of childhood in full bloom. A huge red-and-white-spotted inflatable dog float is the focal point of roughhousing, macho posturing, flirting, and wholesome friendly exuberance from a group of kids who for the most part have known each other for more than half their lives. Mr. Dog provides a friendly invitation to be children, and the kids splash, jump, and dive from the canine raft, squealing and laughing with delight. Outside the pool, bodies that range from prepubescent to provocative move easily without the burden of inordinate self-consciousness. Parents watch through glass windows, smiling at the scene. Chris leaves reluctantly.

Summer comes. Chris goes to Reston Day Camp as he has done every year since he was five, as his brothers had before. He loves the freedom and fun, and especially the counselors, a group of teenagers and college students selected for their enthusiasm in working with kids. One of his favorites is Jonathan Tompkins. Chris learns how to weave friendship bracelets. He delights in creeking—a muddy free-for-all in a nearby nature area—and the sleepover in nearby Lake Fairfax Park, a coveted event every session with hot dogs, s'mores, and barely any sleep. On the last day, always sad for him, he wears his counselor's T-shirt, given to him as a gift, and by the end of the day it is fully autographed by kids and counselors alike. Like others he had collected previous years, this will be saved in its natural form, never to be washed.

In the evening, he often goes down to the tennis courts and plays tennis with his dad and his dad's partners, who all have grown children and have adopted Chris as their surrogate child. Summer nights, Chris camps out in front of the television and watches baseball or a movie. But all the time, he feels the pressure of the upcoming Big Change. He and his best friend Brad discuss it endlessly. But they know there are no answers until September comes. He and his mom go to visit Hughes to walk around again and study how it is laid out. As he practices his combination lock over the summer, he can never quite get over the gnawing in his stomach. What would it be like in middle school? Would he be okay? What was it going to be like to be a Real Adolescent? When would he feel like one?

August rolls around and he starts Reston Youth League football. He has his mother measure him to see if he's grown. He and his buddies compare muscles and football bruises and the scratches on their helmets signifying collisions they have withstood. His practices, held on the fields of Langston Hughes, have new meaning for him. There it is. His school. His new world. And across the way, the high school. He can see the South Lakes team practicing. Last summer he didn't think much about it, but this summer his future is in front of him. His dreams are closer. He hopes in two years he will be there in that high school stadium on the team. But first, in two weeks, it will be him in this middle school. He tells his mom he doesn't want too many new clothes until he checks out what the kids are wearing. He and Brad decide after much deliberation to buy Converse shoes. Although his mom has him fully equipped school supply–wise, he chooses to put only the bare minimum in his new backpack so as not to look too prepared, too eager for work.

The day of school finally arrives and Chris wakes up fully dressed. He pets his dogs and goes into the kitchen to hug his mom. No breakfast today—how about a vitamin pill and a glass of milk? He goes back into his room and watches the tube for a few minutes until it is time to leave. His mom embraces him a little longer and then secretly watches from the window as Chris goes out to stand with the other adolescents as they wait for the bus to take them to Langston Hughes and South Lakes.

Two miles across Reston, he will step over a great divide. He knows it. His parents know it. The community knows it. The end of childhood, the official beginning of adolescence. Chris and his peers are about to enter a time of life that can be understood, according to one South Lakes High School senior looking back, as "a long dark tunnel with many twists and turns and a narrow exit."

# Speaking Out / Acting Out

Thirteen-year-old Jessica Jones sashays into her bedroom balancing a glass of milk and a plate with a bologna sandwich on top of an open notebook, pausing at the door to fling back her blond shoulder-length hair. Once at her desk, she sweeps a stack of books to the floor with her elbow and puts down her snack. Then she flops on her belly on her bed, nestling herself among the pillows edged in lace, the soft white angora stuffed cat with a bell on its tail, the well-worn Curious George, and the Xerox copies of magazine articles on teen pregnancy. She stretches out her arm to turn on her boom box for the sounds of Boyz II Men, and settles in to work.

Her mother has finally stopped lecturing her on how she ought to use her desk for homework. In fact, the desktop could be the start of an archaeological dig for the totems of young female adolescents circa 1992. The bologna sandwich and glass of milk sit surrounded by a four-inch stack of photo packets containing snapshots of her best friend Annie's birthday party last spring, the excursion with five girlfriends to Kings Dominion over the summer, mock modeling poses taken by her friend Mitch, the family trip to Newport, and at the bottom of the pile, pictures of ice skating at Town Center last winter. There is a hodgepodge of schoolbooks, teen novels, school papers, letters, cups of pencils, baskets of barrettes and bobby pins. Dirty laundry is draped over the chair back and seat awaiting the free moment or the dire necessity that would inspire Jessica to do her own wash—a recently acquired responsibility. On the floor lie *Seventeen, Allure,* and some notes from her friends. There definitely is no chance that she will do homework on this desk.

The fresh white wallpaper sprinkled with tiny pink rosebuds, the pink trim, the crisp white eyelet bedspread with matching pillows and bed ruffle are merely backdrop to Jessica's personal decorating scheme. Posters above her desk display a sleek black panther and one of the eight remaining white tigers in the world. Reggae artist Bob Marley and the rap group Digital Underground are prominent among numerous clipped magazine advertisements pinned to the walls near her bed and across the top of the closet. Pubescent sexuality is expressed boldly on the wall beside her pillow: a couple of big posters of "incredibly hot hunks"—two men stripped to the waist, one labeled "Breakfast in Bed" and the other, wearing jeans with a prominent unbuttoned fly, "A Hard Man Is Good to Find." There are photos stuck everywhere—school photos, mug shots of friends hamming it up, family pictures, some from when she was a little girl. Her softball mitt hangs over her bat in the corner, her closet is bursting with clothes ranging from overalls to a slinky red strapless dress. Like a giant collage of early adolescence, her room displays her memories, her present jumble of hopes, expectations, and loves. It is sweet and sexy, playful and passionate, exploring and exhibitionistic, a statement of Jessica Jones at thirteen years and three months, upfront, in your face, full of life and contradictions. And most important, it is a private space where she can see what matters to her.

It is her room, her choice how to live in it. And since she almost always gets As, who can complain about her homework style? "I plan to be a good student. I really care about my grades and that's my future. I know what I want to do in life," she states with customary stubbornness. She wants a ring in her navel, to be a high school football player (not a cheerleader), to get straight As, to be a marine biologist, to be an actress, to take care of her friends. She wants cooler clothes but needs more money, she wishes math were easier, that Reston had an ocean, and that she could be tan all year.

Actually, the only advantage to working at a desk instead of on her bed might be that it wouldn't be as easy to fall asleep. She often dozes when doing homework and then has to stay up even later. It isn't her fault. The hours of school are so outrageous. Anybody with any sense knows that teenagers cannot function for classes that start at 7:35 in the morning when they rarely get to sleep before 11:00.

But today she is buzzed. The assignment given to her civics class is truly cool. All the kids have to write a political speech on an important topic the candidates in the 1992 election have not addressed. And then, the best thing, a bunch of speeches will actually be delivered in a special assembly to which representatives of both parties are invited. So cool! It is a real-life opportunity for her classmates' opinions to be heard. Jessica loves being center stage. She'd been torn between writing about rape or teen pregnancy. She discussed it with Annie, who is in her class. Annie thought Jessica should write about teenage pregnancy, and Jessica agreed: "I thought it was a good idea because I actually had it happening to someone close to me."

This is one of the best assignments her teacher, Mrs. Nance, ever gave in civics, Jessica thinks as she props herself up on her elbows, tucks a curl behind her ear, and begins to write. The words tumble out: "Some of you are probably thinking this doesn't apply to you, so you don't have to listen. Let me tell you now, you should listen. Maybe it doesn't apply to you now but it hits us all at one point. Someone's sister, girlfriend, friend, relative, or even your brother getting a girl pregnant—believe me, it hits you. You think it can never happen to you but it can." Jessica knows. This was her seventeen-year-old sister Kelly's room until just a short time ago when she moved out with her new baby to live in an apartment with her boyfriend.

Jessica still thinks a lot about the night her parents told her: "In the winter, Kelly and Matt went into my parents' room and shut the door and I was like, Oh my God, something must be going on because that's what happens when we have big talks in my family. You go in there and shut the door." A few weeks later, when she'd forgotten the incident, her parents called her in. "I'll never forget this ever in my life—there was this somber kind of attitude when I walked in. I lay down at the bottom of the bed like I always do when we talk, but I was scared. They both were sitting at the top, and they didn't say anything at first, like they were searching for the right words. Then my dad said, 'There is no easy way to tell you this, Jessica,' and I thought someone had died because that is what usually happens. Then my dad said, 'Kelly's pregnant.' At first, I was kind of happy because nobody had died and I always kind of wanted a little brother or sister. But I was mad that they told my big brother first. All this had been going on and I was the last to know!" Her happiness was short-lived.

The baby was born in early September, she writes, and it was really hard. "When I found out that my sister was pregnant, people told me it would be cute and so fun, but they didn't know that having a baby means taking my sister's time so that she can't be with me anymore. I wish I could take my sister's pregnancy back. It's really hard for me to talk about this because in the last couple of months my life has changed so radically." She stops and reaches for her private "grieving box," a shoebox she keeps tucked beside her bed filled with photos of her sister and her together all through their lives until the baby was born. She looks at them, feeling the loss strongly, then goes back to writing.

She is so absorbed in her task that she is startled when her mom calls her to dinner. She'd been working for almost two hours! She bounds down the stairs into the kitchen eager to read the speech to her parents.

The Jones family loves to hang out in the kitchen. The big oak table is the gathering spot for conversations, the place where the kids have done their school projects, where the family wraps Christmas gifts for the poor. After school, Jessica likes to have a snack with her mom and talk about the school day. The bay window, framed by mint-green-and-peach colonial print café curtains, looks out on a large front yard filled with dozens of trees. In the window hangs a wreath of twigs that encircles a shamrock of stained glass, and Jessica loves this symbol of the family's Irish ancestry. The Jones kids have grown up here, and some days the table seems too huge for just Jessica and her mom and dad now that her brother is at college and Kelly has moved out. But the family is present in pictures on the wall, school calendars, and schedules posted on the refrigerator.

This evening, as always, there is a filling meal in pots on the stove, but the routine is strictly 1990s: help-yourself. The Joneses hardly ever eat together during the week anymore—too many demands and activities. There are church groups, sports in season, flute lessons, exercise, errands, friends, and now, of course, baby-sitting. The Jones house is warm and hospitable and often friends and extended family come by. There's always plenty on the stove for them too.

Jessica's parents are still reeling from the shock of their middle child's pregnancy, and found only a modicum of solace at a recent church function where they sat at a table with no less than four other couples, good involved parents like themselves, whose kids were pregnant or already parents. But they are people of faith, deeply committed to unconditionally loving their children and standing by them. It is a matter of perspective. In the past two years, they have suffered many of the tragedies of contemporary life: Jessica's dad had a brother die of AIDS, her mom had a mentally ill brother die in an accident, and the daughter of her dad's longtime secretary was murdered on the streets of D.C. That's why Jessica was so scared she was going to find out someone had died again, and why, in the whole scheme of things, her parents were relieved Kelly's pregnancy was about life and not death. They supported Kelly by listening without getting hysterical, by encouraging the young couple to get counseling, even to consider abortion although it was antithetical to their Catholic faith. So many things had happened in their family that the fact that Matt was black did not concern them except so far as the world might be more difficult for a biracial child. Fortunately, the two kids had been dating for several years, and having them live together seemed like a good trial run for the wedding they planned in July. It certainly was not the scenario anybody in the Jones household had imagined. Jessica's mom thought her heart would break when she helped Kelly and the baby move out, but the baby was now a part of all of them.

While all this was going on, Jessica felt displaced and overlooked, so she is pleased to have her parents' full attention again. She can tell as she reads that her mom and dad really like the speech. They praise her research and her honesty. Her dad offers to type it up before he goes to bed.

In the morning, as usual, her dad has breakfast with her before he goes downtown. Her mom goes to her job in Reston early so she can be back for Jessica after school. After breakfast, her dad gives her the typed speech and reiterates his pride in her work. She thanks him, tucks the pages in her backpack, gives him a kiss and a hug, and dashes out the door to meet her bus.

Squeals greet Jessica as she walks in the school doors. Her friends Annie, Susan, and Rachel envelop her with chatter as they walk in unison to her locker. It is the end of October and Langston Hughes Middle School is in full swing. While seventh graders like Chris Hughes still walk around in a daze, the eighth graders are full of themselves. They feel catapulted to the top of a progression from Little Kid to Big Kid. Just look at them: from the chrysalis of the summer months they have emerged as new beings. Some of the boys have grown as much as four inches, and now lope around in vastly different bodies anchored by gargantuan shoes. Many of the girls—who generally achieve their growth spurts earlier—have become more womanly, a look exaggerated in many cases through the use of dramatic makeup and stylized attire. Their self-consciousness about the changes in their bodies makes even more sweet the opportunity to exult in being "the Bosses of the School."

A large banner hangs inside the front doors of Hughes: IMAGE IS EVERYTHING. The school is saturated with the aura of self-conscious posing among middle school students. They walk around hyperalert to what is cool and what is not, who to be like, who is or is not one's friend, what to wear, what to do, how to act. Students are in a state of constant vigilance not always conducive to learning.

While Chris Hughes and his classmates step gingerly into the maelstrom that is middle school, cautious about doing the "right" thing as defined by their peers, the eighth graders are cocky. They are the trendsetters, top dogs at the school with high school still ten months away—something you can brag about being close to without worrying that you have to go there soon! They bask in the comfort of their return to Hughes. Last year they were worried little seventh graders, recalls Jessica. No problem this year—they have seen the eighth-grade menace and it is them.

Beyond the bravado, however, is a more serious undercurrent. The exaggerated self-confidence, the arrogance of eighth graders covers an awareness of the moment as fleeting, because, says Jessica, "Next year everything counts." Kids have heard forever that high school is the beginning of the Great Divide. What you do, what you achieve from the minute you enter ninth grade determines your future: what college, if college at all, what money you will be able to make, whether you can achieve happiness in life. The message is hammered into them until many honestly believe their lives will be determined by how they perform in school starting at approximately age fourteen. Eighth graders know in their own ways of understanding that this is their last year to be a Real Kid. At the same time, "eighth grade is the turning point," explains Katy. "It is the point where you go upward or downward or straight up the middle. I came into eighth grade thinking, Wow! I rule the school. The high schoolers aren't making fun of me anymore. Now I feel that this is the year when you choose where you are going." Sometimes all this leaves eighth graders feeling they're in suspended animation. For many, the lesson derived is have a hell of a time in eighth grade before you have to get *really* serious.

The Eighth Grade Attitude is immediately obvious on entering Beverly Nance's fourth-period civics class. There is an atmosphere of good-natured defiance, an unspoken challenge to the teacher to win the students' attention. Girls huddle together in secret conferences, furtively looking around to make sure no one is eavesdropping. A couple in the corner sneaks a quick squeeze of their hands. One girl runs a brush through her hair. Three boys loudly squabble about why Mark Rypien is or is not a quarterback worth having on the Redskins; one ends up tipping his chair and falling with a thud on the floor. Laughter. At the very moment the tardy bell rings, Jessica and Annie collapse theatrically in their seats, still chattering and with a final wave to a friend in the hall. The bell stops ringing and still nobody pays attention. Annie is rummaging through her backpack for her speech. Jessica is freshening her lipstick.

"Ladies and gentlemen!" says Mrs. Nance above the din. "Could we please take our seats!" She looks straight at Jessica, who dramatically flings her hair off her face. Nance can be irritable, but Jessica clearly has an attitude this year that the teachers are trying to corral. On several occasions during their daily meetings, the teachers of the Silver Streak team have discussed her sister's baby and how the whole situation upstages Jessica, but there is only so much slack they can cut when she acts sassy, something that is occurring with regularity.

The third time Nance says it, the class very slowly settles down. A few chatterboxes persist, but finally there is quiet.

"Today, ladies and gentlemen," Mrs. Nance announces, "we will continue with our political speeches. Each one of you will get a chance to read your speech in front of the class. We will all critique it to help you make it forceful and clear. Some of you will be selected to read in our assembly later this week. Remember, this is your opportunity to address the issues you think are important that are being overlooked by Bush, Clinton, and Perot."

Election fever has hit Langston Hughes. The school is ablaze with red, white, and blue. Political cartoons, essays on democracy and the use of statistics in elections, posters, buttons, stickers, and critiques on the debates are woven throughout the curriculum and displayed on bulletin boards in classrooms, and in the library, cafeteria, and main lobby. This is the middle school team concept at its best: each team's core teachers in math, English, social studies, and science co-ordinate activities around the central election theme. This affords students a great learning opportunity and creates involvement and excitement about a major national event that will reach a crescendo when the Hughes students cast their ballots the day before the national election.

In Mrs. Nance's room, two walls of bulletin boards display colorful posters that exhort the unseeing adult world: "Choose or Lose! The Choice Is Yours" and "Vote! It's a Privilege!" "Discover the Power of the Vote!" and their adolescent spin on the election of 1992, "Don't drink then vote!" Posters for Clinton, Bush, and Perot excite arguments as the kids support their stands. Many delight in being of the opposite party from their parents—a superb opportunity to disagree in a whole new area. This all serves as backdrop to the main event: their political speeches.

The students like this assignment. Everybody is prepared. Remarkably, some students bring in two speeches, having done *twice* the homework assigned. Nance is counting on Jessica's gifted and talented class to provide the best speeches to showcase in the upcoming assembly for parents and two representatives from the Democratic and Republican Parties of Fairfax County. Nance begins the day with a freckle-faced, cherubic young man who argues passionately that the voting age should be lowered to sixteen: "Why should children who have good ideas, are good citizens, and are interested in the elections not be allowed to vote because of their age? The new president will be trying to help the deficit that will affect us, solve problems that will affect us, and create jobs that will affect us, the children. So if you have good ideas for the government, you should be able to give your ideas, not be prevented because of your age." More radical is his classmate who feels thirteen-year-olds capable of passing an eligibility test that proves adequate knowledge of current events and politics should be allowed to vote. "It's not right," protests the next speaker, a bright, opinionated young woman, "that guns—such a powerful tool—are sold so easily. When I watch the news and hear reports about accidental shootings, I wonder why it is that people sell these weapons to such irresponsible people. Why is it that kids have access to such powerful weapons?" The kids all know there are guns around, and two incidents last spring, one at South Lakes and one at Hughes, brought the message frighteningly close to these students.

This is a side rarely seen. One after another, the students transform from chatty, oppositional, silly, blasé eighth graders to serious, concerned citizens. Developmentally their speeches reflect their increased ability to tackle issues logically and with higher abstract-thinking skills. Emotionally both the speeches and the students' reactions to them give insight into issues of concern to them that go well beyond customary perceptions of adolescents as self-absorbed.

These youngsters on the Silver Streak Team worry about their environment, AIDS, homelessness, gun control, the justice system, and budget cuts in their schools. Probably few adults had considered that the school budget controversy swirling around students matters to them, but several speakers focus on how students are as much the victims as teachers. They talk about how supplies and textbooks are rationed, how teachers are less inclined to take on after-school activities. They think it is wrong for teachers to be underpaid and that devaluing teachers not only devalues their school experience but also gives students a mixed message about the importance of education. They exhibit a sense of fairness: "Teachers teach the world. They teach people how to read and write. They teach doctors to be doctors and lawyers to be lawyers. Then the doctors and the lawyers go off to excellent-paying jobs and teachers don't even get recognized." They resent the debates to cut nonessential academics: "Math, science, English, and history are the building blocks of the educational process, but home economics, art, music, and shop *should not* be ignored. They are the mortar that holds it all together. They help kids experience life better." Dan Quayle had just made his attack on Murphy Brown, inspiring the speech of a girl who admits that Murphy Brown may glamorize single motherhood, but: "Get real. Does she really make it seem glamorous? Being a single parent is a tough job. You must do double duty, which sometimes means working two jobs just to support your child. A family isn't defined by how many parents there are but by how much love and support there is." In a school where approximately half the students come from single-parent families, Quayle's remarks sting.

In between speeches, the talking and horsing around continue. But the assignment has power and interest. The students listen; they argue; they applaud each other. Adolescents no longer live in a protected sphere. They read newspapers for current events, watch the news. The woes of the world belong to them too.

When they talk about homelessness or budget cuts or health care, Mrs. Nance looks proud. But when they take on the issues of their adolescent world, Mrs. Nance and the administrators freak. The paradox of the middle school concept is that it derives from an understanding of early adolescence as a time of special vulnerability, especially in a world where young people face unprecedented choices and pressures. Middle school is designed to meet the specific developmental, emotional, and educational needs of young adolescents, to nurture them and prevent the proliferation of risky behaviors related to sex, substances, absenteeism, and violence. "This is the age when young people begin to wonder about and want to understand great themes such as power, justice, beauty, compassion, courage and faith," writes psychologist Peter Scales in *Boxed in and Bored*, the Search Institute's latest study on middle schools. "They can be deeply engaged by discussions of sex, race, gender, wealth and poverty, prejudice and privilege, and any number of moral and ethical issues found in current events." But as the speeches in Mrs. Nance's class reveal, there is a tug-of-war between the nitty-gritty of what young adolescents deal with and the readiness of the schools and larger society to deal with kids directly.

One issue looming large for them is drugs. One fourth of Jessica's class, for example, prepared speeches on kids and drugs, and of those, several focused on substance abuse in school. In this area where adults and adolescents desperately need a dialogue, the response is less than embracing. Mrs. Nance is nervous.

She'd already had quite a bit of fallout from Susan's speech in her first-period class. The speech, "Looking Beneath the Surface," carefully detailed the use of substances *in* middle school, which Susan felt "teachers fail to address." "I know you're saying, kids can't drink and not get caught. Oh yes they can. How? Most of the kids in Reston have parents that drink, who have bars in the basement, or have wine cellars in the home." With a generous supply available, carrying liquor to school is easy. "All they have to do is take some rum and put it in a water bottle and add some soda. Or maybe mix some vodka and orange juice. The teachers think they are having breakfast." Susan warned that the drinkers may not be obvious—"Many are A or B students."

By the time she got to drugs, the adults in the classroom were practically apoplectic. "Last year, there was selling of drugs in the locker commons, outside and even during classes. Lots of kids know exactly how much it will cost, and when they can get things cheaper because a dealer is having a bad day." She even addressed how some kids get drugs from their parents who also do drugs: "It is not that such parents *give* the drugs to their kids. The kids just steal it from Mom and Dad, and they know they won't be asked or accused because the parents don't want their kids to know that they do drugs." Even though a lot of kids think it is really dumb to do cocaine or crack, they think pot is okay—that it's just a little worse than cigarettes. Sometimes kids who leave class to smoke are smoking pot.

But the teachers don't put it all together, Susan said. "I know you are asking yourself: How can kids use drugs, drink, and smoke at school without getting caught? They are smarter than you think. They watch teachers and see when they're going to certain places, and at what time. Or they steal office passes and say they had to talk to a teacher, and when they come in later, they don't get into trouble."

Susan ended with a plea that would be repeated over and over in conversations with adolescents, a plea that asks for boundaries and the structure that comes from being known: "Just remember, that quiet girl in the back of the class may not be what she appears. That boy that never talks to anyone and loves to read in his spare time may be extremely out-of-control on Friday nights. You adults need to give us more attention. We are not as innocent as you may think. . . . You need to talk to us and watch us and be alert. . . . It is very easy to fool you. It is very easy to lie to you. Teachers and parents need to be smarter about us and stop denying what is really going on."

Within an hour of this speech, it was all over the school. The students are astounded at her frankness and admire her for it. Many students openly concur with what she said. Jessica and Katy talk about the speech during a break in their class. "Almost every single party you go to has a bottle of vodka," confides Katy. Jessica is exasperated that no grownup at Hughes seems inclined to pay serious attention to her friend's speech: "I'm sorry, the teachers have to be stupid or something not to know that kids are coming to school on drugs."

The kids' eagerness to share what they know is surprising to teachers swept into conversation, but the teachers are clearly reluctant to get too involved because, as one confides off the record, "It sets into motion a whole line of reporting responsibilities." Another adult reaction is to focus solely on Susan and believe that the problems she described are her own, or are wildly exaggerated. Yet an informal survey done later of all the classes on the team corroborated the contents of the speech. Students were asked to write anonymously three things that they "absolutely, positively knew, saw, or experienced concerning drugs and alcohol among kids in Reston," and only two could not think of any.

Ironically, at precisely the same time as Susan's speech there is a big move among adults in the school to convene drug discussion groups at parents' homes, since every time the school or PTA has called an adult meeting on the topic, few showed up. The October *Parents' Bulletin* states: "Reducing alcohol, drug and tobacco use among public school students is a priority to school officials, parents and community members." It exhorts parents to sign the Parent's Pledge for Drug Free Youth. The Fairfax County Public Schools biennial substance abuse survey is conducted in classrooms all over the county the same month, and it yields the information that the most dramatic increase in "gateway drugs"—cigarettes, alcohol, marijuana—occurs between seventh and eighth grades and that one third of all middle school students consume beer. National figures corroborate the story in Reston.

Yet nobody wanted to listen to the kids. Copies of Susan's speech and a compilation of the classroom survey were never circulated to an adult audience even while teachers, administrators, and parents professed to grapple with the problem. When the school convened its home meetings on drugs and youth, hardly anybody came.

Jessica, who has been in a huff over how Susan was doubted and ignored, is having her own problems as well. She and her buddy Annie have waited two days for their turn to deliver their speeches. Every time Mrs. Nance asks for volunteers, they wave their hands. By now everybody in the class knows what they want to talk about and there is a movement in the classroom to move them up to the dais.

Katy is angry too. When she was told point-blank no speeches about abortion, she fired one back on freedom of speech. "This speech was going to be on abortion but the school outlawed the topic and decided a student couldn't talk about it. So I am going to talk instead about freedom of speech. When my class was given this assignment we were told to talk about what was on our minds. But how can we talk about what is on our minds when they limit the issues that we can talk about? . . . When you are a teenager, you are supposed to be finding out about who you are, but if opinions are outlawed, how will you find out how you *feel*?"

Finally, Annie gets her chance. She is a willowy young woman of

Caribbean parentage, and her smooth dark skin accents large brown eyes that look directly at her audience. When she begins by posing the question of what is the line between harmless flirtation and harassment, there is a lot of squirming, nervous laughter, and rolling of eyes among some of the boys, which comes to a quick halt with emphatic *Shhhhhhs* from the girls, who lean forward to hear every word. "My opinion is that if someone says or does something sexually related that makes you uncomfortable and this has been communicated to the person, if the treatment persists then they have crossed the line between flirtation and harassment. 'Sexual harassment' may seem like a strong phrase for a little grabbing or a few words, but think about what it can lead to. If you let such treatment continue, you are putting yourself in danger. In most cases of harassment, the less you say, the more rights the harasser will think they have. Then by the time that the harassment gets violent and crosses over the line of assault, it is usually too late. This is the exact reason why you should make your expectations for a relationship or even a date clear from the start. Our grandparents and even our parents were taught to be coy with each other. . . . Nowadays we can't afford to confuse each other. 'No!' doesn't mean yes or try harder or maybe you can convince me, it means 'No!' "

The audience bursts into discussion among themselves, interrupted by Nance calling for quiet. She critiques Annie's language as too strong. Annie erupts: "It happens to everybody! You hear girls talking and its, 'Oh yeah, her too, me too,' and nothing is being done!" Katy chimes in: "They talk about your body parts, they cop a feel, they drop pencils to try and look up your dress. It's like mildly raping someone." But unless an authority sees it happening, nothing is done.

Annie can't understand why she is told that the topic is inappropriate for the assembly. "Lots of guys don't know this. Maybe some of those people who do it would learn something." Although she does not reveal it, Annie had recently been at a small gathering of friends where the line was crossed with her.

In June of 1993, the American Association of University Women had released *Hostile Hallways: The AAUW Survey on Sexual Harassment in America's Schools* to a blaze of publicity. The report stated that four of five eighth through eleventh graders had experienced some form of sexual harassment in their school life—85 percent of girls and 75 percent of boys. The National School Safety

Center News Service called sexual harassment the most "overlooked and underreported offense today." But Annie and her classmates are not allowed to discuss it.

Three days after Jessica bounded down the stairs to read her parents her speech, she is at last allowed to read it in class. It is a whole new spin on teen pregnancy. You can see in the students' faces that they had never considered how a teen pregnancy could change an entire family. They relate to Jessica's loneliness for her sister. Her words are not the usual harangue against teen sex but an explanation of possible consequences that touches their hearts. When Jessica finishes, several students spontaneously get up and hug her. Her teacher says the speech is moving but, of course, it cannot be part of the assembly. Maybe Jessica could deliver it in a sex education class if the assistant principal gives permission.

The three girls, Jessica, Annie, and Katy, denied what they consider their rightful due, march directly up to Mrs. Nance's desk after class and demand their rights vehemently but politely. They refer to the First Amendment, hint at discrimination, and openly plead that they be allowed to present their speeches based on the need their peers have to know about these things.

Mrs. Nance and the colleague assisting her answer in precise and condescending tones. "This is a real eye-opener," says Mrs. Nance, choosing her words carefully. "We are already getting the administration in on it so we can have meetings after school if people so desire to discuss these topics."

"We want to hear your observations, girls," adds the colleague. "You do have a voice and you have a right to say it but once you come onto school property you are in an organization that represents our society and we have an obligation to reflect our society and be constrained by its rules."

Amazingly, the girls do not interrupt as Mrs. Nance continues: "You'll never accomplish what you want by being bulls in a china shop. If you feel that children should be more informed at an earlier age, you have to figure out a way to do it. You don't just do it by jumping the gun. All I can tell you is continue with your writing, continue with what you believe in, but don't be pushy and not use insight. Thank you, ladies."

Jessica marches out of the room. "I was really upset. I went to the assistant principal and said I want to read my speech. She said, 'Jessica, your speech brought tears to my eyes but I can't let you read it because it would stir up so much controversy.' Then she said I could say it in sex ed class. When I later asked for a date, she reneged and told me, 'I'm sorry, I forgot we have to run everything through the Board and it takes like five years.' They were just trying to shut me up."

The day of the assembly arrives and representatives of the Silver Streak Team deliver their speeches on "approved" topics like health care policy, education, homelessness, unemployment, crime, and the national debt. The official representatives of the two political parties respond, and the meeting is open for discussion from the floor.

Without missing a nanosecond, Katy asks their opinion on abortion, Jessica on teen pregnancy. Over their "mealymouth answers" Katy shrieks: "Why aren't you addressing these issues and why don't you care about what we care about?" The kids scream in wild approval, while teachers try uselessly to hush them. Jessica tries to get the adults to acknowledge the ties between teenage pregnancy and abortion, homelessness, and censorship. "The reason so many girls are getting pregnant is because they need to be informed," she insists. Pretty soon the kids have taken charge, to the teachers' chagrin. They want answers on drugs, on juvenile crime, on issues that directly concern them. When the bell rings for the next class, they keep talking and asking questions, ignoring their teachers. They are insistent and want answers from these adults who represent the political parties. They follow the speakers out of the auditorium until finally they agree to come into their classroom for the remaining minutes between periods.

That night Jessica recalls the incident in a discussion with her parents: "I was so pissed off. They say, 'We want to hear what your opinions are,' but the things that apply to us most they won't let us talk about." Then her face lights up as she realizes she actually did win something in the assembly. "They had to answer us, at least for a little while. That was cool."

With that, she gives each of her parents a hug, goes up to her bedroom, flops on her bed, and calls up Annie. They don't mention the speeches anymore, but they talk for over an hour about boys and clothes, their favorite drama class and how they will become famous actresses—important stuff to a girl thirteen years and three months old. At least at that moment.

# High School
# Is for Making Memories

It's School Color Day at South Lakes High School, the Friday before Homecoming, and freshman Brendon Lamont is happy. High school is turning out to be so much fun, so much to do, so many people. There has been nothing scary about the transition. He finds it a relief to be out of Hughes. All anybody cared about there was rules. South Lakes is a happening place. Every day this week has been something different: today most of the kids and teachers are wearing blue and green, the colors of the South Lakes Seahawks. Tuesday was Hat Day and people wore everything from berets to sombreros to the wildest he saw: a guy with the floppy striped top hat of the Cat in the Hat. On College Day, students wore shirts with college names, which isn't unusual, but Beach Day was funny, with students walking in flip-flops, shorts, and skimpy tops, dragging around beach towels during this unusually cool fall week. On Tuesday after school, there was the Powder Puff game between junior and senior girls with guys as the cheerleaders. Middle school had nothing going on—it was go to classes, get yelled at, go home, watch the tube. High school has so much more to offer.

Ever since Brendon began high school almost two months ago, he's been busier than ever. As if choosing from an à la carte menu, Brendon is sampling high school life. He's on the freshman football team and even though he mostly sits on the sidelines, he knows practice is great conditioning for his important sport, wrestling. Sometimes he works on his pieces in the art room after school, before practice. Art is his favorite subject and the opportunity to spend additional time on his passion is soothing. He says he doesn't ever mind being alone if he has his drawing materials. But he doesn't want to be alone. He wants badly to be in the mainstream of school and he is trying like crazy. The way he sees it, "High school is for making memories."

He's been involved after school and in the evenings every day for weeks now on building the freshman float for the Homecoming parade. The theme of the parade is cartoons, and his class is doing the Flintstones. He loves the socializing, hanging out with his classmates. He feels alive, part of something. He smiles and explains, "That's what school spirit is about."

The route he takes to popularity is another matter. His audacity is what strikes his teachers. This Friday, more wound up than usual because of Homecoming, he saunters into his world history class, twirls his chair around backwards, sits down and leans forward until only two chair legs are on the ground, chomps emphatically on a wad of gum, and challenges an adult visitor in the classroom loudly: "Are you an inspector?" Caught off guard, the visitor mumbles some disclaimer, but Brendon is on a roll. He makes cracks about the "school police" and good naturedly gibes the now embarrassed outsider until he gets a rise out of the students around him. His teacher finally intervenes and he looks down with exaggerated sheepishness, slowly rearranges himself correctly in the chair, and quiets down—until the next outburst. His impishness, coupled with his dark-haired, dark-eyed good looks, gives him an irresistible charm.

Brendon's trademark Boston Red Sox hat turned backwards is a testament to the new freedom he feels—all hats were banned at Langston Hughes. "In high school, it's my choice," he says triumphantly. What he doesn't know is that administrators have to choose their issues. The Parent/Student Handbook devotes a single line to fashion—"Students are required to be appropriately dressed at all times"—while sections on substance abuse, weapons possession, and cheating/plagiarizing continue to grow. Maybe he went over the line when he strolled into his class wearing Mickey Mouse ears last week, but hey! his teacher should have a sense of humor.

He is the class clown, irrepressible, funny, outgoing, spontaneous, with a devil-may-care attitude that is the bane of his teachers at the same time it makes them smile inside. In a school environment where attitude often reeks with the threat of real violence, he is comic relief—an irritant, not a threat, to his teachers. Just last week, for example, he got detention for coming late to detention assigned for being late (again) for a class. But his goofiness feels familiar, like a throwback to simpler days. In a school where the system of discipline is overloaded with more serious offenses, a kid like Brendon gets away with behaviors that harm mostly himself by denying him the lessons of better self-control and adherence to standards. Only time will tell where they'll lead him.

Brendon, who always refers to his three older siblings in explaining himself, comes by his self-proclaimed style—"cutting up and laughing"—naturally. His brother Steven, a senior, is known as a partying guy, as was his oldest brother, Jess, before he left for college. Only his sister, Jenny, a sophomore, is of a different mold. The boys call her "Miss Perfect," sometimes with a little jealousy, a bit of annoyance, but mostly admiration. "She's classy," explains Brendon. "She's crazy sometimes too," but not too often. A fabulous student, athlete, and artist, well behaved and deeply religious, she always stands directly ahead of him in school and, although he tries to ignore it, she points to his failures by her successes. He feels he can never live up to her talents, or to her basic goodness, so the way of his brothers is the way for him. With the family roots in Cajun country, there is a "wild streak" in the Lamont family, he explains. They all like to have a good time. Family visits to Louisiana remind him how it is to be "laid back" and "into the good life." That's how he wants his life to be. Life is to "have a ball."

Courtney Smith thinks Brendon's a stitch. And very cute. She's had a crush on him for weeks, ever since they started sneaking smokes behind the school during lunch break. The problem is that he likes her good friend Suzanne, and Courtney's supposed to like Rick. But she really doesn't like Rick that much, and Suzanne isn't that crazy about Brendon. Courtney worries that Suzanne will get mad if she hooks up with Brendon, "like she owns him or something." Courtney is going to have to do something about the situation. She doesn't want to make her friend angry, but she wants Brendon to "really like her." Maybe he does like her, but does he *really* like her? It was hard to tell when they were smoking with a lot of people. At least they like the same things, like hanging out and smoking. Maybe this weekend when they all sit together at the Homecoming dance . . . well, you can never tell what might happen.

Petite, raven-haired, blue-eyed Courtney is the quintessential

American high school girl. This Friday she's dressed in unassuming green jeans and an oversize Champion sweatshirt with a tiny edge of a teal T-shirt peeking out. Her appealing, fresh-scrubbed look is complemented by her enthusiastic chatter. She is crazy about being in high school. It's the freedom and the newness of it all. She loves novelty, and Hughes got old "real fast." When she was in her eighth-grade English class, which faced the high school, she'd stare out the window and wish she were there. She'd sit in the bus and listen to the high school kids talk about parties, driving, and how they went to the beach together with no parents, and she'd imagine herself one of them. It was so cool. The thing is, her older sister Ann, a sophomore, isn't a good example for her: "She doesn't do anything because she's such a goody-goody." But not Courtney. Courtney is determined to have fun. She likes Ann all right, after all they are sisters, but Ann is always on her case for smoking, and forgetting to lock the front door in the morning, and staying out too late.

Courtney is not totally hang-loose. She admits she was a little bit worried when high school began. "The bigness was awesome," with eighteen hundred students and such a huge building. But not for long. She knew she could figure it out. She's definitely not a worrier like her sister. There is a hint of self-consciousness behind her free-spirit airs. One of the reasons she likes high school better is that at Hughes she felt "pushed to do worse things. . . . You are in a smaller school with less people so you are just pressured because people pay more attention to what other people say, what kinds of clothes you wear and what you look like." The bigness of South Lakes makes her feel less self-conscious and more in control of what she wants to do.

Her problem is she doesn't know exactly what. Whereas in Brendon's family, extracurricular activities are expected to be important, and Brendon loves his hobbies of drawing and fly-fishing, Courtney is at loose ends. Her family doesn't care if she does anything extra in school or out of school; in fact, her sister is being docked from track, which she loves, because she got a C on her report card. Not only is Ann crushed, but the coach is upset that his personal plea to the parents was ignored. Courtney and Ann's mom and stepfather are busy with their own lives, and their dad, living in Florida with his second wife, doesn't have much day-to-day influence. So with no encouragement or any real guidance from home, Courtney decides her extracurricular activities are "getting away with stuff and talking on the phone."

To Courtney, school is about friends: "I love gym. It's the only time you ever get to talk, interact with other kids. In English you get to talk for two minutes when the teacher is gone to the bathroom or looks the other way, and in between classes you have no time." Lunch, which is about socializing, is Courtney's favorite period.

This sunny autumn day at 10:06 A.M.—in one of the oddest scheduling decisions in the high school—it is time for lunch. Hundreds of students pour from the classrooms into the four cafeterias at South Lakes. But not Courtney and her friends. Her best friend Allie's older sister has a car, and usually all three dash out the door the minute class ends, before the school guards (called "Narcs" by the kids) reach their posts. "Susie would forge a note to the dentist and we'd meet her on the other side of the school and head for McDonald's. If we got to our next class late, I'd just tell the teacher I was in the bathroom." She doesn't drive to lunch every day, but, as a matter of principle: "We never eat in the cafeteria. I'll eat outside even when it snows. In the beginning of the school year, the outside was pretty full. But now we sit on one side of the school and nobody is there but us. We just don't like the atmosphere of the lunchroom. I guess it's because all through elementary school and last year we were forced into eating where we were told to." Courtney just doesn't like playing by the rules.

When school is the main arena for growing up, lunch becomes a major symbol of freedom. In elementary school, students march in a line to the cafeteria. In middle school at Hughes, the students are assigned tables for the year, a source of enormous resentment when who you want to "hang with" isn't there. At South Lakes, the four lunchrooms, one for each class—designated in funky graffiti lettering—take the challenge one step further. Classes mostly eat in their respective lunchrooms although a few cross the "class" lines, particularly to go to the salad bar, which is in the juniors' cafeteria. Seniors use their privileged position to take their meals (composed of nutritional disasters like double orders of curly french fries, punch, and a chocolate chip cookie) to the floor of the senior subschool in utter defiance of the rules. (Administrators sometimes let them get away with this.) Lots of kids like Courtney and her friends leave the school grounds, ignoring school policy. On nice days, kids are scattered everywhere outside the school in small groups, which is fine. But those who seek cover in the surrounding woods and at the far corner of the building, which are hard to see from school, usually are there to smoke cigarettes or pot, or to leave school altogether. Courtney and Brendon have become regulars among the cigarette smokers. Kids are rarely caught. The lack of windows at South Lakes and over sixty doors around the school make the outside difficult to monitor.

Built as a sleek, modern, functional high school in 1978, South Lakes looks from the outside like a giant windowless factory of yellow-beige brick with a snazzy red brick stripe wrapped around its middle. Inside, laid out on two levels, it is divided into four "subschools," one for each grade. Designed to personalize the experience for students in a potentially anonymous environment, the subschools are each staffed by a principal, guidance counselors, and class secretary that move with a group of kids over the entire four years. The subschools are differentiated by colors—green (freshmen), blue (sophomores), yellow (juniors), and orange (seniors)—and all are connected by a series of ramps and hallways that are marked by color stripes to direct students to the right areas. It is at first utterly confusing, leading one student to comment that when he moved from Hughes to South Lakes, he shifted from "a beltway to a rat maze." There is an institutional feel imparted by corridors of painted concrete blocks, exposed pipes in the ceilings, and the lack of natural light. It was "like living in a science fiction movie," commented a South Lakes graduate, "with students moved along like parts on a giant educational assembly line." Many classrooms have movable walls, an innovation to reconfigure space. In reality, besides occasionally falling down, the walls create a terrible noise problem and the peculiar situation of no classroom doors.

What the school lacks is a center. The main corridor is the only area alive with natural light, bright colors, and eye-catching displays: from the ceiling hang ninety-one colorful flags representing the nationalities of students at the school; bright student-painted murals on the concrete block walls are permanent decorations; a student gallery and wall cases exhibit the products of the school's outstanding art department; and other showcases have various student honors on display. Although the vibrancy of student talents and achievements bathes the hall with personality and spirit, this is not a gathering area but a passageway. Students are scattered all around the school traveling the mazes, forced into small cramped stairways that are shortcuts to different areas, and rarely ever collect as one student body.

To some kids, the physical environment of the school is a hurdle to be overcome, not merely in terms of navigating but also in terms of how it impinges on their spirit. "When I got there, I was astonished by how much it was like a prison," says Brendon. "They painted all the walls white and there were no windows in any of my classes except the art class." The artist in Brendon makes him acutely sensitive to his surroundings, which can affect his mood. That sort of influence is not given much attention in measuring school success, but the staleness of the air, the relentless fluorescent lights, the noise, the closeness can become almost claustrophobic to some students. To others, like Courtney, none of this matters at all.

Freshman Charles Sutter accepts the school's physical environment as a given, a backdrop to what matters to him: class spirit. That is why this lunch hour, unlike Courtney and Brendon, who are outside smoking, he is with the freshman adviser going over the last-minute checklist for the Homecoming preparations. Building the float is going well, he thinks, and it is "pulling the class together." School is Charles's arena for making a mark and he is committed to being an integral part of what goes on. Elected a few weeks earlier to be class vice president, he takes his responsibilities seriously. His trajectory in high school is already following that of his older sister Nika: class officer, athlete, good student. He loves the bigger community of high school. It's not the freedom so much as the variety of activities to participate in. He wants to be a leader and to do well. His freshman subschool principal, Jim Hoy, is thrilled to have kids like Charles and the other class officers. Over his many years as an administrator, Hoy has seen fewer and fewer kids turning to school involvement as a primary loyalty and a rewarding arena for participation, just as it has become harder and harder for the school to elicit class sponsors from the faculty and volunteers from among the parents.

For South Lakes freshmen like Brendon, Courtney, and Charles, Homecoming is their first major event as high schoolers, and the pep rally on this Friday afternoon would traditionally cement their belonging to this huge place. The whole student body pours into the gymnasium, sitting together as classes in specified sections of bleachers. When they take seats as part of the South Lakes High School Class of 1996, even the most jaded of freshmen find it hard not to be caught up in the moment. The rally proceeds like a remnant of some long-forgotten golden period of childhood. The band plays, the student government president greets them, the Homecoming court is introduced, the Dance Team performs a number, the football players are cheered as they run across the floor. Finally there is the class spirit competition, where each class tries to outscream the others. The seniors are victorious! And, in spite of themselves, over a thousand other students, many of whom usually couldn't care less about school spirit, wish at that moment that they had screamed louder. For almost an hour, this pep rally embraces the adolescent community in something simple, fun, *wholesome*. Then as quickly as the school enthusiasm revs up and the class bonding becomes palpable, it disappears. It is as if a huge switch has been turned off. The mood simply disappears as the kids leave as fast as they can.

After school, Brendon and Charles go over to the Kileys', the home where the float is being built, to continue work on it. The flatbed will have been delivered and they can finally assemble the papier-mâché Dino inside the Bedrock hut and the rest of the Stone Age scene. All the costumes will be handed out for tomorrow. Both boys are excited about completing the project.

Courtney goes home and sulks. It's about the dress she has to wear to the dance. Every time she thinks of it she is depressed. "It is an ugly blue scalloped-neckline dress, off-the-shoulder, trimmed in blue floral print. It comes above the knees and I look like I'm wearing drapery," she whines. She gets so disgusted with her body. When she and her mom go shopping, she explains, "I have to buy a 3–4 extra small because I'm so little on top. At least in jeans, a size 6 usually fits. Every dress makes me look so stupid. This dress was like the last one I tried on and it barely fit but it was the closest we'd come. It was ugly but we got it anyway and I didn't even care." Now she has to wear it. Everybody will see her in it. She'll feel stupid. How will Brendon ever think she is pretty?

Work on the float continues late into the night. The kids have a ball even though the work is hard. They do Flintstones interpretations; they consume pizza, chips, and Coke; they do last-minute painting and construction. They feel proud because they complete their whole float all by themselves, unlike other classes who have huge inputs from adults. Brendon and Charles agree with the decision to add one final touch, a sign painted on a collapsed cardboard box: MADE BY STUDENTS. NO PARENTS, SPONSORS, OR ADULTS. They tape it with uneven strips of masking tape on the side of the flatbed.

Finally the day of Homecoming dawns, a brilliant autumn Saturday in Reston, fresh and sparkling, cool, crisp, and inviting. The kind of day that stirs memories. Halloween is around the corner, school is rolling. Everywhere, there are families outside—at neighborhood soccer games, washing cars, raking leaves. It is a perfect day for Homecoming.

In various locations around the town, class floats are being readied for the parade. While Courtney and Brendon snooze away, Charles is awake and at work at the Kiley house. He ticks off his list of tasks with his usual precision: "Check the float, get everything together, then ride the float over to where the parade starts, make sure everybody is in their place, and has their candy to throw, and everybody knows what to do." As a class officer, he then has to change into his dressy clothes to ride along with the other officers in a convertible. He joins the parade participants convening at one of the shopping centers.

Meanwhile, along the streets near the school, people of the community are gathering, many dressed in school colors. Small children romp around their parents. Spectators bring lawn chairs, sit on curbs, and many are wearing the South Lakes letter jackets of their children. Students emerge sleepy-eyed to participate in the fun. There is a small-town feel that easily fools the eyes into seeing the event as more central than it really is. But at the moment the drumbeats are heard in the distance signaling the coming of the parade, the delightful shared sense of anticipation is as exciting as it has been for all times.

The youngest children lean forward and crane their necks to capture the first glimpse. The band leads the way, marching in perfect formation. The cheerleaders follow, accompanied by a rollicking Mr. Seahawk, the school mascot. The Homecoming princesses sit smiling and waving with their princes in four convertibles. The class officers come by in their cars, and there sits Charles—"already the little politician," according to his mother—smiling and waving and occasionally jumping off his perch to go out among the people and shake hands. Walking the whole parade route is principal Diana Schmelzer, smartly dressed in one of her vast wardrobe of blue-and-green outfits, sporting a luscious corsage in the school colors, waving, stopping to speak to kids and adults by name, casting her strong presence.

As the floats pass, participants throw candy to the children on the curb. A receptive audience oohs and ahhs at the students' creations. First is the seniors' Little Mermaid float, decorated with waves of balloons, a bevy of sexy mermaids, and a giant clamshell, with "Under the Sea" playing in the background. The juniors' Smurf Village, which would later win first place, is complete with a mushroom house and blue Smurfs. Next comes the sophomores' Batman float with its backdrop of Gotham City, a Batmobile, and Batcave completed by visual soundbursts reading "Pow! Zing! Biff! Bang. At last the freshman float rolls by, with Brendon Lamont dressed as Fred Flintstone. Although shivering in his orange "animal skin" outfit, he is beaming and waving. "I felt really cool being on the float, happy, accepted," he said later. "It was a blast."

The students on the floats call out to their classmates to join them, and soon a ragtag contingent is following each float.

Finally the parade winds its way into the stadium, where the excitement is mounting. The stands are full—a situation unique to this game. There is the smell of popcorn, mustard, and hot dogs coming from the Booster Club refreshment booth. People are milling in a buzz of socializing that continues throughout the game.

At halftime, the princesses are led on the field by their fathers, stepfathers, brothers, and even a mother, so that the queen can be announced to screams, tears, and hugs. Except this time there is a three-way tie, and a triumvirate of royalty is crowned.

South Lakes, in an exciting overtime, falls to the Langley Saxons 20–17. But except for the football players and their families, the defeat hardly seems to diminish the fun of the occasion. Brendon never even watches the game, he is so busy running around and visiting with friends. He doesn't seem to be bothered by leaving his skimpy Barney costume on, even though the weather is unusually cool. Charles relaxes until it is time to clean up, and enjoys the game as always. He hardly ever misses a school sporting event, and often his sister and parents are there too. Courtney, as usual, hasn't bothered to come: "It was a big thing to go to football games in eighth grade but I guess by high school you don't care about activities anymore."

Evening arrives and Brendon is transformed from an impish boy to a proper young man dressed in tuxedo and boutonniere. As he goes to pick up his date for dinner, Courtney, waiting for her date, is having huge second thoughts about the whole evening. "I didn't even want to go anymore. Two days before I told my date I didn't want to go because we weren't even good friends." But ugly dress and all, she had no way out. "We went to Paolo's and the food was good, but Caitlen and I—we doubled with her and her date—went to the bathroom around six times because we thought it was funny how they say that girls always go to the bathroom together, and we were kind of bored. My date got real mad. He was being real stubborn, a spoil-sport, like I'd open the door and he'd be mad because he wanted to open the door—it was crazy."

The eleventh annual Homecoming dance, "All Night Long," converts the gym, decorated with black and gold balloons, into another world. Mermaids, Cavemen, Smurfs, and Batpeople are transformed into femmes fatale and suave gentlemen. Although occasionally a suit is topped by a baseball cap, for the most part there is an elegance that carries over to manners as well. Except for a few raucous students who clearly got past security drunk, couples sit at tables in conversation; twirl, shake, and glide across the dance floor; and occasionally sing along with a song played by the disc jockey. In a change from earlier generations, some kids come to the dance alone or in same-sex groups, and girls are not at all embarrassed to dance together if the music moves them. But few stay at the dance very long—mostly just the freshmen still dependent on rides from parents. The real excitement of Homecoming is not at school but at parties, many in hotel rooms in the area. Some rooms are rented to students by clerks who look the other way, and, surprisingly, some are rented by parents, who feel better knowing their kids are not out driving around to parties.

Both Brendon and Courtney consider the dance a bust. "It was no different from any lame junior high dance," complains Brendon. "Really bad music, really annoying people. Being on a big stage with a spotlight shining down on you. I guess that's how I see everything. I feel like I'm constantly on a stage, always evaluated and always on display." Courtney decides she will never go again with a "friend" when it is "this little couple-y thing. Because people were like, why aren't you talking to your date? Why would he get so mad, we're just friends, you can talk to other people too." The only good thing was that she and Brendon talked to each other and maybe something will happen.

Charles misses the dance altogether. He'd stayed at school after the game cleaning up and putting things away until six at night. He was exhausted and went home to nap. "I got up at midnight. I'm like, Oh well, the dance was tonight." He'd been asked earlier to go by several girls, but he's not ready yet.

Soon after Homecoming, Courtney and Brendon, in the parlance of the nineties, "hook up." But it doesn't go well. The problem is he wants sex, she doesn't. "I don't know," she says, "I won't be fourteen until the end of December. I just want to wait. He's like, 'I want to but I don't want things to change. I don't want to be too serious.' I told him, then don't do something to make it serious. He broke up with me but it was a big deal to have it a mutual thing. He said, 'I don't want it to seem like I'm dogging you.' "

"As far as sex goes, I'm not a sex maniac," explains Brendon. "I'm a popular guy but I'm not a love machine. My two relationships this year have ended short because I get bored . . . and the girls are like, 'Boo-hoo, waa,' and I'm like, 'I don't care.' I'm a heartbreaker. Some of us refuse to admit it, but guys are just horny in general."

Charles meanwhile is increasingly troubled at his inability to cement class spirit. Once Homecoming is over, class connections unravel. In his class of 425, maybe 50 remain consistently involved in activities. The spirit of Homecoming was a mirage.

The fact is, the number of kids involved in school activities has shrunk dramatically over the years. Some administrators put it at less than 25 percent—and that on an irregular basis. Luckily, there always remain kids like Charles and his sister Nika who devote their lives to school, otherwise there would be no organization. The lack of student involvement is not unrelated to the finding recently reported in *Running in Place*, a study issued by the research organization Child Trends, that parents of nearly half of the nation's high school students stay away from virtually every school function, from back-to-school nights and PTA meetings to school plays and football games. And the participation decreases more with each grade. "I think their lives are affected by lots of other things," explains South Lakes principal Schmelzer. "The school is a place offering lots of activities but it is not the center of their lives. The real difference for kids today is that they are involved in so much beyond the school and many of their lives are so complicated that aside from Homecoming and Prom, we can't get them to come. I also think it is a part of the culture that kids go to other people's houses where they can drink, where they are loosely supervised or unsupervised. Why come to school where they can get caught or get into trouble?"

So Brendon's remark lingers as a question: What memories are they making? Just as the architecture of South Lakes lacks a true center, so do the lives of many of the kids. While the cocoon of warm memories that surrounds adults along the parade route and in the stadium leads them to think what they are seeing is no different than Homecoming ever was, a closer look would reveal that like the pep rally it is a blip on the screen of today's high school experience, in which planned school activities are no longer central to adolescent loyalties and social life. In many ways, secondary school becomes a personal quest with little direction—one option among many even if attending is technically a requirement. Within months of entering, kids are on different pathways. Charles never questions that it is his job to do well, work for his class, and participate in the full range of school activities. He abides by the rules unquestioningly and evaluates his teachers by how they challenge him. Brendon and Courtney see school as a game to outfox the adults. They quickly figure out who checks homework, who disciplines for real, where there are weaknesses in enforcement of the rules, and soon they are among the "Skippers and the Smokers," a sizable group of kids who are not troublemakers so much as limit-pushers. With schools concerned about the frightening problems of weapons, drugs, and other criminal, potentially deadly activity, limit-pushers often get away with things that are benign even though against the rules.

There's a sense of entitlement when Brendon explains, "I like cutting up in school because I just figure I have to be there. I don't really cut up in classes that I like either. . . . Teachers who are dead set that they are right when they're wrong, it's an opportunity for me to come knocking at the door and explode at them. I hate world studies. I guess world studies is just a dumb class the way they teach it." He decides so-so grades are okay because he could get good grades if he wanted. "I'm the kind of person who does the minimum. I don't want to put out the effort because I have better things to do, like just hanging out and watching TV."

His parents indulge his search for the teacher that works for him. They persuade his guidance counselor to approve changing Brendon's world studies teachers three times until Brendon decides it is the subject that was the problem. Teacher Larry Ward calls this behavior the "remote control syndrome" rampant among today's students: "If you don't like it you can change it right away, and nowadays that is how students often come into the classroom. They spend more energy trying to change things than buckling down. They never give anything the time to decide if it is worth doing."

Courtney, who doesn't care about classes any more than Brendon does, has a different strategy. She needs to get decent grades to get away with her chosen lifestyle. "If we get Cs in my house, we're grounded for nine weeks," she says. "If my mom found out half the stuff I do just to spend time with other people my own age, she would kill me."

Brendon views the first semester of his freshman year as a set of cascading disappointments. The last school activity he participates in outside of sports is the Mr. Seahawk contest during the winter, an uproarious beauty/talent contest for boys. "Mr. Seahawk was the end of my trying to be part of the school scene. People seem really cool on the surface but they have no interest in a one-on-one friendship."

There is almost a longing in Brendon for the old-fashioned mode of high school, but the reality is that what he really wanted didn't exist after Homecoming. Underneath the class clown surface, he is lost as to how to weave the high school life he imagined, and he is unwilling to work to make it happen. He still feels high school is for making memories, but he will have to seek his own. Courtney remains intent on having fun, and Charles remains firmly grounded in making his school "the best it can be." Of the three freshmen, only Charles keeps his remote control on school; the others stay in the mainstream briefly, than decide to switch channels.

Just into their freshman year, Courtney, Charles, and Brendon have begun to act out the individual drama that will be each one's distinct high school experience. Yet they walk down the hallways unnoticed, three regular kids overshadowed by the hip-hop culture that surrounds them.

# The Negative Is Positive

The front doors of South Lakes High School burst open and the "ghetto boys" swagger in. Like Old West outlaws charging through the saloon doors, these dudes of all races command attention as crowds of students milling in the vestibule part to let them through. Sometimes defiant, challenging with a look or a gesture, they just as often keep their faces set in expressionless poses, their hands shoved in their pockets as they make their way through the halls. "Yo, wassup man," they call out to friends. The response is a cool, smooth high-five. Modern-day Pied Pipers of Bad, these young men set the style of the nineties high school.

A black basketball star strolls by, his adoring white girlfriend on his arm. Two students in dark shades, earphone wires trailing to their backpacks, strut past, shaking in rhythm to sounds unheard by others, slapping the backs of their "bro's" as they move down the hall. In the cafeteria, one white student can be heard taunting another over a chess game: "I'll kick yo' white ass."

It's a run-of-the-mill morning at South Lakes. Just as crickets break through the silence of a summer evening, in a sudden whir, the somnolent adolescents of the street corners, once at school, come to life in a loud buzz of energy that surges through the hallways, reaching a crescendo near the lockers. In every subschool, the locker area serves as combination town square, local hangout, and boxing ring. Several hundred students are roaming around, checking out the scene, joking, jiving, loving, leering. They sit on the floor, slouch against the walls, crush against the students who are trying to load and unload books and papers, often by shoving with hands and feet the things that tumble from their messy lockers each time they open them. Sometimes a fight breaks out as somebody steps on somebody else, an elbow lands, words are exchanged. Often at the center of these altercations are the hard-drivin' gangsta-rappin' boyz-from-the-hood.

Cramped by design, hundreds of lockers have been lined up in a corner section of each of the four subschools in a misguided attempt to avoid the locker-lined corridors of traditional high school architecture. The idea is to disperse the students, but the arrangement merely locates chaos in clusters. Arranged like a tight labyrinth with only two entrances, the area is just wide enough for two people to move through at a time. Teachers and administrators view it as a staging area for battle, and each morning standing guard are the subschool principals, chatting, admonishing, and especially watching for drugs, weapons, and dangerous behavior. The halls and stairwells are guarded by teacher sentries—yet another duty added to the already heavy burden of educators these days. Although South Lakes is not yet a metal detector school, county police have been placed permanently on school duty at the middle schools and high schools in Fairfax County, and the message is that the adults are ready for something to happen. In a time when school violence has burst on the scene as a frightening problem, the locker areas are viewed with prime suspicion. But the reality is, most of the time the kids are just having fun.

It's hip-hop in suburbia, the culture of rap. Everywhere students wear baseball caps turned backwards or pulled down over their eyes, oversize T-shirts, ridiculously baggy jeans or shorts with dropped crotches that hang to mid-shin, and waists that sag to reveal the tops of brightly colored boxers. Expensive name-brand high-tops complete the outfit. Variations on the theme are hooded sweatshirts, with the hood worn during school, and "do rags," bandannas tied on the head, a style copied from street gangs. Just as ubiquitous are the free-flying swearwords, sound bursts landing kamikaze style, just out of reach of hall guards and teacher monitors. *No shit . . . bitch . . . Fuck you . . . Get your ass over here* and sundry other vulgarities spring forth like the King's English in another time and place, transforming even the cleanest-cut adolescents into people of the street.

In the latest exasperating challenge to adult society, black rage is in as a cultural style for white middle-class kids. As in the sixties, when the sons and daughters of the middle class tossed out their tweed jackets and ladylike sheath dresses for the generational uniform of Levi's and work shirts and peacoats in their celebration of blue collar workers, "the Real Americans," so today's adolescents have coopted inner-city black street style as the authentic way to be. To act black, as the kids define it, is to be strong, confrontational, a little scary. "Everybody would be proud to be black lately," explains a saucy blonde with dreadlocks, "because they are finding out it is an insult to be called white." In hip-hop, white kids accept their integrated world by admiring blackness. It brings "soul" to a flat world where kids are always "bored" and seeking stimulation.

For white teenage boys, copying hip-hop—a subculture that began in brutally straight talk by urban black kids about the realities of inner city life—lets them try on an expressive, aggressive masculinity, a new costume for the perennial adolescent rebellion. "We are living in the gangsta generation," one white high school senior wearing his Malcolm X baseball cap turned backwards explains. "It is all about getting it. I look at what these cool dudes do and how it affects other people. These people are doing more than any faggoty white kid who plays basketball and gets accepted at Duke and has been rich his whole life and maybe gets drunk on the weekend. These kids put their ass on the line every day."

It's not that the whole school becomes one undulating inner-city "hood," it's just that the ersatz ghetto boys preempt the scene, their presence obscuring the steady stream of hundreds of students strolling by unremarkably on their way to class.

Unnoticed is fourteen-year-old freshman Charles Sutter, walking briskly through the locker area so as not to be late for class. He wears wire-rimmed glasses and a lacrosse jacket and is loaded down with a backpack full of books. This hip-hop business is turning out to be a real liability for his class. He just left a before-school meeting with the other class officers and Mr. Hoy about what to do to improve freshman class image. The atmosphere is laid on so thick that his class, in which 20 percent of the students are black, has been nicknamed "the Ghetto" for its reputed bad attitude and its swaggering, in-your-face ways. They came over to South Lakes from Hughes with a notorious reputation, and it has proven to be true. Just recently, for example, a group of nine students, most of them freshmen, drove

over to rival Herndon High School during lunch, broke in a back
door, pushed over the 110-pound woman teacher guarding the entrance, and stormed their way to the cafeteria, beating up anyone
who got in their way.

It never was resolved whether the attack was retribution for a racial
standoff that had occurred between students of the two schools over
the weekend at the Reston Town Center or whether it was a prank,
"just for the fun of it." The South Lakes students ran outside and got
away before they could be caught, and this led to a strange new use of
the South Lakes yearbook. The Herndon assistant principal acquired
one and brought in the witnesses and victims of the attack to peruse its
pages showcasing high school life in full bloom—the football games,
the float-building, the team members, the club participants, all the
smiling students portrayed in timeless high school poses—to identify
the perpetrators of the senseless violent attack.

What really bothers Charles is that nobody in his class is particularly indignant about the event. "It's like Whatever. It's dumb, and
that's that." His generation is highly tolerant of individual behavior
to the point of feeling somebody's destructive behavior is "not their
business." Courtney, for example, knows one of the attackers. She
shrugs and explains that he is a "really sweet guy, but you have to
get to know him." So he's bad sometimes; everybody has their faults.
This kind of tolerance amounts to a new ethic of situational excuses,
a hazy sense of right and wrong.

The fact is, the real troublemakers are a small minority in this
racially diverse class, as well as in South Lakes in general, but their
impact reverberates through hallways and classrooms so that it becomes difficult to tell who has the *real* attitude, and who's putting it
on for show.

As Charles vanishes into his next class, the bell rings and the
stragglers move on. The locker areas empty out but the ghetto boys
don't hurry. Behaving as if they are hanging out at 7-Eleven instead
of in school, they trade insults, bob their heads to sounds from their
Walkmans (which are not allowed in school), and, in a stunning pose
of aggressive nonchalance, move nowhere. An administrator has to
shoo them on. On their way, they poke their faces into classrooms,
occasionally reach in to bop a friend on the side of the head, yell a
quick "wassup" or "motherfucker" as they turn a corner—everywhere
they go creating a low-level of disruption.

It's cool. It's what's happening. And for white teenagers, the pose is relatively risk-free. They can act black without having to actually be black. As one white teenager told a reporter for *The Washington Post*, "You can just enjoy it and be a part of it without dealing with the downside. You can be black without having the racism they deal with." Freshman principal Jim Hoy is beside himself with aggravation. Why is it, he wonders, that in a school that recently spawned Grant Hill—sensational basketball star at Duke and later a Detroit Piston, a fine student, elegant athlete, positive role model—the "gangstas" catch on?

In hip-hop, fueled by the powerful political and sexual images of rap, the ghetto becomes the symbol of a struggle between good and evil, victims and oppressors, powerlessness and taking control. Hip-hop's in-your-face attitude looks strong and free to kids who feel constrained by expectations of the mundane middle-class world they have grown up in. Rappers have become the most popular attractions on MTV. In an interview on his album *Home Invasion*, rapper Ice T refers to the "cultural invasion" that is occurring while unknowing adults sit around with their racist attitudes and their kids sit quietly in their bedrooms, his words pouring into their brains through their headphones: "Once I get 'em under my fuckin' spell / They may start giving you fuckin' hell," he raps. "Start changin' the way they walk, they talk, they act / Now whose fault is that?" The rap world of "ho's and pimps, bitches, muthafuckers, homeys and police" is an attractive diversion from the "ordinary" sphere of dental braces, college boards, and dating. The ghetto—experienced second-hand in movies and music and on the evening news, viewed from the comfort of nice suburban family rooms—holds enormous drama and appeal for young people. The wish to be accepted as a "bro" is an underpinning of the adolescent community of the nineties.

A kid like Charles Sutter, however, cannot afford to play that game. Although he likes rap and he wears his jeans well below his waist, he's black and he knows it makes a difference even in integrated Reston. He's insulted by the equation of all black culture with the poverty-stricken and violent dimension of the ghetto. He can't stand his class's being tagged "the Ghetto," and as a class officer he feels a sense of responsibility to remedy the situation. "They are trying to say that all blacks are angry and poor," he says. "They are trying to say we want to be violent and that is not true. It makes me want to advertise everything I do well to prove them wrong about the stereotype that black students fail most of their classes."

Focused on success, Charles is determined he will not go down with them. He understands, and his father has told him repeatedly, that black teenagers don't get second chances, even in an integrated community like Reston. White teenagers who lack a distinctive sub-culture of their own may romanticize the tough kids of the ghetto, but adults with power over his future don't. "I don't want to take the chance of ruining my chances to go to college by getting a police record," he says. "It seems like if you mess up once, it sticks with you forever."

On his last day of middle school last year, Charles had a close call. In an out-of-character moment, he spontaneously cut classes with a few friends and crossed the parking lot to the high school. "We decided not to do anything but roam the halls. Then our group somehow got bigger and bigger until there were like twenty people," he recalls. "I was feeling real nervous like something was going to happen, and it did. Somebody in the group beat up a kid outside the gym for no reason." Charles and the others found themselves running every which way, narrowly avoiding a police car. Some of his friends were exhilarated by the danger, but he was filled with terror.

Since entering high school, Charles has distanced himself from these childhood buddies who believe that to be authentically black, you should act like somebody from the inner city. "The fad is to be tough, to stand up for yourself, and to do as little as possible to get by," says Charles. "The pressure is that you are not much of a person if you get good grades because then you won't get a chance to do things," says Charles. So his old friends do things without him. They aren't bad kids, but they like to take chances, skipping school to go out for lunch at McDonald's, smart-talking their teachers, interrupting classes—all things Charles wouldn't even consider. He has learned his lesson. So he sees his old friends around in school and misses them. "But they can do well," he emphasizes. "Some of them feel that they are expected *not* to achieve and the only way they can be noticed is by acting out in class. They do that from force of habit. They just feel like they are in a downward spiral." Except now these friends represent the essence of hip-hop attitude, "the pride of not doing well," Charles explains. "It's mostly what they see on MTV and the videos. Rappers are doing it for the money. Kids think they have to do what the rappers are doing. I don't want to see them still being freshmen and sophomores when we are graduating." He adds sadly, revealing the irony of the situation, "they think Charles *can* be like us but he doesn't want to because he has a future because of his grades."

By refusing to go along, Charles pays a price in isolation and loneliness every day. "There are maybe four or five of us [black] students who have chosen not to be losers," he says. They aren't close friends but there is a bond of understanding among them. "We've decided we want to go to college and do as much as we can for ourselves and our community. And if it means we are going to be lonely, we're going to do what we have to do."

This realistic, old-beyond-his-years approach may be the healthiest one Charles can take to his dilemma. It is something his parents have carefully inculcated in him. As his mom has told him again and again, "There's nothing wrong with failing or making a mistake, but if you are black the mistake will follow you."

On the surface, Charles seems to have it all. The child of two black professionals, he has grown up in Reston in a spacious colonial house on an integrated street of large homes. Since elementary school he has been in gifted and talented classes, played several sports, and served as a class leader. Charles, his seventeen-year-old sister Nika, and their parents look, to the world, like proof that the American Dream works for all. In fact, Charles *plays* to the world that his life is good: as a class officer, he "knows everybody," has "lots of friends," is instrumental in attracting kids to his favorite sport, lacrosse, and is doing well in school. But under the bravado is a tightly wound young man acutely aware of the restraints and responsibilities his race imposes.

He never feels at ease in his classes because he is never free of the burden of proving he is Mr. Perfect Black. In his gifted and talented classes, his is the rare black face. But Mr. Perfect Black is never good enough. He senses condescension. "I feel left out because the kids never think I actually belong there. They always think that I'm not as smart as the rest of them." It is a presumption made perhaps unconsciously about black students that haunts them and their families. His mom recalls going to middle school to pave the way for her son: " 'I'm sending you a good student, a leader,' " she explained to the administrator. " 'What are you going to do to nurture him?' And he started telling me about the mentor program. I find the schools automatically assume that all black kids come from dire straits."

"I have figured if I have to perform, I'm going to perform," says Charles. "If people try to stop me, I'll just prove that I am better than them. I will do what I have to do." He cleared a space for himself by beating up a kid in seventh grade who hounded him relentlessly. His old buddies respect that if he needs to, he can defend himself, and in the time-honored passage of boys, he earned the respect to be himself. But he knows he cannot let down his guard for a minute: "If I ruin my only chance, then I won't have another."

Unfortunately, the odds are stacked against Charles in a world that sees a black male adolescent as potential Trouble. It is an everyday thing for him to walk into a convenience store for a candy bar, or a record store for a tape, and be eyed suspiciously. "Oh, yeah, people in stores always see a black male as stealing," Charles says. "Whenever we go to High's, they make us leave our backpacks at the door. I've been in stores with my friend Jerome, who's Indian but looks Hispanic, and nobody ever trusts us. People are always following us." Does it make him angry? He sighs. "It's more like an annoyance than an anger because it is a fact of life that people are going to see me that way." Two classmates describe in the same calm voices being tailed by salesclerks, being stopped by police on the shallowest of pretenses when in cars with black friends. Restraint is the only way to protect their status. So these boys use words like "ignorance" or "stupidity" or "acting dumb" to describe acts of racial prejudice that are enraging. They swallow indignities, they walk away, distance themselves. To react with rage to what amounts to an almost constant stalking by white society would be to validate what everybody expects.

Charles's dilemma represents the world of striving black middle-class adolescents. It is life lived on the defensive, a constant tightrope to be navigated between two cultures: a white culture that never fully embraces them, and a black peer group that disdains black achievers. If hip-hop extols the black underclass, then where does a kid like Charles belong? "It's a mess," says Langston Hughes eighth grader Annie Jeffreys. "I don't even know how the stereotype got started. Because the whole civil rights struggle was because there were intelligent black people who deserved rights and could do the same things that whites do. But after we fought for all these rights, we're trying as hard as we can to get back to the stereotype."

Just like earlier teen subcultures peopled by beatniks, rock 'n' rollers, and others, members of the hip-hop generation adopt a shocking veneer not just to unnerve adults, but to cover the acute self-consciousness and painful vulnerability of being an adolescent. To most kids, this is a "style." But hip-hop has a new dangerous twist: race. Like the many-headed Hydra, it frightens outsiders with its tangled dimensions of negativity, violence, offensive language, celebration of the inner city, and adulation of the black outlaw.

Hip-hop keeps at a low boil the legacy of racism in a country where it needs no encouragement. Maybe kids can separate the style from reality, but adults can't. So if a bunch of white, Asian, and black kids are "pimpin' " (a style of walking) down the hall, the adults see the black kid first. The brutal truth is that black students are disciplined, suspended, and expelled at a higher rate than white students.

As with the Hydra, when one problem is dealt with, one head lopped off, others grow in its place. The racism now brought into the heart of adolescence in the suburbs creates a tension played out in school. For a small group of kids, the negativity at the core of hip-hop gives them license to not do well, and for some, unleashes destructive anger and even violence. Hip-hop confuses issues and inflames stereotypes, escalates levels of fear in complex times when the problems of society play out in the schools. An increasing number of students come to school already weighted down with problems like racism, poverty, lack of guidance, loss of hope in the future, and anger at family situations, abuse, lack of attention. Hip-hop doesn't *create* the problems, it merely gives them a voice and a stage. But the popularity of the style among all kinds of kids "creates an undertone to school life," according to Jim Hoy. "The subculture keeps things not quite right."

Disruptiveness is a big problem. "Parents don't have a clue to what school is like these days. If all I had to do was go to classes and learn it would be a huge relief," says Courtney's older sister Ann. "But every day, we have to deal with being knocked around the halls, having to look over our shoulders, having classes absolutely taken over by rude kids. School is basically chaotic and it is really hard to learn."

The pervasive new attitude takes an inordinate amount of administrative time, according to Hoy. Most of the kids, white or black, try to go right to the line. They'll find each teacher's line in class, "and one day the teacher's having a bad day, or they go too far, and they end up with me and punishment follows." They go to their classes but they don't bring books, paper, or pencil. They often sleep or ignore basic rules for behavior. A teacher might say, "Hey, you're talking too much. Stop talking." They'll answer, "Why are you picking on me?" and then there is a verbal back-and-forth. The teacher tries to move their seat, they refuse. Not doing their work is a point of honor. The attitude is: I do what I want when I want. "It seems their parents decided to let them go whatever way they wanted," says Charles. "Maybe it is a cry for help from themselves to their family that they should be stricter. The kids think, 'It seems you don't care what I do, so why should I care?' "

The disruptive students are there because they have to be there, explains Charles. "They figure if they don't want to learn, they don't think anyone else should learn, and they can bully people around." In one incident Charles recalls, a student brought a crowbar to our school because someone had been bullying him. "The teacher thought he was someone disruptive. They didn't know it was a good student who was trying to defend himself. That's all it was."

Charles is certain this is also the root cause of several gun incidents at South Lakes that fortunately never led to harm. "That's why there's people bringing guns to school. It's not the people that don't want to be there, it's the people that want to be there trying to defend themselves. Or people just being there, trying to make their lives a little more fun in school. The incident with the shotgun this year in our class was someone trying to have fun in school. I know the person who did it. He said they just brought it to shoot people in the butt and have a few laughs." The class officer knows the armed student. That's the high school of the nineties.

Former Reston precinct police captain Justin Murphy in a 1992 interview concurs on the "show-and-tell" motivation for incidents. But in a chilling reflection, he verbalized his worst nightmare: One day, if the flow of weapons in the nation is not stopped, a student at South Lakes will reach into his locker and grab a loaded weapon and start firing, and when he stops and looks around, "God knows what heart-shattering scene will surround him."

The Centers for Disease Control biennial "Youth Risk Behavior Surveillance Survey" monitors adolescent behaviors that lead to intentional and unintentional injuries. According to the report issued in 1991, in answer to a question about whether they had carried "a weapon such as a gun, knife or club at least 1 day during the 30 days preceding the survey," among all students ninth through twelfth grade, 26 percent answered affirmatively. Among all students, 42 percent were in at least one physical fight during the previous 12 months. Blacks scored higher in both categories. By 1995, weapon carrying finally showed some signs of abating—only 20 percent of all students carried a weapon in the thirty days preceding the survey, but the percentage of students who engaged in fighting remained the same.

The effects go beyond the walls of the school. Ironically, the disruptive kids aren't concerned about consequences, the good kids are. "I have to take a lot of things into consideration before I go somewhere," says Charles, "like who is going to be there, what kind of people, if there is a potential for trouble. I have to worry everywhere because I'd rather be safe than sorry." This is not the life Mr. and Mrs. Sutter imagined for their children when they fought for civil rights in the sixties. They provide a safe home, love, a wide range of opportunities in an integrated middle-class environment, and their young son has to walk a tightrope to success.

One of his sister's black friends recently found out that success has a price when five black students jumped and beat him at another friend's party. "They were just being ignorant," the victim says of the assault that left him injured. "Some people want to fight other people because they think they act white." Charles speculates that the kids who beat up Bryce "were upset about his doing well legitimately. If they weren't smart enough to get it, they were going to take it from him. However, that is something you just can't take from a person—the mindset to succeed."

For these boys, there is no escaping the burden of being "part of an endangered species." A recent South Lakes graduate whose dad is a former member of the United States Congress plans to have a party with several black male friends when they reach twenty-five, "because we survived the statistics . . . statistically I should either be in jail, have been in jail, or be a drug addict or dead. It's not what you call a morale booster."

Sometimes it gets to be too much for Charles. Just a few weeks earlier there were tryouts for basketball. The competition was fierce. He was the last kid cut. The last boys that made the team were among the kids later involved in the beating at Herndon High School. After a few days one of them quit, saying he "didn't have time to play," but really, it was because he didn't want to be bothered. After the Herndon incident, the other one was expelled from school. The day of the tryouts, Charles's mom picked him up. As he was telling her what happened, he began to cry. He cried because he was humiliated at having failed to make the team, out of anger and frustration because being good never seemed to count for much—and because he was humiliated that he was crying. He told his mom he wished he could go to the coach and tell him: "You let me go and I'm coachable. I would always do what you said. I have no attitude. You would have me for the whole season." His mother tried to explain that maybe the coach was trying to "save" those two kids, hoping that being on the team would provide some discipline. She told Charles he was lucky, because "Not everybody has a family like yours that's positive and cares about you." But when you are a boy with a passion for sports, with childhood dreams of playing basketball for South Lakes, a mom's words don't really comfort.

Charles sulked for a while, feeling very sorry for himself. But with his parents' support and his usual resilience, he decided to manage the girls' varsity basketball team instead. His sister was one of the star players and he had a plan. He figured he could earn his varsity letter his freshman year through involvement in all three seasons of sports—football, girls' basketball, and lacrosse.

The school day ends and Charles gets ready for basketball. He goes to his locker to get his books and walks down the main hall past the strutting, swaggering ghetto boys. Charles darts and weaves his way through the throng of students, a young man in a hurry with a destination in mind. Once outside in the student parking lot, he goes to his sister's car to drop off his books. He opens the car door, then quickly jumps back to avoid a pulsating black Nissan, its windows wide open, its radio blasting, its white teenage driver chanting along with rapper Dr. Dre, "I can't be faded, I'm a nigger from the muthafuckin' street." Charles watches him zoom out of the parking lot. Then he closes the door of Nika's car and runs back to the school, ready for his responsibilities as team manager.

# Honor and Other Relative Things

A day off from the regular routine is welcome, and to spend it
with local television personality Jim Vance is a kick even if
the topic is ethics—not a big interest of most of the kids participating. It is the second annual "Ethical Decisionmaking in the Workplace and Society" seminar for South Lakes seniors cosponsored by
the Reston Board of Commerce.

Inside the bright, airy community room at St. John Neumann
Catholic Church, one of two locations, adults scurry around readying
the room. The group leaders, professionals from the community who
have volunteered their time, take their places and wait for the kids.
The event has been months in the planning, requiring hundreds of
hours of volunteer time, including a one-day training session for the
group leaders and thousands of dollars' worth of donated equipment
and food. The adults are excited about the prospect of this day making a difference. You can feel it in the air.

Finally the school buses pull up, and half of the South Lakes senior class, in good spirits, amble into the room. There are several
minutes of confusion as they find their way to their assigned seats at
tables each headed by an adult in a profession in which they have expressed interest. The students had listed three career preferences
weeks before the event. Jonathan and his friend Alan find their places
with local freelance writer Peter Slavin. Both boys are mildly disappointed that they didn't get their first choice, a teacher, but, "Hey, it's

not like we aren't with teachers every day." They nod to the four classmates at the table and sit down, never stopping their discussion about the Environmental Club's agenda for the year. Jonathan, a club officer, is impassioned about the possibilities for cleaning the streams in Reston and wishes that polluters could be seriously punished for their careless disregard for the purity of water. Since his Vision Quest, he has become even more intolerant of those who abuse the environment.

Slavin welcomes the students to his table and finds they are initially difficult to connect with; they prefer their chitchat with peers. Slavin's not worried. He's worked with teens before and understands this beginning awkwardness and distance. Twelfth graders are a challenging group to engage anyway, since they feel halfway out the doors of high school, but not yet comfortably inside anywhere else. The wild acting-out behaviors, the frenetic energy of early high school years has been tempered by greater maturity and a better developed sense of who they are. But their blasé attitude only lightly overlays tension over what the next year holds. They are not particularly accessible for this ethics business. Although definitely happy about being out of the school building, they are not in the mood to learn something new. "A whole day of ethics?" says Jonathan. "It is unbelievable that we have to have an ethics seminar, that people think the average teen's ethics are that far distorted."

The contrast between the adult and adolescent attitudes is notable as the popular keynote speaker, Washington, D.C., news anchor Jim Vance, comes to the dais. Around the room, kids slowly stop chattering among themselves and start to pay attention, though without enthusiasm. Their unspoken challenge is not hostile but clear: Interest us. Vance hones right in on the situation. When he watched people coming in that morning, he says, he saw "some faces and some people with attitudes because it's early and you aren't real sure what you are doing or what's gonna happen to you and you are probably presuming already that you will be bored to death and that this thing sucks and why did anybody ever make you get involved." Whoa. The listeners are jolted to attention by this straight-talking guy. And he's got their number down. "Choices separate us from the animals. We are in a time when a lot of people don't make good choices."

"How condescending," Jonathan whispers to Alan. "It is really small-minded to say animals don't make choices." In a society that apparently places little value on human life, many youngsters are absolutely fanatical about animal rights.

"Choices need to be based on more than what's happening or what's hip," Vance continues. This day-long seminar has the goal of teaching these students how to make the right choices. Eyes roll. They know about choices all right. That is at the heart of being a senior, and is for many a full-time preoccupation. But their choices are about money for college, where to go, what to do, whether to go to college at all. The audience clearly doesn't get it. "You probably are thinking, 'What do I care if I make the proper ethical decision?'" Vance says. "I assure you it will make a huge difference in your quality of life." Vance comes by this honestly. Most everybody knows that he had suffered a cocaine addiction in his past and after twice failing to recover, losing his prominent news anchor job, messing up very publicly, he finally turned his life around and regained the respect of his community. The guy has more credibility than most.

The chair of the event speaks next, emphasizing that this day is a "gift from a community that cares about its kids." At Jonathan's table, they are restless. One of the girls leans over and whispers to her friend, "Is this going to get any more interesting?" Even though teachers have been preparing their students for the event, the notion of ethical decision making remains for this group, as it had for last year's seniors, as remote as the meaning of quarks. Religion they understand. Personal satisfaction they use as a measure. But ethics as something you need for your job? It is a stretch.

It seems as foreign as the language they are encountering in their twelfth-grade English requirement, *The Canterbury Tales*. What is it going to do for us? is the question that hangs in the air. The day starts with painful slowness. The first exercise is to answer the basic question, What do you value? The group edges along. It is obvious they are not used to thinking this way. At first the answers are "clothes," "friends," "sports," "money." Jonathan notices that his fellow students have no sense that these answers are superficial or low-minded. Then, with a grin, he shares his list: "environment, friends, outdoor sports." The facilitators work to bring the group to a deeper level and finally drag more out of them: school, family, religion, self, life, success, happiness. Visiting county supervisor Bob Dix groans and mutters to the person beside him, "I can't believe 'country' hasn't come up."

The adults are agitated. A huge chasm has opened up between their fine plans and the student audience. Psychologist John Hawley, a group leader participating for the second time, recalls: "The shock value of having sat in my office and listened to kids making poor decisions and seemingly having little in the way of values, then to walk into a school function and have the kids spew back that they really don't care, that they were not terribly interested in the topics, and that the whole notion of how one did form a value was way out in the ozone, led to this kind of collective disbelief by all of the adults there of, what have we gotten ourselves into?"

Moving on, members of the drama department at South Lakes present a series of vignettes that illustrate ethical dilemmas where the audience needs to reach a consensus. As the minidramas unfold and the tables discuss the issues, the process finally gets going. With bumps and starts, the kids grapple with making a connection between values, ethics, and the kind of person they are or want to be. Slavin, watching his group work, is hopeful. "I expected to be surprised or disappointed at first but I figured they would see the light."

The chemistry of the event takes over. Even if the kids are dunces at ethics, they begin to soften in response to the generosity on the part of the adults in the room. It is rare these days that teachers, students, and members of a community interact for hours in ways that allow them to get to know each other. The intimacy works for everyone: the teachers, usually isolated within the school walls, feel acknowledged by the outside community; the professionals glimpse what the next generation is like in a more human way; the kids feel cared for and linked to a larger community. Because the professionals don't have preconceived notions about individual students, many kids labeled as cutups or losers in the school find voices as equal participants. The goals of the seminar are clear and structured, and the students know the adults feel the topic is very important. In fact, they could be discussing widgets. What matters is that there exists a rare balance of the "old-fashioned" elements of community and traditional priorities. By 10 A.M., most students have settled in, not eager but ready to try.

The actors and actresses have presented the first situation and now the question is, Who gets the heart transplant? A choice has to be made by consensus or everybody dies. The first potential recipient, Alfred, is a brilliant research physicist on the verge of a major cancer discovery who is seriously stressed by his work and his own illness, and this is placing a strain on his family. The stress, the moderator notes, may require him to see a psychiatrist in the future. The second is Bill, a black auto mechanic with only a high school education, who has a pregnant wife and a three-year-old daughter. Decent and hard-working, though with little chance of career growth, he loves his family and wants his wife to quit her secretarial job to become a full-time mother. Cora, the third character, is a full-time mom of five young children, a high school graduate who is deeply religious and committed to her family. David is a brilliant college student with almost a straight-A average, an ardent activist in a number of causes, who is majoring in philosophy and literature. He is engaged to be married and hopes to be a college professor. The final candidate is Edna, a tough-minded, successful single career woman, active and effective at work and in the community. The moderator loads the portrait by saying that even though Edna is well regarded by all who know her, "It is clear that her natural aggressiveness and combative tendencies worked against any sort of marital attachment." Slavin is pleased with his group. They zero right in on the values aspect: How many years does each person have to live? What is his or her contribution to society? But reaching a consensus among the students is draining.

When all the tables are done, the entire room shares their conclusions, and now the whole group has to agree. The once detached audience is alive and engaged. The mike is open to the floor and kids are boisterous in defense of their own group's decisions. They line up to speak, fighting for who they believe in, greeted by cheers and vehement arguments. At first, the groups compete for the "right" answer as if this were a quiz show and the correct answer would win the prize, or as if it were a Nintendo game where the object is to eliminate the weaker challengers. They don't get the anguishing side of such ethical decisions.

"Not the woman with the kids," says one girl. "She'll have no kind of impact." Cora is totally expendable, a nonperson; not one table agrees she should get the heart. The reasoning is that since her mother lives with the family, when Cora dies her mother can take care of the children. The next to go is Edna—what value is a single female executive? "Who is she going to help?" they wonder. She's "too self-centered, too involved in her work." The nineteen-year-old college student loses out because literature and philosophy are not important, being a professor not so admirable, and he doesn't have a family. His protesting might get him thrown in jail, and besides—the group's lack of empathy is striking—he's "just a kid." Then someone stands up and says, "Wait a minute! We can't just choose people based on their contribution to society—others have the same right to live." One lone student, a girl, makes an impassioned plea on David's behalf. She orders the group: "Think of his dad's pain at losing him. All of us are young, all of us have a future, and all of us can succeed." It stirs nobody. Alfred had won at several tables because of his potential to cure cancer and thereby have the farthest-reaching impact; besides, "lots of scientists are crazy but maybe on a higher level." Most, however, dumped him because of his "mental instability, although sympathetic to his stress." The main contenders are Alfred and Bill. Ultimately the room reaches consensus, less because of any sense of social responsibility to make sure someone receives the heart than to end the exercise.

The big winner is Bill. At a time when the country is in a tizzy over television character Murphy Brown's baby and the ensuing debate over family values, this group of South Lakes seniors—who are for the most part the children of working parents, many of whom are divorced; who live in a comfortable upwardly mobile middle-class community full of high achievers—warmed to a high school–educated African American who loved his family and wanted his wife to stay home with the kids. "Without Bill, the family will sink," one student argues.

There's news here about kids' values. They like family and nurturing and commitment; the color of a person's skin is not a factor one way or another; they don't understand their own potential; they are uncertain about how to prioritize and value women's roles. They discount the importance of a full-time mother, yet warm to a man who puts his family first. Their parents may be on the fast track, but to this group of youngsters, family togetherness is the big winner.

As the scenarios move on to decisions closer to their world, the seniors' ethics are murkier. The final minidrama concerns a star college basketball player who is just back from a sensational victory, exhausted, but looking forward to the next day's game, which will be attended by an NBA scout. His dilemma is that he is pooped and wants to be rested for the game, but has a calculus test tomorrow too. He's doing poorly in the class and needs to pass to keep his scholarship. He has three options: study the best he can with the willing help of his roommate and give it a try, knowing he's in sorry shape; pay a tutor and work most of the night to learn enough to get a C; or, get the answer key to the test and memorize it so he can pass the test and still get his rest for the game.

There is immediate, almost unanimous agreement on the solution to the young man's problem: Cheat. Slavin polls his table. An honor student answers unequivocally: "Ethically, I would cheat." The two girls are adamant about taking care of number one, that he needs to honor his idea of what is important: "It's not like it's laziness." "Fake an illness that improves right before the game," suggests Alan. Or the basketball player should cheat as long as he understands, "If he cheats it is his responsibility and he has to accept the possible consequences of getting caught." Jonathan alone disagrees: "We have to take responsibility for our actions and if he screwed up, it is his problem and he has to accept the consequences. If he cheats, it is not taking responsibility. If he stays up all night studying, he does."

The day has taken a toll on Jonathan. He is slumped in his chair, and somehow looks out of place. "It was scary, I knew that I wouldn't do this thing, but the whole table couldn't understand what I was saying about taking personal responsibility." The issue of taking responsibility had come up for him in day camp when he wondered why he couldn't take his group on certain hikes or camping trips, and was told about issues of liability. Once again, his interest in nature had yielded a lesson for his life: "Don't do something if you can't live up to it. If you don't study for a test, you fail it. If you fall in the backcountry and you break your foot, you don't sue the guy leading the hike."

The kids' matter-of-fact responses have most of the adults gasping in disbelief. It is not just the consensus on cheating as the route to the basketball star's dreams, but the fact that the students are at ease and adamant in supporting their point of view. The room is frighteningly devoid of conscience. Psychologist Hawley is not surprised. For several years he had been noticing a difference between the answers of today's adolescents and those of the past on the intelligence tests he administers. "One of the standard questions is, 'If you find someone's wallet or pocketbook at the store, what should you do?' Invariably the kids now ask, 'What should I do or what *would* I do?' The implication is consistently that it is okay to lie, cheat, or steal provided it benefits me and provided I can get away with it. It is the idea of 'getting away.' If one can escape judgment, then it is okay."

A number of national surveys corroborate the responses of Reston teens. In 1992, a *USA Weekend* survey of over 236,000 young people revealed that 25 to 40 percent of teens see nothing wrong with cheating on exams, stealing from employers, or keeping money that isn't theirs. A 1989 Girl Scouts survey of 5,000 kids found 65 percent would cheat on an important test. A survey by the Josephson Institute of Ethics in 1992 similarly revealed that 75 percent of high school students admit to cheating. The same year, only 10 percent of students polled by *The South Lakes Sentinel* said they would never consider cheating, and 90 percent said they cheated anywhere from "once in a while, to some of the time, to anytime I can get away with it." The biggest reason, according to 65 percent of the students, was that it was more important to get good grades than to be honest. The editor of that issue explains: "People are under lots of pressure. The attitude is that everybody does it, people don't look upon cheating as bad, none of your friends look at you as bad because you cheated." Everybody knows it is the wrong thing to do, "but I am not convinced that it is unfair when you are in a class you are never going to need again in your whole life but . . . the difference between a C and an A will make a difference in what college you get into." From the minute achieving students enter South Lakes as freshmen, they are painfully, often frantically aware that everything is centered around getting into a good college, into "building your résumé."

Paradoxically, there is an ethic of cheating. This is how most students explain it, according to the honor student: It is easy and it is not always straight-out cheating. It is the little sneaky stuff like asking somebody from the period before what is on the test, or being absent so you know what is on it the next day. "Real cheating is having the answers in front of you while you are taking the test, looking at someone's paper."

The truth, and everybody knows it, is that to get into college an A or B is always better than something lower, and students' lives are so full of pressure and activity, especially for the smartest and most ambitious, that something has to give. "Even though we are told it will hurt us in the long run, that is a bunch of baloney," says the straight-A honor student. "Unless you are actually planning to keep the pattern of cheating, you can cheat in that English class that doesn't matter toward your goal, let's say, of being a doctor. Maybe you are hurting other people and that may be unfair, but you are not hurting yourself. Why not take the easy way out if you can go home and be with friends for three hours or work in a subject that really matters to you, like I work on my science courses—why sit there and struggle over English that is five hundred years old?" The bottom line is that "grades are more important because they get you someplace—getting good grades, not being ethical."

This may be the crux of the matter. In the Girl Scouts of America survey, it was found that by a huge margin the youth problems of the headlines—peer pressure, drugs, alcohol, sex, gangs—were not the "crisis issues" for kids. Their major concerns were "the social expectations of the adult world which all have to do with *pressure*: the pressure to obey parents and teachers (80%), to get good grades in school (78%), to prepare for the future (69%), and to earn money (62%)." In times when society lacks clear ethical guidelines, when parents neither spend the time to educate about time-honored values such as honesty, integrity, and personal responsibility nor necessarily model consistent values in their own lives, kids are responding to the one message they hear loud and strong from the adult world: Succeed. Do well. Do whatever you need to do. One of the girls at Jonathan's table is almost apologetic. "We know what the right answer is. We know the difference between right and wrong but we have to live in the real world."

"There have been more ethical scandals in the last five years than in the previous five decades combined," writes Michael Josephson in *Ethical Values, Attitudes, and Behaviors in American Schools.* "In every field of endeavor—business, politics, entertainment, sports, law, accounting, religion, and even the nonprofit community—prominent organizations and famous people have found their name in the news because of illegal or unethical conduct." The ethics of this generation are but an "amplified echo," according to Josephson, "of the worst moral messages of their elders." Kids have grown up with a regular diet of people like Leona Helmsley, who ripped off the government; Mayor Marion Barry, who was reelected after being in prison for cocaine possession; Michael Milken and his junk bonds; Ivan Boesky and insider trading; Pete Rose and gambling. The list seems endless: Watergate, Clarence Thomas and Anita Hill, Lorena and John Bobbitt, Whitewater. Stories of killings for sneakers, parents who abandon their children, drive-by shootings. The students see inconsistent punishments or no consequences at all. Their ethical discussions have less to do with issues like Would you die for your country? than Is it justified for an abused woman to whack off her husband's penis with a kitchen knife? They have grown up in the quicksand of an ambivalent moral society.

It's no wonder many youths draw darkly cynical conclusions.

"Life is all about getting it," explains one of the seniors. "Some kids may go to college to get it; some go to Colombia. Legal, illegal—it just depends what side of the law you want to be on."

It starts young and adults don't even know it. Sometime during his sixth-grade year Chris Hughes told his mother, in a discussion about how a repair person had cheated her: "Well, as Arnold Schwarzenegger said, 'Basically everybody is out to get everybody else.'" Shocked, she asked him why he thought this. "That is the way it looks," he said with great seriousness. Somehow people keep on expecting kids to have a certain belief system or a commitment to certain kinds of values that are not evidenced with any regularity in their environment. Values do not spring fully formed out of nowhere. And cheating, among all the things people are doing that are not right, turns out to be fairly benign.

Jonathan, who craves honesty and moral purity—not because he is a holier-than-thou type but rather because he wants a rudder to navigate the world that lies ahead—in the end conceded that maybe calculus wasn't so important to a guy who wanted to be a basketball star. "They got me to thinking how important is calculus in life anyway, so I got a little confused." He later lamented: "I was so different, especially after the Vision Quest. It was both the worst and the best thing I'd done in my life. It was the worst thing because it isolated me so much from the average person in high school that I just felt like some kind of creep."

The day comes to an end. Later, in private reactions, kids admitted a feeling that it was all too late. They have fended alone when perhaps their world would have felt safer, more certain if they'd had some clear rules to follow. The sadness is that by the time they are seniors, their innocence is long gone and they feel like their destiny is about to be sealed.

It's not that they are jaded, or, says Josephson, "moral mutants," but rather that they hold morality tightly to their immediate lives, where they might have a glimmer of control. Mostly, they gauge morality in terms of their friends. "I think as long as you don't betray your friends, it is okay," explains a former school paper editor. "Betrayal of your friends would be stealing or lying to them, being two-faced, pretending you are friends with them then going behind their back, making them lose respect in the eyes of other people." This is why recent school scandals such as a class officer attending Homecoming drunk, the head of the student government being charged with tampering with the votes for homecoming queen, and the number of students cheating do not bother the students at South Lakes. The issues are not viewed as "really important" in the scheme of things. "I found a disconnect between what the kids were concerned about and the seminar," says Slavin. "Even though the case histories were realistic, except for the cheating one they were far removed from the kids." They shot down "altruism" as an SAT word, he continues, and when asked if they ever evaluated a decision listing pros and cons, very few responded affirmatively.

Trying to look on the bright side, Jonathan conjectures: "I think each of us has our moral values, whether we know it or not, that we use to make our decisions. But very few people make them in the manner they describe in the seminar. They just make their decision based on their prior experience." If part of growing up is figuring out what matters, in an era of situational ethics adolescents have to make sense of everything. Nothing is sacrosanct, everything is up for debate—from the meaning of calculus to the meaning of life itself.

The best thing about the seminar, according to Jonathan, is that "people we normally don't hang out with see how we think." The discussions were more about life than most of what is done in school. He quotes a Pete Seeger song to make his point: "Schools are like prisons because they don't teach you how to live."

"I find it disgusting that the high school is offering, in their senior year as the kids are walking out the door, a one-day seminar on ethics and values when they had twelve years or thirteen years to educate these kids," says John Hawley. "What the hell are we doing as adults if we are not doing something to foster a set of values?"

The thing that makes the biggest impression on Jonathan is something Jim Vance says in his final remarks. "The deal is this, folks: of the many things that I am grateful for, one of them is that I am not you. I am exceedingly grateful that I was seventeen in 1959 and not today. You have more in front of you, and over you, and behind your back than I even had to consider when I was seventeen years old. I can tell you sincerely from the bottom of my heart that I have consummate respect for each and every one of you for being able to cope and survive in this jungle that you have to deal with today."

The influence of a single adult reaching a youngster at the right moment cannot be underestimated. This was the hope of every adult at the start of the day, the power of the exercise. "All of the society I've been introduced to creates doubts for me, and most of the doubts are about myself," says Jonathan. "When I go out to the river or the mountains I see the doubts shouldn't be about myself but about the society we're being raised in. When Jim Vance said what he did, I felt maybe I was right."

Before he finishes, Vance has one other thing he needs to say: "When you came in here this morning, the very first thing I noticed was that some of you were in a state of attire that I do not allow in my presence. There are some of you young men who have hats on. When I was teaching, and in my house and in my office, you come in, you gotta lose the hat. I was that close to telling all you young men to take off your hats and show some respect." He didn't because he did not want to get the day off on the wrong foot, because he wanted the kids to be at ease, and because he was a guest.

As his remarks come to a close, so does the seminar. There is genuine attentiveness on the part of the students, now feeling some ownership and pride in the occasion. It turns out that it was interesting and fun to be challenged in these new ways—even if they are seniors. The seminar, it turns out, was as much about an intergenerational dialogue as about ethics.

When Vance finishes, the kids jump to their feet in an ovation for him and for the other adults who have shared this day. They will remember the feeling of the event, the embrace of this larger community, if not the details. In the end, however, not a single boy took off his hat.

The kids file out, and the world that they return to is no different than before. The same pressure to achieve creates anxiety for them. If the world doesn't change, wonders Jonathan, how can we?

# The School Paper and a Whole New Adolescent World

Long after the last class has ended this Thursday afternoon in mid-December, junior Joan Garcia and sophomore Ann Smith huddle over a computer in the "pressroom"—actually the computer lab during the school day. They are closing the December issue of *The South Lakes Sentinel*. Ann is at the keyboard, Joan pulled close in a chair beside her, as they decide the layout of Joan's graphics on the opinion page of the paper. They are intent on their task, speaking quietly, moving things around, trying to get the job done right.

At first glance, they could be representatives of two distinct phyla of adolescence. Joan's outfit—long purple flowered skirt, Doc Martens combat boots, black T-shirt accented by two strands of homemade beads, and plaid flannel shirt—is in dramatic contrast to Ann's freshly pressed long-sleeved white blouse tucked neatly into camel-color wool slacks, worn with a thin leather belt, penny loafers, and socks. A passerby could easily label them "Grunge" and "Preppie" and list the things that separate them. But they are a picture of cooperation.

Joan speaks softly, with the slightest lisp, and when she laughs her almond-shaped eyes crinkle and almost disappear behind her dark-rimmed glasses. She's good company as far as Ann is concerned, "a very nice person, and great listener. She is extremely sweet and non-judgmental. That is why everybody finds it easy to get along with her, although she is a little environmental and that bothers people after a while, but that is just one of her quirks like we all have."

Most striking about Ann is her long, lustrous, golden-brown hair, which she usually pulls back austerely in a ponytail or braid that hangs halfway down her back. It's the kind of hair that begs to fall free so it can flow around her shoulders. But Ann rarely wears it down, and when she does she pulls it straight back off her face with a barrette. She seems tightly controlled, severe, serious. Her habit of blurting out her definite opinions, and never mincing words, intimidated Joan at first. Joan would listen to Ann in class and secretly admire how "she didn't take bullshit from people and told it like it is." Ann looked confident to Joan. "People probably describe me as a bitch, really strong-willed," Ann says. "I say what I want and if you don't agree, that is not my problem and I don't really care. I also like to have a good time but I don't think people really know that about me." Ann calls herself "bossy." But when she smiles, her face softens and her pink cheeks, the sprinkle of freckles across her nose, and her vulnerability are accentuated.

Working on the paper has allowed the girls to get to know each other better and feel more comfortable. They still aren't exactly friends, but they love the camaraderie of these high-pressure after-school sessions to get the newspaper out.

In the quiet hours after 2:30, when the only people at school are students and staff involved in sports and other activities, Joan finds South Lakes "more warm and welcoming." Maybe because there is so much going on during the day, it isn't possible for students like her and Ann to sort out what it all means to them. The two girls feel anonymous during regular school hours, in a day fractured by movement through seven unrelated classes, among noisy, surging streams of students. It is not all bad, not all good, but a way of life that leaves them feeling ungrounded and off-center. That is, until their seventh-period journalism class with Mr. Ward, which has been something each could count on since their freshman year.

Larry Ward says his strength as a teacher is "relating and making kids comfortable in the classroom." Even though his class location has switched several times, the feeling in the room where he teaches English and journalism remains the same. His desk has a lived-in look; it is covered with piles of papers awaiting his attention, and has several pictures of his wife and young son that are turned to face his students. Bookcases behind his desk are stacked with books, papers, and, notably, thirty or forty empty fruit drink bottles to recycle. The kids are always bringing in more. Cartons of school newspapers add to the confusion. The disorder is more a testament to his involvement with students and his family than sloppiness. Notes or assignments on the blackboard are neatly written and always ready each day for class, and he makes a point of trying to address each student personally at least once during a school week. In his mid-thirties, Ward is tall, trim, all-American-handsome, and he dresses comfortably in casual clothes that announce his accessibility but never cross the line into trying to be a kid himself. He is not the kind of teacher to win Teacher of the Year or Funniest Teacher or Most Popular Teacher. He's neither a star nor an aggravation. He uses no gimmicks to amuse the kids, but he commands loyalty and gets results in the classroom by his straightforward, low-key, firm yet easygoing style. Kids sense his commitment to them and respond.

One of the things students like about Mr. Ward, Ann explains, is that they feel they know him and he knows them. They know, for example, that he worked as a professional dog trainer and a policeman before he took up teaching in the late eighties. And last spring, every day for weeks there was scrawled across the assignments on the blackboard, "Zippy not here yet"—a reference to his soon-to-be-born first child. The kids in the class had bets going as to the date, and if they were right, the deal was that they would get extra credit. "We'd all go to him, 'Come on Mr. Ward, Zippy's got to be born today because I need the extra credit,'" Ann recalls. "But really it wasn't the extra credit. We wanted the baby to be born because we wanted to know what it was, to know its sex and its name." When the day finally came and his wife had their son, all his students were genuinely happy and excited. Ward was bombarded by well-wishers when he returned to school. In journalism class, his students lined up at his desk in a touching display of affection. They congratulated him individually, and many brought small gifts for Christopher, the new baby—balloons, a signed baseball card, a rubber duck, a book, a Dave Barry column about boy and girl toys, a handmade card. That day was the start of a tradition. "We love Christopher stories," Ann says. "The whole class gets quiet. It is great having a man teacher share all of this, and I don't think it could be anybody but Mr. Ward because he is such a warm, open person about that type of thing. It is nice because you feel you are not just his student but a little more. If you had a problem you could turn to Mr. Ward and he would help you in

any way. You also have him for more than one year and that estab-
lishes a bond. It brings us closer when he can discuss his family and
we can discuss subjects like teenage pregnancy with him."

Ward says simply, "I remember the teachers who combined learning with life." He thinks he becomes a better teacher because of his
students. "Kids are irrepressible. They will find the way to bring out
the human in anybody."

Whatever the reasons, the chemistry in his classroom works. The
atmosphere is good-natured and respectful and gets the job done.
Ann, who "doesn't do homework as a matter of principle," works
long hours on the paper, always volunteering to stay after school to
help. She is proud of her finesse on the computer. The newspaper
staff struggled with the computerization of their work earlier this
year, and she took a leadership role, helping the others adjust. The
newspaper requires commitment, responsibility, and teamwork that
results in a tangible product. In other subjects, sometimes she has a
hard time seeing the point.

Joan too is a committed team player on the paper, more willing to
participate constructively here than in any of her other classes with
the exception of creative writing. But in that class the focus is very
personal. She pours out poetry and stories from her heart, often il-
lustrating them with brilliantly colored drawings. In journalism,
Joan feels like she belongs—a big issue for her. She works hard to do
anything she can, from writing to layout to taking pictures. The students in this class are unaware of how surly and uncooperative she
can be in other classes. They would be shocked. They also have no
idea of the depth of her yearning to be accepted.

She never questions her commitment to the paper, saying of Mr.
Ward, "I owe him one." She explains that when she was a freshman
she was "terrible, but Mr. Ward would always look out for me. He'd
see me in the hallway and say, 'How are you doing?' Or kids would
do mean things to me in class, and he'd always ask me about it and
give me advice. He was kind of fatherly. Sometimes he seemed like a
pushover but he's not—he just knows what he's doing, how to handle people."

Like Ann, the thing that Joan likes best about Mr. Ward is how he
shares his family, and no matter how many times the class asks him
to tell the story of how he met his wife, he tells it. Joan, like a small
child reciting a treasured book, rattles it off herself: He went to the
beach one summer and Natalie's younger brother and his friends

cooked up a scheme to get Mr. Ward to call Natalie for a date. They met in August and by October, were engaged. The rest is history. "It's sort of one of those too-good-to-be-true, oh-yeah stories," Joan says. "He is so emotional and sensitive about it. That is what is so appealing about Mr. Ward—he's not like a macho guy—when he tells the story you can feel that he loves this woman."

One day Joan was working at the computer listening to the Grateful Dead while she typed, quietly singing along to "Cumberland Blues." While she sang, "I can't stay much longer Melinda / The sun is getting high / I won't help you with your troubles / If you won't help me with mine," Mr. Ward sat down next to her and started singing too. "I was like, oh shit, you like these songs? You just wouldn't suspect it." Maybe some of her other teachers like the Grateful Dead too. But only Mr. Ward gives that peek inside.

Ann makes a few deft strokes on the Mac and *voilà!* yet another arrangement of the layout of Joan's simple male/female symbols to illustrate the Point-Counterpoint page of the paper comes into view. The topic is condom distribution in high schools, a hot topic nationwide, and recently creating a furor in northern Virginia as one school begins to make them available. As the two girls work, they talk—Joan about the Environmental Club and the school's wetlands project in Reston, Ann about how stupid and unfair it is that her mom made her drop track just because she got a few Cs on her report card. Ann is always complaining about her mom and stepfather. She feels they just act on their own ideas and don't consider her feelings and her life. "My mom thought her adolescence was easy, and therefore mine is too. She thinks you don't have to worry about sex, friends, whatever. She is in total denial and avoidance. She doesn't have a clue." Joan doesn't talk a lot about her family. She keeps a distance that Ann recognizes and doesn't push, because "We aren't good enough friends to ask what the deal is with that."

They talk about movies and classmates, and of course there is endless talk about sex. They go on and on, and then Ann summarizes: "It is such a blasé kind of thing. You just do it, and you can keep it to yourself and nobody thinks anything of it. And if you don't, you don't, and that is fine too."

Even though neither girl has engaged in sex, they agree with Mary's piece in support of condom distribution: "Rather than blindly turning away from the problems teenagers face today, the school should be able to offer safe alternatives. Although ideal, it cannot be expected that everyone gets help from their parents. . . . High school students aren't going to stop having sexual relations simply because the risk factor is high, they are simply going to have dangerous sexual relations."

The girls recall how everybody was yelling at Mick in class about his point of view, but now Ann slaps her forehead in exaggerated disbelief that his article actually argues that students are warned in school health classes about the dangers of fire, skin cancer, and riding bicycles without the proper safety gear, and yet they are not given smoke detectors, sunscreen, and helmets. That being the case, classes on safe sex should inform but not hand out the safety apparatus. "Does anyone really believe that a student who is too uncomfortable to spend a few dollars to anonymously purchase condoms at the drug store," he writes, "will be comfortable enough to walk up to the school nurse, discuss sexual activity, and ask for a condom?" The problem with condom distribution in school is not that it would encourage sexual activity among teenagers, Mick writes, "but that it would be impractical." How could he possibly say that, especially with the cover story on teen moms? The mock-up lies on the desk beside them.

TWO SENIORS CHOOSE TO GROW UP FAST headlines a full-page story on teen motherhood. Unlike the dark diatribes on the topic in the mainstream press, this tale is of two bright, white honor students en route to top universities after graduation who briefly interrupted the beginning of this, their senior year, to give birth. The faces that smile happily in the photos are of two fresh-faced young women who could as easily be holding pom-poms on the football field as babies. The one pictured with her "boyfriend" Matt is Kelly Jones, Jessica's sister. The story opens: "Motherhood is the most complicated and challenging task a woman can face—especially if the woman is seventeen and still in high school." The moms tell about their surprise at the cost and time babies take, and how hard it is to lose the excess weight they gained, but both find being a high school mother is working out because they "both started out as strong students, and the babies' fathers didn't run away from responsibility." That is what they consider the big news. They brag about the support their boyfriends are giving them, pointing out, "It's a fact that the father stays with the girl only 10 percent of the time." One girl's parents essentially disowned her and she lives with her boyfriend, also a senior, and their son at his parents' house. Kelly and Matt live in their own apartment and plan to be married in July. What is not mentioned is notable: *out of wedlock* is irrelevant; *mistake* is beside the point; *biracial baby* is not worthy of notice.

*The South Lakes Sentinel,* like other school newspapers around the country, documents the world of adolescents in their own voices. What it covers reaches way beyond the school grounds, and includes teen pregnancy, condoms, drugs, AIDS, alcoholism, gangs, cheating, dating violence, the presidential election, homelessness, and the environment, right alongside the usual news of sports, Homecoming, SATs, school plays, and class elections. "Whether we are planning the paper, or just talking to each other," explains one of the staffers, "conversations go from things like what are you doing this weekend, have you finished your term paper, to what do you think about God, Bosnia, the environment, violence against women. We have all the stuff about high school but we also have much bigger lives."

The real difference between school journalism a decade ago and today is that stories then reflected a world of adolescence as a circumscribed portion of childhood—a place to stop in-between, a place to stay awhile before becoming an adult. The occasional coverage of issues like drugs, divorce, and vandalism a decade ago was surrounded by a sense of the unusual. In the seventies, the headline grabbers in Reston were stories about students breaking the no-smoking rule on school grounds, and the fact that South Lakes was way ahead of other schools in declaring that students would not have a smoking area in the school. In April of 1979, there was a story entitled, "We Play Cat and Mouse," that tells of the sleuthing of an Awareness Aide who "seeks out smokers in the parking lots, bathrooms, stairwells, the locker areas, underneath the air conditioner outside and behind the stadium." She knew "approximately forty students who smoke regularly." In the nineties, Awareness Aides (now referred to affectionately as Narcs) are joined by the police in watching for weapons, drugs, and fights in all the same places. A search of newspapers since 1978, when South Lakes opened, does not portray a pristine atmosphere in high school, but a more defined realm where teens grew up with clearer and safer boundaries. By the nineties there was no demarcation—the world encroached and adolescence was a part of the bigger story. "When they hit the teen years," says Ward, "it is as if they can't be children anymore. The outside world has invaded the school environment."

Joining the paper is as it always has been—for extracurricular credit with an eye to college and because the kids love to write—and the new twist, because they want to go into broadcast journalism. The students on the staff are for the most part bright, articulate, motivated. There are also hidden agendas that get to the core of their motivation. Joan and Ann, for example, are both considering journalism as something they might want to do later in life. But each girl has personal reasons as well.

Joan seeks a forum for her voice to be heard. She loved reading the paper from the moment she came to South Lakes. She felt tangential to the world it described, even though she was right there in the place where it was all happening. She wanted to be a part of it. What better way than to cover it, and to help define the types of stories. Ward sees Joan as somebody who genuinely wants to make a difference. "When she was a freshman she was simply trying to survive, to keep her head above water and know that everything would be all right," he recalls. "When she worked her way through that, she started realizing there were things that she could do to change the world literally. She saw the paper as a place where that could be done." Joan is never at a loss for ideas. The newspaper allows her to make her mark.

She hopes her article on stereotypes for this issue will open the eyes of students. In the article she discusses how "teenage society is a colorful one filled with diversity," which can best be viewed within the halls of high school. "One of the biggest problems to emerge in teenage society is acceptance. Many of us reject or get rejected because of style, looks, political beliefs, and religious beliefs. All these things are secondary. . . . We should all start looking at the inner self." She has felt stereotyped herself all through high school: "People think of me as a sixties, love-in, pot-smoking flower child wannabe who is not in her right mind. So they don't want to talk to me because they think I am half-baked, or they do talk to me because they think I am really funny. Few people ever take the time to really get to know me. I wrote about stereotypes so that everyone could see my point of view with my byline under it." Although Joan is reticent, there is passion seething inside.

Journalism is Ann's favorite class of the day. "I didn't choose the paper just because I needed an extracurricular activity but because it is something I feel really strongly about: reporting what happens. People have a right to know what is going on, and I want to be part of that." She comes to life in these classes, thrilled to be part of searching out information directly from sources, and then having the responsibility to inform others by a fair and balanced account. She loves a forum where the goal is communicating truthfully—something apparently shaky at her house. "If you ask me a question, I am at least going to give you an honest answer. That is my whole thing in life: I want an honest answer." Whereas her sister Courtney, only in her first semester of ninth grade, has already decided to get away with as much as possible and to define her own version of high school, Ann wants to be a part of what is going on, in the heart of it through reporting. Someday Ann hopes to be an editor.

Both Joan and Ann are excited about this issue because it delves more deeply into teen concerns. The pregnancy issue, says Ann, is "huge and terrible." She recounts how when she was in seventh grade at Hughes, the newly elected eighth-grade class president was impeached because she got pregnant. "She was in my math class and it was weird—in eighth grade you aren't allowed to touch each other! If you hugged somebody, an administrator would come and pull you apart. Then you come to find out that in eighth grade a lot of people are doing things. And these days, it's gotten a lot worse." At South Lakes, there are always a few girls walking around with bulging bellies. Signs go up on cafeteria walls after a birth congratulating the new moms. At Back-to-School night this fall there still were a few signs left on walls around the school congratulating Kelly and Sally, the two mothers featured in this issue. Can you imagine what a parent might think passing a sign written in big, bold letters on poster board: "Congratulations Sally and Andy, 6 lbs. 3 oz." with pictures of baby bottles and a teddy bear? Some adult in the school blew that one by missing a few of the signs normally ripped down as fast as an administrator sees them. Ann is crazy about babies herself. She works as many hours as she can as a sitter but she would be "scared to death" to have a baby of her own now.

The story meeting a few weeks ago with the *Sentinel* staff started out as always with the class in a last-minute frenzy to come up with the required three ideas. It was editor-in-chief Joanne Barlow's idea on teen moms that energized the class. She'd been thinking about it for a while, she said, every time she saw her childhood friend Sally with her belly getting bigger and bigger. And now Sally is a mother. It just blew her away. She asked Sally if she would mind being interviewed for a story. Sally agreed and approached Kelly, since Joanne didn't know her. "I wasn't really embarrassed to ask them the questions that I did," Joanne later explains, "because it is something that is around a lot and something I can relate to because I am their age and I understand it can happen but I don't think it should. I love babies too, so I was interested to hear the good side as well as the bad."

The group listened without shock or moral judgment. These adolescents tend to evaluate situations on an individual basis, not in terms of any overarching morality. "When I wrote the article," Joanne says, "people were wondering how we could write something that makes everything seem okay. But I don't know anybody who thinks it is okay. When Sally or somebody else is pregnant, everyone is glad they are not in that person's shoes." It just happens, she continues, but students don't think it is a good thing. It is just not as bad as it was years ago when people were ostracized and considered disgraced. "They don't lose their friends over it."

The debate in the story meeting focused not on the advisability of the story, but on whether it should be considered a feature or news. The decision: It is news for this generation of adolescents, it describes part of what goes on, and it merits front-page coverage. The staff discussed the value of the story for making a statement that teen moms are not necessarily "the poor minorities or the stupid." "We all recognize the fact that this is not the right way to bring up kids and not the right direction for society to be going," observes one staffer. "So it needed some attention."

Mr. Ward respected that. He approved the story and did not run it past the principal, Dr. Schmelzer. "I didn't see this article falling into the category of legal concerns even though I perceived there might be moral objections to it. We weren't advocating having babies. We were interviewing two people who said this is what life with a baby is like."

So the story has made it to the cover of this issue, and Joan and Ann are almost finished laying it out. But it is 6 P.M., time to join their colleagues for some food and gossip. The traditional all-cheese Domino's pizzas are set out on four desks pushed together, there are a couple of six-packs of Cokes, and lots of laughter among the eight kids putting the issue to bed. A quick check to see that Mr. Ward is out of earshot and they can't wait to chatter. They go on and on about dating, schoolwork, college applications, and what's coming up over the Christmas break. Mary and Joanne are off on a fantasy of "Reston 22091," a television series starring them. Mick tells the latest in his resignation from Honor Society over the issue of honor students cheating on their required volunteer hours. There are the usual discussions about straight-A student Melanie and her exclusively black boyfriends who are often failing and in trouble, Arlene's latest drunken sexscapade, and on and on until they have depleted the stock of rumors flying around that week. Joan and Ann recall with fondness that there was lots of gossip but nothing vicious. "It is a means of connecting with each other," says Ann. "It is all you really know about anybody—what goes around."

When it comes to Christmas vacation plans, they know they have to be a little restrained because of Mary. While working on the traditional Holiday Remembrances section of this issue, where members of the staff recall favorite holiday moments or family traditions, they learned that Mary's dad died just this September. Mary's piece describes how even though her parents were long divorced, they remained best friends and celebrated holidays together. She tells of how, each Christmas, her dad would call early in the morning and sing a carol to her. He would always be at her mom's house by 10 A.M. with surprises. One she remembers in particular was Shel Silverstein's *A Light in the Attic*, which her dad inscribed: "On your seventh Christmas, may the crazy, happy, sad, and wonderful ideas in this book give you many crazy, happy, sad, and wonderful moments in your life. And most especially, may it cause you to think about the world in which you live and the people who live in it with you. I love you very much, Dad."

Kids may be accused of being uncaring when in fact they simply don't know what is going on because people are so isolated from each other. Mick recalls that no one on the staff had even known that Mary's dad had terminal cancer. They only knew her parents were divorced and she lived with her mom. "Even though we work together at school," Mick continues, "none of us has a clue to what the rest of our lives are like. All I knew about Mary was that she came back to school bright and cheery as usual and thanked us for the card—she never talked about it and neither did we."

The Holiday Remembrances section focuses on the simple pleasures of life rather than the complications. As if uncovering beautiful gems, held in a safe place, the staff writers allow a glance inside intimate family moments, recollections from when they were small, times each year when the world seems in balance and they feel loved and cared for in old-fashioned ways. They write of watching the Thanksgiving Day Parade from start to finish every single November, of a favorite Christmas in Colorado a decade ago when the snow kept the whole family inside, cheered by drinking hot chocolate in front of the fire; of waking parents up on Christmas morning and ripping the paper off presents. "The morning wears on just so, whether sunshine or snow, all of us laughing, sticking bows on cheeks and foreheads, munching hot orange-and-raisin sticky-sweet rolls," writes one reporter. "It is the most wonderful time of year." This is also why they warm so to Ward's willingness to share his love of his wife and his "Christopher stories." The world may be crazy, but in their hearts these kids know what is beautiful and appropriate. They are aware of the differences between what Ward says about his family, and what the teen moms say about theirs.

The December issue of the *Sentinel* finally comes out a few days before Christmas break and the whole staff feels good about it. Nobody thinks it is a problem. But the next day in class, Ward tells them that there are a lot of adults in the school angrily accusing the paper not only of promoting teen sex and teen pregnancy because of the condom editorials, but also of glorifying teen pregnancy by putting it on the front page.

A number of teachers particularly objected that ninth graders be exposed to such stories. Patty Warstler, a ninth-grade social studies teacher, who coincidentally knows the father of one of the babies and praises him for his maturity, is furious that the *Sentinel* published such stories. "Where are our ethics?" she demands. "Why highlight something that is outside what you should be doing at that age in your life? It is not a wise thing to be a mother at fifteen. It is not a wise thing to be suffering through all that at that age, to highlight it and say, this is the happy couple. We've got people going, 'Gee, that is freedom of the press.' I think all of us adults need to look at how wise their behaviors are. Not right or wrong but how wise. Is this a dumb move or is it smart? There is no distinction between dumb and smart anymore. It's like, 'Do what you want to do, and isn't that cute?' "

Such criticism puzzles Ward. The objections pummeling the newspaper were that "we weren't strongly saying this is not the way to go. But the two girls said having babies was wonderful—what were we supposed to do? Say, No, you have to tell us it is not wonderful?"

They were so wrong, says Ann. "We never thought this would be a scandal or even controversial. It was like, okay, the teen mom story is a good idea and later 'Oh well, we have another page to fill, let's write about condoms.' "

Joan is so angry at the adult response that she shoots back a letter to the editor, so full of emotion her handwriting scrawls across the page—her errors not crossed out but heavily scribbled as if heaving anger in the dark spiraling lines: "*The South Lakes Sentinel* staff have received complaints about the front page of the December issue concerning two seniors who have become mothers. Teachers have said things like 'You are glorifying teen pregnancy' and 'You glamorize it' and 'You are promoting teen sex.' I do not think telling the story of what two teen mothers have gone through is promoting pregnancy or sex. It is simply taking two girls and telling everyone about their lives. It seems to me like most adults want us to be blind to the truth, to ignore it. They don't realize that we are in contact with people like this, or that maybe we have even experienced something close to it. Ignoring the truth is the worst thing that we can do."

"It was never a moral question," says Ann. "It is just something that can happen and it is not the end of the world. I used to think that it was, when I was a freshman, but now that I am a sophomore I know it is a reality and nothing is foolproof." Teen pregnancy, she continues, deserves a front-page story because it is a fact that there are a large number of pregnancies and abortions right in this school and this reality is never addressed. The two girls in the story are part of the one million young women who get pregnant annually, according to the latest figures reported by the Alan Guttmacher Institute. "We need to cover more of what is really truly happening," Ann says.

The conflict at its core is over an idealized world versus reality, a belief in limiting exposure to what is going on versus a need for a forum for kids to report what is really of concern. Ward wrestles with these dilemmas each time story ideas are considered for the paper. He believes in freedom of the press; he respects his students' right of expression. As was true for the teen mom story, he encourages them to discuss carefully the meaning and implications of their work and to make good decisions. But often, in the end, he is "allowed to go only as far as the politics of this place will allow. Many teachers here do not see the newspaper as a high school activity. They think they can control information in the newspaper. I have had teachers tell me not to run stories, teachers tell students they can't put something in, teachers tell students to let them see a story before it gets published." He pinpoints community pressure on the school as the source of the tension inside. "It is endemic in Fairfax County and probably throughout the country, that if parents don't like something, they come in wielding the ax of litigation, and the schools are afraid of that."

The inability of the adult world to deal directly with adolescents' concerns in the name of protecting them can backfire. It sets up a conflict about what is whose truth, or leads to an escalation of attention-seeking behaviors to get adults to wake up to what is happening, or totally secret lives. Adolescent life is a bizarre mixture of everything that adults remember plus a whole other layer of things affecting their kids. When adults say, in words or actions, "We don't want to accept your reality. We just want to fix things and make the nasty business go away," it forces extremes.

"It makes me want to say to everyone who objects, Look, we are not trying to shock you," explains Ann. "We are not printing stuff that is not true and there are more issues we need to cover because they are things we deal with every single day and nobody talks about them. Like drinking and drugs—more kids do them than don't. Doesn't that strike anybody as a little strange? Lots of kids, like the guy I went to Homecoming with, play both sides of the coin. He readily admits he goes and hangs out with people who drink and do drugs and he does too, and then he goes and hangs out with some kids who are totally straitlaced and he does what they do. We have two extremes. There is no middle ground for the few of us who sit in the middle. I am one of them and I don't fit anywhere."

While adults seem obsessed with controlling what adolescents see, hear, learn, and do, adolescents have to cope day-to-day in a mixed-up world. They live with and are sometimes involved in drugs, fights, cheating, and pregnancy right along with the usual sporting events, trips to the local library, and snacks after school at Taco Bell. They recycle without thinking, automatically tossing their cans into special bins—some even scout trash cans in classrooms to make sure they get them all. They worry about their earth, they parent each other, yet simultaneously don't value property or themselves. They are full of paradox, confusion, and a lack of integration. They talk mean, they defend turf, yet they also keep in their rooms old toys that comfort them, and in their hearts old memories of more innocent days. The school newspaper reflects all of this.

As reaction to the December issue continues to swirl around them, the staff of the *Sentinel* is on to the next issue. At the story meeting, Joan is assigned to page one coverage of President Clinton's inauguration. Ann will write an editorial on stopping teen violence, as well as the Counterpoint in favor of the death penalty. Other pieces for the issue will include an editorial on American military intervention; coverage of the Mr. Seahawk contest, the benefits of a recent stress management workshop for seniors, and how Alateen helps teen alcoholics to heal; a report on vandalism in the school; an update on Prom plans and Beachweek; a feature on a teacher who includes transcendentalism in her eleventh-grade English course; coverage of senior slump, controversy in the National Honor Society at South Lakes, winter sports, and so on. The issue will also carry ads for the East Coast Surf Shop, Birkenstocks, and the upcoming teen job fair, and a police Wanted poster for the man who killed two people and wounded three at the main gate of the CIA facility in nearby McLean, Virginia.

So it will continue, eight issues a year. The newspaper becomes a symbol of adolescence itself, a head-spinning, heart-thumping, soul-searching array of all sorts of things happening simultaneously. Understanding contemporary adolescence is not just knowing that this bad kid is doing this or that good kid is doing that; it is not about classifying the nerds and punks, the skateboarders and Valley Girls, the grungy and the preppy. Contemporary adolescence is a story of kids growing up involved in a world we don't fully understand.

The bell rings and the journalism class disperses. Once out the classroom door, they blend into the surge of bodies streaming through the hallways, down the stairs, and out the doors. They go out to cars or to meet their buses stretched in a long line along South Lakes Drive. In minutes, there is a long ribbon of students, seventh-grade through high school, filing into buses and cars, winding down pathways, through the school grounds, and across surrounding streets.

Chris runs from the door at Hughes to catch his bus way down at the far end of South Lakes. He learned quickly that if he got his books before the last period, he'd have more time to complete his commute without being scared he'd miss the bus.

Jessica is with her friends Annie, Susan, and Rachel in the center of a group of high school boys, in no hurry to go anywhere because her mom is coming to pick them up to take them to her house. She asks one of the boys to get her an extra copy of the paper with her sister's picture on the cover. She thinks it is so cool.

Courtney and Brendon take off for the electrical box on a nearby path, where the smokers congregate. If Courtney times it right, she'll have time for a smoke before she gets on her bus. Joan walks toward the group at the box, hoping one of them will see her and invite her over. She waits for a moment or two, then decides she might as well go directly home.

Charles is still inside the school at basketball practice with his sister's team. They won't be home for hours.

Ann chats with her best friend for a few minutes at her locker, moves efficiently through the halls, and is one of the first on her bus, an eye out for her sister, who always runs late.

Jonathan hops into his friend Bill's amazing orange Volkswagen bus decorated with scores of hand-painted fish, a scene straight out of Ken Kesey.

And so it goes, the ordinary daily commotion as the adolescents of Reston are sorted back out and shipped to their empty neighborhoods. The school has been doing its best to keep them safe, engaged, and learning all day long. But now most are on their own as they enter into their community of youth.

Within a half hour, the buses and student cars have driven away and there is stillness.

# MAKING

# CONTACT

*A*fter a day at school, I was bushed. But it was not even 3 P.M. and, like the kids, I wasn't done yet. The problem was that after school the kids vanish. Except for the presence of those staying for activities, the emptiness and the quiet were both welcome and unnerving. Now what?

I had won my way into their world at school, but outside school they certainly were not accustomed to having an adult like me nosing around in their lives. There was a new awkwardness between us that had to be overcome. I was ready to launch the next stage of my story, to explore their private worlds, find out what made them tick. If they could tell me about anything, what would they choose as central to their lives? This was the trickiest part. I wanted to get the real scoop without leading them or suggesting an agenda. I wanted to see the larger context without intruding and changing the dynamic. I had to gear myself to be an open listener when being told of things I would not approve of as an adult and mother. I had to make sure they understood that I might write down, to the most private detail, whatever they revealed. One thing was certain. I couldn't do it sitting at my desk. I had to go to them.

It helped that I had done lots of homework about adolescent life in Reston. By now, I had months of daily involvement in their schools and related activities. There was lots we could talk

about. It won me access. What helped most was my attitude of
partnership. I didn't presume. I went to them and let them know I
needed them.

Out of school I could be more real too, free of the scrutiny of
people who thought I was spying on them, evaluating, judging. I
wore jeans, carried a backpack, sat on the floor, expressed my emotions openly—and eventually so did the kids. I wasn't mute. I was a
participant in a developing dialogue.

My passport into their private lives was food. Lots of it. I ate subs
by the lake with Jessica while she expounded her theories of love
and friendship; I had M&M's with Courtney while she told me
about her new boyfriend, leftover Chinese with Ann while she went
on and on about her parents. Charles and I discussed race over pizza,
Chris and I consumed Chicken McNuggets at McDonald's while dis-
secting seventh grade. I had more McDonald's, Roy Rogers, Taco
Bell, and Pizza Hut in the years of this book than during the previous decade. Sometimes we ate in the restaurant, sometimes we carried out. I learned to stock my refrigerator at home with real Coke,
not diet, and not to lecture on nutrition. I talked to the kids over so
many meals that some graduated to real food—Joan and I even had
sushi!

When not eating, we spoke in their homes, my home and sometimes in parks. Some opened up instantly, eager to share; others took
some time. But one on one, they learned they could be real with me.
They tested me; sometimes it was uncomfortable. But I wanted it to
work, so we kept trying. I learned to accept silences while they got
their thoughts together, to pace our visits to their tolerance level. It
didn't take long before the interviews lasted hours, and sometimes
they brought friends so we could get all the details or an additional
opinion. With some of the kids, my relationship felt parental, with
others collegial. Some were more blunt, aiming to get my reaction—
as when Brendon told me it would be a great idea to interview him
when he was on LSD (I declined)—others took a long time, dancing
around issues, testing the waters. Some things recounted in this section I heard at different times. For the sake of the action of the book,
I wove all of them together to re-create the immediacy of the scene;
the stories are all true and as they were told to me. The ground rule
was honesty. The kids knew if they regretted telling me anything,
they could let me know and I would respect their wishes. With some

of the most sensitive material I checked and double-checked with them. Nobody recanted anything.

I always had my tape recorder with me because many times we would finish talking and just as we were getting in the car to drive home, they would reveal something new and interesting. It got to the point where they were so comfortable with my recorder that they would remind me to turn it on and check to make sure the battery light was bright red.

This section is like a kaleidoscope of adolescence, rich in many different designs and colors. What the kids chose to tell me was widely variable and often surprising. By the time we'd finished we had covered all the big areas of adolescence, including education, sports, home life, friendships, sex, love, music, and mayhem. But in 3-D, as kids actually live and perceive them.

I found it interesting that each youngster's life had a theme that emerged as we talked. For example, Jessica always cared about doing well in school but she virtually never discussed school beyond that overall goal. Her obsession was friendship and love, experiencing life fully. That she worked hard in school and got good grades was a backdrop to the social part. In Chris's case it was the opposite. School and success were primary and friends were absolutely essential, but he spent more time talking about academics and the hurdles to being himself, as well as his passion for sports. Jonathan was consistent in tying nature to everything meaningful, and in his philosophical stance. Charles had his eye on the prize from start to finish, matching Chris in his passion for sports. Ann was the little-mother nurturer while her sister Courtney was the wild child. Both complained about school, but for each in her own way, it was the center of her life. They both were talkers—but something was not being said. Joan always seemed to be acting out her internal struggles with belonging. Even though she was quite self-revealing, there was a layer deep within that she didn't reveal. All the kids were unique, facing their own lives and realities.

In Part Two, I make contact with the adolescent community. If there are tribal mores, this is the section that best captures them. The chapters relate to each other through the motifs of adolescence, the ever changing kaleidoscope.

Sometimes the kids are living strikingly separate lives from their families, as are Brendon and Courtney. Even when youngsters *are closely attached to family, as Chris, Charles, and Jessica are, the lives they lead and the issues they face proceed unabated by the parental connection. This section is about another expression of the different selves children reveal in the different domains of their lives. It is the ongoing task of adolescence to find how these pieces fit together.*

# Out of the Whirlwind and
# on to the Playing Field

Chris Hughes is glum. The bus ride home from school is an ordeal. When you're a seventh-grade rider at the bottom of the hierarchy that stretches through high school, you are exposed to all sorts of wisecracks and looks that make you feel like an ant. At best, you are ignored. Either way, the commute makes Chris feel uncomfortable. He focuses on his friends, or disappears into his head, listening to his Walkman. Sometimes he pines for the days of power in sixth grade. As his bus swings past Forest Edge, he looks at the school and knows he doesn't really want to go back, knows there is no turning back, but then again he misses the comfort. Groan. He feels so young and short. Finally at his stop, he gets off and trudges home.

His mom meets him in front of the house and he brightens. It is nothing out of the ordinary for Chris to be greeted after school. When he was little, his mom or his sitter always waited for him at the bus stop. He takes it for granted that there is always somebody happy to see him. Thank goodness for the ordinary when everything else seems out of whack.

Since he started seventh grade a couple of months ago, he and his mom have developed this little ritual. She always goes to the front door, and usually walks outside to meet him. She can time it perfectly because, from her desk, she can hear the bus grinding up the hill. She gives him a big hug hello and he breaks into a grin. They walk to the house together, his mom's arm draped over his shoulders if none of the other students is in sight. (Chris, always loving and receptive to his parents, still is after all a preteen.) It makes him feel good to see how his mom cares.

Chris comes into the house, greets the dogs, and yells hello to his father, who is downstairs in his office. His brothers used to be around too, but they are both off at college—not that it matters, although, he sheepishly admits, he sometimes misses them. He drops his backpack on his bedroom floor, wades through dirty clothes, books, magazines, papers, empty soda cans to get to the hooks mounted on his closet door, where he carefully hangs up his Penguins Starter jacket. Obviously not a star in the neatness department, he is careful with his precious jacket, the only one of its kind so far at school. He is so pleased with himself for figuring out which team to buy. Chris likes to be different within a structure. The Starter jacket is de rigueur among young adolescents, and to Chris's mind, having a team that is unique makes his really special. He admires it for a moment before he makes a mad dash for the bathroom. No way he'd use the one at school—it's too nasty. On the way he grabs the latest issue of *Sports Illustrated*, one of the highlights of his week. When he emerges, he goes to the kitchen for a snack. He comes home starved, another victim of the 10 A.M. lunch.

He flips on the television to *Looney Toons*, and he and his mom sit at the kitchen table. Chris knows that his mom is eager for all the news of school and sometimes she feels a little left out, but it is often just hard to recall. The days register as a whir of sensations in his brain. So, as usual, they go over his homework strategy. He likes to tell her his plan of action: he'll do English, Teen Living, and science before football practice, then pre-algebra, current events, and history when he gets home. Telling the plan seems to give it substance.

Today he has some extra worries. His mom senses it. But he doesn't want to share just yet. Back in his room before he starts his homework, he tries calling his best friend Brad. No luck. He's probably at Kindercare picking up his little sister. Chris really needs to talk to him about Kim. This girl thing gives him an instant stomachache. He'll try to talk tonight at football practice. He's got to figure out what to do.

At first, he thought having a girlfriend was terrific. Was it only a month ago that he had been so excited about his first dance, held after school on the Friday before the high school Homecoming?

The dance was after school and before the late buses, not exactly an introduction to "night life." Most of them were terrified. It was for virtually all of them their first dance, and for Chris it was a huge leap from the only other mixed-sex party he'd been to—the sixth-grade pool party.

He remembers how he and his buddies filed into the darkened gym to the undulating sounds of rap and instantly felt good. That music, the hallmark of their age group, has a style that is all they are not: confident, outspoken, brash, packaged in a deep rhythm and attitude that says things he wouldn't dare say, speaks of doing things he wouldn't dare do. It takes away thinking, awkwardness, transforms the room by its overwhelming beat and volume. Real talk is drowned out; the focus is on the sound, not them. What adults don't understand is that music—whether it be rock, heavy metal, or rap—overrides the painful self-consciousness of adolescence; it eases the need for suave interactions and creates an instant community among listeners.

Kids making their way down the uncertain pathway of friendship look for signposts along the way. Music preferences are a major means of identification. "I can tell a lot about a person by the music groups they like," says Chris. The music can smooth over the awkwardness of a car ride, provide common ground for discussion, and, as in this case, jolt a room to life. Chris thinks it's dumb for grown-ups to get so worked up about it. Getting a Dr. Dre tape the day it is released is exciting, and luckily his mom takes him to buy the tapes he wants without any hassles. She even lets him play the tapes while they are driving, although she doesn't like most of them. She sometimes asks a lot of questions about the lyrics. Chris tells her it's not the words but the sound, although he informs her about the "bad words" ahead of time, "so it doesn't seem as bad as it is because it shows I know right from wrong." Thank goodness his parents understand he's not going to become a gangster just from listening to music.

The dance would appear to an outsider like a total free-for-all. The participants' anticipatory anxiety is released by the music, the whooping and hollering, the rambunctious but benign physicality. The kids have a blast. A herd of youngsters gather in several huge lines to do the Electric Slide—this generation's Bunny Hop—where to the students' amazement a few teachers join in. The dance etiquette is free-form: people dancing together in groups as the mood dictates, girls dancing together, individuals dancing alone. The unusual sight is a couple, and especially rare are slow dances of any sort. Any departure from rap by the disc jockey is booed. Mostly among the boys there is horseplay, and standing up against the walls. "I don't know if anybody knew what they should do," recalls Brad. "I didn't know what to do so I just stood against the wall and listened to the music."

While Brad hangs on a wall, Chris, distancing himself from his mother, who is a chaperone, spends most of the dance running around trying to figure out how to talk to Kim. "I was shy," he explains. "I wanted to talk to her but I didn't know what to say. Mark was pressuring me—joking around, 'Dance with her, dance with her,' but I just couldn't do it." Kim is busy mingling. In the last five minutes of the dance Chris pulls himself up as tall as he can and ambles over to Kim. She smiles with delight and they talk briefly.

His mother waits in the car to take Chris and his friends home. When the last one is dropped off he confides, "Now don't make a big deal out of this and get all excited, but I am going out with Kim." This, of course, does not mean he is *going out*, but rather that they are going to be identified as a couple.

The next Monday he gets off the bus looking bemused. It takes him a while to get up the gumption to tell his mom the news. "Remember what I told you yesterday? Well, Kim is my girlfriend." It happened in English class, where she sits behind him. "She handed me a note under the desk that said, 'Do you want to be my boyfriend?' I was really excited. I wrote her a note back that said, 'Yes,' and then we were boyfriend and girlfriend." His mom is afraid to say more than "That's nice," because he clearly needs some time to sort this out.

Before he can elaborate, the phone rings, and it is Kim, the first of what will be many long calls between them each day. Before long her friends start calling too and have long conversations with Chris about how the relationship is going. His friends call to see what's happening. The permutations seem endless. There are conference calls. Several people backed up on call waiting. Chris's bedroom phone is at the center of a huge communication network.

He has a ball at first. Everybody knows that one of the hallmarks of being a Real Adolescent is talking on the phone a lot. He and Kim go out on a date. He is wearing his new Penguins jacket when he and his mom go to pick up Kim to see *Honeymoon in Vegas*. As they drive across Reston, his mom tries to gently instruct him in the etiquette of dating. He goes to Kim's door to get her after his mom explains that it is impolite to honk, even though Kim knew, as ever-practical Chris points out, that he was on his way. When they come back to the car, Kim gets in back and Chris returns to his seat in the front. They sit in silence the whole way to the Town Center. Then Chris, suddenly debonaire, opens the back door to let Kim out and they walk away chattering, delighted with each other's company. (When his mom comes to pick them up, she locks the front car door so Chris has to get in back with Kim.)

Being Kim's boyfriend was wonderful for almost a month before a subtle pressure began to destroy the innocence. Their relationship quickly became group property, full of pressure and innuendos scripted directly off the tube and the movie screen, pressure from the same kids who had been without a clue about how to handle a middle school dance but whose minds are bursting with sexual and romantic images from the media. "Suddenly my friends were pressuring me, 'You kissing her, you get her in bed or something?' and they just kept asking me stuff. When we were watching movies in English class they kept pushing me to hold her hand, to put my arm around her. During class time!" Their meddling is shocking to Chris's sense of appropriateness. The self-consciousness he feels is excruciating. "Everybody's looking at me and saying, 'Hold hands,' and everything like that." Kim doesn't seem to mind, Chris says. "But when you are in seventh grade, you are not mature enough to be dating. That is what I think."

He is feeling trapped, sad, and confused. For the first time, he feels he can't tell his parents something, because he is ashamed for being so immature. Parents just can't understand what it is like at school. "It's too much trouble, too hard," Chris has confessed to Brad. "I don't really like her anymore." But he is scared of her eighth-grade friends, who have been taunting him that if he breaks up with her they will beat him up. Threats and violence are constant companions in middle school. He is convinced they mean it.

He turns to his homework, which is simultaneously a pain and a relief from the big dilemma about Kim. He consults his DAB—an acronym for the Daily Assignment Book, distributed to all Hughes students in a pioneering attempt to help them learn to keep track of their work and organize their time. In social studies, his assignment is to read the first three paragraphs of each front-page story in *The Washington Post* for a weekly current events quiz. He spreads out the paper, does a quick survey, and puts it away. It would be nice to do alone but it is too confusing: tax bills, Bosnian atrocities, corporate mergers, countries he's never heard of—even though he is great in geography! As usual, he will discuss it at dinner with his parents and take notes. His mom and dad are great about being available to help him if he needs it. Of course, he'll have to tell his dad again that he will not read more than the three paragraphs required. Chris takes his assignments literally and does what is expected exactly, not more, not less.

Next, homework for Teen Living is a breeze to complete. In a far cry from the old-fashioned home economics, both sexes take this course, which the teachers call a "real life survival course"; it educates them in self-care, care for others, cooking, sewing, and other skills they need in an era in which children take on more responsibilities at a younger age. Today's assignment relates to self-concept. Asked for words "that would describe the way you look to a stranger," Chris thinks for a minute and writes, "a short, young, athletic boy with braces, blue-gray eyes, short brown hair, and strong legs." When asked how he sees himself, he writes, "I am a chubby responsible boy with small feet." His self-image is basically positive, he writes, but if he could change the way he looks any one way, he would make himself taller. He is aware that his friends wouldn't like him any better because being taller "wouldn't change my personality."

The next assignment asks, "What's Inside Me?" Chris has already decorated a small brown lunch bag with magazine pictures of Deion Sanders, Isiah Thomas, John McEnroe, a red Corvette, a silver Miata, a telephone, a huge candy kiss, Chips Ahoy!, Kix cereal, a large-screen television, a VCR, and a boom box—a collage of images that appeal to a twelve-year-old boy. "I worry about death," he writes, "because I don't want to leave this world. I daydream about playing professional football and baseball because it has been my dream for years. If I were rich I would buy a lot of cars and houses because I need them. A little thing that makes me angry is cleaning my room. A big thing that makes me angry is homework because it is hard. Even though it could never happen, I have a secret desire to rule the world because I could have anything I want." Maybe if he were in charge of the world, he would feel in control of his life in seventh grade. He folds his sheet over and over until it becomes a tiny rectangle, places it inside the brown bag, and staples it shut about ten times.

Poor Chris of the ordered life. Forget orientation. Forget the practice locker. There was no way to be prepared for this. Middle school has swooped Chris deep into the center of a whirlwind, with changes coming at dizzying speed requiring all his energy to remain in charge of himself. He appears to be doing fine: his grades are good, he is on top of his work, he has lots of friends. But the shape of the world is confusing. He is just a chubby, responsible boy with small feet. He's not interested in sex with a girl, or cuddling during a class. He thinks it is wrong for Kim's friends to be threatening him. Nothing makes sense anymore.

At first it was just routine anxiety. "I was kind of nervous when I started school. Trying to fit in, maybe. Not getting hurt by an eighth grader." He quickly found middle school an environment difficult to navigate. Searching for words he says, "You get there and it's like an explosion and you separate." Suddenly the old support system is shattered as kids are placed on different teams. A new center has no time to gel because as soon as the kids come in and adjust in seventh grade, they have one foot out the door in eighth. Hughes is a revolving door, and the kids feel it from the start.

They pour into Hughes from different schools and neighborhoods all over the town, over five hundred seventh graders, with one major preoccupation: friends. Yet rather than encourage the creation of a new community of middle schoolers, at the very time the youngsters need many points of connection, the school narrows their options. At Hughes, with the exception of the band, the newspaper, and the yearbook, school clubs meet only monthly and intermural sports are not well attended. Budget limitations and a lack of interest severely limit extracurricular opportunities. Kids are at loose ends within the school environment.

It is not that Hughes is physically a chaotic place. On the contrary, the impression Chris and his classmates picked up during orientation last year turns out to be no mirage. For kids bursting at the seams anyway, the traffic lanes marked down the hallways at Hughes, the constant reminders to sit still and listen, the restraints on socializing during lunch, send a clear message. Not only are they logistically unreasonable for children who biologically need motion and psychologically need socializing, but they also are heavy with judgment that by failing to sit still, to be quiet, to be obedient, they are *bad*. A kid like Chris can keep himself under control in the face of such frustration. Other kids are more keyed-up, have less self-discipline. "You see people you've known your whole life transforming before your very eyes," says Chris, watching several old friends turn rowdy. It makes each classroom a pressure cooker, each hallway a contest of wills.

The changes are sudden and dramatic. The first day, students are welcomed to their teams, which have friendly names like Soaring Eagles, Whiz Kids, and the Panther Pack, and special logos, colors, and mottos. The new students get special leeway if they are late, help with their lockers, coddling. Then, Boom! It is time for the ABCs of the nineties—the Acceptable Behavior Code, delivered by one of the administrators, Charles Everett, whom Chris describes as "old but strong as an ox" after witnessing Everett wrestle a knife-toting student to the ground the first week of school.

The seventh graders stream into the Little Theater where only a few months ago they had been welcomed warmly. Everett begins solemnly: "Today I have to go over the county rules of what is expected of you." His voice drones on and on, chronicling the punishments for misbehavior that runs the gamut from tardiness, cutting classes, cheating and forgery, to improper attire, running in the halls, and smoking, to substance abuse, physical and sexual assault, and possession of weapons including explosives and anything used as a projectile. He tells the kids they will be suspended for ten days for carrying a gun and might be expelled. No beepers will be allowed. Everett ends by emphasizing that the verbal abuse rule would be enforced this year. His audience is not intimidated. Those who would commit the offenses really don't care, and the huge majority of students present who are good decent kids feel put down and bored.

The adults are reacting to documented truths: a report released by the Virginia Department of Education in the winter of Chris's seventh-grade year states: "Incidents of weapons possession, tobacco possession and referrals to substance abuse programs peak during the middle school years." The report says that "violent and unruly behavior" peak in eighth and ninth grades, that approximately 70 percent of weapons found in public schools statewide are found in middle schools. School personnel deal with increasingly violent environments.

The reality and the fear of "bad kids" and "problem behavior" have come to dominate middle school in America. On the one hand, teachers give little self-esteem assignments like the ones for Teen Living, which some might say are just fluff and take away from academic goals. On the other hand, Chris tells his parents, the adults at Hughes act as if the kids are a bunch of wild animals that need an abundance of rules: "Every teacher assumes we are going to be bad, wild, and crazy. They are so strict, they won't give you slack for anything because they fear we will get out of control."

The lure of the outlaw in adolescence is not new, but its overwhelming power today is amplified by higher numbers of kids in trouble and the inadvertent collusion of the adult world. All kids want to be noticed and they see clearly who gets attention. "Why doesn't anybody care about me?" asks Brad. "I made an A on a paper, he got into a fight. Everybody is talking about him." He goes on to say that fighting is wrong but, "you want to be associated with that person. I did." Good kids secretly wish they had "the guts to be bad." It's hip-hop in middle school, but even more out of control because of the immaturity of the dudes.

The administrative tactic of an iron hand behind childlike approaches in many classes creates a focus that is all wrong. In the effort to save kids from negative behaviors, the spirit of middle schoolers is often crushed. Just when creative outlets for their robust appetites are so necessary, their avenues for expression become more limited. "Through early adolescence, up to and including ninth grade, there really needs to be more of an emphasis on exploration," says psychologist Peter Scales of the Search Institute. "Young people need to have the chance to sample a lot of content, a lot of different subjects and topics and themes and activities to find out, 'What in the world am I good at? What do I like to do? What talents do I have, what interests do I have?' And along the way finding out, 'What values do I have?'" Instead, the invitation to explore is more often drowned out by the demands to behave.

Chris is the first on his team to be named Student of the Month, an honor given to one person on each of the teams in the school. The selection criteria reflect the values apparent at orientation: "Is on time; controls hands, feet, and body; dresses appropriately; respects rights and properties of others; attends all classes; leaves teenage toys and snack foods at home; helps maintain a safe school environment; has a hall pass when outside the classroom during class time. In addition, the nominated student *has not* had more than two detentions for the current quarter, been suspended, has not been placed in the Temporary Learning Center." Big whoop-de-do. Like Chris doesn't know all of that is what you are supposed to do in school. Thank goodness his social studies teacher, Mrs. Roche, had something to add. She writes, "This student is nominated for being a Super Student! Besides fulfilling the criteria above, Chris is kind and courteous to all his peers and faculty members. He always has a supportive word for classmates who need extra encouragement. Chris is conscientious with his schoolwork, always turning in assignments on time and making good grades. Chris is concerned about issues currently occurring in the media and expresses an interest in helping make his world better. Chris is truly a pleasure to have in class!"

The ceremony in school is a big zero, a total nonevent. The winning students are called out of class into the Little Theater. The principal and vice principal give little speeches, hand out award packets, period. No big assembly for the school to set a good example. Nothing.

His parents tell Chris they are proud to have a son who is not only a good student but a good citizen in school, that he is a fine person and that matters in life. His mom puts the certificate in a scrapbook. He is happy to please his parents, but to him it is no big deal because nobody in school cares about it.

The integrity of early adolescence as a developmental pathway is ruptured for this generation. The kids, at a fragile stage of development, have before them wildly contrasting definitions of what it means to be an adolescent. These seventh graders face a revolution in their bodies, their minds, and their environment. In their classes, their self-concept is tossed around by highly divergent ways of relating: in one class they are treated like babies, with rote learning, mindless projects, spoon-feeding; another class is a sarcastic free-for-all where kids chew gum, jump around, sass each other and the teacher. Some teachers treat them with respect and creative challenges, others with distrust and rigid discipline. Most of the kids want to please and do well. But who they are and what is expected is a mystery.

Witness the principal's office. On a chair is a well-worn pink panther (the Hughes mascot) wearing a Hughes T-shirt. On the wall is a copy of a Norman Rockwell painting of a little boy wearing a Boy Scout uniform far too big, saluting an American flag. His Cub Scout uniform is draped on a chair beside him. The picture is entitled "Can't Wait." To one side of the picture is a large conference table used most days by police officers and troubled parents for meeting after meeting about truancy, violence, drugs, abuse, abandonment.

It's no wonder Chris likes to come home to people happy to see him and to routines that are comfortable and familiar. He loves to zone out, to pull on his big red Florida Seminoles shirt over his boxers, take a nice big glass of orange juice to his room and turn on the tube. His home is orderly and friendly, and it's good to be there.

Chris is lucky. He seems equipped with a strong inner core. He has by luck—because of their jobs—parents who are available to take care of his needs. He may not be consciously aware of it, but the fact that he can relax, feel at home, relinquish care for himself to his mom and dad gives him the space to do the growing up he needs to do at his pace—not an unnatural one. He never worries like many of his friends that he won't have a ride to practice, to the library, to wherever he needs to go. He is not required to cook his meals or the family meals. He has no younger siblings to be responsible for, like his friend Brad. He is expected to pitch in with the dishes, do yard work, and walk one of the dogs. Basically, he can worry about what he has to do: his homework, his sports, his bar mitzvah this year, and take the rest for granted. His world, so full of mixed messages in school, is not entirely upside down. He can still count on watching sports with his dad, trips to the family farm. Just like always, they'll go sledding in the winter, get videos on weekends, rake leaves in the fall.

Chris's responsibilities are far different from those of many of his peers. In one class, his teacher did a survey of the twenty-eight students and found that 75 percent of them had breakfast alone or with siblings they were responsible for. Only 25 percent had their mom or dad available. One-fourth of the seventh graders in the group made dinner regularly for the family too. This wasn't about neglect but about schedules, changes in the fabric of growing up.

The first part of his homework finished, Chris goes downstairs to remind his dad that they have to leave for practice in fifteen minutes. They chat about the second half of the Monday-night game, which Chris missed the night before. Chris generally goes to bed by ten, but he gets to stay up on Monday nights for the first half of the football game.

Chris has a passion for sports—all sports, but especially football. He has an inexplicable loyalty, in rabid Washington Redskins territory, for the Buffalo Bills. He still can't believe that head coach Marv Levy was once his dad's camp counselor at Camp Interlaken in Wisconsin. Thurman Thomas and Jim Kelly are his heroes. Huge posters of them are right beside his bed where he can see them and dream of the days when he'll be a football star. He is a compendium of sports information with amazing historic depth. He knows names, positions, teams, and numbers of all the players in football; the rosters of all teams; statistics and standings of any sport in its season.

He and his dad have the best time quizzing each other on sports trivia, watching games, and even having an occasional friendly wager. This day, the conversation brings him back to a world he understands—he can forget the girl stuff, clear his mind of the middle school confusion, and look ahead to football practice.

Chris and his dad get into the car. Chris asks, as usual, if he can listen to "his station" on the radio. When they get to Brad's apartment, he and his sister are waiting outside. She is a cheerleader for the youngest football team in the Reston Youth League, referred to affectionately as the "ankle biters" because they are only six and seven years old. The boys talk about the day in school, homework, and the upcoming game. Brad and Chris are both grateful to be on the Panther Pack team together. Their friendship goes back to third grade and provides a sense of security and fun for both. Chris will bring up the subject of Kim later when they are alone.

At the field, the kids bound out of the car, happy to see their teammates. They talk about the past weekend's game, where they crushed their opponent. Chris is still giddy with success: "I got into a fight with a center and that was the best time I ever had—I was talking so much trash, we were crushing Springfield—the center started crying and he was swinging at my helmet with bare hands." It's controlled violence, Chris and Brad explain. "If you get run over, blocked or something like that, you want to get back. The same thing happened at Lake Braddock—I cut-blocked this guy and he said, 'Come on, obscenity, try again.' So I did it again," says Chris. "That part of the game is fun to me," adds Brad. "I like the talking part, but at the end of the game you come together and you shake hands and say good job and that resolves the problem. So in that period of time you can be mean and violent and dangerous. And then it is over."

No more time for talk. Practice begins. The boys run their warm-up lap, then participate in "grueling" calisthenics led by team members. That's the worst part. Now comes the nitty gritty. There are hitting drills, tackling drills, and sled drills, team offense and defense drills. Chris, a lineman, takes on the sled. With a manly bellow, he charges it, running into the first pad, rolling and slamming the second pad, and onward until he has roared and flung his body at each of the seven pads. Then, since he is the last of the group, he joins six of his teammates and they roar simultaneously, slamming into the pads, pushing the contraption down the field now almost completely dark.

Practice over, the boys gather around their coaches for a meeting. Play sheets are handed out. Some schedule changes. Then the closing cheer. His friend Denny leads: "Who are we?" The team shouts back, "Reston!" "How do we feel?" The boys reply, "Fired up!" "What are we going to do?" This is their favorite part. "Kick their butt!" "Who?" "Vienna!" "How?" "Easy!" They repeat it even louder and end with an earsplitting whoop. Then the tired, sweaty boys go contentedly into the darkness to get their rides home.

Chris willingly goes through the laps, the drills, day after day from the middle of August for the sheer joy of playing the game. "I just love football," he says with seldom-expressed passion. "I don't care what position. I just want to play. I just want to start and play the full game." For Chris and Brad, football deals with problems and challenges in an atmosphere of rules and order. It embraces them with a feeling of camaraderie, gives them an identity. Football, like other team sports, provides markers they can see and feel, and a perspective they can use to understand other aspects of their lives. Chris, who only started in the Reston Youth League in sixth grade, experiences himself growing as a player. He sees hard work pay off. He loves victory, but he is learning to measure the strength of his own effort and to see the value of a personally good game even in defeat. In football, he says, "I came and I worked as hard as I could just to get up to my position."

Football teaches cooperation. "When you are little," explains Brad, "you want to play quarterback or you want to play halfback because you want to get the ball and score a touchdown and be the star. You don't understand it is a team game and everybody has to contribute to win." However, you quickly learn to "root for each person to be good at what they do." You understand, Chris says, that "because we want to win, we can't have somebody not play well." He adds: "You don't want to let your team members down." Unlike school, according to both boys, where a kid who has an attitude and is disruptive is considered cool, a team needs unity. "You can't be bad," says Chris, "the coaches will kill you. There is more discipline in football than there is in school."

The weeks go by, and it is almost Thanksgiving, time for a series
of bowl games. Their victory over Southwest is a highlight of the
season for Chris. They play so well as a team, it is as if everybody is
in sync and can do no wrong. When the final touchdown has been
scored, Brad and teammate Anwar dance in "celebration" in the end
zone just like Deion Sanders. With no thought of personal glory, just
the sheer exhilaration of being a part of a winning team, happy for
his friends, Chris savors the win. But he also makes a promise to
himself that someday he will have a "celebration" when he has a
moment so fine.

The traditional end-of-year party follows the game, this time at
Fuddruckers. As the kids and their families sit around eating burgers
and drinking milk shakes, talking and laughing, rehashing the season, communicating about their lives, there is an unmistakable old-
fashioned feel. Like Homecoming, Christmas, or Thanksgiving, these
gatherings of families are satisfying to all involved. But they are too
infrequent. And at this party, as was true of the games all season,
many kids are there without their parents. The involved parents pick
up the slack by driving car pools, by even paying for the unattended
kids at a party like this. They work hard to make sure all the kids feel
they belong. This is happening across the board in school sports and
outside activities. But the number of parents who are never there
still is dismaying, especially when the pattern is in place by middle
school.

It's finally time for the coaches to speak. Even though it has not
been a winning season, they give out participation trophies with a
personal recognition of every player. It takes forever but each kid
waits patiently for his name, and readily claps for each teammate.
Now it is Chris's turn. He comes forward to stand beside the coach,
smiling shyly. The coach puts his arm around Chris's shoulder and
credits him as "another second-year player who shines, the starting
left guard: he was always at practice, always willing to jump in there
and give his most to the team." He talks about how Chris has
"heart." Everyone applauds.

Football season ends, Thanksgiving comes and goes, and Chris still
struggles silently about Kim. The threats of possible violence become
a torture. His parents notice that he seems troubled; after weeks of
silence, he tells them his problem. They suggest that maybe the time
to do something is during Christmas break because by the time it

ends, the whole topic might lose its interest for Kim's friends. They tell him that he doesn't have to be mean, that he can let Kim down gently. Maybe he can even give her a Christmas present to let her know that he still likes her as a person, but that he just doesn't want to be her boyfriend anymore. That way, she will tell those threatening friends that Chris is nice and should not be beaten up. Chris likes the idea. He suggests they buy a stuffed animal.

The Saturday after vacation starts, Chris and his mom go to the toy store at Town Center. Chris chooses a small white stuffed bear. His mom gets it wrapped.

It still takes a few days to get his nerve up. He sits on his bed and looks at the phone. He picks it up and puts it down. He gets up and goes into the kitchen. His mom says to just do it, he'll feel better. He goes back and looks at the phone. His stomach is in knots. His heart is galloping in his chest. He goes back to his mom to go over what he will say.

It's fast-food night at his house, so he mentions he's hungry. They go and get dinner, and he takes it back into his room and looks at the phone. No way he can eat. He takes a deep breath and dials her number. She answers. The call takes maybe ten seconds: He wants to break up but he really likes her as a person and he has a Christmas present for her. Can they still be friends? She says okay. He feels so relieved he cannot believe it. He even feels hungry. He eats his Chicken McNuggets with a lighter heart than he has had for months. The next afternoon, he drops off her Christmas present. It is still almost a week until school begins. Enough time for things to smooth over. Nobody ever tries to beat him up over Kim.

The undercurrent of violence takes its toll on Chris. Long after the relationship is over, he avoids taking chances. Every day he comes home from school, meets his mom, does his work. In the spring, he and Brad try Reston Youth League baseball, which is great fun, but not their sport like football is. The two of them spend time at Chris's farm, where they can act like the children they still are, doing things they would never share with their other friends: catching frogs and salamanders, petting the new calves, playing Monopoly and Sorry, mending fences with Chris's dad. Things that are fun and fulfilling, simple and traditional that they allow themselves to do when far from the adolescent community.

In June, the Panther Pack has its year-end celebration and awards assembly. There is a palpable air of relief in the room, a thank-goodness-this-is-over-and-we-will-never-have-to-be-seventh-graders-again feeling. Next year they will be the bosses of the school. For a few hours the undercurrents of seventh grade vanish and they are welcomed as children to a party. Some parents are there, maybe of 25 percent of the kids. The centerpiece of the occasion—a big cake in the shape of a paw—is decorated with the message "Panther Pack, Have a Purrrfect Summer."

The team awards are distributed before the refreshments. Chris ends up with a stack of awards for outstanding achievement in all his subjects. It is an affirmation that he has made it in middle school. Most important, his classmates have voted him the Most Likely to Succeed Boy. "The academic awards are important," he says, "because good grades are important in life. I like to shine." But the award from his classmates means that the person he is and tries to be is accepted, maybe even admired. That is the best.

With focus and discipline, Chris makes it through the cauldron of seventh grade, growing gradually into a better sense of himself while others begin to lose their way. It has been a year of the absurd, a year of childish assignments, adult-sized evil, and devaluation of the students in an environment that is out of sync with who they are. Chris flourishes because of the clarity and reinforcement in his home, a consistency in his out-of-school environment, and adults in his world who don't just tell him what to do but also model positive behaviors.

The last day of school he bounds off the bus, down the street into the house with Brad. They are jubilant it is over and the long days of summer stretch ahead. No homework, especially no need to read those damn first three paragraphs of the stories on the front page! They have lunch watching the tube, change into their bathing suits, and pick up Brad's sister at day care to go to the pool. All afternoon they talk and throw a Nerf football, the sun beating down, the water cooling them, the pool itself a colony of young people in the middle of a workday. As they wait to be picked up, Chris discloses his interest in Katy, and how he is looking forward to seeing her at Reston Teen Camp.

That night his parents take him out to dinner to celebrate a job well done. They toast him for a great year, recognizing all that he did. The only mistake they make is that his dad orders for him. Chris announces in no uncertain terms that he can handle it himself. He is, after all, an eighth grader now.

After dinner, he thanks his parents and goes into his room and closes the door. He calls Katy, who seems happy to hear from him. He watches the Orioles game on television and goes to sleep luxuriating in thoughts of summer. He wonders how much he'll grow by the fall. The only thing better than being an eighth grader would be to be a tall eighth grader.

# A Circle of Friends:
# It's Not Peer Pressure,
# It's the Adolescent Way of Life

Jessica and her mom sit at a table in Roy Rogers after school on a frosty November afternoon. While Jessica scarfs down a cheeseburger, fries, and a Coke, she delivers a running commentary: School today was good. . . . She got another 100 on a math quiz. . . . In PE they didn't have to go outside because it was too cold. . . . Some cute boy talked to her when she was over at the high school for French. . . . Annie wants to help with the Thanksgiving baskets for the homeless this year. . . . Tonight she wants to go with Annie, Susan, and Rachel to a movie at Town Center; can she go and would Dad drive? . . . And one more thing, could she spend tomorrow night at Rachel's? Yes, Rachel's parents will be home.

Her mom is used to this cascade of talk. While her other two kids are quiet, keeping their feelings to themselves, Jessica is an open book. She is a people person like her dad, delighting in relationships, winning in her manner, and enthusiastic about experiencing life fully. As she approaches high school, she sees a wider world opening to her and she can't wait to partake of it. "Jessica would like to sample everything in life," says her mom, "and hopefully she has enough sense to know there is danger in certain things—you cannot do everything." The two of them hang out at Roy's for almost an hour talking, laughing, making plans to go shopping during the day Saturday and visit Kelly and the baby on Sunday after church. They have a good time.

Jessica's mom is pleased at her daughter's characteristic exuberance because lately she never knows what to expect. Jessica goes in a flash from animated child to surly adolescent, from talking nonstop to silent sulk. Part of the problem has been the situation with her sister, first living in the house with the new baby and now moving out. It's not like they were so close exactly, but Jessica feels that Kelly is supposed to still be there, just being her Big Sister. Now her sister's been lost to motherhood. That is what her speech in Mrs. Nance's class was about. It still makes her angry that she didn't get to give it at the assembly. Oh well, she's got her friends.

Jessica can hardly believe her luck having such great friends. When she came back from St. Luke's in seventh grade, she had lost touch with the local kids. She tried to reconnect with friends she had known in third grade, but the relationships didn't go well. Things limped along until the holidays, when she found out they had a party and she wasn't invited. She felt so rejected and alone. Kelly was helpful. She told her to "get real about these kids." Kelly told her straight to stop depending on people who didn't value her.

Jessica turned her attention to some new kids. She already knew Annie from her science class, and one day they went to the mall together, where they ran into Rachel, a friend of Annie's. When Rachel had a party at her house the next week to watch the Super Bowl, she invited Jessica. It was really fun and opened the doors to a whole new group. Rachel's parents and a bunch of youngsters watched the game with a feast of junk food, Cokes, chips and dips, and lots of conversation. It was heaven to Jessica. She met one guy, Chuck, who she hooked up with briefly, and another, Tad, who she ended up going with for several months.

Her life had turned around and she was happy. She had a circle of friends, guys who liked her. They talked on the phone, took in movies, and visited each other's houses. She kissed her boyfriends and held hands. Jessica finally had a social life. Now she didn't feel so lonely.

The kids loved to come to Jessica's house. Everyone thought her parents were cool. They were warm and friendly yet never intrusive, and they were generous with time, rides, food. Everyone thinks her dad is a stitch, "always making cracks, so corny," says Jessica, rolling her eyes affectionately.

Seventh grade ended and school days became lazy summer days by the neighborhood pool. "About six of us teenagers sat off by ourselves. We'd smear on baby oil and fry. I love to get a tan. And we'd play games like Shark and Fish and Marco Polo." They'd splash in the water, chase each other, compete just as they had always done since they were six or seven. Outside the pool, oiled and dressed in bikinis, the girls appeared nymphlike and displayed the innocent seductiveness of youngsters developing into young women. She didn't see Annie and Rachel much because Annie was in charge of her little sisters for the summer and Rachel's older stepsiblings were around. But that was okay. She hung out with Mary, whom she knew from St. Luke's, and Mary knew Bob and Seth because they lived on her street. And they knew this other guy named Ian, whom Jessica ended up going out with. "We hung out at the pool, and we'd go out bowling and to movies. Ian dumped me because he went to soccer camp and, I guess, found someone else. I was upset for a little while and then I wasn't because I didn't *love* him."

When summer drew to a close, social groups shifted and realigned. Jessica got back together with Annie and Rachel, and Susan got in with them too. Then Jessica met Mitch through Brian, from the pool. Rachel had known him a long time. He was one of the "car drivers" so essential to younger teens who want some freedom. It was the ultimate: four eighth-grade girls hanging out with junior and senior boys from high school. The girls dubbed themselves "the Crew."

Things changed right away in eighth grade. The fulcrum of social activity moved to Rachel's house because, as Jessica noted, "It was looser at Rachel's—her parents didn't watch us or pay attention to what we did very much." The girls could even smoke cigarettes if they wanted to as long as they did it outside. Jessica wasn't looking to rebel or anything. She just liked the delectable feeling of having more freedom, of growing up.

Jessica's parents are uneasy when the kids change locations. They don't know the other parents. "A lot of times I feel like I am walking this line," her mom says nervously, "because I want to help Jessica develop who she is, yet I want to be able to pull her back before she falls over the edge." Her parents comfort themselves with the feeling that they have brought up Jessica right, that she tells them what is going on, and that she seems so successful in her life.

The girls have a great time at the movies Friday. They hang out for an hour afterwards with the ocean of teens at Reston Town Center on the single main street and the open green spaces that this perfectly planned miniature downtown provides. Promptly at 11 o'clock, Jessica's dad appears and takes the giggling group to their respective homes.

The next night, Jessica goes to Rachel's as planned. Susan and Annie are already there. Her mom drops her off and peeks out the car window to see that Rachel's mom answers the door. What her mom could never have imagined was what greeted her daughter inside. Jessica recalls, "Rachel was high that night and her parents knew. They looked at her bloodshot eyes and said, 'Rachel!' then started laughing. They were like, 'Don't leave the house because you are high.' " Jessica laughed with them, but she was thinking, "If my parents ever found me high it would be like go up to your room, all your friends are leaving, you are grounded forever."

This is curious new territory for her. Rachel's parents even have their own bong right out in the open like some throwback to the sixties. Jessica isn't dumb. She knows it is a special pipe used for smoking marijuana. It knocks her socks off. "I mean, parents are grown-ups and grown-ups are supposed to be responsible." She doesn't say a word to Rachel about her feelings. Jessica wants to be cool.

After they give their stoned daughter instructions to stay home, Rachel's parents go out for the evening. They don't mind leaving a houseful of kids. Jessica feels a twinge of guilt. She wasn't supposed to be at a friend's with no parents home, but it isn't her fault. She did not plan this, and what self-respecting eighth grader would do a lame thing like calling her parents to come pick her up? Oh well, maybe Mr. and Mrs. Drake will be back soon.

The group goes down to the family room and watches television. Several hours later, the phone rings. "We are sitting around downstairs having fun, and this guy Cal calls up messed up beyond the point of knowing what he was doing. He says to Rachel, 'If you guys don't bring Mitch over, I'm going to kick your ass.' " The kids try to think of a way to respond to the threat. Mitch, who has seen Cal in the past get indiscriminately violent when he is drunk, tries to put him off. First he tells Cal he'll call his mom to see if he can stay out later to come over. Then he calls Cal back, and says he's sorry, but he has to go home now or his mom will take the car away. Cal coldly responds, "Fine, 'bye," which hints darkly that Mitch has now made his choice and is going to have to pay for it. Everybody at Rachel's senses there is going to be trouble. They run upstairs and arm themselves with kitchen knives, double-lock the front door, and turn off all the lights. The boys call their parents and say they have to stay a little longer. The group sits crouched in a hallway, knives ready for the attack. A long time passes, maybe half an hour. Nothing happens. The boys say it is okay to get up now and turn on the lights. Everything seems fine. Maybe Cal was bluffing.

The boys say good night and go to their cars. While Mitch is unlocking his car door, he feels a hand on his shoulder. In an instant, Cal shoves Mitch against his vehicle. Maybe it would have stopped there, but Cal has some friends with him, also drunk, egging him on. So Cal starts punching. Mitch is smaller and has no idea how to fight. He's down on the ground and Cal, supposedly his friend, is kicking him. The girls peering from a window are terrified. Jessica calls her dad and Rachel calls a family friend. The two adults arrive within minutes. As they pull up in their respective cars, Cal runs off with his friends and is swallowed up by darkness. The two adults try to calm the girls and tend to Mitch, who is banged up and has a bloody nose. Jessica's dad calls Mitch's father.

All the adults were in a tizzy, recalls Jessica, but Mitch wouldn't let his dad call the police. He said Cal just gets rough when he is drunk, so it really isn't his fault. "My parents didn't think of it as our fault either," explains Jessica, "because Cal burst in on us. We didn't have anything to do with it. Their concern was more a question, 'Why do you know these people? How do you know someone who would do that?' But then I didn't know him." Somehow, in the hubbub, it never came up that Rachel's parents weren't there.

The story plays well in the halls of middle school. What an adventure! The girls wear that night of excitement like a badge of honor in the category of life experiences. It is so "unboring."

A couple of weeks later, Jessica tells her first big lie to her parents. She wants to spend Saturday night at Susan's. The other girls will be staying there too. She goes through the usual assurance, true up until she says that Susan's mom will be there. Her adrenaline surges through her veins, her heart pounding as she blatantly fibs to her mom. This is scary, but she also has to admit, exciting.

The Crew has been plotting this evening for ten days. Susan's mom had to go out of town to a business meeting. Susan begged her not to send her and her brother to their dad's house, to let them stay alone. She told her mom she had too much to do—with school, cheerleading, and baby-sitting—to waste time commuting from her dad's. Hadn't she proven her reliability by taking charge of the house for years while her mother worked? Hadn't she cooked dinner and cleaned and watched out for her brother? Furthermore, she and Billy are both in the eighth grade now. They hate going to Dad's anyway because he doesn't understand them like she does. Susan had learned how easy it was in a divorce to use one parent against the other. The ploy worked. Mission accomplished.

The other girls carry out their plans too. Rachel's parents, eager for a respite from their daughter, who is testing them to the limit only six weeks into the semester, easily agree to her staying with Susan, never asking whether her mom will be home. Annie and Jessica get permission for Saturday night's "slumber party."

As the sun goes down, the girls luxuriate in their total independence. Sprawled on the living room floor watching MTV, empty Domino's boxes around them, they take long drags on their Marlboros and discuss plans for the evening. Susan is using this opportunity to invite over a few close friends. She tells Jessica that she won't know a lot of the kids, but no sweat, after a beer or two they will seem like old friends. Jessica feels a rush of anticipation. Though she has sipped champagne at weddings, this would be her first official drinking party.

By 9:00, about thirty kids show up at the quiet townhouse where Susan lives, several bringing picnic coolers full of beer. After two or three beers, Jessica feels strange. Actually she feels horny. How bizarre. How interesting. She assesses the roomful of people and zeros in on a totally adorable guy leaning against the dining room wall. She walks over and begins a conversation with him. He is so handsome and has the most beautiful blond curly hair and the strongest arms. He tells her his name is Marty and he is a sophomore at South Lakes. He plays football. They amble over to a couch and sit down, shoulders touching. She snuggles. He wraps his arm around her. She can't believe what she does next. "I made the first move," she recalls. "I kissed him."

He says they ought to go to a place where it is quieter. He leads her into Susan's bedroom. She glides as if in a dream into the room where she has spent countless hours gossiping and laughing with her friends, sharing secret wishes about boyfriends and marriage and motherhood. But now the room seems so quiet and dark. She's a little frightened. She nervously says, "Okay. Let's talk." He lies beside her on the bed holding her hand, being so nice that she relaxes a bit. After all, she's thirteen now and should be able to handle guy situations.

The next thing she knows, he is on top of her, kissing her, his hands wandering up her shirt. She pushes him off and they talk. Before she knows it, he is on top of her again. She pushes him off again and starts chattering about her sister, what happened with her and how upsetting it is. All the while she is jabbering on and on, she is telling herself, I'm not going to sleep with him, not going to let him take advantage of me. Over and over. I'm not going to sleep with him. Then he mounts her again, and she is convinced in her drunken stupor that he is having sex with her. "It was dark," she remembers, "and when he was on top of me and doing things, I was afraid. When he was humping me, I was really scared because that was something I never did before. She shrieks, "What are you doing!" He jumps up and says, "Look! I still have my pants on!" She tells him to just stay off of her, and she shoves him with all her might. But it is not until his friend comes to tell him that they have to go that he stops trying.

He rolls off the bed, stands up, and straightens his clothes. All of a sudden Jessica is sad to see him go. "Are you going to come back?" she implores. He says he will. "I wanted to see him again," she remembers. "It wasn't until I looked back on it that I saw it as dumb, and wondered why I went into that room with him because I knew what he wanted. It is like, when you go to a party and get drunk, you get horny. That is just what happens and you hook up with people. Most people have sex. I didn't. He was just someone to be with, he was leaving, and I wanted him back. I thought I was in control of the situation, but I really wasn't." She gets up from the bed, tucks her blouse back into her jeans, and goes downstairs.

She runs into Rachel at the bottom of the stairs. Rachel and Annie had left for a while and come back, so when they entered the house the party was in full swing. "I walked in the house and everyone was messed up except me and Annie because we were the only two who hadn't been there," recalls Rachel. "Two guys I didn't even know were laying in the middle of the floor with all these people walking around them. They're like, 'Here, come lay down with us.' I grabbed a beer and I did. We were just on the floor laughing. Then I got up. It was dark so I asked, Who's on the couch? A guy rose up like some sort of ghost, came up to me and got me up in a corner. He leans forward to kiss me, and all of a sudden I hear, 'You'd better leave my friend alone.' People were chasing each other all over the place."

Jessica, feeling forlorn, goes outside and runs into another guy she doesn't know, who happens to be very polite and gentle. He notices right away that she looks sad and she spills the whole story about what had just happened. He is sweetly sympathetic and explains how Marty goes to parties all the time, hooks up with girls, and sleeps with them. She finds out she had been totally tricked when he told her he was sixteen. Marty was actually almost eighteen and a senior. The boy told her not to expect Marty to come back. "I was like, Wow. This guy is being really nice. I didn't know until later that he was Cal, the guy who beat up the kid at Rachel's." It had been so dark that night she never really got a good look at him. When he seemed so nice at the party, "I just figured maybe it had just been a bad day for him."

The party goes on into the wee hours. Around 3:00 in the morning, Jessica is sipping another beer, thinking to herself that it really tastes disgusting. Every time anybody says something to her she says, "I'm not going to sleep with you. I'm not going to have sex." Rachel jumps up at the sound of an approaching scooter. Donny has come to pick her up for a ride. "He was drunk as anything but he drove fine—you could have a conversation with him," says Rachel. "He drives better than any sober person I've ever seen. Lots of people know how to drive drunk."

Susan wanders back from wherever she had gone with some guy and is none too happy. "I had three people at the house who were supposed to chill, stay sober, and watch the house for me. I came back, my brother was passed out on the floor. So we had to put him up in his room and lock the door so no one would 'prey on him.' " (This is a common amusement at parties, where the helplessly drunk get doused with hot water, cold water, and other imaginative concoctions, "so they never do it again.") Jessica is slumped over, sleeping against the couch. Susan and Annie shake her awake and get her upstairs into Susan's room. She collapses on the floor like a rag doll, so they lay her out gently, arranging her head on a pillow, and then cover her with blankets.

Finally, Susan and Rachel are the only ones awake. With the booze wearing off, they are shocked at the scene. The house is a shambles. Garbage, food, bottles, cans, cigarette butts are everywhere. A chair in the kitchen is smashed and left in the corner of the room. The portable phone has been stolen. It is a disaster. They decide to deal with it after a few hours of sleep.

Much too soon, it seems, morning comes. Jessica gets up by 9:00 because her mom is picking her up to go to church. She has a horrible headache. She brushes her teeth three times and hopes she looks normal. She leaves quietly and meets her mom outside.

The other girls sleep late. Susan meant to set an alarm so they could clean before her mother came home. Big mistake. In midafternoon while the three remaining girls and Susan's brother are groggily assessing the disaster, Susan's mom walks in. She freezes in her steps. Susan and her brother begin to cry. Annie and Rachel wish they could disappear. Their mother says icily, "I'm going to go out, and when I come back I want all of you out of here." She slams the door on her way out, hops into her car and zooms away. The kids, now wide awake, scurry around room to room doing the best they can.

When Susan's mom returns several hours later, she angrily threatens to call the other parents. Susan refuses to give names and numbers. She tells her mom that it was her responsibility because she gave the party. Once her tears have dried, Susan feels no remorse. She stakes out her position: "My mom says I have not said I'm sorry about the party. I'm not. I'm sorry that the phone was taken and that I didn't get the house cleaned up. I told her that the only reason that she found out was that my time management wasn't very good."

A few days after the party, Jessica's dad asks if they will go trick-or-treating as usual this year. At first she hesitates. Then she declines because she is thinking thirteen is too old. But when he says, "Fine," in that I'm-laying-a-guilt-trip-on-you kind of way, she grins and agrees to go. The truth is she always looks forward to Halloween with her dad. They've been going together every year since she was a toddler, while her mom stays home and hands out the treats. They immediately get to work devising costumes. The two of them relish any opportunity to ham it up.

Halloween arrives, and Dr. Giggles and the Vampire Witch step out of the Joneses' front door. The doctor emerged when Jessica's dad traded in his everyday lawyer suit for a medical shirt and jacket her mom brought home from the dental office where she works, a stethoscope borrowed from a doctor friend, and a wild mask resurrected from the household collection. Ms. Vampire Witch is attired in a short black dress, with fishnet stockings and high heels, a bright-colored tinsel wig, and garish makeup.

They stay out for hours, as long as Jessica's aching feet can stand it. It is like it has always been, a happy fun-filled adventure with her dad. She loves him so. And these shared hours reassure him that Jessica's growing up doesn't mean losing her. Back home, they enter the house laughing and joking. They dump the pile of booty on the kitchen table, to her mom's customary exclamations over the quantity.

While Jessica is arranging her candy by variety, enjoying the evening with her parents, her friend Rachel is having sex with Cal at a Halloween party. Telling Jessica the next day, Rachel admits she is astonished that she did it. "At the beginning of seventh grade I shared my first kiss, and then suddenly a year later I lose my virginity!"

Jessica is furious. It doesn't make any sense to her. First Rachel was going with Brian; they were about to do it, but the condom ripped when he was putting it on. Then they break up and right away she decides to do it with someone she just met, and he is the guy who beat up Mitch! Maybe Cal was nice to Jessica the night of Susan's party, but none of the girls really know him and now Rachel has had sex with him. While she listens to her friend's story over the phone, Jessica eats her Halloween candy piece by piece.

The two girls are sitting in Rachel's living room several days later and Rachel says to her mother, "Mom, by the way, I'm not a virgin anymore." Jessica's mouth drops open in shock. Later Rachel explains to her stunned friend, "My mom had already decided she was going to put me on birth control pills because I had come close before with Brian. I thought I'd tell her so we could make the appointment with a gynecologist." But it turns out her parents' approval is not so crystal clear. First, they give her pills and let her smoke weed. Then they get mad at her for her grades and her attitude. "With everything going on," Rachel says, "they are holding it against me. 'You are too young to do this and that. You are too young to have sex.' My dad hates the guy I did it with. My mom is pretty cool. It gets confusing."

Jessica tells her own mom, inadvertently creating more worry. "It's tough," reports her mom. "Because of the situation with Kelly we are walking on eggs and we don't want to get paranoid about Jessica." What she and her husband do is try to be proactive by encouraging wholesome activities. They suggest the kids go to youth group functions, to the movies, to Town Center to hang out and get a cup of hot chocolate. They know how much Jessica loves to ice skate but can't seem to get the group involved. They try inviting the kids to their house. "With this latest episode, I told Jessica that I just don't trust Rachel," her mom says. "For example, the other day Rachel came over with a guy and I know she's grounded, but I didn't call the mom and say, 'Do you know your daughter is here?' because I don't feel I know her well enough." How does one mother of a thirteen-year-old who thinks the kids should be skating and drinking hot chocolate communicate with another who gives her thirteen-year-old birth control pills? Jessica's parents feel they are in a tug-of-war, pulling their daughter back from an adolescence that is not what they wish for her.

Jessica meanwhile is happy as can be. She's active in her church group going to retreats and meetings. She spends lots of time with her family. She does her work and gets good grades. And she parties on weekends with her crowd unless she has too much homework.

The best times are at Cal's house. He finally wins them all over by his boldness and sophistication. Just as Rachel has become the self-appointed leader of the Crew, fifteen-year-old Cal is head honcho of the group's social scene. "It was so neat," says Jessica. "He had like this whole little apartment of his own in his townhouse." A family room had been converted into his bedroom, with two beds with a table in between and two old grungy couches. It is dirty and messy but the kids are oblivious. It is a teen mecca. They can drink, smoke, and spend the night and his parents don't care. "His parents were really cool," recalls Jessica. "They would yell down, 'Cal, you need another beer ride?' And people would give money and they would go buy it for them. A lot of parents get beer for their kids." Jessica thinks it is so cool when a parent says, "I'd rather have them drinking it at home than stealing it and getting in trouble."

This December night, there are five eighth-grade girls and six high school boys. Jessica and Annie are supposed to be at Rachel's, and Rachel at Susan's. They pile into Cal's room—coats, hats, and gloves in a tangle on one of the beds. The boys have already started drinking. First the group plays drinking games. "You have to suck a paper to your mouth and pass it boy to girl. You kiss the person through the paper and blow it on to their mouth. Whoever drops it has to drink," Jessica explains. As the game goes round and round, there are occasional paperless kisses exchanged. Then Cal turns off the lights and people dance.

Jessica is already sleepy from two beers, enough for a 105-pound girl to feel quite mellow. She stretches out on a couch, her head perched on the opposite end from Donny, mindlessly rubbing her stocking feet against his. He sits up and says sternly, "Don't play with me unless you are going to have sex with me." Jessica withdraws her feet.

Later Cal takes her hand, pulls her up from the couch, and holds her close to him in a dance. He presses his crotch against hers and whispers, "I want to kiss you, okay?" She straightens up and says, "Well, you were with all of my friends. You had sex with Rachel and Susan, so I don't think so." He leaves for a moment and asks Rachel's permission—Rachel, who is presently drunk out of her mind. That's how he got Susan so he's hoping his luck will hold. He comes back and tells Jessica that Rachel says it would be fine. "Then I told him, 'Cal, I don't think it would be right.' So I never did anything with him and I am proud of myself for that."

The hours go by. All the time, Cal's parents are upstairs, never once checking, never once suggesting it is late and the girls should go home. Couples slip into the weight room adjoining his bedroom. Others caress each other on the beds in full view. The drinking continues for hours. The young girls disintegrate from their early studied poses—beer sipped with style, cigarettes puffed just so—bravado building as the alcohol surges through their young bodies. The boys keep going, but after a while the girls get silly, they get sleepy, and finally Jessica, Annie, and Rachel collapse on a bed. Susan never makes it. She sinks down on the carpet and vomits all over the floor and herself. "It wasn't little baby throw-up like my nephew's but big disgusting barf," Jessica remembers. "Susan couldn't get up so we had to clean it, and it was totally gross."

Finally, it is quiet. Cal's friends leave, and he is passed out on one bed on top of all the coats and hats and gloves. Susan is on the floor covered with a blanket. On the other bed are the three girls, sleeping peacefully.

Jessica has no second thoughts about her social life. "I'm a good student, that's why I get away with so much. I really care about my grades and my future, and I care because I know what I want to do in life. I want to get married, have a few kids, and be a doctor or a marine biologist. Just because I drink and mess around with guys a bit doesn't mean I'm bad. I'm just experimenting. I'm not good but I'm not bad. I just like to have fun." She insists she is not succumbing to peer pressure: her friends don't care if she smokes, they don't care if she drinks, they don't care whether she has sex. "They are my friends. I don't know anybody that says, Jessica, smoke! Smoke right now! Are you being a wimp or something? I wouldn't hang out with anybody like that."

"Everything we do is regular," says Susan. She is not far off the mark. Behaviors once at the fringe of adolescent rebelliousness have not only permeated the mainstream culture of high school but are seeping into the fabric of middle school. By the eighth grade, 67 percent of youth report having tried alcohol, 13 percent marijuana, and 45 percent have smoked cigarettes, according to the 1993 "Monitoring the Future" study conducted by the University of Michigan's Institute for Social Research. The tenth-grade boys Jessica and her friends socialize with are among the 81 percent who have tried alcohol, the 24 percent who have tried marijuana, and the 56 percent who have smoked cigarettes. Susan and Rachel are among the 16 percent of thirteen-year-old girls who, according to the Alan Guttmacher Institute, have had intercourse. "This is what you are supposed to do," says Jessica. "It is our teenage phase. You are only a kid once."

New Year's Eve arrives. The Crew has big plans. The girls start at Rachel's and walk over to Cal's house. Actually Rachel is grounded from seeing any of her high school friends, so they tell her parents they will be at another kid's party. That, of course, is never the intention. At Cal's, they meet up with the usual group of guys, who are deep into their holiday celebration already. When the girls arrive, plans change. They will all drive to Lovettsville, where Cal's uncle has a cabin. Everybody is excited but Jessica. While sipping her wine cooler, she mulls over the situation. "I had this sick feeling in my stomach, and I said, Jessica, you are going to get caught. You are going past Leesburg. You are going to a party an hour away on New Year's Eve when your parents expect you to be somewhere else. You thought you were going to be in Reston. That way there is somewhere you can go if there are problems, but if you get stuck out in Lovettsville, you're a goner. There's no way. You call your parents, and that's a real possibility, and you say, Mom, Dad pick me up. I'm in Lovettsville. I don't know where the hell I am." Besides, Jessica sees that everybody has been drinking. "Cal, who didn't have a license, was going to drive because his parents left him the car but he was definitely too drunk," she recalls. "Then Mitch said he would drive Cal's parents' car, but Will insisted it was his duty to drive because he would be getting his license sooner than Mitch." So the drunken fifteen-year-old Will becomes the designated driver.

Jessica knows she must get out of this situation. When they pile into the car she says, "Guys, I feel really sick. I think I'm going to throw up. Please take me home." She knows if she had told the truth—"If I'd said, Guys, I don't want to go. I'm scared I'm going to get in trouble, and besides you are all too drunk to drive"—they would have never taken her home. And the fact is, she does feel sick to her stomach.

She walks into her house a few minutes before New Year's and, standing alone in the doorway for just a moment, feels enormous relief. She looks at the Christmas tree in the corner of the living room aglow with white lights, crystal balls, and icicles. There are still scraps of wrapping paper and ribbons beneath the real pine branches. Everyone is downstairs in the family room around the "children's tree," always decorated with colored lights and all the ornaments she and her brother and sister have made over the years. She walks down into the family room and everybody converges—her parents and grandparents, her aunts and uncles and family friends—hugging and kissing her, saying "We are so glad you are home, glad you are with us to welcome in the New Year." Then it is the New Year. Everybody lets out a whoop and her new nephew cries. She picks him up and kisses and holds him and tells him everything will be okay.

She brings Darien up to the kitchen where it is quiet and sits rocking him in a kitchen chair beneath a plaque that reads, LORD AND MASTER, PROTECT THIS HOUSE AND EVERYONE WHO GOES IN AND OUT. As she gazes at her sleeping nephew, she thinks how glad she is to be home, but how sad she feels to be missing out on New Year's with her friends.

# Graffiti, God,
## and Other Meaningful Things

The late winter night is crystal clear, the moon lighting Reston like a giant spotlight. Sailing along on his bicycle at two in the morning down the trails in the silent woods near his home with his buddy Tad, fourteen-year-old Brendon Lamont has never felt better. His body buzzed by three Colt 45s consumed in his living room with his older brother while his parents slept, he feels warm and alive. He likes the buzz of the alcohol topped by the "blunt" or two smoked on Tad's deck before they left. "Joints are for sissies," he says. The rage is stuffing marijuana into a hollowed-out Phillies Blunt cigar—more pot, a bigger high. It's cool: "Pot is like relaxation, an escape from everybody to make yourself happy." As he flies along on his bicycle, not thinking, "not being mental," the frigid air on his face feels like a slap jolting him to a life free of restraints—no thoughts of school, no thoughts of problems, no sadness.

Brendon likes to escape, not to care, not to feel his feelings. He tries many modes: his classroom clowning, his truancy, his school activities, his art, his dope, his cigarettes, his booze. They are all hedges against an anger that lurks beneath the surface, a dark side that sometimes flashes across his face. In less than six months he has relinquished the idea of being just another Joe Highschool, his fate sealed with the embarrassment he suffered in his lame act at the Mr. Seahawk talent show at school this month. His optimism and excitement have vanished since the innocent football games, floats, and

Homecoming dance of the fall. His attitude has taken a nosedive. People disappointed him. The friendships he thought he had were all surface friendships. Teachers are fucked. He hates being forced to go to school by society. It is never his fault.

But he has not withdrawn from the conventional entirely. Tonight, like every night, he sat down to dinner with his parents and siblings. On Sunday, as always, he will dutifully attend church and youth group. Most Tuesday evenings he goes to his Boy Scouts meeting, halfheartedly working on his goal to become an Eagle Scout like his father and brothers before him. He is devoted to wrestling, following a tradition set by his father's success as a collegiate wrestler and carried on by his brothers when they were in high school. The family appears in many ways the embodiment of traditional family values, eating together and praying together, two parents and their children living under the same roof. His dad cooks breakfast for the kids in the morning. His mom acts as the peacemaker when there are problems, often running interference for the children. Both parents share preparing the evening meal and attending the kids' activities. But all is not what it appears. As in a warped mirror, the reflection of this model family is distorted by the pain of economic loss.

Victims of the national economic stagnation of the eighties, Brendon's family began to have problems in 1985, when they were forced to move from Houston to Reston because his dad lost his job. Brendon was only a little boy; yet, in the family mythology, the Texas years were the golden years when the family was truly happy. They had a comfortable life, extended family nearby in Louisiana, and security. Three years after coming to Reston, his dad lost his job again, and in order to have control over his life, he started his own computer business. The way Brendon sees it, his dad tried to get things moving and underestimated the time that it would take. He struggles to rationalize his tremendous disappointment in his dad. "My dad has a master's degree and he has the potential to get a good job, but he is just following out his dreams. I guess that's good for him but. . . . He knows it is going to come together but we just don't know when." The problem has dragged on for years with no end in sight, and has caused the family tremendous heartache.

The economic hit has been devastating. Constant money issues are like a creeping poison changing the whole family dynamic. His mom had to go to work—"She is pretty much forced to bring home the bread"—and spend her time in jobs that have nothing to do with the artistic endeavors that she is interested in. Being under so much stress, she is no longer effective as the arbiter of family problems. "My brother and my dad have really vicious arguments," says Brendon, "my brother Steven and I have had vicious arguments, and me and my dad even more vicious arguments. And I guess my mom doesn't have the energy to put up with it. She is just as sick at waiting for the money as we are." His parents' relationship has been affected, and the boys are angry at their dad and defensive of their mom. Brendon is still shocked that his dad didn't give his mom a Christmas present. "She was so upset," he recalls. "And my brothers didn't give her one either. Only me and my sister did. Our holiday, to say the least, was a big gyp for the whole family."

The whole atmosphere of the household has slowly broken down. The four kids, left alone after school year after year, have taken out their aggression more on each other. Nothing abusive, but there is a lack of harmony. His sister misses the time she could share with her mom and partake of her talents and essential religiosity. Brendon feels that the stress makes his mom less available to communicate with, so more and more he keeps things to himself. As the youngest child, he also has been affected longer by the empty house and the never-ending economic insecurity.

When their parents come home from work, says his sister, they "aren't rude but they are short-tempered and snappy." They come home hassled, and since the kids have no clue what goes on at work, and they only hear the stories of the bad stuff, it makes work seem like drudgery. The scene of the family sitting around the table suddenly doesn't have the same Norman Rockwell appeal. "They are tired and exhausted from dealing with people in bad moods, and they come home in a bad mood and we are hungry and want to eat dinner," explains Jenny. By high school, all the kids' activities and social lives shrink the already limited family time to hardly any at all.

Brendon doesn't care, he says. Out here in the night, life is sublime. He and Tad zoom down the pathway. As they pass a generator box, in a dance of defiance they lean over and quickly, happily make their mark. Like male dogs pissing, they spew paint from their aerosol cans, claiming the territory. It's "bombing," in graffiti parlance. As they travel, they bomb the pool, all the tunnels, all the generators in their path. Graffiti is a turf war of paint, cover, and clean, played out by opposing armies. The artists decorate, the vandals desecrate, and the cops try to eliminate. Until violent gangs got into the picture across the country, it had been a basically benign but annoying thorn in the side of "civilized society." Graffiti is to Brendon the ultimate game of chicken—and art. He loves the danger, the rush of sensations that obliterate daily concerns. There's nothing like a little vandalism on the way to the big event.

"I don't consider myself a troublemaker," Brendon says. "But it is really fun to make trouble." He and his childhood friends delighted in throwing water balloons at cars, egging houses. From the time he was little, he grabbed a smoke or a beer with his older brothers. Graffiti fits the pattern. Getting away with stuff is a natural high. He's quickly transforming himself from class clown to class pain in the ass to bona fide delinquent. But he doesn't see it that way at all. He'll make his own high school memories on the sly, he says grinning, taking a deep drag on his cigarette. It is his choice.

An insomniac by nature, out here he joins the people of the night. They gather in posses or crews, groups of kids from the local area who hang together but who are not gangs. "You'd be surprised how many kids you can meet out there, ranging from their teens to early twenties, who love the night like I do," he says. Most of them party or drink until they go out at two or three. There is a special thrill in owning the darkness, and among the graffiti artists it is the time they ply their trade.

This is the subterranean world of Brendon, a secret interest shared with a coterie of fellow outlaws who double as regular kids during the school week. One is a varsity basketball player, another an avid environmentalist, another a top student; several are marginal in academic subjects, but all are recognized in school as accomplished artists. Most participate in school activities while maintaining a parallel life of drinking, drugs, vandalism, and theft. "The posse I'm most friends with is TFS—The Fuckin' Stoners, although it really stands for The Forgiven Sinners. We drink 45s, bottles of tequila. It takes me three or four 40's to get ripped. I have a high tolerance." He also does dope with them. "I don't see any crime in it. I don't do drugs for anybody else or to be cool. Parents try to protect us, but there is nothing they can do about it. If we are going to do something we are going to do it. One of the things I resent about society in general is age limits," says this precocious fourteen-year-old. "When I look at *Roe versus Wade*, the courts are saying the women can do what they want to do with their bodies, so why can't kids do what they want with their bodies? We're not stupid, and we are not going to kill ourselves. I think adults think that we are incompetent and we don't know what we are doing."

Brendon's greatest natural high is his art. "If you really want to see what I'm about, you're going to have to wait until the art starts rolling," he says. His family is rich in artistic sensibility: his mom's skill with dried flowers, his dad's woodwork, his siblings' talents at drawing and painting. His oldest brother, Jess, is studying to become an architect. His other brother, Steven, master fisherman, not only paints extraordinary demons that have fishes' heads, but also creates masterful ties for fly-fishing. His sister's artworks are displayed in the school art gallery and exhibits, but unlike her brothers' often angry art, her works reflect a world of natural beauty. His family's bright cozy townhouse nestled against the woods is alive with the personal touches of his family. Wreathes decorated with dried flowers made by his mom hang on the walls, along with framed artwork done by the kids, doilies crocheted by his grandmother and great-grandmother, and a collection of duck pictures that have been framed by his dad. Leaning in the corner are several quaint straw brooms his mom trimmed with ribbons and flowers. The hutch displays a collection of antique baby dishes she has collected through the years. This is a family that loves to collect, create, and display both its heirlooms and the creations of the present. The walls speak to how they value self-expression.

Brendon is convinced he is following in the family tradition. It's just that the walls he chooses are not in the living room but on the byways of Reston. His feelings are too big for a piece of paper. Graffiti is emotion writ large and provides an outlet to let the angry feelings flow. It is "bad and it requires a spirit of rebellion, creativity, and skill," says Brendon. His art expresses his feelings directly when words fail him and his actions subvert him.

Brendon, outlaw artist and Boy Scout, wrestler and substance abuser, exists in a world both threatening and supportive. He has not dropped out, but he teeters on the boundary. While he keeps one foot firmly planted on the wrestling mat this cold winter season, still aiming to win, he has his other foot on a rocky road, one that leads him to act out ways to foil the system.

After fifteen minutes or so of raucous fun desecrating property in their path, Brendon and Tad reach their real destination, the tunnel near a convenience store. Graffiti artists don't reach a wall and wait for inspiration. They always have something in mind. Brendon has been planning this all week, sitting in his classes not listening, sketching in his notebook, a small bound journal that unlike his disorganized, messed-up school supplies is neat, with the drawings meticulously rendered. He loves his book. In it are not only his own sketches but also stickers and miniature designs done by other graffiti artists he admires. The book travels with him everywhere, especially to alternative concerts and clubs where graffiti artists congregate and exchange their journals like the autograph books their parents probably toted around at the end of each school year.

Brendon and Tad are totally prepared today, having an abundance of supplies. Tad and another friend pulled off a major heist at the local hardware store last week. They sneaked can after can of spray paint under their jackets and into a shopping cart that they'd hidden among the outside displays of gardening supplies. In the middle of the night, the other boy scaled the cyclone fence and tossed the cans over to Tad. The magnitude of the theft was impressive. Brendon brags that he hardly ever buys caps, the tips of various sizes placed on the nozzle of a spray can to regulate the width of lines. He steals them at Kmart or gets them from other painters. He always has a bunch in his backpack because they get clogged up as he uses them.

Spending time with Tad, two years his senior, is the best. Tad is an admired graffiti artist on the local scene, and Brendon considers him a mentor. "You need someone to show you how to be a graffiti artist," says Brendon. "I got taught and picked things up but it is a never-ending learning process, it is experience. You need to go out and get a lot of practice with somebody of a significantly higher skill level." He and Tad distinguish themselves from vandals who scribble pornographic messages and from gang "taggers" who are making their territory known. Although they enjoy bombing as they ride, basically Tad and Brendon consider themselves true artists of the night.

Brendon has a clear philosophy about the medium of graffiti as distinguished from the pieces in his portfolio at school and at home. With traditional art, "It's like this art, it's mine. I show it to people sometimes. But graffiti art is for everyone to see and for everyone to know how you're feeling." Although it is signed with a tag and not his real name, artistically it is most honestly the creator's. He bristles at graffiti's reputation as defacement rendered by juvenile bandits. If people understood the art form it would not be considered illegal. "There are not enough people who understand graffiti to realize what it's like, that it takes a whole lot of time and a whole lot of effort, and that it's not done to destroy something. If we wanted to, we could go spray paint cars, but we don't. What's the harm in painting a tunnel? None of it's vulgar. Everybody draws and draws and draws, and takes their best product and redraws it and redraws it, trying to make it something that's nice for people to see. It just pisses me off how in our country anything that's art can be considered wrong."

The two boys jump off their bicycles, drop them on the ground, and get to work. In utter silence they create their pieces, a quiet broken only by the hissing sound of the spray cans. Brendon's hands are freezing cold but he doesn't stop. He's been imagining this all week. In ten minutes or so it is done. He stands back and admires his drawing, a man with horns like a devil, a big frown for a mouth, and weird eyes like sideways Vs. The best part is the upper body, arms crossed and wrapped around the figure's back as in a straitjacket. It is not one of the "fill-in" drawings that are outlined and then filled in with color, often in elaborate designs. Brendon prefers painting "hollows and throwups"—big unfilled drawings in a simple style. They feel like essences, raw emotion to him. The style of the characters becomes as much of a signature as the names the artists call themselves: Base, Fellon, Gage, Creator, Thirst are part of the local crowd. Sometimes, they simply draw their tag, as Tad did today, a highly stylized rendering of their moniker. Brendon's artistic signature is the lack of eyes, expressing "something not developed." In his book, he has also been preparing a picture of eyeless clowns, to which he's added a poem, "Laughing Hands": "These are the hands of a demented circus clown. / Outside I'm laughing / but inside I'm wearing a frown." He says, "Why do you want to draw something that looks human? You can do that in art class." But that's too simple an explanation. These are his most secret thoughts. Under the bravado, the I-don't-give-a-fuck attitude he tries to project to his friends, is someone desperately searching to find himself.

Brendon likes to play it free and loose. "I don't know what the standards are," he says, "but I guess it is pretty much what you feel inside." That's how he justifies his choices. But by acknowledging there are standards, he guarantees turmoil within his mixed-up life. He defies convention and clings to it. Like a hiker lost in a dense forest, he follows others' trails, desperate to find a way out. He says: "I'm doing wrestling just as much for my dad as for anyone else. It makes him proud. I think that's the motivation. He was state champion in Louisiana. So I just want someone to continue the legacy, pretty much." On the other hand: "I guess sports are all right, but after all the hard practices you wonder what you are missing, like people calling you up, hanging out with your friends." His dad also inspired his membership in the Boy Scouts, which Brendon sees less as a way of life than as a chance to go camping. He attends meetings, which he thinks are pretty dumb, only sporadically. His parents don't hassle him about attendance. The amazing thing is that he goes at all.

He spends long hours discussing God and faith with his sister, who has become a born-again Christian. He doesn't feel the same way about God as she does. He feels like God has let him down. "What good is a God that you can't come to terms with in your own way, and you have to follow some set of rules?" he wonders. When she tells him she never had any trouble dealing with that issue, he envies her strength and inner peace. "I wish I could have it," he says wistfully. "My sister realizes what's out in the world. She's not naive. She's had every opportunity to drink and smoke, and she doesn't do any of that. She's got her head on straight. It's good that someone in our family is not screwed up." Maybe the problems in the family are guy-things. His mother has her head on straight too.

His anger swells at the failure of his youth group to give him the answers he needs. It is not spiritually satisfying. It is not ethically satisfying. It is not even fun. "It is a waste of my time, but I constantly find myself going to it because I have nothing better to do," Brendon says. "They try to pump you full of morals but they don't have any clue what you are going through—like all the problems I feel with hate for school, and the problems I experience with my family and the cynicism for God. They just naturally expect you to be Christian because your parents are and you go to church." Brendon wants, actually demands that church give him answers to his restlessness, stave off his disappointments and make him peaceful. It is as if he commands faith to enter him and if it doesn't, church is to blame.

He wants instant gratification. He is quick to judge the failure of institutions to make him feel good. He thinks he gives them a chance, often many chances, and they fail him again and again.

School is a waste. Friends betray him. Family aggravates him. One chance and you are out in his world. Sort of. His oppositional behavior subverts him and alienates others.

Under it all is the deep economic wound and loss of roots that pervades this family and racks Brendon's soul. One result is a home that feels like a way station. "My mom and I talk about how we can't get over the fact that we have lived in this house for so long," his sister Jenny says. "When we moved we were supposed to be here a year, a year and a half max and then buy a house that would be our permanent place. We don't even own this house, and everybody is in and out and it is too small for us. It has never really felt permanent."

Whenever anybody in the extended family comes, they have coffee and sit around the table and talk about the memories. "My mom's father died when she was seventeen. My dad's mom had a depression problem when he was growing up. My parents got married and my mom didn't finish college," explains Jenny. "It all sets the stage for so many 'what ifs.' " Life was grand in Texas, growing up was simple, satisfying, innocent. In Reston, things are different—the tone of life, the attitudes of people. "It is faster, quicker, more blunt, more intense," says Jenny. "I almost feel that our family would work better if we just lived somewhere else. My dad shouldn't be in a computer software company. He should live in a big house with a woodworking studio and my mom should be able to just be a mom. We are an anachronism, in the wrong time and place."

They crave being close to their extended family and grieve at the miles that separate them. They know how family is supposed to be because of their religious faith, and their deviation from the standards they believe in makes life more difficult. The fatalism that runs through the family holds them up to standards they believe in but feel powerless to achieve.

Brendon soaks this all into his being and then tries to push it away by making everything a simple matter of dollars and cents. "I just wish the money would come in so that things would ease up," he says. Living in Reston you see daily all the different social classes from the subsidized housing to the huge homes, the nice cars and cool clothes of the kids, and you can't help saying, "Yeah, I want it."

Brendon is one of the walking wounded of the middle class. He feels he has a right to more than dashed expectations, feelings of loss, sacrifices—from his mom working to his second brother having to delay college. All the kids are hounded by an increased pressure to earn, when they can, money toward their own schooling. The family is mired in uneasiness, disappointment, and apprehension. "One of the most difficult things," says Brendon, "is asking for something and being told no, or being told there is not enough money."

He wishes he could alleviate his own financial needs by getting a job. But he needs to be fifteen for a work permit, and even then things look bleak. This year, South Lakes canceled its student job fair because so many local businesses had no jobs and what work there is, says Principal Schmelzer, "the adults are taking."

There is a dream that surrounds everybody in Brendon's house with what could be. They are haunted, torn apart by it, and it makes Brendon crazy, furious, impulsive. He tries to act like everything rolls off his back, but it tears at his insides. His life is in limbo as long as he is dependent, and he can't shake free of his yearning for a storybook family. So he seeks freedom on the trails, in substances, in Scouts, in church. He is a study in contradictions—a struggle for depth belied by surfaces. Though his longing of only a few months ago to be Joe Highschool is becoming paved over, there are rays of hope. The family wound is at the juncture of where Brendon seeks peace from God and repose from drugs; where he tries to please his dad by continuing family traditions; and where he flies in the face of expectations by screwing up in school. He lets out his frustration in big marks that deface the spaces of the town that he wishes were not his.

The saddest thing is that nobody knows his anguish. He reveals only the facets of his splintered personality that connect with the group he is part of at any given moment. Who will he be and for whom? Will the anger win out? He dabbles and submerges, comes up for air and runs away. Even his art becomes a symbolic struggle between the portfolio in school that can get him into a good college and the art on the tunnel walls that can land him in court.

When they finish their drawings, he and Tad get back on their bikes and ride over to the ultimate graffiti gallery in Reston, the high slanted walls under the Dulles Toll Road. They are just looking tonight and arrive to find that once again it has been painted over by the police. Usually filled with stupendous drawings because of its large surfaces and its distance from residential areas, it is a nighttime favorite. The art will be back, but not tonight at the risk of being caught. Also, it is late. They know the longer they stay out, the greater the chances of running into trouble from gangs or the police.

They ride home happy with their night's activity. Brendon quietly slips into his family's townhouse, slowly closing the front door decorated with a welcoming straw wreath made by his mom. He tiptoes upstairs to his bunk bed, almost tripping over his bright red childhood stool that has his name in bold letters above a quote from Psalm 100:3: "We are His people and the sheep of His pasture." The moon shines in his window, illuminating two G.I. Joes hanging on the blinds, and a series of hockey and baseball cards lined up on the windowsill. He takes off his shoes and socks and drops his jacket on his desk chair that holds his Bible. He flops into bed still in his jeans and sweatshirt, ready finally to sleep. As he lies there in the darkness, he thinks to himself how he wishes "we could bomb everywhere as long as the art is good. It brings concrete alive, especially in sterile, upstanding Fairfax County. I wish I could redecorate the world." But in the space of moments, he feels the fulfilling sensations of his adventure slip away, to be replaced by deep sadness. Nobody in the house stirs. His parents are asleep, apparently ignorant or not wanting to know of their youngest son's nightlife.

# Sex: Let's Get It Out of the Way, but Don't Look at Me Naked

Courtney is getting real tired of the male sex drive. First there was Brendon breaking up with her because she didn't want to do it just for fun. She likes to be close and to feel cared for like anybody else, but having sex—well, she remembers how she thought sex seemed like it might be cool when she was in seventh grade, but she isn't so sure now. She and her little middle school girlfriends, she recalls, were totally sex-crazed. Their attitude was, Ah, sex, let's try it. She recalls: "In seventh grade you know all the facts about it. You see TV and movies and you're like, Oh, we could have sex and get married and have children. It's a big fantasy. And you think it would be perfect. But you don't really think about the actual act of sex. You don't know how it's going to feel, or that you have to trust someone. You just think, He's a hot guy, let's have sex. And of course, in seventh grade, you don't really mean it."

Now that she is fourteen and a half and has a regular boyfriend, Nat, it could easily be real. Although scared and uncomfortable, she feels it is inevitable.

After she broke up with Brendon, she wasn't looking to go through that again. He was so immature. But then she met Nat through her best friend Dee. The end of the summer, the two girls were at Uno's at Town Center sharing a pizza when Nat came over to their table to say hello. Courtney knew who he was from her friends, but when he sat down and joined them, she had an opportunity to get acquainted herself.

That night, Courtney slept over at Dee's. She told her friend she thought Nat was cool and she'd like to see him again. She didn't have to wait long. The next afternoon, Nat met them at South Lakes Shopping Center, a popular hangout for young teens in Reston. They sat around for hours by the lake talking. It was all the usual stuff about mutual friends, the kinds of things kids talk about to get to know each other and size each other up. Courtney found out that Nat had the same attitude as she did about school: You go if you can't figure a way to get out of it. She found out they liked to smoke dope occasionally with the same people, because it was fun. They eventually got to sex. She was kind of shocked to find out that Nat was not a virgin. "I was surprised because Nat's a little guy, but he gets a lot of girlfriends. We all knew that. Most people at this age if they are having sex, then they'll just be really immature about it and brag. They just do it to just do it. It doesn't mean anything. They'll have sex with you and move on," says Courtney.

But Nat told her, "I wish I was still a virgin. It would be so much more meaningful." He said: "I don't understand why someone would want to have sex with someone and then leave them and not talk to them after. I would be just as happy with a relationship if all we did was kiss as I would be if we had sex all the time. I think if you have sex all the time then your relationship gets based only on sex."

Courtney thought Nat sounded so mature. She remembered how Brendon told her he wanted to have sex that didn't mean anything; that it was "something cool to do." When she listened to Nat, she liked him more and more. She didn't want to seem too eager but could not hide her admiration. "I said, 'How old are you again?' I was thinking if I were going to lose my virginity to someone, it would be good to have a person like Nat."

The day went by in a flash the way it does when someone new and exciting has entered your life. As darkness descended, they grabbed a burger at Roy Rogers and split to their respective homes.

The next day, while Courtney was baby-sitting, Nat called. This call blew Courtney away. "He told me that he liked me, and I thought that was good that he didn't go through friends like most people do. I thought that was mature of him to tell me himself." She told him she liked him too.

The next morning, he walked all the way to her house so they could be together. They watched a movie and talked about how they liked each other. They sat awkwardly on the sofa in the family room and gradually worked their way toward each other, eyes glued to the television screen. He put his arm around her. She put her hand on his knee. It was a little uncomfortable but okay. Courtney kept telling herself to relax, that she was finally with somebody who knew what he was doing. Then her sister Ann messed them up by telling them to move downstairs to her stepdad's den, a totally macho fifties-style room with a black-and-white check linoleum floor, an old-time jukebox, and a pool table. Like her stepdad, it is masculine, bold bordering on brash, especially compared to the rest of the house which reflects her mom's elegant taste. They retreated downstairs and continued fooling around.

By now, Nat had been at the house most of the day, a big no-no in the family rules. When Ann heard their mom pull into the driveway after work, she alerted Nat and Courtney, who tore upstairs to the kitchen.

When her mom walked in, the two were leaning casually against the counter talking. Courtney introduced Nat and told her mom that he had only been there for half an hour. Ann lied for her. "Oh yeah, he just got here." Courtney's heart was doing flip-flops. She didn't think her mom was going to like him. "He looks like he would be some druggie because he's got long hair, he wears big clothes. He's not a very presentable-to-adults kind of kid, which I think is bad because I don't think adults should stereotype." She was certain her mom would size him up as a bad kid.

Her mom baffled her by being nice to Nat. She wasn't mean about him being there. She even offered to drive him home when he was ready to leave, a gesture so rare that Courtney cannot even remember the last time her mom did such a thing. It never occurred to Courtney that her mom was so grateful that she had brought home someone apart from the crowd she spent her freshman year with that it actually made her hospitable.

As far as her parents are concerned, it will probably take the rest of her life to make up for her freshman year. Her mom lets loose with the list of offenses like the Ten Commandments of Bad: "Cutting school, lying, stealing, cheating, smoking, drugs, cutting out of the house in the middle of the night. Going joyriding with a guy

who 'borrows' his parents' car. Courtney knows better." Most confounding to her parents were the kids themselves, "good kids. They're
not something you pick up off the street."

Parents are rightfully confused. Who's a troublemaker and who is
not is never clear anymore. "It's not like when we were kids," one
mom laments. "There are no Greasers versus Preppie-types; there
is no such thing as the clean-cut college type and the low-class
dropout, certainly no rules for what 'nice' girls do or don't do."

Courtney's mother takes the time-honored position that the problems come from elsewhere, sweeping her daughter along. She goes
on about all the bad influences around her daughter, how she
"hooked up with these kids every day after school, never came
home." Her mother blames the kids who lack adult supervision, not
understanding that all the calls to check in with her that she requires
of Courtney and Ann are nothing but pro forma. She tries to say
there is a great family feeling in this obviously strained household
because they eat together when Courtney interjects, "We don't cook
meals, we eat cereal." Her mom says defensively, "So we bring it
home and sit around the table." She also alludes to racial influences
on misbehavior: "There are some ethnic groups that put pressure on.
I've heard many times from Courtney and her friends that if you
don't have a couple of blacks in your group, you are going to get into
trouble." The mother and daughter get into a major squabble over
this issue, which is especially testy in a home where one sister, Ann,
loves an African-American male.

Courtney has in no way been deterred from following her impulses. She still sees nothing wrong with being out in the middle of
the night: "If we did what we did at two o'clock Saturday afternoon,
then we'd be like, 'This is boring, this is really dumb.' But because it
is in the middle of the night and we are the only people up, that's the
only thing that makes it worth it." The middle of the night "is so
much more laid back. You get to know people better." There is no
hassle about having to ask your parents' permission but there are
still rules: "Everybody knows we have to be home by four-thirty in
the morning before parents get up." It is so easy to get away with because "it is not something parents think their children will do."

This pattern is not new for Courtney. "I sneaked out the year before too but just to walk places. That's when you are only with girls
and you go out in the middle of the night for half an hour just to see
if you can get away with it. You go out in seventh grade bundled up

in your pajamas, sit in a park and talk and then run home. You're gone for twenty minutes, and you think you're big rebels."

After freshman year, her mother was not budging. "We had a lot of acting-out behavior. Got in with the wrong crowd, made some real bad choices, which I knew she knew better than to make." There was talk of therapy, which Courtney's dad, a social worker who lives in Florida, thought was desirable. But her mom and stepfather wanted a quick fix and they were definitely not interested in family therapy. Things finally came to a head with an ultimatum at the end of school: "No ma'am, you're not staying here this summer."

Courtney's mother wishes to make all problems go away, clearly finding them a major interference in her life with her second husband. She sent Courtney to a Christian Outward Bound camp. Courtney didn't fuss because her mom bought her a lot of new clothes. "I figured if I was going to get all this new stuff then I could just go to camp and do something bad there. If I hated it that much, then I could always find a way to get sent back home."

She made it through, even liked it, and came home not at all chastised. The key lesson she learned was, Don't be so obvious. This wasn't too hard because she felt that her parents didn't really know her and they preferred not being called on to participate much in their daughters' lives. They never attended school meetings; found it terribly inconvenient to drive their girls places, including the library; didn't believe in home-cooked family meals; and were not particularly curious about their children unless they threw something in their faces that demanded attention.

How utterly out-of-the-loop Courtney's mother was became clear immediately after camp, when Dee began spending lots of time at her house. Her mother suddenly was enthusiastic about Dee even though not so long before she had forbidden Courtney to see her. She embraced Dee now, grateful that she was not part of the middle-of-the-night crew. Courtney and Dee laughed plenty over that. Dee was over so much simply because she had the time, now that her boyfriend Paul, the "car thief" who'd ended up getting Courtney and her crowd into trouble, had been sent away to military school.

Courtney's mom is always trying to separate her daughters from people she labels as trouble. "Why should she blame the other person?" Courtney asks. "No one has a gun to our heads. She shouldn't blame our friends, she should blame us. Who's to say we don't pressure our friends?" Courtney feels lucky her mom likes Dee and Nat.

Right from the start of their relationship, Courtney became aware of some odd things about Nat. In the manner of her generation, she doesn't judge him but she notices. He lives near South Lakes High School but he goes to Cedar Lane, a county school for the emotionally disturbed. She knows he sees a psychiatrist and is on medication. He's been hospitalized a few times for depression. But what's new about that? Lots of kids are in therapy.

Nat doesn't really go home, he just goes from one person's house to the next. He hates going home and Courtney doesn't know why. He comes from a large family but his older siblings are all grown. His parents don't get along but they are not divorced. His dad, who travels a lot, comes home about once every four months, "so they don't bother getting divorced," Nat told her. He likes his mom. She is nice to him and they get along, especially since she lets him do anything he wants. He says it is because "I have a bad temper and she's afraid that if she tells me what to do, I'll get mad at her and I'll like beat her up or something." If he is over at Courtney's and has to leave before her mom gets home, "he just goes to Brendon's or someone else's house," says Courtney. "Spends the night here, sleeps there." It's kind of annoying, someone just drifting around like that. But that is just the way it is. He's nice to her. Courtney says: "I don't think anybody knows another person. I think you can know how they act around you. They could act totally different around somebody else."

While Courtney's mom lets down her guard a bit, accepting that Dee and Nat are nice kids, she is completely ignorant of the consuming issue in her daughter's life. Courtney is not thinking about doing drugs or how she'll do in school this fall. She's wrestling with the Big Decision about sex. Ironically, her parents only think about Ann having sex with her black boyfriend. They have it all wrong.

At first Courtney is in seventh heaven. Nat is different because "most of the guys I go out with, I'm always the one who calls them, and I'm always the one who wants to see them." Nat calls her wherever she is and always stops by to visit. "Most people I have gone out with," she says, "say they like me but then don't really and it ends up being a two-week relationship." Nat is consistently nice and the relationship has gone on for a month.

She does have a little trouble with his devotion. He always wants to be with her. "He's like, 'I want to see you, I haven't seen you in a day.' I say, 'Can't you wait another day?' I'm nice about it, but it gets on my nerves sometimes." On the other hand, if she doesn't talk to him, she misses him. It's the same thing with kissing. Even though he always kisses her when they're around her friends, the first time they were alone he didn't. She doesn't understand herself. She's so nervous about things going too fast but when he didn't kiss her, she wanted him to.

One night when Dee comes over, Courtney and she have their millionth discussion about sex. While the noise of the television drones in the background, they munch on M&M's and grapes. They go over the same ground as if it is new. Dee starts, "I haven't had sex yet, but hopefully I will love him."

"Yeah," says Courtney. "You've got to be sure they're smart enough to know about a girl's body."

"Right," says Dee. "You don't want to have sex with someone stupid."

"I told you I didn't know where this was leading with Nat," says Courtney with a sigh. "I don't know if it's going to lead to sex. I'm not sure."

"I think a lot of teenagers are stupid," says Dee, trying to make her friend's decision easier. "They think everyone's having sex so you have to too. A lot of people are having sex, but not that many. Personally, I don't think I'm mature enough to have sex anyway. I'm not comfortable enough with my body, let alone theirs, to have sex."

"The thing is," says Courtney, "I know I'd get so mad if I had sex with a guy and then they didn't speak to me again. I know I'd proba-bly prefer them not to have sex with me at this stage in my life." She is ashamed of not wanting to have sex, thinking it shows how imma-ture she is. She goes back and forth about Nat as her first partner. On the one hand, she thinks he is exactly the right person. On the other hand, his attentiveness often drives her crazy. She thinks she must also be immature not to like his constant attention.

The conversation goes around and around as the two fourteen-year-olds strain to impart wisdom to each other. They do not feel free to talk to any adult about issues of sex and relationships, and their families never bring up the topic in an information-sharing manner. It is always emotionally loaded. "You don't tell your parents about sex," says Dee. "They just freak out. If you tell them, they think you're a whore or something."

They are so contradictory, says Courtney. "If you tell them that you're not ready to have sex they conclude, 'Oh God, sex is on their mind. They're trying to cover up for it.' They get hysterical. If you tell them that you think you are ready, they're like, 'You're not going out tonight.' "

What her parents couldn't guess and Courtney can't risk telling them is that they are giving her a muddled message. Her concerns hint at a need for boundaries. Courtney, who acts like she hates rules says, "Usually on school nights they won't let me go over to a friend's house, unless they live in the neighborhood, unless we are doing a project." Yet they let her go to Nat's house just to watch television until 10 o'clock on school nights. "They let me go over to my boyfriend's house when they know his parents aren't home. That is weird. I am surprised they let him come over all the time. They're really good about him, they've accepted him, and they always let me hang out with him." It seems just when she wishes there were some limits, her parents have given her an abundance of space.

With all the opportunities she and Nat have to be alone in empty houses, it is getting more difficult for Courtney to draw the line. Nat is increasingly aggressive. "We haven't done anything that's a big deal. He's kissed me. He's gone up my shirt and stuff, but that's all. But you can tell it's going to go farther," she tells Dee.

Courtney, petite and thin, is painfully self-conscious about her whole body, and particularly her stomach. Like too many girls her age she has a distorted body image, imagining she is paunchy. "I have this obsession with stomachs. I'm going to get a flat stomach," Courtney says. "I don't even like to look at myself naked, so why would I expect other people to?" Every time Nat pulls up her shirt, she pulls it down. He asks her why she is so self-conscious. He tells her that her body is beautiful. "I'm like, 'No, no, no.' So he gets frustrated."

One day when Dee and Nat are over, Nat keeps kissing Courtney right in front of Dee. He is all over Courtney, saying he is going to marry her. It is terribly awkward. Finally, in desperation, Courtney uses her period as an excuse. Dee understands right away what she is doing. There is a commercial on television about tampons and Courtney tells Dee that she likes Playtex best. "I use those," Courtney says. Dee responds without missing a beat, "Are you using those now?" The two girls are on a roll. Courtney responds, "Yes, actually, I am." Courtney is delighted with their finesse. "That was kind of an easy way to get out of anything, any sort of pressure because he knew I was on my period," she explains. "That was kind of an unspoken 'no.' "

But the issue keeps coming up. She is relieved when school starts and they can't be together as much. She's still hoping that it "will definitely be okay if I say no, because I don't think I'm ready to have sex in the next few weeks."

Just fifteen, Nat has already had sex with at least three girls. He tells his friends he lost his virginity when he was twelve. Courtney and Dee still think their age, fourteen, is too young. "I don't really think about my age when I think about it. I just think about me," says Courtney. "I think fourteen definitely sounds young, but I think tenth grade is about average. I'm not really excited about it because I don't think many girls enjoy it their first time, and I think it will be painful. But it's something that you want to get over with. I think it's a little too young to come up in relationships, but it is coming up. It's something you have to face. I think you have to deal with it at fourteen, decide."

She has concerns about Nat that never get noticed, while everything about her sister Ann's boyfriend is magnified. Her parents never notice that Ron is many things Nat is not—a good student, dependable, responsible. Ron comes from a great family while Nat's has big problems. Courtney found out the reason Nat doesn't like his dad is that he hits him and his mom. She heard from one of her friends that Nat isn't always faithful to his girlfriends. Soon after school began, his behavior became erratic and he ended up being hospitalized again for depression. She doesn't talk to her parents about these things.

Courtney goes back and forth in her mind about Nat. She sometimes has bad feelings about him and is definitely sure she doesn't want to have sex. But she always comes back around. When he was in the mental hospital, she says, she stopped taking him for granted.

She likes him a lot. Maybe she is even infatuated, but she doesn't think she really loves him. "He always used to tell me that he loved me, and he'd always get mad because I wouldn't tell him I loved him," says Courtney. "I only did when he was in the hospital, because I figured, He's in a mental hospital, what else can I do?"

When he is released from the hospital, they continue as before. He'll ask. She'll say, "I don't think so." Then he'll say, "Oh, let's have sex, I want to have sex with you." Then they talk about it.

There is tension. She likes him; she feels she doesn't want to touch so much. That's another thing Nat gets mad about. "He can't wait to touch a girl's body, and then he gets mad at me when I just sit there." Courtney tells him, "I'm sorry. Maybe next time."

For her, making out is enough. "I don't know any girls that are as eager about it as guys," says Courtney. "When girls have sex, they're giving in to guys. Maybe they wanted to, but not as much. I think they just want it because the guy wants it. If they didn't have sex, I don't think they'd be upset. But with guys, I think it upsets them if they don't." Nat is always telling her she has no sex drive. She tells him she's sorry, but that is the way she's always been with all her boyfriends. She's fine with kissing, but she just goes along with anything else. Nat tells her that if a girl with him doesn't "get into it," then he feels like he is forcing himself on her. Courtney doesn't know what to do.

About two and a half months after she starts dating Nat, Courtney runs out of excuses. "I just did it because he really kept bothering me about it." Deep inside she knows part of her hesitation is because she doesn't trust him "not to cheat on me, not to break up with me." But she is worn down. So finally in November when there are two Teacher's Workdays, where South Lakes students are out of school at the end of the quarter, she does it.

On the Friday before, the two of them are "making out like crazy in the rec room. We had talked about it before and I was like, 'My parents are upstairs. It's not a good idea.' I was trying to stop talking about it." She tells him that maybe when her parents aren't home it would be okay. He jumps at the opportunity.

"I'll come over on Monday," he tells her.

Courtney knows his school has no holiday and immediately tries to persuade him to go. Who's she kidding? He doesn't care at all about school. He insists on coming over Monday. She finally agrees. Now it is planned.

Saturday and Sunday she pushes it out of her mind. "I wasn't really scared. I just didn't think about it."

Then Monday comes and true to his word, Nat arrives at her door. She has the hugest butterflies in her stomach. The worst feelings are about how she is ugly, and now she is going to be naked, and it is going to hurt, but she has to get it out of the way.

They start out sitting on the family room couch watching television. He says, "Let's go upstairs."

She gulps. "Uhhh, why?"

He says, "I don't know, it's better up there."

Courtney wishes her sister would come home, her mother would call, the house would fall down! She whispers, "Fine."

They go upstairs to her bright feminine bedroom complete with pink-and-white mattress-ticking curtains, lace pillows, and crisp white sheets. The room smells of smoke. Smoking is something that she is forbidden to do but that her parents choose to overlook. Her sister Ann says with disgust, "They see what they want to see." Courtney's desk is cluttered with papers, schoolbooks, an ashtray made by a friend in art, tiny ceramic animals. Her bookshelves are lined with photos, an old-time bubblegum machine, earrings, cards, stuff. Unlike her sister, she has only a few books, mostly on astrology. Most prominent is a grand collage, an ongoing project on her closet door created from magazines, many of the words lifted from her sister's collection; the collage speaks the language of adolescence: *nightlife, surfer girl, allure, love games, romance, moods, just great, junkies, fitness, running for cover, the immune system, wild, hair, body news, free!* A cigarette is at the center.

Today this familiar haven feels strangely foreign. It is her feminine, teenage preserve and now she is bringing this boy to her bed.

He undresses. She averts her eyes. She takes off everything but her sweatshirt. She feels so incredibly vulnerable sitting there. "I get really self-conscious. I think that kind of bothers him because he's not self-conscious at all. And that's pretty funny to me because I think the male body is actually pretty ugly."

She keeps on reminding herself that Nat is good to be with because he's been in this situation before. He tries to take off her sweatshirt. She pulls it down over her small breasts. He tells her not to be self-conscious, that he likes her so much and thinks she is perfect. "He was really nice about it," she recalls. "That's good if you're going to have sex with someone to have someone who is ego-boosting about your body." But she never lets him take her shirt off.

She keeps telling herself it is okay, it's not that big a deal. But she has this feeling she is doing it for the wrong reasons.

They lie down and he goes for it vigorously. She never gets involved in the act. It's almost as if it is happening to someone else. It is awkward and clumsy. "He skipped steps," Courtney, more experienced now, remembers. "He'd kiss and then want to have sex. That's not good for me. You've got to work up to it." She tries to let him know she's not ready, but he is oblivious.

Just before penetration, Nat asks her for a condom. If he hadn't mentioned protection, she says, she would have insisted on it. She's not dumb and she has tons of rubbers. Just to be prepared for such an eventuality, she and Dee had stolen a big box from Safeway, so they each had a dozen Trojans in their desk drawers. She never thinks about the fact that Nat hadn't brought his own.

The actual sex is a bust. "If a girl's a virgin, it hurts, and it doesn't always work your first try. So we didn't really fully succeed, and I felt dumb. I still don't know if I consider it sex. Technically we had sex," says Courtney, "but it didn't go all the way in."

She senses his disappointment. She feels like a failure. But they don't talk about it at all. There is nothing tender or reassuring. When it is over, he sits up, pulls on his clothes and says, "My mom's picking me up because I have a doctor's appointment. I'll see you later."

Courtney dresses and says, "Okay, 'bye." She feels horrible—embarrassed, unsuccessful, and terribly alone. She doesn't move until she hears the front door close.

The next morning Courtney wakes up feeling totally humiliated. She just wants to forget it ever happened, but she can't stop thinking about it. Since it is still a school holiday she has no classes. She meets her friend Allie. As they walk to the pet store to buy fish food, she tells her everything that happened with Nat. Fourteen-year-old Allie says, "Oh yeah, the same thing happened to me." Courtney is floored.

Courtney tells her how dumb she felt, how they tried but it didn't work. Allie understands perfectly. Courtney discloses how utterly embarrassed she feels—"Like it was my fault, but it's not really my fault." Allie agrees, explaining that he should know if he's ever had sex with a virgin that it doesn't always work. They concur that guys don't know enough about a girl's body. "I just think from my own personal feelings," says Courtney, "that he should be very aware of it, and he should know about a girl's body before he's going to go meddling with it, you know. I think that's like the rule. Everything that a girl knows, a guy should know. How girls' bodies are different. The whole thing of why they get their period. When's a good time to have sex and when's not. Make sure he knows everything about everything."

Then Nat breaks up with her. Not right afterwards but several weeks later. Her friends say not to worry about it. She cuts a few classes to commiserate with Brendon, now her buddy; even though he tells her that Nat is messed up and confused and needs to grow up, she feels a cold hard knot in the pit of her stomach. "I was having a hard time facing that he and I broke up. I'd always think, I should tell Nat about this, if something happened. Then I'd remember, I don't talk to Nat."

In time Courtney and Nat get back together briefly, but the old magic is gone. "I don't even know whether this is going to be a good relationship, if we're going to go out for another three months or whether it will only be a few weeks," says Courtney. Before, Nat used to tell her he loved her all the time. Now he never says it and she wishes he did. But she never tells him how she feels.

Nat and Courtney break up for good the day before Valentine's Day. He had been cheating on her even while they continued to have sex. Still fifteen, Nat is now on his fifth or sixth sexual partner.

Courtney is sad. "I kind of miss having a boyfriend, but not Nat himself. I miss someone in the role of a boyfriend—going out at night, talking to him on the phone, going to his house. I used to hang out with my friends and my boyfriend. I have my friends but where is my boyfriend?"

Only fourteen, Courtney has had sex, has carried on a full-blown social life in the middle of the night, smoked cigarettes and pot, cut classes, been with somebody who "stole" his parents' car and somebody who has been hospitalized for psychiatric problems. By her freshman year, she was bored with legitimate school activities.

As for sex, she thinks that maybe when she is older, "like in college or after college, I'll have a steady boyfriend, and then sex would be like a bigger part of my life. But now that I've had this bad experience, I'm not sure anymore."

# Lacrosse and Other Challenges

On this cold, gray February day, Charles Sutter is feeling totally happy. He is feeling so fine that he's even nice to his sister the whole ride home from school. The reason is simple: lacrosse season is about to begin. All through seventh and eighth grade he was in awe of the high school players. He already knows some of them through his sister. Her class built their Homecoming float at the Sutter house last year and a couple of the lacrosse guys took some time to encourage his interest. They tossed the ball around with him and he was in heaven. Now he will be on their team.

He has been waiting for this moment all year—through football season, through track. He waited through basketball when he played in Reston Youth League. He liked the other sports all right, but in truth he had merely been whiling away the time waiting for lacrosse. The big snows and never-ending ice made the winter seem unusually long. Even though it is still wintery, Charles can imagine the sun beating on his head, the sweat running down his back, the feeling of speed and power as he sprints down the field toward the goal. He can feel the crash of bodies, hear the cheering. He is filled with anticipation.

He closes the car door, lopes into the house, drops his bookbag in the front hall, and without missing a beat picks up his long defenseman stick and starts cradling the ball. He walks to the kitchen still cradling, goes to the refrigerator to get an apple still cradling, flips on the television still cradling, and sits down to watch it, continuing to cradle the ball while eating his apple. Lacrosse is tonic to his soul, an obsession that took hold of him four years ago.

He discovered lacrosse, a relatively new sport to catch on in northern Virginia, through an earlier disappointment. When he was ten, his future in football was compromised by a knee injury. The event is indelible in his mind because on the same day his dad hurt the very same knee, the same ligament, while refereeing a basketball game. Father and son, Charles Clinton Sutter III and IV, ended up in the emergency room side by side. When the doctor walked in holding both charts with identical names and identical complaints, he asked if this was a joke. His dad remembers that his son was running around a few days later and it took his knee months to rebound.

Charles, even at ten, knew his football days were numbered, and even though he still had basketball, he wasn't as good at it. He had to find something or he'd go nuts. "I'm like, What am I going to do? There's only basketball." Then his friend Dan, who had already started playing lacrosse the year before, suggested he try it. Charles's parents bought him a stick, and a neighbor who had once been a college player taught him how to play. He practiced with the neighbor diligently all fall, then in late January his parents signed him up in one of the local leagues, in Vienna, Virginia.

The day they passed out equipment he was hooked. "I'm like, Whoa, the equipment looks like football. Maybe I get to hit people like football. My coach was like, 'You're not supposed to hit people like football, but you can, and we'll teach you how to play this.' "

Lacrosse has been likened to a blend of football, basketball, soccer, and hockey. The game originated in the North American Indian ceremony called *baggataway*. The basic concept has not changed: two teams trying to score a goal by catching and throwing a small hard ball with sticks that have a curved net at the end. Like soccer, modern lacrosse is played over a large field. Two teams of ten players utilize the physicality of football, the defensive/offensive strategies of basketball, and the goal plays of hockey. Lacrosse demands speed, skill, and aggressiveness. What won over Charles was that "you go around hitting people wielding a stick like a baseball bat." This was a sport Charles could love. What is so great about hitting people, explains Charles, is "that you can move somebody around with your body weight and force, move them and knock them down, rather than just sit there and let them try and knock you down. It's more or less like trying to push something that's not pushable. That's why it's like playing football. When I play lacrosse it's like, Whoa, the guy's moving while you're trying to do this so that puts another edge into it. And I have this stick in my hands so I can start swinging at him too." For a tightly controlled, focused kid like Charles, lacrosse is a great way to cut loose.

His first scrimmage gave him a shot of confidence that he never lost. "I didn't know what I was doing. The guy I was covering had been playing for four years. He thought he was the greatest thing in the world. He thought even though it had rained the night before, he was so good that he wouldn't get muddy at all. He came out there in all white. I came out there and just wore whatever I had."

The guy got the ball and raced toward the goal. Charles screamed, "What am I supposed to do?" The coach yelled, "Hit him!" So Charles charged into him like a bulldozer, stick flapping, and the much larger kid went careening into a huge mud puddle. Charles relishes this tale, which will undoubtedly be passed on to his children and grandchildren. "The other boy was wearing his mom's white turtleneck, which was totally splattered with mud. Everything on him was covered in mud, and he was all mad because he had been knocked down by someone who had only played for a day."

Mud is the essence of one of his mom's recollections. After one of the games years ago, her husband had taken Charles to The Sports Authority to get a new stick. He was still wearing his blue-and-white lacrosse uniform, and a man passing through started talking to them about the sport. He told them his brother was an all-American lacrosse player at North Carolina. Charles was impressed. They must have chatted for twenty minutes. What stuck with Charles was a passing comment the man made that his brother used to sleep with his stick. That night, and for months afterward, so did Charles. It didn't matter what condition it was in. Anything to become a college star. Those were the days, remembers his mom, when her son's always spectacularly messy bedroom also had various amounts of mud and dirt in the bed from his lacrosse stick.

Charles quickly became absorbed in all aspects of the game. Starting in seventh grade, he always assumed the responsibilities of general manager. He calls all the players, collects their money and deposits it in the proper account, makes a team roster, goes with his dad to get cashier's checks to pay the league commissioners. He keeps all the information and statistics in his computer. He wants to do everything necessary to keep lacrosse happening for him and understands he has to be active on his own behalf. He puts teams together, recruiting aggressively, so that there are enough players to play in fall and winter leagues. In the summers, his parents put money aside for him to go to lacrosse camps to hone his skills and build his self-esteem and finesse as a player. By high school, he and his dad already dream about his playing lacrosse in college.

When he recruits, he proselytizes. Lacrosse to him is the perfect sport: "It's like football, but you don't have to be big to play." He has always struggled with size, feeling too small and skinny. Even though the measurements his mom records on the kitchen wall show progress, it is never fast enough. The beauty of lacrosse is that his size doesn't matter. When he's on the field, he's an equal member of the team. "Lacrosse is something for medium-sized to small-sized people to play because if you're fast you have an advantage. You can be small and you don't have to worry about it. Or you can be really big and have good stick skills and you won't have to worry about people hitting you."

The grounds of the Sutter house bear testimony to this consuming passion. Every evening possible Charles goes outside and throws the ball against the wall of the house. Throw and catch, throw and catch. Different angles, different velocities. Over and over and over, he flings the ball against the house until the last shred of light is gone. His family will carry that maddening repetitive sound with them forever. There is a hopeless bald spot on the grass where he stands; there are dents in the siding and a few broken plastic slats in the shutters. His parents console themselves with the knowledge that it all makes Charles a better player.

Inside the house, a friendly, lived-in colonial brimming with life, there is a trail of clutter that leads as surely as Hansel and Gretel's crumbs to the family's command center. The hallway is a jumble of coats, sweats, backpacks, briefcases, basketballs, and lacrosse helmets, pads, and at least four long sticks, including Charles's new space-age titanium one. On either side of the hallway, the living room and dining room speak of order and decorum and the promise of how life can be when they have time to get organized. All the members of the family regularly escape into these areas to sit surrounded by family photos and a collection of African-American art and other objets d'art, some made by the children. They listen to music that ranges from classical to jazz to reggae to rock coming from magnificent handmade speakers. On Sunday mornings, Mrs. Sutter's favorite black spirituals fill the air.

But straight through the hallway of drop-and-run are the kitchen and family room—together the hub of this busy household. The table, which needs to be cleared each night for dinner, is piled with everybody's papers and schoolbooks, newspapers, Mom's tests to grade for her class at the elementary school, mail, forms to fill out, grocery lists, college catalogs, and on and on—an ever-changing display of what is going on and needs to be done.

The house reflects the hectic pace of its dwellers. It is "crazy," according to all of them, but for the Sutters it brings them closer. They eat together almost every night, first pausing to hold hands and say grace. They are not formally religious but know what values matter to them: family including relatives, friends, community, work, school, each other. They scurry around and complain, but they are always in touch, whether it be over dinner, car pooling, doing errands, or just watching television. They talk and tease and chastise in these rooms every day. Although it appears that everybody is always on the run to meetings, games, jobs, and school, they are close and vitally connected.

"They know me better than I know myself sometimes," says Charles of his family. After his sports, Charles says, the most important thing to him is "hanging around with the family just talking sometimes, going someplace, even when me and my sister fight." Charles loves going to the hardware store with his dad, helping him work on projects like the speakers he made. Father and son learned about lacrosse together, studying videos of college championships and endlessly discussing the sport. He goes to school games with his sister, who drives. His mother watches over and orchestrates the whole brood, making sure the schedules go smoothly, rushing home after her teaching job each day to be with her kids. Yet she still spends time pursuing her love of African-American art and fashion, dreaming that someday she can make her avocation a career. They are a passionate, emotional family who yell and scream and joke and love each other with an exuberance that surrounds all of them in a secure embrace.

Sports have always been a family thing, which is why when Charles got interested in lacrosse, his dad learned it too. His dad has always been active in his children's sports as coach, referee, or parent volunteer. He recalls that when Charles was seven, and began with the "ankle biters" division in Reston Youth League football, a neighbor who had a son playing South Lakes football advised him that "if your kid gets involved in sports, you get involved too because that way you can be sure they don't do anything to hurt your kid." Charles's dad never forgot that advice. The two parents never miss a game. When Charles's and Nika's events overlap, Mom and Dad split between them; otherwise the whole family attends together.

Mr. Sutter's commitment to his children's activities has a higher motivation as well. He stays involved, remembering his own father's admonition: "From those to whom much is given, much is expected in return."

He learned from his father. In 1965, when he was eighteen, his dad went with him to get his first car. He was so proud, having saved from his summer jobs for several years to buy it. Then he picked up some friends to go for a spin in his snazzy 1955 two-toned Chevrolet station wagon. Two hundred feet down the street the engine exploded. He was devastated, but his dad would have none of it. The next day, Sunday morning, his dad and he got eleven of his buddies to help push the car into the Sutter backyard. He and his friends, instructed by his dad, spent every night of that hot, humid Washington summer putting the car in working order again. Night after night, his dad worked patiently with these young men, teaching them all he knew about cars. That summer, working side by side around a broken car, under the patient tutelage of a caring adult, eleven teenagers made the journey from boyhood to manhood. His dad was passing on a legacy, and the group never forgot what it meant. Three years later, when Charles Sutter III was in the marines, his dad lay dying of cancer. The young men came and stayed with his dad in the hospital, showing their care and concern, their respect and love the best they could. When Charles came home on leave and held his dying father in his arms, he began to understand fully what his dad's words and example meant to him. He vowed never to forget.

When Charles Sutter III gets involved in his son's and daughter's activities, he continues his dad's legacy. He says he wants to prevent his kids and others from becoming part of the "IDI"—I-Deserve-It—generation. "I get involved because I don't want to live in a world where kids can do anything they want with no sense of responsibility to elders, to the community, to their fellow men. I want them to learn that sometimes you have to compromise." So he coaches football and lacrosse. He referees basketball games. And he and his wife have been active in Reston, their home and community, for seventeen years. They get involved in politics, in the schools, and through their work.

So does Charles Sutter IV. He referees basketball like his dad, helps him coach lacrosse, manages teams, is a class officer, and plays a sport every season. He says he knows he is "good with little people because I have been small and skinny for so long." Actually, it is because he is a strong teacher like his dad. Not that it is all sweetness and light with his dad. His father has high expectations and he is always there demanding the best effort of his son. He rails, he chides—but he often comes bearing the Skittles candy they both love. Charles has a dad whose constant presence is nurturing, even though he often seems only to be critical. Then Charles the son turns around and works with the other kids in the same demanding yet supportive way.

Charles knows his parents are his inspiration. "Mostly it is coming from my parents," Charles says, "because they always say that you have to give back to the community like when I help coach the little kids in lacrosse. I work with them hoping that somebody that starts in youth leagues can get to where I am. I remember looking up to those high school players as a little kid. I figure if it meant a lot to me, it could mean just the same to someone else."

Charles and his family's life centers on meaningful involvement. "It is more fun being involved than just hanging around the school." To Nika and Charles, the school is alive with interesting activity, whether it be sports, after-school art, or a pickup game.

Charles's dad feels he clears a way for his children, creating a supportive network by becoming known for good deeds in the community. He says he may not make a lot of money but he will "never be a nobody." He goes on: "I want to create a supportive web to open doors, so if my children want to be doctors or scientists or architects they won't have to push the door open again—they will find it open to them, the resources available."

But sometimes dedication and effort are not enough.

Once the lacrosse season gets into full swing, it whizzes by as always. Before Charles knows it, they are on their way to the last game of the season at Madison High School. The season has had its frustrations, notably that Charles is not allowed to play the position he loves, midfielder. "This year they moved me back to defense, and I really didn't like it because now I remember why I left defense. I feel like all I can do is wait for the person to come here. Playing midfield, you can actually try and stop the person from getting down on defense." Also, it has been a losing season.

The weather is overcast and unusually cool for May when his mom drops him off at South Lakes to meet his team. Charles wears his headphones during the bus ride, listening to rap—Snoop Doggy Dogg and A Tribe Called Quest. He turns the music real loud, blocking out everything around him—his usual way to get fired up. He thinks about what kind of defense they will play, he visualizes things that might happen in the game. His team had won only three games during the season, so this last game doesn't have that much importance except that they are coming off a win so they are psyched, wanting to end the season with a grand finale.

As the South Lakes team straggles off the bus, they exhibit the wacky and wild spirit around lacrosse. They're a ragtag bunch of players in anything but traditional attire. Charles wears shorts, combat boots, and a striped wool hat. There is method in their madness, he explains. His hat gives a psychological edge because "people don't know what you are going to do." The weird way they look makes other teams scared of them, "makes them think twice about messing with us in a game."

South Lakes is leading by a goal as they enter the fourth quarter. Charles is feeling terrific. "I was playing one of my greatest lacrosse games ever," he recalls, "and I hit this one boy on the other team and he called me 'stupid nigger.' " Charles is momentarily dumbstruck: "You know, in a sport in sudden rage you might say "asshole" or something else that slips off the tongue. But 'stupid nigger,' you have to take a second to think about who hit you and then what to say back to them." Charles scoops the ball and starts downfield when he is viciously slashed from the rear by the same kid who bad-mouthed him. The referee drops a flag and Charles continues down the field until he loses control of the ball and the referee blows the whistle.

When play stops, the Madison player raises both hands like Rocky, at which point Charles loses it. He runs after the kid and starts beating him with his stick. People from both teams run over to restrain him, while the crowd roars, "Throw him out! Throw him out!"

"We were the only ones near each other when it happened," says Charles. "Nobody else knew until I came off the field."

His parents know something is terribly wrong. They run down

the bleachers and Charles runs to the fence to meet them, his eyes smarting with tears. "You don't understand!" he cries out to them. "You don't understand what he said!"

He tells them and his mom screams, "He called you *what?*"

A hush settles on the stands, and some of the parents from the other team come over and apologize. The boy's father comes over and apologizes. Later the boy's mom apologizes. But never the boy who uttered the words.

Charles's teammates are stunned. At first they'd wondered why he was fighting this kid when they were still in the game. They were surprised to see their teammate get so violent. When they find out what happened, they want to go after the boy. "All they could talk about was how they could get this boy back," says Charles. "They were more concerned with what he did than the game."

The varsity team was warming up on the sidelines. They saw what happened and applauded Charles for going after the guy. A couple of them came over, and Bart Duncan, the only African-American player on varsity, talks to him. Charles recalls: "He said, 'Don't worry about it. It's all part of the game.' He'd had it happen to him. He said don't think about it—go on with the game. People try to get inside your head, that's what they want to do and don't pay them any mind. Get them back by scoring goals on them, not going after them. Make them think they didn't get to you."

Both boys get penalties. As the game nears its end, Charles is left to himself. "They took away from me anything I could use as a projectile—my stick, my gloves, my helmet." He is fuming. "The kid tried to seriously hurt me—first what he said, and then by him hitting me—it was like him spitting in my face. I have always been taught you don't let someone say that to you," says Charles. "I was going to let it be and get back cleanly, but when he hit me, it was like he had no respect for me. There was nothing I could do about it but hit him back real fast before I lost the anger about it."

Charles has a six-minute penalty and there are five minutes and thirty seconds left in the last quarter. Madison scores right away while a man down, tying the game up. The Madison player gets released. A South Lakes player tries to hit him, "take his head off," and while he is falling he shoots the ball and makes a goal. Madison wins in overtime.

On the way home, Charles's mom tells him that what he did was dangerous, that it got him thrown out of the game and made it possible for the other kid to score the winning goal. Her heart aches and she is not going to reprimand him for beating the kid. She reminds him that there were other ways he could have handled the situation. But she also tells him, "We have taught you that you don't allow anybody to call you that, whatever it takes." By the time they reach McDonald's, Charles's anger has subsided. He and his teammates will figure out a way to get back. The thought of retaliation makes him feel better.

In the balancing act between two cultures that is his life, to be called a nigger was the one thing Charles never imagined. "It would have been different in the fifties," he says. "It was common language back then but there is no place for it anymore." Some sense of security about how things are getting better was ripped from Charles in that game, something was taken that cannot be given back. It was particularly horrible in lacrosse, which is "the melting pot sport because it wasn't started by white people but by Native Americans," Charles says. If an Indian had called him a name, he reasons, it would have been less horrible somehow because they know what it is to be discriminated against.

"It seems like this one person is completely misinformed about his surroundings at the moment," Charles goes on. Just recently the media had been flooded with news of the Rodney King beating, the riots and the verdicts. Charles feels that the outrage over the Rodney King beating means that prejudice and injustice are on their way out. He wonders if maybe the Madison player's problem was that he had never seen a black person play lacrosse, but that still is no excuse. "Now it is going to stick with me the rest of my life," says Charles. "I was wrong for taking it out on him the way I did, but if I hadn't done anything, it would have been saying it was all right. I said to myself, whatever he does, I can't let him do that."

That night his parents talk to him. Carefully choosing their words, they tell him: "There will always be people like that, and it seems the more and more you think you've come, the more you haven't come. You think this wouldn't happen again and when it does happen, it is shocking." They also tell him that he is "feeling what other people have felt before, like Jim Brown with football and Hank Aaron with baseball." But Charles thinks his experience is different because "there was nothing they could do about it because it was a sign of the times. But there is no place for it anymore."

The incident confirms for his parents their own experience and how fragile their status is. "The rage is there," says his mom. "People say, 'You're doing okay. You've got a house.' But you don't know what I'm struggling with. Yes, I'm doing better than my parents did, but it is not all that it could be. And the anger is that I've played the game and done what I'm supposed to do, and it's gotten no better. And it may not be better for my kids. We are allegedly middle-class but my children will have to earn the right to be here all over again."

Charles Sutter III exhibits the same restrained raged. When he gave up his dashiki twenty-five years ago for a Marine Corps uniform and then a business suit, he expected things would be better. He had faith then that hard work and achievement would bring acceptance. Instead he finds the battles continue. His advice on the lacrosse field incident was simply to expect it: "I told my son that if you are going to play this sport or any sport, you are going to hear it all the days of your life." He tells of how young black athletes in lacrosse and football are often overlooked in the schools because tradition supports the grooming of white stars for certain positions. He tells how it never ends: "The bigotry comes full circle, the double standards that exist in this country and are not going away, they are just not always in the open." He's a tough realist with his children because he feels that they need to develop a protective shell for the slights they will endure. But a look of devastating pain and rage crosses his face as he recalls how, going back from the Madison lacrosse game, he gave two kids on the team a ride home. One of the kids had started playing just six months before and now was playing midfield, the position Charles hungers to play. The kid was chatting about how he'd been asked to play varsity in the tournament. Charles Sutter III controls his voice as he explains the reason he thinks this boy is playing and his son is not: "He's got blond hair and blue eyes."

Charles Sutter III tries to keep his bitterness in check by reminding his son of what they used to say to the kids in basketball: "I don't say can't, there's no excuse. When I want something done, I put my brain to use." If nothing else, he wants his son to learn that "he can use his mind to move mountains if he so chooses. It doesn't require that you hit with a stick."

The same week as the infamous lacrosse game, Charles runs for class president. No rotten incident on the lacrosse field will knock out of him what his parents have inculcated so lovingly. He still believes in his heart that "more and more people are coming together as a human race rather than as individual races." Besides, he can set the incident aside until next year, when he and his team will exact revenge. They'll make that kid sorry for what he did.

The day of the election, Charles stands proud and tall on the dais and delivers his succinct speech in the cracking voice of a boy becoming a man: "Class of '96, good morning. I am here to remind you that change is not always a good thing: look at how well our float did with little preparation and how well our car wash did this year. So remember for a class that ran well and a class that will run well, vote Charles Sutter for president."

His classmates file out and cast their votes. The next morning it is announced. Charles Sutter IV has been elected the sophomore class president.

# Taking Care of Each Other and Other Grown-up Preoccupations

As soon as Ann gets into the house after school this Wednesday afternoon, she heads straight for the Northern Virginia Yellow Pages. She flips to "Abortion Services" and starts scanning the columns. She doesn't have to look past the *A*s. There is a big advertisement that says right up front, "Parental Consent Not Required."

Perfect. She picks up the phone and makes an appointment for Saturday morning. "It was just like calling for a dentist appointment except that they asked the date of your last normal period." Thank goodness they had time available because it was impossible to get over there during the school week, and after Saturday it would have been too late in the pregnancy to have an abortion in the state of Virginia. She writes down the appointment time in her constant companion, her Day Runner.

It's weird, here she is a junior and before now she knew nobody except her eighth-grade president who'd gotten pregnant. With the cover story in the school newspaper last winter, she feels she has the inside scoop on what it is like to be a teen mom, but what is really strange is that none of her other good friends is even having sex. She does a quick mental check: Ellen doesn't even have a boyfriend, never has. So if she's having sex, that would surprise Ann. Linda is still a virgin. She recently broke up with her boyfriend of many years because she wouldn't have sex with him. Rene doesn't have a boyfriend, never even been kissed by a guy. The only exception on the list is Sallie. Ann says that she knows her friends are not the "cool crowd," implying teens her age having sex are more with-it.

Call waiting beeps while she's making the appointment. It's Ron, her boyfriend, calling from school in Texas. She rings him back when she's done. He's checking to see if she got the roses for their anniversary. She tells him she cried when she got them and now they are on the table next to her bed. He still has not received her gift, a silver herringbone necklace. She details what is going on, and asks his feelings. He says, "I'd support you either way. If you were a senior in high school, I'd say keep it, but I wouldn't have to carry it, so it would be your decision." It is so typical, him respecting her that way.

She can hardly believe how wonderful their relationship is. They met during her freshman year at a track meet. He was a senior and captain of the cross-country team. "We just slowly got to know each other." Especially during the annual twenty-four-hour relay early in the school year, where they and several other teammates sat around talking, joking, and laughing all night long, interrupted only by their scheduled runs around the track. The two of them just clicked.

They never asked each other out. One day a team member asked if Ron and Ann were dating. Ann turned to Ron and he said, "I guess so." It was as simple and spontaneous as that. "It honestly did not dawn on me that he was black until I sat down and thought, He's black and I'm white. It never really mattered. We never even gave a second thought to it." But her parents did. She's had nothing but grief from them ever since.

The relationship has lasted two years, over the separation and against all odds. "I'm really unusual," she comments. "There are people that have known their marriage partners less time than I've known Ron."

Even more unusual is that she is not having sex with Ron. The abortion is for Sallie, the "exception" among her friends.

When Ann finishes her conversation with Ron, she calls Sallie and tells her the appointment is made. The two girls then figure out the logistics. They cook up a scheme based on a fictitious seventeenth-birthday celebration for Sallie that entails Ann spending the night at her house.

Such maneuverings are necessary in her life. Since Ron became her boyfriend, her parents, hating that he is black and older, have been relentlessly on her case, strictly curtailing her activities. Especially her mom. "I was forbidden to see him," Ann says. "Plain and

simple." No discussion. No reasoning. "People under house arrest
get more freedom than I do," she complains. "Last year, my friends
totally ditched me because I could never do anything. I didn't have
any close friends except Linda and Jill, and Jill finally said, 'You need
to talk to somebody else. I just can't help you.' "

The injustice of her confinement in the face of her sister's wild-
ness makes her furious. She believes Courtney "controls our parents.
And I cannot kiss butt. I've never learned that art form, don't want
to." Ann tells how she was the one who got spanked as a child.
"Courtney hardly gets a hand laid on her. I guess I always took
it. Courtney screamed bloody murder before you got a hundred feet
in front of her." Her parents are in constant battle with Courtney.
"Some of the fights are better than a soap opera. Free, too. Even my
stepmom admits it, and my dad." Ann feels the whole family shares
responsibility in her sister's behavior since she was always allowed
to get her way "because she bitched and complained and cried and
threw fits, and it was easier to give her what she wanted than to listen to her and say no." Her sister is "the queen of temper tantrums."

Ann, however, doesn't believe Courtney is "any more messed up
than probably half of the other kids in her class, or any class." But as
with so many kids, her number-one need is for discipline, which is
hard to impose after all these years. "They indulge her more. They
throw up their hands with her more. She gets a whole lot more freedom. The thing that bothers me is, You don't have to love me or anything like that, but just treat me fairly."

Her parents have loosened up a bit since Ron left for Texas, but
Ann still is wary. Her mother shocks her by giving her permission to
spend the night at Sallie's without the usual third degree.

Upon arriving at Sallie's, Ann finds out Donald, Sallie's boyfriend
and the father of the child, is meeting them in the morning. Originally he was not going to come because he has moved to New Jersey.
Not that the move has kept them apart. He's already been to Reston
eight times on the weekends. "His parents think he's been down here
half that number," says Ann. He tells them he is going to spend the
night at a new friend's house in Trenton, drives to Virginia instead,
and stays at his best friend's. He then drives back the next day. The
girls tell Sallie's parents they are going to take their friend Laura out
to breakfast. That's why they have to leave at 7 A.M. The lying is ex-
tensive and complex. None of the kids gives it a second thought. It
comes as second nature, not as a means of "getting away" with

something but rather as "creating space" for the lives they want to live. This behavior is commonplace among their generation: the Josephson Institute of Ethics reports that seven out of ten high school students admit that they lie to parents.

Early the next morning, Sallie drives to where Donald is staying and lets him drive to Alexandria. It is a nervous ride with only half-hearted attempts at conversation. Sallie is scared, but Ann is convinced she and Donald are even more scared. They arrive at the abortion clinic to face a group of noisy protesters in front. Thank goodness there is a new law that says they can't block an entrance. "I saw them," says Ann, "and I was like, Shit, what are we going to do now? Sallie was not fazed at all. I would have been petrified." Ann tells Donald to maneuver Sallie inside quickly, and she scoots in behind them.

At approximately 8 A.M., the three kids walk into a homely room filled with women sitting in ugly green Naugahyde chairs. A coffee table is stacked high with months' worth of *Family Circle*, *Vogue*, *Time*, and other staples of waiting rooms all over America. Sallie goes to the desk to sign in, and pays $212 in cash she withdrew from her personal savings account; $210 is for the procedure and $2 goes to the National Coalition of Abortion Providers to keep abortion safe and legal. The clinic is a cash-only operation. Donald doesn't contribute because "he doesn't have a job right at this second because he just moved." He says he will pay Sallie back. Ann thinks that is sweet.

They sit down in the crowded room. Ann looks around. There is a preponderance of college-age kids, as well as a surprising number of unaccompanied "older women in their thirties." There are only a few couples. Some of the women are crying. The strangest thing, Ann thinks, is that everybody is sitting close to each other—not like in a dentist's office, where people leave empty chairs between them. "It was like we all knew we were here for the same purpose. We're all going through our own feelings about why we're here, what we're doing, and how we feel about it. We're not afraid to get close to one another."

Ann's take-charge attitude about her friend's abortion is just one example of how kids take care of each other in the adolescent community. Parents would be shocked to find out how kids guide each other, however ineptly or naively, through divorces, abuse, dating violence, drug overdose—all sorts of things that affect them even when the problems are not theirs personally. When Family Life Education opponents, for example, work to clamp down on the information flow to teens in schools, a kid like Ann is never their target. The prevailing wisdom is, give kids information about sex and they will have more of it. Yet Ann is a virgin, free of any wild lifestyle, and she is orchestrating her friend's abortion, choosing a medical establishment on whether they tattle to parents. How many other scenarios are like Ann's and Sallie's, given that 40 percent of one million teen pregnancies annually end in abortion?

Ann had known Sallie since sixth grade, but Sallie transferred to another school her freshman year and they lost contact. Their mutual friend Laura stayed in touch after she moved. It was through Laura that they got back together.

Over the summer, Sallie and Ann picked up where they'd left off. Being her "motherly self," Ann found out that Sallie was pregnant while talking with Laura one day on the way to the mall. "I bitched and moaned to Laura for like thirty minutes about how could she let this happen," recalls Ann, "because apparently they weren't using birth control all the time."

About a month later, Ann spent time with Sallie and Donald as part of a group that went to a movie. Ann pulled Laura aside and asked if "anything happened." Laura had already told her that Sallie was supposed to get an abortion, but hadn't, when she was in Florida being a nanny.

Ann gave Laura a message for Sallie: "Tell her if she wants me to go, I'll go."

"I know Sallie," Ann says. "She wanted to have it done, kind of, and if her mom found out, she was going to kill Donald and make her go have it anyway. I knew this because her sister got pregnant when she was sixteen, and her mom made her go have an abortion. So it was just a basic assumption that she was going to make her have it. She wouldn't tell her mother because her mother would have been really upset that she was sleeping with Donald, A. And B, her mom would have been really disappointed in her."

The passage of time on this problem worried Ann. She knew something had to be done, so finally when talking to Sallie she blurted out, "Do you want me to call and make the appointment?" Sallie said yes.

Being motherly comes easily to Ann. "It's just my nature," she says. "That's why I baby-sit and why friends are always asking advice." She's been parenting her sister for years—although in this case it's against her will. "I have to watch her when my parents aren't home. Not that she's going to listen to me. But my mom will call. 'Where's Courtney?' I tell her, 'I don't know. She's not home.' 'You don't know where she is?' my mom says. I get angry and tell her she wasn't home when I got home. Then my mom starts yelling at me." Often Courtney asks her to cover for her and when her parents come looking, Ann has to lie and then scramble around to find her.

Even worse, Courtney tells her everything. "I tell her, 'Please don't tell me, I don't want to know.' Like when she tells me she's going to sneak out, I'm up all night worrying that something bad's going to happen, and it drives me crazy. So I told her, 'If you're going to sneak out, don't tell me about it. I need some sleep.' " At least with her friends and the kids she sits for, Ann is in control of the mothering and nurturing, and she receives the positive feedback that she is doing good work.

That is why as she and Donald wait in the clinic for Sallie, Ann has the feeling of a job well done. They sit for hours. Midway through, Ann realizes she'd better check in with her parents to tell them where she is. She calls from the clinic phone at around 10:30.

"We just got back from breakfast," she tells her mom.

"Where are you?" her mother asks.

Ann is caught off guard by the specific question and stumbles a bit. "Well, I don't know. I can't really see the sign right now."

"What city are you in?"

"Reston-Herndon."

"By the Kmart shopping center?"

"Yeah, I think so." Whew! She thinks if her mom didn't catch her on that one she probably wasn't going to. She hangs up the phone laughing. "I would have told my kid, Well, go find out where you are."

Back in the waiting room, Donald chats with Ann as if they were in a movie theater waiting for the show to start. He says, "Would you please help Sallie find a really nice guy?" "Wait a minute," Ann says. "You're not going to break up with her, are you?" She can't believe what she is hearing—and here, of all places! He answers, "No, but I just want you to find a really nice guy for her because I'm not always going to be around." Ann has no idea what he means so she says nothing.

Sallie comes out pale and stooped, with terrible cramps. She fills her friends in on what has been going on. They have spent four hours at the clinic for a procedure that takes only minutes. They sit together another half hour making small talk. Sallie gets checked out, makes a follow-up appointment, and is told she can leave.

Ann is exhausted partly because of lack of sleep and partly because of the stress. The girls drop Donald off at his friend's, then go back to Sallie's house briefly so Ann can check in with her parents again. Sallie complains to her about the cramps, pops several Advil, then decides she wants to see Donald before he leaves for New Jersey. Again they lie telling Sallie's parents they are going out to take pictures for photography class. Her parents say fine. "No one's picked up on this by now," says Ann with some amazement. "So they're never going to, hopefully."

After they pick up Donald, they drive to a local park and just sit in the parking lot. Ann tells the couple that they can talk and she will go to sleep in the back seat. She dozes off for maybe twenty minutes, and awakens to the sound of Sallie crying. "I think it just hit her what had happened," Ann recalls. Sallie was crying that she would have liked to keep the baby, given the choice. But she couldn't. She knew if her mother had found out, there was no way she could have kept it. She didn't even have a high school diploma. Ann hears Donald tell Sallie that he wishes they were five years older so that they wouldn't have to go through this. Ann winces at his hypocrisy.

After a while, they drop Ann off. She has to be at her sitting job at five. This sixteen-year-old is having quite a day, one in which she is quite sure she does more authentic mothering than her own mom.

Ginny's mom opens the door, and the nine-year-old comes running to give Ann a hug. Ginny is one of Ann's favorites. They have marathon checker games and many long conversations. "I love kids," Ann says simply. "I form a bond."

She has a natural sensitivity to the needs of children—like John, for whom she is sitting tomorrow. She knows he has a "genuine fear" of being in the house without his parents. Most sitters would disregard his feelings, according to Ann, and tell him, "Just go to bed." "But I come and check on him and I sit with him and rub his back, because I know he's scared and I want him to feel comfortable."

She thinks she enjoys baby-sitting so much because she gets to be a "little mother." She takes the role seriously, to the point where she may be overprotective.

That's why, even though she is adamantly pro-choice, she knows she could never have an abortion. As she sits in front of the television this Saturday night, with Ginny cuddled close beside her, she thinks about the day. "I'm going to become a nun. I figure I haven't had sex, so I won't know what I'm missing. Besides, I never want to go through that. Loving kids as much as I do, I couldn't have an abortion. I know that's another life. That's a little baby. And then I couldn't give it up for adoption, not my little baby. As much as I know some people want babies, I just couldn't give it up. So I would be stuck. So I'm just going to become a nun."

But she thinks Sallie made the right choice in her circumstances. "The way it was, had she brought this child into the world, the child would never have been happy anyway, nor would she. Anybody who has a child unwanted and unplanned, they're always thinking in the back of their minds, 'I didn't want you.' That kid's going to feel like shit forever."

She also believes that some unmarried people really want children, and some married people really don't. Like her mom. "She's one of those people that wasn't meant to be a parent," says Ann.

Her mom is a total control person, very domineering. She thinks she is always right, explains Ann, and can never admit when she's wrong. "If you're a parent, that's a really bad thing to be," Ann says. "You've got to tell your kid, 'Okay, I screwed up, sorry.' With Mom? No thanks. It's my fault. She could never do that." No matter how hard she tries to be responsible, to work hard, her mom never praises her. "She's just never been one to say 'I love you, come here, you did good.' "

Her mom never hugs. "Not since I was eight or nine. Like when we leave for the airport, 'bye Mom. But it's never good night, a good night kiss."

Mostly there is anger in the house. Both girls find it not a very nice place to be. "Why do you think I baby-sit twenty-four hours a day?" says Ann.

Theirs is a home where everybody lives together separately, the lines of demarcation drawn by the parents. They generally eat individually, the girls grabbing a sandwich or cereal or Ann's favorite invention, "macaroni and cheese without the cheese and with spaghetti sauce." The house is staked out into territories for the children and the adults—only the dog is welcome everywhere. They fight over the television, the rule being that the stylish family room off the kitchen is the domain of the girls' mom and stepdad when they are home. Ann and Courtney are required to go downstairs. There is no place they feel at home except their bedrooms, and even there their mom feels free to intrude and snoop at will. "What parents would say, 'This is our room, you can't watch TV in here,' " says Ann. "It's crazy, no family in the family room."

The girls complain that they are not allowed in their mom and stepdad's bedroom. Ann has this fantasy of being close to her mom, doing things together, sharing clothes. She envies her friends who borrow their mom's clothes—even some stepmoms share with their teens. She thinks her mom is a great dresser. "She could open up a store in her closet," Ann says, obviously smarting, "but I'm not allowed in there. Mom says, 'You guys will move out of this house and down to your father's before I have to put a padlock on my door to keep you out of there.' "

The issue is a lack of parental attention. Ann has simply given up on it, feeling that whatever she does it makes no difference to her parents. But she thinks it is a big issue for her sister. It is part of the reason Courtney stays out until 4:00 in the morning, explains Ann. "Every parent should look at what the child is doing and then think, 'There's obviously a reason for this.' Don't just say the kid has 'bad friends.' That's the standard answer. No, *your* kid's bad. Why is it their kids are bad? Why isn't it them? All parents are always like, 'It's the other kids, get them out of the environment and they'll be okay.' "

Ann is truly worried about her sister. "Courtney needs something. I don't know what it is but she needs something. She's out of control." Courtney got caught smoking pot. A friend's mother called their mom, but their parents never took action. "I guess they don't think she really is, but she is," says Ann. "But I'm not going to say anything because it's a trust thing." Ann finally told her parents she wouldn't sit for her sister anymore. That's when they sent Courtney to camp.

Ann is still trapped though. When she complains to her dad in Florida, he is sympathetic because he obviously didn't get along with her mom either. He tells Ann he feels sorry for her because "he put in his time" and she is "kind of stuck there." Sometimes the girls implore him to let them move in with him, but his second wife doesn't want the girls full-time. She tells them outright that she has already raised her family.

The coldness in Ann's home makes her love her little charges more. She thinks she learned to be loving and nurturing from her grandparents. "My grandparents were always huggy and stuff like that, and I was very, very close to them. I was their favorite grandchild," says Ann. When her grandmother died of cancer Ann was in sixth grade. The following year her grandfather died. It was a painful loss to Ann, who now had nobody left to love her gently and with warm embraces.

But there is more to the story. As wonderful a grandmother as she was to Ann, apparently she had been a cold, rejecting parent to her own daughter, Ann's mother. Then her mom married her stepdad, a tough ex-marine who made the girls run laps if their rooms didn't pass inspection. He orders the girls around and they hate it. Ann hopes to break the cycle. "I feel I'm going to be a pretty decent parent. I've been around other kids and I know how I react."

Her parents are "the model-to-not-end-up-like." She studies her friends' families, searching for role models. Her best friend Linda's parents are really loving. "They're nice to each other. Actually, it's surprising. I have a lot of friends whose parents are still together. It's really strange." She studies the parents of the children she sits for and watches to see if the children are happy.

Ann is cynical about marriage. "You say your vows to each other. So if you get up and say it in front of two hundred people, that's supposed to make it more important than if you just say it to each other? Come on now." She does not think marriage is necessary, although like most girls she fantasizes about the wedding chapel and the beautiful gown. She would like to get married someday, but "if it doesn't happen, it just doesn't happen." After all, she says, she is her own independent person just like her mother, who has said many times that she does not need her husband, that she "could be by herself and be happy."

Ann's life is one of inhibition, judgment, rejection and restraint; her sister acts out but Ann buries her feelings inside and tries to meet her needs in the homes of others. If she cannot find nurturance at home, she discovers it in herself and gives it to friends and the children she cares for. She works hard to get away, and follows her own inner compass with her boyfriend. She's a solid, no-nonsense kid who is embarrassed about how straight she is. "I don't know why it is," she complains. "I'm like nailed to something. People say I need to cut loose. Sometimes I wish I could go out and do something totally out of character, like go to a club or something, just do something purely for the fun of it, but I just can't."

When she finally gets to sleep late at night on this busy Saturday, she thinks about the roses, about Ron coming home soon, how she misses him, how she loves being close. Sometimes she feels guilty because she knows he had sex early, when he was in eighth grade. He seems to be okay with their waiting, but she wonders if he will continue to hang in with her. She is firm about delaying sex until she's around twenty, "because the way my luck goes it will either be I can't ever have children, something's wrong with me, or I'll get pregnant like every time I have sex. That would be my luck. So when I have sex I'm going to use four birth control items to make it foolproof."

Over time, the experience with Sallie recedes to become just another item on another day in Ann's Day Runner. Every morning she consults her planner, and several times during the day she updates it to keep her life running smoothly. She stumbles in her work at school, refusing to do homework; she amuses her friends by her constant bitching about her parents, rarely letting any of them know what anguish they cause her; and she is cherished by the parents of the children she sits for because of her skill and warmth.

She hasn't kept up contact with Sallie now that the school year is lurching toward the end of first quarter. Laura tells her that Sallie and Donald still see each other, but not as much. It seems Donald is finding it more difficult to get down to Reston. Laura also tells her that Sallie is sleeping with other guys on the side. "Now she's got three or four," says Ann. Ann thinks it is because Sallie has discovered she can have sex and not care about the person.

Before Ann knows it, Thanksgiving is around the corner. Ron completes his courses at technical school and comes back to Reston. As he ponders what to do next, the two of them talk on the phone constantly and see each other surreptitiously now and then. Even lying together naked side by side in Ann's bedroom, they never have intercourse even though they think they will burst with longing. Ann continues to grudgingly look after her sister. She stings with hurt over her parents' neglect.

Sometimes she thinks about the abortion. What is amazing to her is that she acted without any judgment or thought. "It was like, 'If that's what you want, I'll go with you.' I didn't judge Sallie, I reacted automatically. It was just, 'Okay, you can't handle it, so I will be there and do that for you.' She doesn't even consider her offer unusual. When youngsters feel their friends have no adults to turn to in a life crisis, they come together to fill the void.

"I never judged her for what she was doing," Ann says. "Never thought, Oh my gosh, you got yourself into this mess, you have to get out of it. But sometimes that's the innocence you need. Without it, I would have gone, What am I doing! But with that innocence I can take it and run with it." She only wishes she had the same clarity about the issues in her own life.

# Moshing Is a Way to Belong

The walls of the Reston Community Center tremble to the sounds of Arctic Shepherd, a local hard-core rock group. Their words are indistinguishable in the roar of music, the beat that surges through the crowd. A mass of teens from the counterculture of the nineties pushes closer and closer to the stage; their carefully cultivated defiant dress features overalls, lots of long hair, multiple earrings on boys and girls, partially shaved heads on both sexes. An array of T-shirts flashes past, the wearers like human billboards proclaiming their tastes—Metallica, Guns n' Roses, Pearl Jam, Red Hot Chile Peppers, Pro-Pain, Primus, and Megadeath, the preferred heavy metal and alternative rock groups. No rap music lovers here. Once inside the room, several kids whisk off flannel shirts, uncovering T-shirts decorated with cannabis leaves and the message "Step into a Whole New Realm."

Joan and her friends have been waiting for this group to play. They stand happily at the perimeter of the dance floor grooving to the music. Joan is sizing up the scene, watching especially to see how the girls are faring. Her petite friend Carol is a monster on the floor, her arms like propellers, her footwork like a boxer's. Sweaty, dirty, bloody and bruised, she keeps "dancing." She is jerked out momentarily when a cut on her nose bleeds onto her shirt, then is back in the middle a few moments later, a Mickey Mouse Band-Aid on her wound. One boy leaves with what appears to be a broken nose. Boys and girls, faces frozen in furious grimaces, circle about, shoving, jabbing, hurling themselves against one another, their hair damp and matted. In this rolling sea of flesh, occasionally someone gets pushed to the floor and stomped on. Alert fellow dancers or one of the brave wide-eyed adult chaperones at the edges of this community-supported concert will dart in and scoop up the victim. One very preppie honor student wearing a rust-color ribbed top straight out of a Lands End catalog looks like she wandered into the wrong dance. But looks are deceiving. She goes in and within moments her sleeve is torn as she whips around slamming into people until she disappears, having slipped and fallen. She emerges from underfoot tearfully, with the help of a chaperone. Her friends rush to comfort her, and a few minutes later she goes back into the fray.

Kids are passed over the heads of the dancers—hoisted up by friends, moved along hand to hand to be dumped on the stage; it's a groping, manhandling cooperative effort called "stagediving." Once onstage they do a little jig and then jump back off to be swallowed up again. Some don't make it, like one young man who is dropped on his tailbone and limps away.

To Joan, it looks like a great way to feel like part of something. She steps forward and is swept into the current of bodies. Like a windup doll, she hits the wave of flesh and starts moving her legs up and down, her arms side to side in a spinning motion to protect herself and hit other participants in this strange ritual. She gets lost to her watching friends in a canopy of bodies, her head down to protect her face. She rises up, sees someone she feels like hitting, and lets loose, arms flying again.

To an outsider the scene appears an incredible display of dancehall violence. Teens know it as a mosh pit, a kind of modern day war dance, a rumble to music, a trendy free-for-all. Like the era it reflects, it has no synchronicity, no steps, just action, sensation, and physicality. Adults see it as some peculiar, sadistic, self-flagellating ritual that instantly confirms this is an alien generation. There is no precedent that an adult can conjure up to understand what this moshing is about and why anyone in their right mind would want to participate. In fact, adults would never even witness it except in a situation like this concert, where they are chaperoning. No matter what the adults think, the kids love it.

Joan is punched twice, and each time simply punches back the next body moving across her line of fire. She furiously maneuvers around the floor, sometimes moving only up and down because the bodies get packed so tight, and she always stands firm. Her friends watch her with admiration, puzzling at how this gentle sweet girl who they know as a poet and friend of the earth can be so aggressive. They should know.

It's the annual Jam for Man concert, started in Reston in 1988 by local teen rock groups to raise money and collect food for the homeless. Admission is three dollars and a can of food. Held in a community room and limited to 350 Reston kids allowed in with picture identification cards, the concert is well chaperoned by adults and two Fairfax County police officers. A stream of cars moves along the curb near the community center with moms and dads cheerfully letting off their kids for the event. The parents are focused on the wholesomeness of a concert with a larger purpose. The kids are wondering if the bands will blow out the community center and if the Pit will be "intense."

Joan emerges from the Pit breathless and laughing her high-pitched laugh, her clothes out of kilter. She twists her fringed jeans around straight and runs her fingers through her hair. "It's fun," she enthuses, because "anything goes. You can get your frustrations out. I like pushing people with the music playing. When you're there, society doesn't tell you, 'This is bad, you can't do it.' " One nearby girl gushes, "I like being with lots of people really crowded and pushed together." "I'm a really nice person, easy to get along with," says a wide-eyed boy with a much-too-large flannel shirt, dripping hair, and a long scratch on his cheek. "But when I am in there, I express all the stuff that is happening inside. When I was in there today, I was knocking people out of the way. You don't really do it to hurt them, you just have fun. You get an adrenaline rush and you just keep going, you don't get tired, you don't feel it when you get hit." The anxiety-reducing benefits are celebrated over and over: "You know some people get out their anger when they jog. I get it out moshing. I feel like a load is lifted off my shoulders. I feel so much happier. You can ask people. When I got here I was tense, but now it's like, 'Hey, what's up?' I'm having fun. It pumps me up."

When the music stops the vicious looks fade, the kids put happy faces back on, and everyone hugs. As the evening proceeds, the kids use every number as a vehicle for walloping each other, even the slow numbers that would in the past have found couples nuzzling close on the dance floor.

Ultimately the mosh pit is for these participants a place where they belong and are supported in a chaos of their own making. Joan feels uninhibited, part of the action, and especially part of a group of peers, something she longs for. For youngsters growing up in a world of out-of-control violence, the mosh pit is their own sweet form of brutality. Most of the kids say they relish moshing for a simple reason: they "like to be close to people."

The rules passed to everybody as they walk in are strewn around the room, laughable "guidelines" on sheets of bright pink paper underfoot:

• Dance with safety in mind—look out for your fellow dancers. Please don't knock anybody down or hit them too hard.

• Keep air-passing of dancers to a minimum and remember that anyone who doesn't want to be passed should be left alone.

• Stay off the stage for the safety of the performers and chaperones—we're here to keep it safe.

Yeah. Right. The grown-ups do the best they can. Take the refreshments, for example. Domino's and McDonald's have contributed food and drink; the drugs, absolutely forbidden of course, are Bring Your Own, or purchased from several dealers who move through the crowd, indistinguishable from their peers. The rule is clear: once in the building nobody is allowed to leave and reenter. The doors of the center are guarded. Yet even the best attempts at control are less than perfect. The spaced-out youngsters drifting through, some of the most frantic moshers, even some kids who hide it well, are definitely not substance-free. "You can't smoke weed," says Joan. "The only thing you can probably do is acid or another drug. The weed would smell. A lot of people just come stoned."

While the adults fret, Joan is ecstatic to be out with her friends. It doesn't matter that she got punched twice while in the Pit. It doesn't matter that before she could leave her house tonight she had to clean, cook dinner, and finish paying the bills for her dad and brother. The main thing is that she is here surrounded by her people.

All in all, it has been a great day for her. There was an Environmental Club meeting after school, which is always fun. Joan is outraged and outspoken on behalf of the environment. Today she explained to members that even though technically they can't join the radical group Greenpeace as part of a school club, since she is a member she can sign them on. "We don't want to be just a social group," she implored the club members. "We want to do something!" Hearing her own passion startled her. Could she become the strong person of that voice?

The feeling carried her through her tasks at home, and at the end there was the delightful surprise that her dad would let her go out with her friends. She never knows what will happen at her house, what kind of mood Papa will be in. And the cultural differences between him, with his Ecuadorian origins, and her teen world often create tension.

When Joan was ten, her mom left to do the laundry and never came back. She ran off pregnant with Joan's father's best friend. There was no communication with Joan and her brother. For two years, their mother vanished. When she resurfaced, she had a new daughter and husband. Joan would never get over that abandonment, and to this day has an arm's-length relationship with her mother.

The minute her mother exited, Joan was expected to become the woman of the house, to clean, cook, and take care of her little brother. Since she knew English and her father didn't, she also had to manage the finances. "All of a sudden," she recalls, "I went from being spoiled one day, to the next day when I'm told to clean the house or my dad would yell at me." She did everything expected "out of fear."

She was told repeatedly, "This is what women are supposed to do." Inside she knew it was unjust. She grew up isolated and lonely. "I never met any kids. I was supposed to go from school to home. I wasn't allowed to talk to children, and if I did they had to go through my father first and see if it was okay." She didn't do much of anything when she was growing up except the chores. Nobody seemed to care that she was just a little girl, devastated by loss. Over time, she turned her anger on herself. Food was her only solace. She gained a lot of weight, and that made other children cruel.

This evening with her friends is still more the exception than the rule. "Even now," she admits, "I don't do much." Her father maintains many old-world controls over her.

After her mom left, for two years she was trampled and defeated by her life conditions. She craved recognition and respect. She was too scared to ask for love.

Over time she came up with a solution. The problem, as she saw it, was that she had taken whatever life dished out. No more. She decided she was going to fight back. When she was twelve, she moved to Reston with her father and brother. "It was an opportunity for me to make a whole new person of myself," she remembers. She would enter Langston Hughes "a big bad wamma," a tough white person who acts like she's black. " 'You touch me, I will kick your ass.' That's who I became." If she even thought somebody was talking about her, she would turn around and say in her new voice, "Yo, what the fuck are you talking about? Are you talking about me or what?" She watched kids turn around with fear in their eyes, muttering "Oh, no." But she would insist anyway, saying, "Yeah, you are talking about me. Yo, you better shut the fuck up before I kick your ass." She felt powerful. "People would just be like, 'Get away from me.' "

She continued the pose into high school, bringing with her a string of school detentions, poor grades, and a reputation for having a bad attitude. The biggest joke was that technically she was not a "wamma" because she was a Latina. "You have to understand that if you're Hispanic you are not white for them," she explains. "You have the right to act this way." While black friends would ask other wamma friends why they were trying to be black, they never challenged her. "I was all set. It didn't matter what I did."

She moved from the sidelines of fights to provoking them. She recalls her favorite. She and her friend Jack, recently out of detention, were sitting in math class her freshman year exuding attitude, "like, 'Yo, you know, we're cool.' " This was a remedial math class, and the kids considered themselves losers and always gave the teacher a bad time. This day, Jack called Alice, a new girl in class, a bitch. For some reason, Alice thought Joan said it. She turned around and exploded at Joan: "You shut the fuck up."

Joan jumped up and said, "What the fuck are you talking about? Try and tell me to shut up."

Alice demanded that Joan "sit her ass down." Joan didn't move. Nobody was paying attention to the teacher, who was trying to get both girls to cool it. Alice, her face bright red with rage, finally said, "Let's step outside."

That did it for Joan. She had a short fuse when it came to threats; there were too many at home. "You want to step outside?" she said. "I ain't stepping outside, I'm going to hit you right here right now." She smacked Alice in the face. "I got her right there. I grabbed her head and smashed it against the wall, and it was just wrestlemania.

The funniest part was when the teacher came and held Alice back so that we would stop, and while she was holding her back nobody was holding me back, so I was getting jabs at her."

The teacher pulled Alice out of the room because she was bleeding. The freshman principal came in and dragged Joan to his office. "I remember yelling all the way down the hall, 'I'll get you after school. I'll get you after school.' "

A lot of things happen when you're a wamma. People instigate a lot. "They say so-and-so said this about you, when they really didn't. Then they'll run to the other person and say, well, Joan said this about you." To confront the person is a point of honor. "Even though you don't really know if this person knows about it, you have to step up to them."

When Joan was in this crowd she regularly popped lockers and stole things from other kids and shoplifted in stores. There was little forethought. She'd be walking with a friend and it would seem "a cool thing to do at the time." She says that with her present friends it is exactly the same. "We'll just be sitting there and someone says, 'Hey, why don't we light a joint?' You don't think about how you could get in trouble or this is bad, you just do it." In other words, whatever behavior is common to a group of kids feels normal to them, whether it be doing drugs or doing homework. Whether the adult world sees the lifestyle as positive or negative is not the standard the kids are using.

Gradually Joan began to question herself. She was beginning to see that all she had done was "hide my feelings and be tough and kick everyone's ass because I didn't know any other way to do it." If adolescence is about trying on different identities, maybe it was time for her to be someone else.

Her heart was opening. She remembers an incident with Jonathan Tompkins that was part of her transformation. There was a fracas going on between two of Joan's friends in the locker area of the subschool. She stood nearby egging them on with smartass remarks and innuendos. Jonathan, getting his books from his locker, called her on her inflammatory remarks. One thing led to another, and Joan and Jonathan were battling it out verbally when she uttered something so mean to him that he stood silent. While all around her everybody was taunting him for letting a girl get the better of him, she couldn't stop looking at his downturned face. "I saw how I had hurt him and I felt terrible." She felt the pain of another and remembered after years of numbness her own pain and hurt. "I didn't want to hurt people anymore." She had become sick of seeing people get hurt because of what she or a member of her crowd did.

She realized that she wanted a future for herself. She didn't want to "grow up and get welfare and have a baby and have a husband who can't stay out of jail or who's going to dump me for some other whore next week, or not even have a job, not even graduate from high school." It could happen. She saw that girlfriends were sitting home with babies. She could end up like many friends, on their own because their families don't want them. "All because we wanted to be cool," she says. "I'm glad I got out of it, because I wouldn't be here."

Joan had run away twice and had been found once by her dad and once by the police. But most of the time her dad was oblivious to her troubled ways. He knew she got suspended, that she was often in detention, "but it was like it didn't matter who I was in my world." She was, after all, only a girl. "All he cared about was that I was keeper of his house." She had to be responsible for herself. If she hadn't changed, "I guarantee you, I might be sitting here with a baby, or maybe in jail myself. I could have killed somebody, it could have been worse."

She also wanted to let out some of the tender soul she had defended so strongly to avoid pain. "People can trust me," she says. "Some people don't want to believe that right now, and some people never knew me before, and they just can't imagine me any other way. But I don't want to steal your stuff. I don't want to cuss you out because you're looking at me." She was worn out from being tough.

Joan was engaging in the riskiest behavior of all: learning to be herself. "It was very hard," she recalls, "because it's like you turn around and there's no more friends. A lot of them won't talk to me anymore, and some of them I don't even know where they are. They just backed off totally. I started thinking maybe this was the wrong thing to do."

She renewed a friendship from middle school that made all the difference. She started talking to Helmut Singh in school, and especially on the phone at night. A gentle, soft-spoken young man who had troubles of his own, Helmut told her to be who she wanted to be, to dress the way she wanted to dress, and "just don't give a shit about anybody, just do it. Just go out and talk to people. People are going to like you because it's going to be because you're yourself. You're not going to be playing a role anymore." That phone line became a lifeline. It got her through her transition. "I started forgetting about what people wanted me to be or what was appropriate and what wasn't," she recalls. "I just did what I wanted to do."

In the last months of her freshman year, the real Joan began to emerge. She started dressing in long skirts and Indian tops. She changed her hairstyle. "My old friends would look at me and say, 'What's wrong with you? You're like a grandma.' Or they'd say, 'Have you been hanging out with white people?' Stuff like that. I'd be like, 'This is what I want to wear, respect it.' " So they started respecting her but they backed away. She stayed true to herself, communicating in kinder ways, smiling more, doing things for people, and pretty soon she developed a new set of closer, more gentle friends. One of her favorites was Jonathan. Over time, she let him know what role he had played in her metamorphosis. She wanted him to understand that she now knew "People need to be treated better than I used to treat people." She says, "I know that was a stupid way to act and I know not to act that way. I know there are things that you just don't do."

She doesn't regret her "bad" years, feeling they got her through some difficult emotional times. Luckily, she straightened out before she ruined her life. By being tough, however, she learned to be smart for today's world, "what's going on, what to watch out for, where I'm safe and where I'm not."

She finds it amusing that the people who are her friends now could never fathom how she used to be—unlike Mr. Ward, for example, who has been around for the whole show. School is her connection to the larger world. Even though she considers most of the people she knows at school as the "hey, what's up" kind of people, "You can talk to them for a while." She loves the ambiance of school, the activity and the laughter. "I have wamma friends, I have black friends, I have bamma friends, I have hippie friends. I have the political 'I love Bush' kind of friends. It's fun, because you can talk about different things." She doesn't like to be limited to one group, but her closest friends are the hippies. And those are the friends she is with tonight at the concert.

The only problem is that deep inside, she is still fearful. She is always afraid that she will do something to lose the friends she has.

Even surrounded by friends who care for her, she worries that it is an illusion. "It's really hard for me to accept that they're my friends. For me, it's like they have to prove it. I don't tell them that, but I see how they act in different situations. Like if I have a problem, if they help me. Or if they call me or they invite me to go out. I've always known people that say, 'Oh, I'm your friend,' and then they don't call me to go out." If she calls them, she tests to see if they lie or make up excuses.

Action dissipates the worries, so she turns and asks her friend Leslie to dance. They walk out beyond the Pit into the open space, lock arms, and swing around together as fast as they can. Then they let go and fly backward. They come up to each other shaking their bodies and heads to the music, and lock arms again and swing around wildly, this time only letting go with one hand so they flip around. They do this as long as the beat continues, a kind of aerobic routine on a tilt-a-whirl ride. "You do whatever you want is basically the idea," says Joan as the two come laughing together off the floor. This dance is restricted to the outside area. As the girls are explaining, a couple in their early twenties come staggering out of the Pit, shaking their heads in disbelief at how "out of control this generation has gotten."

The clock registers 9:40. The chaperones begin to relax. The evening has been raucous, and they feel badgered from guarding the Pit, but all in all it has gone well. In less than an hour, it will be over and deemed a success.

Joan and her friends sit on the floor munching pizza. A number of people have already left and the room has opened up. Most kids are looking ahead to whatever comes next, since the night is young by teen standards. Joan knows she has to go home, but her friends have plans.

Suddenly, there is a burst of noise and activity from the enclosed patio off the main floor. Kids are racing around frantically getting the adults. A girl has overdosed on drugs. Adults scurry out there and come back carrying Kerry King. They rush her down the corridor and into the bathroom. Adults cordon off the hallway to keep other kids away. Kids everywhere are crying and carrying on. Joan's friend Leslie runs up to one of the chaperones and tells her she found out that Kerry had taken LSD. The chaperone runs into the bathroom to tell those tending her. In the bathroom, Kerry is sitting propped on the sink counter—her body twitching, her eyes wild and bulging with unimaginable terror. "Find out how much," someone shouts as the emergency crew rushes in to get the girl.

Leslie clams up. She says she doesn't want to get her friend in trouble. The chaperones work hard to convince Leslie that her friend is already in trouble and cannot be helped unless that information is obtained. Leslie reports, "It was three hits"—a huge amount for the tiny ninth-grader.

Theories about why Kerry did it are flying around the room. Teens argue about whether it was basic stupidity, miscalculation, or attempted suicide. Many people seem to know Kerry. She is considered to be a somewhat troubled adolescent. The fact that she is already taking medication from her therapist makes the drug overdose that much more dangerous.

The assistant director of the Community Center goes to call Kerry's parents, and a couple of her friends grab his arm as he walks toward the office. They insist that if a man, her stepfather, answers, he must ask for Marianne, her mother. Don't talk to him, they say.

Fortunately her mom answers the phone. The assistant director says her daughter is very sick and is being taken to the hospital. He asks her to meet the emergency crew there and to bring any medications Kerry is taking. The mom asks where he is calling from. He explains about the concert.

At that moment, her daughter Kerry, about whose whereabouts she had been clueless, is on the floor of a hall in the community center of a nice town that had a closely chaperoned "drug and alcohol free" concert for its youth to benefit the homeless. She is surrounded by medics madly working to keep her alive. Kerry passes into a coma and is rushed on a gurney to the waiting ambulance. Helpless, the chaperones watch in horror as the medics hook Kerry up to a heart monitor, close the doors, and race away.

Meanwhile the two young police officers who have been there all evening are asking the kids questions. They want the dealer. The kids know a name and are hedging. The officers are skilled with young people, and it is clear the kids are shaken by the event. Someone comes forward and tells the name. Several others corroborate that the dealer is a senior at South Lakes, an excellent student, who works at the local supermarket after school and who often generously gives LSD to friends as well as sells it. The kids are scared to death that they have tattled. The police would love to arrest him for attempted murder but can do so only if Kerry "makes it" and testifies. When they go to find the dealer, he has vanished. A chaperone remembers him dancing every single dance all evening long in the mosh pit, one of the few who had a placid look on his face in spite of the pummeling he received.

Many of the remaining kids leave. Others hover around in disbelief, in tears, frightened—trying to comfort each other. Leslie, Lisa, Kayla, and Joan decide to go. Leslie is still worried that she is going to get Kerry in trouble by revealing what she did. Her friends assure her the hospital would have found out anyway. Then in a haunting singsong Leslie chants, "She's going to die / She's dyyying for attention / She's dying to be heard." The girls hug Leslie, understanding she is upset.

Kids are milling around outside the Community Center, mistakenly waiting for word from the hospital. Some are angry, aware that this kind of incident screws things up for everybody. Some parents come to get their kids and decide to stick around for a while. The kids gravitate to these adults, who maybe can make sense of what has happened. The grown-ups, of course, are as shaken up as the kids to think that such a thing could happen at a well-chaperoned event. Nobody has any answers but somehow there is comfort in the clusters of teens and adults that dot the plaza for a long time after the Community Center doors are locked.

Joan is beginning to feel she has to get home. She is worried about Papa again. He is nice around everybody, but when he gets mad, he transforms, sometimes when you least expect it. Sometimes he is the most loving man in the world. Other times, he is not. She never knows what to expect.

She keeps up the chatter with her friends but the old insecurities surface. Even though she has had a great evening except for this last incident, she feels the familiar gnawing doubt about whether they really like her and will stay in her life. Are they glad she has to go home earlier than they do, or do they love and accept her with these limitations on her freedom?

Kayla drops her off at her house. It is not quite 11:00. When Joan walks in, her dad calls to her, demanding to know why she is home so late. She walks up the stairs to the living room, reminding him, in Spanish, that he agreed she could stay at the concert until now. They argue back and forth. Finally he concedes. Sitting with Papa, Joan is no longer a regular teen but, again, the keeper of his house.

Kerry recovers from her overdose and is back in school that Monday. Her mother gets angry when her subschool principal suggests that maybe it is too soon, that she needs some counseling. The school once again provides outside counselors from the Community Mental Health Center to help counsel kids who are still shaken. Such outside counselors are becoming a common sight in schools, which are regularly dealing with traumatic events that affect their students.

The adults involved in the concert are profoundly shaken. The incident shows that even the most monitored place can hold danger when there is a will to defy the rules. Future Jam for Man concerts are canceled. There are already too few community-sanctioned events for adolescents, but it is easier to cancel events than to figure out creative new ways of avoiding dangers. After this evening, the risks are too great.

## Shedding Light on Darkness:
## School Is an Uncomfortable
## Place to Learn

The excitement is palpable as the students fly above the ocean in a small plane toward Andros Island in the Bahamas. In hours, they have fled the icy depths of a particularly difficult Virginia winter, stuffed their jackets into their luggage, left their parents behind. The freedom opens them up to delicious expectation. They sense it in their teacher too as they begin their descent.

It is winter break, and Jonathan Tompkins and twenty-eight other marine biology students from South Lakes and Thomas Jefferson high schools are on an eight-day educational adventure led by Mary Ann Brown. An innovative, demanding, hands-on educator in the classroom, Brown has arranged this trip because "teaching marine biology in the Northern Virginia suburbs is like teaching mining from the surface."

The group disembarks at Andros Island cheerful and ready to roll. Most have never been in the tropics, and they find the steamy heat and lush greenery intoxicating. At sixteen hundred square miles the largest island in the Bahamas, Andros is isolated and unknown to most people because it is surrounded by a barrier reef that excludes cruise ships. The population is only about three thousand native inhabitants, many of whom still live in thatched huts without running water.

In no time, unpacked and unfettered, these suburban teens are running on the beach soaking up the beauty, flinging off their sandals and splashing happily in the ocean. Any carefully cultivated blasé demeanor rolls out to sea as the kids exclaim over the incredibly intense colors; the sky never seemed so blue, the water so crystal clear. So what if there are no hotels, no telephones, no televisions, no video games, no Walkmans. So what if they were not allowed to bring anything that makes noise, only cameras to record the trip. They go from a world of mind-numbing deafening noises to one where they actually hear the silence, broken only by the sounds of the surf and their own laughter.

Jonathan sits on the sand and gazes at the vast expanse of ocean that stretches to the horizon. He takes in the white sand sparkling like tiny diamonds in the sunlight, the barnacles freckling the shoreline rocks, the seaweed dripping moist and slimy and sensuous. He takes a deep breath and stretches, arms extended to the heavens. He lets it out, feeling relaxed and content. The sun warms his back and reaches deep into the cold darkness that fills him every winter.

Jonathan hates winter. "You get up in darkness, you don't see the sun rise, you don't see the sun all day." Every winter, depression enters his life like a rolling fog. He feels closed down, his options narrowed, the vitality seeping out of him like air from a balloon. He and his friends discuss depression, and how easy it is for someone to tell you "just get out of it." But for him it is hard. He just pushes forward and waits each year for spring to come with its promise of camping and kayaking. Too bad he can't hibernate like a bear.

In winter, he sees the darkness reflected in those around him. "All through the winter everybody walks around with their blinders on, you don't look at anybody." He sees the change after spring break when people return to school smiling at each other.

In winter, he worries more about his family. His parents separated nine years ago but have remained friends. Jonathan still believes the cold, long darkness of the winters in Alaska, where they used to live, destroyed his parents' marriage. He feels they lost each other in the unrelenting gloom of the endless nights that pushed his dad to escape by living it up with his buddies at the local bar like a character in *Northern Exposure*.

They never formally divorced, and they moved back to Reston together even though they live separately, Jonathan with his mom. Every night, his dad comes over to his mom's house and sits around and talks. "All three of us," says Jonathan. "Or I'll be upstairs doing my homework and my mom and dad will be downstairs. It's the strangest thing you've ever seen, yet it seems perfectly normal to me."

Jonathan feels responsible for jump-starting his parents, but that is difficult in the winter when his energy is depleted. "I feel like I can get them in a good mood faster than they can get me in a good mood." It takes a lot of effort on his part and the problem is, especially in winter, talk is tough. A few days before he left on this trip, the three of them were sharing a pizza and he was thinking they should turn off the TV so they could talk. But, Jonathan recalls, "I guess there wasn't that much to talk about. It was like I was trying to get some quality time in there but everyone is so isolated that it is hard to get things together." In summer when he can share fishing with his dad, gardening with his mother, the talk flows more easily. He loves his parents but the pressure of being an only child, the glue that keeps the family together, along with the knowledge that he will be gone next year gets to him.

School casts an even darker shadow on his life in the winter. Even though he has a B average, he finds school a "boring blur" that inspires little effort. He can't remember the last time he felt he was really learning something there. He gets "so wasted" from school, it takes him all the hours out of school to recover enough to return the next day. At least in spring, he can flee to a nearby park to hike or kayak in the long daylight hours. In winter, he leaves school to be stuck at home.

In the Bahamas Jonathan feels freed from these burdens, as if the brilliance of the sun sears away the inner fog and shadows. He feels connected to what is happening. Like the first full day, when the group takes a boat ride led by two International Field Studies graduate students based at the research station on Andros. The flat-bottomed dive boats skim across the pristine water revealing a magical world of tropical fish. Gemlike wonders swim past, sometimes in schools, then disappear under the coral shelves. It draws Jonathan out toward new frontiers of seeing.

Jonathan and his friends swim among the fish, feeling almost a part of them. On land, the kids explore the flora and fauna. They log the tiny creatures they see, such as the yellow skink that crosses Jonathan's path. Most impressive are the giant mangroves that form a canopy overhead, the dense underbrush, and the zillions of broken coral pieces that cover the surface of the island. Jonathan climbs a huge coconut tree with Andy. They pick coconuts that look like wiz-ened faces, crack them open, and eat the luscious sweet flesh. "It was like another world I can't describe," he later writes in his journal.

The group begins to develop a rhythm. They explore all day with various activities, keeping some time for play. At night the kids coop-eratively cook dinner, serve, and clean up. Everybody has to pitch in and all do so willingly. After dinner, members of the research station provide slide shows and lectures on the marine environment. This night the topic is evolution. It really gets the kids thinking. After-wards, before lights-out at 10:00, they record the day's activities and their impressions. Jonathan writes on evolution: "Everything about an animal can be seen by looking at it. That is to say, it forms to what it is and becomes a piece of the earth not by choice but because it is the only way to survive. Any creature becomes part of the landscape it lives in."

That's the good news in the wild and the bad news in school. To Jonathan, school is an unfriendly environment that shapes its inhab-itants in twisted, nonproductive ways. "People aren't comfortable in school," he says, "so they never learn the joy of putting everything they've got into learning." He gives the example of a recent wilder-ness first aid course he took in New Hampshire where the instructor began with the comfort of his students. He strolled into the barn, greeted the students, and invited them to make themselves comfort-able because, he said, "that is the most important thing about learn-ing." They were in a big barn and people set up hammocks or stretched out on their sleeping bags, settling in with cups of fresh coffee and glasses of juice. There were no expectations to sit in hard chairs in rows for seven hours a day. Jonathan never forgot that lesson he learned along with the first aid.

Just as important is to be comfortable with the people sharing the learning process, both students and teachers. In high school, that doesn't happen. "We don't even introduce ourselves. Teachers just say 'Okay, you're in physics.' Everybody's looking around thinking, That person's cooler than me, that person's not as cool as me, that person's hair doesn't look good today." When Jonathan becomes a teacher, as he plans, the first thing he will do is "take however long it takes until people get comfortable."

The uncaring environment of the school does not facilitate com-munication. In classes and walking down the corridors, this verbal young man goes silent. "I hardly communicate in school. Not at all, not the whole day," says Jonathan. "The most I'll say to someone is, 'How are you doing?' Or maybe I'll talk to Andy or Bill a little bit, but everybody's just sort of down on everything, including myself." Bottom line: he gets a bad feeling talking to people in school, but he knows it is because they don't have a good feeling either. "You walk by people and say, 'How's it going?' and they are like, 'How's it going?' And what are you supposed to say, 'This place sucks, man'? Or are you supposed to say, 'I'm great'?" He thinks people really don't want an honest answer. "Everybody is talking about nothing," Jonathan explains. "I like to talk about something."

In school, Jonathan concludes, "There's really no room for being honest. It just breaks your spirit. You get farther and farther down in a hole." Lost in that educational void is the dynamic substance of Jonathan. His teacher, Mary Ann Brown, who has known him since he was a little boy wandering around the townhouse development where both families live, says, "Jonathan is the kind of kid that if you had a question, you could say to him, 'Okay, find out the answer for me. Go to the library, here's a computer, go online and find out everything you can and share with us.' Ideally, that is the way education should be but it isn't. Not with this many kids. And not many kids are like Jonathan, so self-motivated."

Jonathan's potential languishes in a stultifying school environment. "I spend all my time trying to make up for the losses I get in school," says Jonathan. "It tears your soul to pieces. It is devastating to self-esteem. Everything in there is awkward." In his English class, he was struck by a poem that said, "Man, you're even collective in your isolation." At the end of it, they were supposed to write about it. "One thing I figured out was everything in nature fits into nature best by being what it is. That's not happening with the people at the school, they become dehumanized."

Jonathan wrote a poem that captures how, when people raise their hands in class to talk, they speak in inhuman voices. "There's nothing personal, nothing individual about it," he explains. "They don't want to let who they are come out. It happens to me, too." He likens the phenomenon to a sculpture his class studied in art, a flat sculpture covered with five blobs that look remotely human and then one face. "You can barely tell they're human," he says, "and then one face is at the bottom looking at them. That's what's happening in school."

This trip is proof of how nature is a powerful educator, according to Jonathan. "If you spend some time in nature, something catches your eye and you're like, Geez, how does that work? You don't ever answer that question. You figure out half of it and you ask another question." People in school are dulled by the remoteness to the real world. "High school takes ninth grade kids and turns them into a metal pole. It takes off all the edges."

Every day is a new adventure on the trip. As they drive around the island in open-backed trucks, the bumps in the road, the flying dirt jolt them to life. They duck for tree limbs and hanging vines; they wave to people along the way.

They stop to swim in Church's Blue Hole. The kids learn that it is a unique geological formation where water on the island has drained to a central point and dissolved away a hole through the island, forming a perfect circle, surrounded by cliffs.

The group, dressed in their wet suits, scramble to swim, many using snorkel equipment. What they see is a most spectacular aquarium that is for real. They had studied the fish before they left, but seeing them swimming was sensational: the zebra-striped Sergeant Major, the buttery yellow Blue Tang with the blue mascara, the breathtaking Queen Angelfish.

They manage the thirty-foot drop to the water by swinging on a rope rigged by the local navy base. For kids who have been exposed to the character building of rope-courses, this is the real thing. They whoop and holler as they swing free and drop into the water. They are students, children, adventurers one hundred percent alive in the moment.

On the way back for dinner, as they bump along happy and content from the day's activities, something wonderful happens for Jonathan. He and Andy are sitting together and talking as usual, kidding around and laughing in the way old friends do, and one of the girls says, "So, are you guys best friends?" "We said yes. It was a really special time." They had never actually admitted that to each other before, and to Jonathan it felt like a gift.

The openness among the participants on the trip excites him. "People were just free. It was a beautiful thing to see." It makes him sad to know that there are "so many beautiful people in the school that you never meet, that don't come out. Even close friends don't come out while you're in school."

He looks at this group sharing this experience and wonders how these could be the same kids from South Lakes. A realist painting he studied in art history, *The Lovers*, shows two people with bags over their heads who are kissing. Jonathan sees that barrier even between close friends. "It seems like all these people are running around and they're not feeling anything. Every day I go through school and I'm like, That's fucked up and that's fucked up and that's fucked up."

He tells about the girls at his art table. "They're like, 'Yeah, my mother left me for a week here. I can't wait to move out. She doesn't care about me.' Then they're making fun of the girl at the end of the table. Then they're like, 'Party at my house, we're going to get drunk, invite your boyfriend, you can have this bedroom.' Am I supposed to think these people are fucked up?" He feels "pretty sure what they're talking about isn't right. But at the same time, how do I know I'm right?" Sometimes he judges them; other times he feels sorry for them. But the thing that makes him mad at himself is that he rarely talks to these classmates that he sits with every day in art, to let them know he cares and to share his different perspective. He wants to tell them that "they've lost, and I have too, what's real. We're reaching into the dark."

If school is a dark place, the Bahamas are brilliant with light. Still glowing from the affirmation of his friendship, Jonathan comes back to the lodging and serves on the dinner crew. "It was so much fun. Everybody has come into their place here." After dinner, he and Rob go out and search for hermit crabs along the shore. Before going to sleep he writes in his journal: "I feel so real, like I am in the center of the galaxy."

The next day, he meets nature head on. Andy, Rob, and he take a morning swim. Out a hundred yards from shore, they come face to face with a barracuda, about five feet in length. They edge away and it stalks them. "It was cold and mean-looking," recalls Jonathan. "I was scared to death." Rob's first instinct is to tear-ass in the opposite direction; Andy and Jonathan's is to band together. They tell him to come back and stay in a group. The barracuda follows the boys a good twenty-five yards, moving in closer as they retreat to shallower waters. "I kept my calm like we were the antelopes stalked by wolves. But if there were more than one I would have crapped in my pants, seriously." The boys yell to other people to get out of the water. Finally they reach shore, hearts pounding, bodies trembling, flooded with relief. That's when they find out there was no chance the barracuda would have hurt them. "You're not supposed to be afraid of them," relates Jonathan sheepishly. "They're not supposed to bite."

Another adventure awaits them as the group goes out for a three-day trip on two boats. They are sailing on the ocean side of the island after exiting a sheltered cove in a light rain. They watch with fascination as a storm approaches, the darkness sweeping across the sky, the winds increasing. They are engulfed by rough seas. The boats toss wildly, waves crashing over the sides. Mary Ann Brown is terrified she is going to lose one of the kids. Kids are vomiting, screaming. Luckily, they get through it. When they anchor that evening in another cove, the rain has stopped but the winds remain bone-chilling cold. After dinner, the group discusses what would happen if they fell overboard, no longer an exercise but a vital piece of knowledge to have. "For a lot of the kids," says Brown, "it gave them an immediate sense of the power of nature, how cruel it can be."

The integrity of each piece of the trip forms a unified whole—unlike the seven unrelated periods of a school day—a rhythm rooted in clear boundaries, goals, and schedules. Even though each day is packed with activity, life seems to move slower than at home. In nature, Jonathan theorizes, there is no time, there is just a flow. The natural rhythm brings out the best in people. There is more honest conversation based on shared experiences, and ultimately the participants cohere into a community of learning and living.

The feelings are not unique to being in nature, says Jonathan. The same sense can come through any kind of really compelling interest that's thorough and absorbing. "It could be carving wood, making furniture, dancing, a sport. As long as it comes from inside," he explains. "If it's a parent who says you must play football because I played football and you have to be perfect at it, that won't do."

Too often his generation wants to escape to the quick sensation, "like wanting to have sex because it makes you feel something fast, like an instant gratification." He thinks when kids smoke dope, they're trying to escape from school, from their parents, from society. But along with the escape, "at the same time, drugs allow you to look back on what's going on." They allow the user to step out of civilization and assess it. To Jonathan, marijuana "is an important part of understanding yourself and what's going on in the earth, how strange this place really is." When he smokes, he only does it in the outdoors, not to escape or step outside of nature but to become a part of it.

As the week goes by Jonathan feels the old tension building. He feels the pressure to make every second count, like Thoreau said,

"Now or never." The message is driven home when he wants to go talk to a girl who has been a bright and enthusiastic participant in everything going on. He loves her spirit and wants to know her better. He starts walking toward her, then hesitates. "I had everything together and I chickened out," he recalls. He decides to do it later, and goes and wrestles with his friend Rob instead. In the middle of the horsing around he gashes his foot. He has no idea what happened except that he should have talked to the girl. "Now or never."

As his teacher sees it, Jonathan broke a rule by not wearing something on his feet at all times because of the broken coral everywhere. She is terribly distressed that he needs stitches, since medical care in the area is inadequate. Jonathan cannot understand why she is so upset. What he hopes is he remembers next time to go for the girl.

The last day, Jonathan takes his journal to a private spot on the beach to record his thoughts. "I have found so much here by this ocean," he writes. "I hope I can take it with me over the horizon to my door. I have met happy people who have light in their eyes."

He later admits that he would never have all his thoughts about school and civilization if he had not had the perspective that a week away provided. It was the opportunity to live a different way in a different place that opened doors for him.

As the time of departure nears, the tanned, ragtag kids amble around the airport, close-knit and satisfied with their week. They can't believe how much they learned while having so much fun. Mary Ann Brown watches them with the satisfaction of success. On this kind of adventure, she says, "you make a connection on a very different level." Before they left, they were just teacher and students. But then they cooked, cleaned, and studied together. They saw each other wet, straggly, and everybody was equal. They experienced every day together whether seasick on a boat or swimming in Blue Hole, and it became a shared learning experience because nobody knows it all. "You learn to depend on one another. You learn from them, they learn from you, you all learn from the staff. You come back with a tremendous feeling of camaraderie."

Brown is content in the knowledge that in terms of a learning experience, this trip went way beyond marine biology. For a lot of kids, such an experience awakens dreams, cements an essential connection between life and learning, and opens new vistas to explore.

But once off the plane, kids exchange tearful hugs and kisses good-bye. Even though most live in the same area and will see each other in class on Monday, it can never be the same. "I felt fine at the airport," remembers Jonathan, "but on the plane flying above Andros Island, I became depressed. When I got back I was just trashed out. The second I got off the plane, it seemed like my mind started to fall downhill."

It is dark and cold. His parents meet him and they set off in the car with Jonathan driving. They get into an argument about which route is faster. Jonathan wonders what is the rush. Then as he's driving along somebody comes up behind him and flashes their lights to hurry him out of their way. Jonathan is pissed. "I figured if I felt this messed up after coming back to this place, that maybe this whole place was messed up and maybe my parents were messed up too."

They go out for dinner and Jonathan watches his parents to see if they are okay. He decides his dad is acting weird. He gets worried again about his dad's depressive side and that makes him worry about his own shadows. He thinks of a line from a Bob Dylan song: "And hold your judgment for yourself/Lest you wind up on this road." The cold of the night chills Jonathan through and through even in the warm restaurant.

The next week, Jonathan hands in his personal journal and his trip log. He writes a note to his teacher sharing his sadness: The trip was amazing. He learned so much. "In that one week I spent in the Bahamas, in that one month I spent at National Outdoor Leadership School backpacking in Montana, I did more thinking and learned more about life than I learned in all four years in high school." The outdoors is the only place that he feels whole and at peace. That is why leaving the Bahamas is terribly sad. He wishes that he could come up with a way to always combine learning with nature.

His teacher writes back: "I can really empathize with you. It was very hard for me to come back even though I felt a tremendous responsibility at Andros. I hated coming back to the 'Rat Race.' May your dreams come true, Jonathan!"

# MAKING

# SENSE

*A*s I got to know the kids better our meetings shifted out of my living room, out of their bedrooms, away from fast-food restaurants to my office. I moved an easy chair in, and there in the quiet we spent long hours in conversation. One-on-one we considered their lives. Only Courtney and I kept the conversations at her house because she was hardest to pin down for a meeting.

The most amazing thing had happened. We had shared enough of their lives and mine that we were communicating. What had begun as observation, then moved to interviewing, now blossomed into conversations. I had become a mirror, a sounding board they could use to bounce off ideas, try things out, get another perspective. We had become friends—not buddies, as if I were one of them, but with the intimacy that is possible if an adult cares enough to get to know them.

If Part Two is mostly about behaviors, Part Three is about making sense of these behaviors and moving forward. The mood changed from "revealing all" to "figuring it out," with the kids trying to put pieces together, telling me more, retelling things differently. Some kids, like Brendon, Chris, Charles, and Joan, seemed to be still talking about actions, but their stories were laced with more and more introspection.

Brendon told me, "I think growing up is a lot harder than it needs to be," and others in my sample expressed the same thought. His

statement was made more dramatic by his divulging his drug dealing. It was at the last minute before he left for college. We'd met
one sweltering August afternoon in 1995, to catch up, say goodbye.
I brought him a philosophical book on fly-fishing as a late graduation gift. We chatted for an hour tying up loose ends, looking ahead.
He had been open as usual about school, his escalating drug use,
his anger, and particularly his love for Carol, who had left several
days before for college. He followed me to my car talking and, as
I stood with key in hand, he alluded to the scope of his drug dealing. Startled at the magnitude of what he was disclosing, I asked
if he had any moral compunction. He blew it off, saying, "Somebody will be doing it. There's a market and I can use the money."
Quite frankly, I was appalled at his lack of conscience but curious
to discuss it further. As I often did, I made a date to come back
right away to continue the conversation. He agreed. The next
day, midway through the discussion with my recorder on, I asked
why he was telling me all this. He answered it was because he
trusted me. An hour later, my head spinning with the risks he
was taking and the equanimity he seemed to feel about doing it, I
asked again why he was telling me. This time he said in a weary
voice that he "had to discuss it with someone." It was a dramatic
example of how kids, even the ones we might think are incorrigible,
want guidance. He wanted to be heard and, at some level, to be
stopped.

The kids, if we get to know them, will decimate every long-held
stereotype any adult has ever had about teens. As one teacher told
me, "Regular kids are getting more irregular." They are not all doing
bad things—that is not the point—they are simply more complex
than we could ever imagine.

Brendon's telling me and my listening set loose the deepest parts
of him. We spoke for hours, and I left shaken but convinced that
tenacity is key in breaking through adolescent defenses even as they
try to fend you off. Brendon knew I disapproved of his activities; we
both took a chance on honest communication. What Brendon really
trusted was not that I wouldn't tell (later we spoke and he encouraged me to lay it all out in the book), but rather that I knew all the
parts of him. To me, he was not just an evil drug dealer, a delinquent.
I also knew he was spiritual, artistic, and loving. He counted on me
to remember that once all he wanted was to be a good Christian boy

immersed in school spirit. He knew I remembered and understood that smiling Fred Flintstone on the freshman float was part of him too.

In this section I let the kids reveal themselves in their own words more than in earlier sections. It is in their voices you will hear them grappling with the issues, their revelations, their insights. In this section their actions take a back seat to their secrets, their courage, their struggles. For some of the kids the process is wrenching, for others a more gradual maturation.

I went back to them again and again to make sure I got it right, each conversation encouraging deeper thought on both our parts. I had to respond when Jonathan implored, "Is the future really bleak?" I had to listen to Chris's struggles in eighth grade with the same seriousness as I listened to Ann and Courtney's heartbreaking tale. His life is as important, his struggles as real within his context. I was honored that Jessica was able to share some of her deepest loves with me, and sad that she felt constrained elsewhere. I listened with fascination when she and her friends explained the lure of the underworld. I was part of those soap operas that began the first semester I went to school: Where will Joan end up in her desperate search for acceptance? Will Charles get revenge in lacrosse? Can Jonathan find a meaningful course to pursue after high school? Will Brendon self-destruct from anger, spin out of control, or are his anchors sufficient?

I listened and talked, but I never told them what to do unless they asked my opinion. Sometimes they talked just to hear how something sounded out loud. They were trying to figure out what they thought about themselves. I was simply a witness. Sometimes they would act bold when they were scared, act angry when they were hurt, act like they didn't care when they did. But because I knew and had time, eventually the truth would come out.

It was a gut-wrenching yet exhilarating experience for me. Adolescents are acutely aware, curious, deeply into the pulse of life. They need to know so much and earlier than before, they need to sort out life's complexities. Yet as they grapple, albeit awkwardly, with the same world that confounds us adults, we want to control delivery of information as if that will stop them from arranging their friend's abortion, having sex, doing drugs, sneaking out in the middle of the night, and so on.

*As the writing of this book progressed, I read sections of chapters, even entire chapters, to some of the kids. There was always a sense of wonder—"My god, that is me! How did you know how I was feeling! How could I have done that?" I knew what I knew because they told me in words, in actions, in comportment. Face-to-face over time it was not so difficult to figure out.*

## 15

# *Rearrange Your Room When You Can't Arrange Yourself*

On a late August afternoon, Chris Hughes is standing in the middle of total meltdown in his bedroom. What a mess. The furniture is all pushed to the middle, the posters are off the walls, with nothing left behind but pieces of tape, bits of paper. The books from his bookcase are in several piles on the floor; bedding, clothes, and other things are all lumped together.

His mother peeks in and asks if he wants some help. He declines. She tosses in some garbage bags and storage boxes and leaves. Believe it or not, Chris loves this kind of work. He likes his stuff and his control over it. He happily works for hours with his television going in the background.

He has always been an arranger and sorter. His collections since he was a young child are legendary in the household: from the stuffed animals he had as a tiny boy, to the Ninja Turtles, Masters of the Universe figures, and monsters both natural and imaginary, to his shell, mineral, and sports card collections, he has kept them in order. Even as a youngster, he wanted his toys separated by type, and hated it when a G.I. Joe tank lost a wheel. A funny, happy, kid who appears more carefree than rigid, Chris finds some kind of inner satisfaction from periodically rearranging his possessions.

This summer's project amounts to a major remodeling job. It is no coincidence that it is occurring as he prepares to enter eighth grade, as if some inner voice confirms for him that it will be tough, a decision-

making time and also a time that will challenge who he is. He knows
that by eighth grade a lot of "cool" kids are involved in the fast track
of parties, drinking, even sex, but he is not interested. It's tricky. He
wants to be cool, but is content at just thirteen to remain a young
teen. He's not naive—he's grown up with older brothers and their
friends around, and he hears what's happening. He knows he will be
faced with choices that test his values. Chris is not a boy of many
words. His actions provide the clues to what is going on inside. So
the enormity of the remodeling task he is undertaking underscores
the drama of the upcoming transition.

Bedroom redecorating is an unrecognized ritual in adolescent life
because the Big Mess that torments parents has won top billing.
August seems to be a favorite time. What at first may appear an
antidote to end-of-summer doldrums may actually be a vehicle
for taking control. A bedroom, especially when not shared with a
sibling, is usually seen as a safe haven, an expression of self when
the outside world is messy and confusing. The remaking of the bedroom is carefully thought through and often takes days. It is a
youngster's attempt to "edit self," an externalization of the idea that
each new school year, kids see the possibility of starting fresh, remaking themselves.

Last night Chris's room was a happy reminder of younger days, a
cumulative hodgepodge of his life. There were posters for children's
books, sports heroes, cast-off psychedelic posters once belonging to a
brother, prizes from school fairs, school awards, vacation souvenirs.
His bookshelves were filled with notebooks full of sports cards, books
that ranged from Roald Dahl to Steven King, comic books, school
yearbooks. The drawers under his bed were overflowing with clothes,
toys, things. It was a typical kid's room, bursting with the energy and
wide-ranging interests of its inhabitant. But it cried out for an over-
haul. Chris was ready to pause, rethink, and regroup.

Today, he begins his attack. First, the toys. There are boxes to put
things in the attic to save for "my kids," there is a huge bag to fill for
charity, and there is the trash. Books are all saved, and he packs them
smiling as he remembers some of the stories. Out in the hall are a
growing pile of boxes and rolls of old posters. Chris would never in a
million years admit it, but he is sentimental about the memories
gathered in these storage boxes. It is clear to his parents, who peek in
periodically, that their son is involved in a ceremony of his own design to reach closure on his childhood and enter a new stage.

The summer before eighth grade something wells up in Chris and his friends: what starts as louder and louder boy stuff—the grossness, the cracking knuckles, the rough-and-tumble competing with friends—begins to be paralleled by new concerns about what styles are right, what hobbies are cool, and new notions about what their social lives should be. Large gestures and loud sounds seem to be the male way of signaling more subtle changes inside, or of drowning out the confusing surges of puberty.

The pressure of eighth grade is different from the conformity of seventh grade when the point was more to fit in than to make waves. Eighth graders want to stand out, be positioned appropriately among their peers. But the pose better be right. It is about public fronts and private values in an environment that does not encourage consonance.

If Chris knows who he is at home, that gives him a secure base to depart from as he defines himself among peers. It is in the arena of peers that the struggle for self-definition is waged. The kids hunger for each other, which is why even though many hate school, it is the happening place. As Chris evaluates every item in his room as to its acceptability for a boy his age, he's both full of positive expectation and girding himself for battle.

It has been a great summer for Chris, offering opportunities to stretch boundaries. His parents insisted that his summer be full of activities—not so easy to find for young adolescents. Many of his friends spent the summer sitting for siblings or "just hanging out," which often becomes an invitation to misbehave. The special needs of this age group being addressed in the middle school concept are generally abandoned in the summer and during school holidays.

Luckily for Chris, his summer is planned to provide some new opportunities that are fun. His first real break from home was at Art Monk football camp, an ultimate male-bonding experience led by Real Life Football Players like Monk himself; Tim Johnson, a defensive lineman; and kick-and-punt returner Brian Mitchell. The biggest challenge: going without a friend, a brave departure for a member of an age group dependent on buddies. With characteristic determination, Chris greeted his unknown roommate from downtown D.C. shyly, hugged his parents goodbye, and never looked back. When he called home the next day, he already sounded more confident and independent. It turned out to be a wonderful experience. He lived in a college dorm, ate his meals in a college dining hall, got up at 5:00 in the morning to get a shower without competing against hundreds of other boys, and learned he could be on his own. The timid boy, dropped off by hovering parents, did just fine, and matured even over the few days. When his parents picked him up, Chris was waiting with circles under his eyes and a big smile on his face.

Male bonding was followed by teen camp in Reston, with its coed bonding. This day camp for teens is unique in filling the void. Young teens led by charismatic older teens spend their days rolling around Reston and environs in the teen camp van. The best part was the camping. Exploring nature was easy coupled with (against-the-rules) kissing in a tent, the consequence of "Truth or Dare" games. Chris settled into the easy companionship of this group, even gave hard rock a try. He'd been waiting to be with Katy, Jessica Jones's friend, and he had a ball. Her spirit and daring were seductive. She's smart and funny and has a much freer spirit than he does, and though he may not know of her forays in the middle of the night, he senses them. She opened up a new world and he brought his buddy Brad along.

Brad and Chris become blood brothers of sort in a colossal end-of-summer football crash that occurs on a Sunday afternoon in the Hughes family room, of all places. Acting out their football fantasies for the season, they pass and tackle around the room. Chris crashes into Brad, loosening his own front teeth in a cascade of blood, gashing his friend's knee with his braces.

With camp over, Chris concentrates on his room. He and his mom make a number of shopping trips. He needs storage containers for clothes, magazines. Central to the decorating scheme are new posters that create a pantheon of sports heroes: Reggie White, the Minister of Defense; Randall Cunningham; Joe Montana; Bruce Smith; Ken Griffey Jr.; Michael Jordan; Mario Lemieux; Thurman Thomas; the Bulls; the Dream Team, arranged along his walls and across his ceiling. He takes all his Reston League football pictures and arranges them above his pillow; he clusters his trophies, from childhood soccer through football in the present, on a bookshelf. This is a room where a young boy dreams of his potential to be a superstar.

For days he is lost in the work—things down and up, shifted and moved. He rearranges his furniture. He hangs up all his clothes in his closet by category, permanently removing the closet door so he can see what he has. He wants no just-in-case clothes that never get worn. They go to the homeless. A long shelf over his window which once held a little boy's collection of stuffed animals now houses a growing sports cap collection. Stacked neatly on the bookshelves is his prized *Sports Illustrated* collection. His parents can only gawk at what is going on.

As the new room emerges, so does the school year. Football practice begins. The high school band practices marching routines for hours on the outskirts of the field. Teachers come to school to set up their classrooms. Pools start closing as the college-age lifeguards return to their campuses. Reston is readying itself for fall.

Each day, Chris goes to practice complaining about running laps but enthusiastic about the game. He eagerly waits for the requisite five days to pass before they get to hit and tackle. Out on the field he looks over to the high school. He feels excitement, not fear, that he will actually be there next year in the stadium.

Brad and Chris have one last sleepover at Chris's. They camp out in the family room. They stay up most of the night for a horror movie marathon. At 4:45 A.M., they are still up watching *976-EVIL II*; then they sleep through most of the next day. Early mornings will come soon enough.

Late in the afternoon of Labor Day, Chris emerges from his room with a big smile. His room is finished just in time. "You can do anything when everything is organized," he says. The first Monday-night football signals fall. Tomorrow he will be an eighth grader. He carefully lays out his clothes, a James Madison University T-shirt and long purple shorts. He loads his backpack with one small notebook and a pen, minimalist that he is. Then a final touch: He wants to know if his dad has a leather wallet he can use instead of the Ocean Pacific one he's had for years. With his new if-my-feet-are-growing-I-will-too size 8 shoes and a "man's wallet," Chris is set to go.

The year starts on a high. The buses now separate middle and high school, so the eighth graders are hands-down the Bosses. Chris and his pals in the neighborhood flaunt it by announcing to the seventh graders in the bus that the coveted back seats are reserved for them.

School quickly gets down to business. This year has a change for Chris. His parents had lobbied for him to get certain teachers and it meant changing teams. Usually each year the teams are mixed up, but this year they haven't been, so that means he's the "new kid" even though he knows most everybody on his team. He presents a

stoic face, but he misses the team that had voted him Most Likely To
Succeed Boy. His discomfort is compounded because there is a school-
wide push for excellence at the expense of the kids' community standards. All of a sudden, good students are being showcased in an adult
effort to make excellence "cool." By the end of first quarter, honor
roll students are listed on classroom bulletin boards, are asked to do
special things in the classroom (positioned uncomfortably as "teacher's
pet"), and are even pulled out of class for a special Honor Breakfast.
Chris, absolutely committed to good grades, finds the spotlight an
embarrassment. He becomes preoccupied with calculating what is
necessary to remain socially relevant to his peers and what is required to ace his classes. His own internal drive for excellence is driven underground. "In Forest Edge, my friends and I wanted to get
straight As all the time," he says. "But something happened. It must
be a new attitude. It's not everybody, but some people just don't respect you when you get good grades."

If last year the Big Issue was girl problems, this year it is science
class. The class gets off to a bad start. The first teacher, a meek, well-
intentioned young man, had never taught in public schools, and by
the end of the first month he quit in horror. The second teacher, although seasoned in Fairfax County schools, is weak on discipline and
the class, already unruly from the teacher they scared to death, never
gets into a serious mode. "Her room was bad. She let anything go
by," Chris says. A few of the fellows in the class see Chris as a tempt-
ing target. Anytime he passes by them, especially while "helping the
teacher," the humiliating reward for good grades, they hit him on the
back of the legs. It is Chris's pride that is hurt. Badly.

Chris is torn. He doesn't want to take it, and he doesn't want to
get into trouble. What bothers him the most is that the perpetrators
seem not to like him. He feels that somehow he has to be cooler
to meet their approval. Probably he has to be more like them. But
maybe that won't work either.

He shares his dilemma with his parents. The worst thing, from
their point of view, is the problem is distracting Chris from the science that he likes so much. He withdraws into a shell for months.

Chris's problems, the judgment of his peers in science and the pressures surrounding his relationship with Kim last year, might seem
bush league in a society where kids are dealing with addictions, eating
disorders, depression, and serious violence. But these are the problems
that surround him in his world, and his pain is no less real. The issue

is to help him deal with what life hands him. It gets to the point where he dreads the class, yet he forbids his mom to talk to the teacher because that would make him the butt of more derision. His mom does anyway, but makes the teacher promise not to say anything to the boys. It becomes a minidrama in how disruption and intimidation rule the milieu of school. That same year, a report is presented to the Fairfax County School Board documenting disturbing trends in student behavior and discipline: Only 56 percent of middle school students feel safe in their school. In elementary school, 98 percent of students respect teachers, 95 percent respect peers; in middle school, the rates drop to 46 percent and 42.7 percent; in high school, they increase only marginally.

Chris is navigating these troublesome waters. His science teacher's only solution is for Chris to change classes, which would upset his whole schedule. So he has to live with it and figure out what he can do to change things.

Thank goodness for his civics class with Mr. Lundy. Lundy, with his nine-scoop ice-cream tie and goofy sense of humor, is Chris's favorite. "He was a cop," says Chris respectfully. "He's strict but funny. He lets you talk but he won't let you get too loud. He'll keep you under control." Chris thinks he is a great teacher because he has an ability to excite his students by explaining the subject well, and keeping order in the classroom.

Steve Lundy's secret is that he likes young adolescents. He not only finds them fun and interesting to be around, but also believes in their ability to learn. "People keep saying these kids are on a plateau intellectually and they don't learn anything in seventh and eighth grade, they are all into emotions. That is a bunch of garbage. They may be putting it into a somewhat different context because of their interest in social behavior, but if you include socializing in what you are doing, you will get them to learn a ton. If you push them along into things, they just might get engaged." His approach works.

Chris's art class is the only other class he really enjoys. Like Lundy, the art teachers involve their students positively; they remain in charge of their classrooms by allowing the kids some space to move and socialize and express their energies. Mrs. Cordyak, his last year's teacher, and Mrs. Bruce, this year, have style, spirit, flair, and an openness to their students. They hand-hold with Chris as he works through his artistic insecurities. "He is maybe a little lacking in self-confidence," says Diane Bruce. "He always wants to check it out before adding something to make sure it is okay and I tell him, 'It's your painting, what do you think?' I give him a bunch of choices so that he's making his own choices." Chris's interest in art is a mystery, since he is not naturally talented. It is as if he instinctively knows his creative side needs nurturing. He sits daily with some really talented boys, yet has the tenacity to keep trying. When he gets As in the course, and his bright painting of birds in the tropics is displayed in an art show at the Reston-based United States Geological Survey, he is as proud as if he scored a winning football tackle. His mom and dad frame the painting and hang it in their bedroom.

Almost always attentive and diligent in school, Chris begins to notice something: He can expend less effort and still do well. There is an automatic reward just for being respectful in class and turning up with the work completed. He is beginning to see teachers as human and fallible, and school as much more about who is behaving and doing assignments than about learning. Chris doesn't fall into the self-defeating behaviors where kids sacrifice grades. He is directed by an inner compass that seems to keep him on course. "I choose to do things because I want to get good grades and go to college," Chris says. But he is always confronted with the lure of the mediocre, the acting out, the in-your-face-I-don't-give-a-damn attitude of cool.

Part of the problem of student performance, says Lundy, is the messages they get from society. "It is easy to blame the kids, but they grow up in a paradoxical environment. You can't have people cutting down education all the time and then expect the kids to turn around and say how wonderful it is. . . . They end up not caring either." When teachers held an early-morning open house for the 125 members of Chris's team, parents of only 11 kids showed up. A counselor remarked that in the gifted and talented classes there would be standing room only. Parents who repeatedly punish their children for bad grades or trouble in class may be ignoring the reality that punishment after the fact is no substitute for surrounding them with a home environment that supports and celebrates learning.

So Chris loves and hates school all at once. He loves the social aspects, and looks forward to a few classes. But he is frequently bored, and he dreads science for months. Each day is a roller coaster. It never is relaxed and yet is often painfully dull. Chris is not alone. In *Boxed In and Bored*, Peter Scales of the Search Institute reports that research indicates as many as half of all young adolescents "feel boxed in and bored in their middle schools: boxed in because their opportunities seem too few, and bored because they have neither sufficient supportive adult relationships nor sufficient curricular challenge to feel that school is a welcoming and exciting place to be."

After the pressure cooker of school, Chris likes to come home and relax by slashing a few throats. Several times a week, Chris lumbers into the house with a bunch of friends and greets his parents with something akin to a grunt. The homework business, the how-was-your-day business is shelved until a later moment. These friends who have been around the Hughes house since elementary school suddenly fill the house with their size, deep voices, clumsy gestures, and cavernous hungers. They make Chris's bedroom seem suddenly small. It doesn't take long until the room quiets, and Jeff, Brad, and Chris, all limbs and sweat and noise, become silent and attentive. This is the year of Mortal Kombat Mania.

Their concentration is palpable. In moments, they become fully centered on the game, sweating profusely as they compete. Girls, universally acknowledged to be more socially and sexually mature in early adolescence, may sit around discussing feelings and relationships, but boys, using traditional codes of competition, scores, and shared challenges, sink comfortably into the metaphors of video games. Actually, Chris has resurrected the games after several years of ignoring them. He, unlike his brothers, cannot remember a world without video games. He grew up watching his brothers compete at Pac-Man, Space Invaders, and Missile Command as often as he watched *Sesame Street* and *The Electric Company*. Chris and his friends are truly the first multimedia generation—from Sesame Street to MTV to the Internet. They grew up as visual learners, at ease with technology, enthusiastic and quick at picking up the modes and changes in it. During their lifetime, the personal computer has become a staple in most of their homes and in their classrooms, and though few might realize it, it has been just a baby step from their video games to learning on computers.

Although the technology is displayed on Sega Genesis, several generations away from Atari and Nintendo, the attraction of video games has remained constant since their introduction in the seventies. Video games are an adolescent boy's great escape—hypnotic, somewhat addictive, providing primal satisfaction in their metaphors of heroes and villains, victors and vanquished. Although much maligned by adults, the games have always had positive aspects. They help develop the hand-eye coordination so essential in the computer age, they reward memory and concentration, and they promote sportsmanship whether in Chris's crowded bedroom or the arcade at the mall. "Video games are intellectual," says Chris. "Just being good at them makes you feel good, and it's great to beat other people at them." Mastery is respected, honored by rapt observers. But it is more. The addiction is to play and play until you beat the game itself, a quality certainly honored in sports or business. "You want to learn the moves," says Chris. "You want to be good when you go to the arcade, not sorry. Just doing the moves is hard: you have to do them at a certain speed, you have to remember how to do it all, you have to use both hands a certain way, using the controls simultaneously." Each boy sees it his own way but each feels the need to beat down a challenge and gain self-esteem.

There is cooperation as friends try to work the games out together. The process takes countless meetings and phone calls, a wide-ranging collaborative venture comprising everything from tiny slips of paper with codes to sophisticated computer printouts of complex strategies. The cooperation is often overlooked by critics, who may not be aware of how youngsters share their secrets and work together to solve a game. "It's fun to talk to your friends about the new games, buying magazines, reading about them," says Chris. Like sports, they provide growing boys with a common language, goals, and a vehicle for easy companionship.

The arcade has replaced the corner soda shop. At Tysons Corner Shopping Center, Chris and his friends spend hours at Fun Time arcade, watching as much as playing. In this almost totally male environment, the lights are dimmed, voices are muffled, and the air is electric with tension—and lots of psychedelic blinking lights. There are security guards, but most of the time there is little reason for them. The Game is the great equalizer of ages, races, and attitudes. There is posturing all around but the valued commodity is skill. The main focus of attention is Mortal Kombat, even better and more gross on the large arcade screen. Chris and Jeff stand in awe watching a master. It's the death moves that grab the crowd: Raiden electrocutes with bolts of lightning, Kano rips out his opponent's still-beating heart, Sonya Blade (the token female) gives the burning kiss of death, and—the absolute favorite—Sub-Zero tears his foe's head off and holds it up victorious as the spinal cord dangling from the neck continues to twitch. The gruesome murders are called "finishing moves."

"Mortal Kombat was great because of the gore and blood and guts. But you don't see kids just playing a game and then going down into the shops and killing somebody," explains Chris defensively, responding to Kombat criticism in the media. "It's not real—you don't just go up to somebody and rip their heart out and look at it!" He and his buddies say they like the violence because it "looks good"—meaning the graphics. Brad concludes: "Kids don't think the way adults think they think."

The games never completely preoccupy Chris as they do some of his friends. After an hour or so on a schoolday, Chris always tells his friends to leave. He has homework to do. When the boys are gone he gives his mother a hug hello. They talk about "the homework situation," he goes to the bathroom with the sports page, rummages in the kitchen for his snack, and returns to his redecorated room to work.

The year begins to settle into a rhythm, except for the science problem. He decides that the key is to make friends with the boys bothering him. Finally, in an act of tremendous courage that goes against all his principles, he starts hitting them back every time they hit him, when the teacher isn't looking. It is a Pyrrhic victory because he knows they are the winners by getting him to act against his own behavior code. "They still do it," he says with a sigh, "but it's friendlier because I feel safe to hit them back." In retrospect, he says, "I should have switched. I like the people better in seventh period."

This class irritates Chris's Achilles' heel. He prides himself on having a wide mix of friends. The only kids that he has trouble with are those who come across as supersuave, with an ultracool veneer of indifference and a superior attitude that excludes him. They always make him feel awkward and inferior. It is precisely such boys that get his goat in science.

Football helps. He breaks loose with his aggression, his command of the skills. His fortitude and perfectionism come out on the field. The camaraderie and friendship among the team also free his sense of humor, his playfulness, his determination. Like his male buddies, of course, he explains none of this in detail—just smiles and says, in late November, that it was his "personal best season ever." The season ends and he has the satisfaction of having started offense and defense and getting "a hell of a lot of tackles." That's code for "I did well; it was great."

Winter comes and goes, with the added bonus of a slew of snow days off, which Chris savors along with the entire student population in Fairfax County. Spring arrives, and before they fully enjoy eighth grade, he and his classmates are asked to select their high school courses. A South Lakes counselor comes to talk to them and delivers the hard line. He starts with the reasons kids fail: number one, poor attendance; then substance abuse. Once again, the implication is that adolescents will never behave unless scared. The kids are sick and tired of all the ominous warnings about everything. What they yearn for is to grow and learn alongside each other with time to socialize and space to adjust to their rapidly changing selves.

Health class, required of eighth graders, is supposed to assist. This quarter, physical education class moves from the rules of sports to the darker side of life. With the emphasis on rote learning rather than discussion, it heaps buckets of definitions, explanations, and statistics about abuse—sexual and verbal, sibling, spouse, elder—and the line between neglect and abuse. Chris and his classmates learn that one youngster in four becomes the victim of sexual abuse before he or she reaches eighteen. Sexual topics are touched ever so carefully. They learn to "Just Say No" for about the millionth time and get a rundown on the usual litany of drugs from tobacco and alcohol through heroin. It's so boring.

What the students don't get, according to health teacher Carol Clark, are enough real-life coping skills. The course aims to accomplish so much in a short period of time that "We don't have time to do more than a short unit on decision making. We need to have role play for kids to get them to work it out," whether it be around drinking, smoking, sex, fighting, or teen abuse. One film they are shown, Clark continues, instructs the youngster to cope by filling a beer can with Coke to be socially acceptable. "But it is hard to get these kids to give an excuse because they want to fit in. Some of them aren't strong enough." Each day she teaches, and especially this year because her own daughter is an eighth grader, "In my gut I am scared to death because you can't choose their friends. They have to start making their own choices and decisions."

This course reflects the world accurately, but it is out of sync with the reality of kids like Chris who need opportunities for beginning to mix socially with some independence, and who are confronted repeatedly with the message that the only alternatives are to go from nothing to a social life fraught with dangers. Paradoxically, the reality and the hype of the current social scene slow down the social development of young teens rather than speed it up. There are few popular age-appropriate events like the old sock hops and hayrides their parents might remember. Most kids seem to do nothing, or venture minor forays to the mall or the movies, while the real social-izers move directly to the party scene or social underground. It's no wonder most kids get bored. Boys and girls want to be together at this age, but society fails to create enough safe developmental social opportunities that catch on.

The unit in health class that catches Chris's attention is on values, and only because his teacher, William Bryant, engages them in the process. "When he asked us to define our own personal values and goals, it made me think," remembers Chris. "I never saw them in front of me like that." It takes days. With great ceremony they are typed out for signature by parents and teacher, then placed in indi-vidual picture frames. Values resonate with Chris because they con-firm his instincts about what matters. This is what his final product looks like:

## My Steps in Life

| *Values* | *Short-Range Goals* |
|---|---|
| 1. good grades | 1. good grades |
| 2. family | 2. good grades on finals |
| 3. life | 3. graduate from Hughes |
| 4. friends | 4. drug-free |
| 5. education | 5. do all my homework |
| 6. health | 6. get to class on time |
| 7. success | 7. be courteous to my teachers |
| 8. drug-free | 8. get friends |
| 9. money | 9. don't get in trouble |
| 10. good job | 10. do all my work |

| *Medium-Range Goals* | *Long-Range Goals* |
|---|---|
| 1. good grades | 1. get accepted to good college |
| 2. meet new people | 2. get a scholarship |
| 3. get to class on time | 3. get married |

4. graduate from South
   Lakes
5. always go to class
6. drug-free
7. do all my work
8. good grades on SATs
9. don't get in trouble
10. be courteous to my
    teachers

4. have kids
5. get a job
6. get a house
7. make lots of money
8. pass college
9. live long
10. die peacefully

Chris gives his list to his dad on Father's Day. It is hung on the wall in front of his dad's desk.

Sports again saves the day for Chris when other domains are ambiguous. This spring Charles Sutter introduces him to lacrosse. His parents had suggested he play this game he never heard of. They told him that it might be fun for a football player, and it would be good to have a spring sport since baseball was a flop. He hemmed and hawed. Chris was shy the day his mom dropped him off at the Sutters' to watch some tapes of the game, but he found the combined persuasion of two lacrosse enthusiasts impossible to resist. They watched the tapes and Chris thought it looked pretty cool. Then Charles took Chris outside with a stick and showed him how to catch, as he had been taught years before.

The season gets off to a disappointing start. The tryouts for the team are on a cold, damp March day when the Sutters cannot be there. The boys' team meets at the infamous Mount Trashmore, a field created out of landfill adjacent to the county dump. The smell is horrendous. Chris sits alone, discouraged, and chilled to the bone when his parents arrive to pick him up. He's not going to do it, he tells them. They suggest he try a few more practices before he decides, that he has nothing to lose. The next time the location is better, it is bright and sunny, and best of all, people he knows are with him.

Chris decides he wants to be a goalie. The coach says he has good reflexes, and that the goalie is supposed to be a leader, "the eyes of the team." Chris is ready to step forward as a leader in this domain. He loves the challenge and commits to working hard to become a crackerjack goalie. The game opens new vistas for him.

He writes in his creative writing journal: "I had my first lacrosse game on Saturday, April 11. We played Lake Ridge, which is a really good team. They got a couple of lucky shots. I got a lot of saves but my favorite part of the game goes like this: There is a clear where the goalie runs out and throws the ball up the field. I did that and the other team's player hit the ball out of my stick. While he was going for the ball, I laid him flat out on the ground."

In May, he learns another lesson in how there can be victory in defeat. In a lacrosse game against Lake Braddock, his team is clearly outplayed but Chris is getting control of the leadership position in goal. He yells and screams at his team, prods them on, chastises, tries his hardest. He is furious at himself when goals get through—he slams his stick on the ground in anger—but proud of his stops. His sense of perspective is growing along with his height, strength, and coordination. He does his little ritual at the goal like those he's watched in the high school games—two taps on each side with his goalie stick. He ends the season hooked on this fast-moving, hard-hitting sport and plans to go to lacrosse camp to sharpen his skills.

Another sport, another award ceremony. At a picnic in the warm sunshine of June, parents and kids gathered around on blankets on the grass listen as the coach says a few words about each player. When it is Chris's turn, Coach McKeon says he thinks the boy had "the biggest talent hurdle this year." Warmly, he goes on: "I'd come screaming out on the field pointing a finger and yelling at Chris: Chris, get back there. Chris, don't do this. Chris, get the ball up. . . . He never quit. His clutch saves really kept us in the program. He made an extraordinary transition from the first day out to the last day in the program. . . . You made a difference. I hope you're going to hang in there." Everybody applauds.

It's been a short stop in middle school. Chris breaks loose with his own version of middle school in a final art assignment, on the topic of perspective, in which the students are asked to draw the locker area. Chris needs no hand-holding on this one. He draws the brightly painted lockers in yellow, red, and orange; each is marked by a number and locked with a tiny combination lock. They stand on crumbling cliffs with white-hot flames breaking through the cracks. Stalactites hang down from above. "I guess you could say it is a type of hell," he says. "All the kids know the lockers were a big fight area, where everyone was crunched, a kind of trap." The locker area is ground zero for acceptance in middle school. Chris came in with concerns about lockers and leaves with the symbolic lockers of his experience.

He piles on the achievement awards again at the end of the year but they don't mean as much as with the old team. His parents tell him they are like war decorations signifying how he held on to his values and concentration when all the middle school forces seemed to work against him. He grew five inches in one year (most important), developed a sense of mastery in art and lacrosse, and maintained good grades. He learned there are things that matter in his home world and things that matter in his school world.

Chris is a realist who sees things for what they are. He carries with him a strong sense of right and wrong, a vision of a future where he already understands that what he does and how he handles himself day to day can make a difference. Always interacting with the world through myriad activities that his parents support, he invests his identity not solely in any one area but in several, from sports to school to friendships and family. Unlike many other adolescents, he doesn't act out in secret places outside the range of adult vision but rather shines in arenas openly available to adolescents where the generations interact. Even in this public adolescence he has private struggles, but the stark aloneness other adolescents often feel does not haunt him.

Middle school has been an unpleasant passage. Like most of his classmates, he doesn't bother going to his eighth grade celebration. Bottom line: eighth grade wasn't much fun. He's ready to move on, excited about high school. To this transition he brings a more mature self, proven in sports and school and able to overcome hurdles. His athletic involvement is his greatest joy, a clear sign for him that his prowess is no longer the dream of a little boy but the attainable goal of a hard-working athlete. In his room, he has moved some of the posters of the greats to make room for a gallery of his own team pictures and achievements. Now when he lies in bed, he can look at the wall and see pictures of himself growing and changing through time and dream of what Chris Hughes can be.

At the end of the school year, Brad comes home with him again. They while away a hot afternoon playing video games. Chris is happy and comfortable. His room is in order and so is his life. Just the way he likes it.

# The Dilemmas
# of a Fourteen-Year-Old Girl:
# Contradictions as a Way of Life

A humongous bright red, blue, and yellow dinosaur occupying a huge space in front of St. John Neumann Church seems to be laughing uproariously from its belly. Upon closer scrutiny, one sees flying bodies, a jumble of feet and hands, and millions of red, yellow, and blue balls. The giggles are from Jessica, Annie, and Rachel, jumping and carrying on inside. It is a trampoline rented for the opening celebration of Agape, the church youth group. It is a rare moment of pure play by three young teens seldom invited to be simply kids. Everybody is having a wonderful time. It is a picture-perfect illustration of how adults wish adolescence would be, a gathering of teens for a church activity led by adults who want to work with them. "Father Jim"—as the kids call James M. Turner, the priest in charge—wanders comfortably among his flock sporting a Brine lacrosse cap turned backwards, a T-shirt over gray running shorts, socks with red stripes, and Saucony running shoes.

The girls tumble out of the dinosaur flushed and happy, and sit on the grass to put on their shoes. Dressed in shorts, T-shirts, and sneakers, they are a vision of wholesomeness. Jessica, the social coordinator for her friends, asks if that was fun, and gathers them up for the next event: football with the boys. Then dinner and the convening of the group. Jessica is pleased her friends are joining. She has plans this year for Annie and Rachel to come to her house on Sundays for dinner and then go to the meetings, "like a little family."

As Jessica enters ninth grade, her priorities are her friends, her grades, and getting a Real Boyfriend. Her ambitions for school now exceed her longtime goal of straight As. When she went to her sister's graduation in June and saw the eight honor students specially credited for achieving a 4.0 or better, she was hooked. It's only the third week of her freshman year, and she's already worried about final exams, which are nine months away, and her SATs, which are not for three years. But she is determined as usual.

She's also resolved to have a different kind of social life in high school. "I got my badness over early," she says with great conviction. Behind those words are a series of events that knocked her to her senses. But not right away.

The incident last New Year's Eve did not make much of an impression. Even though she didn't approve of what her friends did, going to Lovettsville, an hour away, with an unlicensed driver who was drunk, she saw it as "just being stupid." Her friends were all grounded a month, but when they were released, things picked up right where they left off. Jessica just wanted to be out with Rachel, Annie, and the guys, going along for the ride like they had on the roller coaster at Kings Dominion. It was fast, risky, and full of thrills. "I must have liked the party scene because otherwise I wouldn't have kept going," she says. Jessica mostly stayed at the edges of what was going on, as if dipping a toe in a raging current. It was as if she dared herself but was not entirely convinced this social scene with Cal and his friends was what she wanted. She was confident she had things under control.

Jessica's secret journey into the wild life skidded to a halt when the unthinkable happened to Rachel. She was raped by their "friend" Donny. The girls think the incident had roots early on in the evening of New Year's Eve, when Rachel was with him and didn't have sex because she had her period. Donny spent the evening walking around with his legs open complaining about how bad he hurt. "Rachel was laughing about how she gave him blue balls." Then in March they were at a party where Rachel was smoking dope and drinking. Donny took her into a bedroom, where he started kissing her. Rachel didn't want to kiss. When she resisted, he pushed her hard against the door, jamming her legs up on his shoulders. She was screaming for help, but her friends couldn't come in and get her because every time they would try to get in, the door would hit her head. All Rachel could do was to tell Donny if he was going to do it, to use a condom.

Jessica thinks it changed Rachel for a while but not for very long. Rachel had sex with two guys in quick succession after the rape, but then she didn't do it with anybody for months. "When she tried to be with someone," says Jessica, "it was hard for her to have a relationship."

Rachel blames herself for the rape. She thinks if she hadn't been stoned and drunk she could have fought her way out of the situation. Maybe if she had been sober, she wouldn't have been so scared. "He was saying, 'I'm not going to hurt you,' " Rachel recalls, "but then he slammed me into the door. It was like, Wait a minute, I'm confused. I was so messed up, I couldn't fight back. I couldn't walk, let alone fight."

The three friends held the secret among themselves for months, trying to make sense of it. They never told any adults. During the summer, Rachel finally opened up to her twenty-three-year-old stepsister, who had just moved back home following a divorce. The sister was sympathetic. It turns out she had once been raped too. This startling coincidence is less surprising in light of the 1992 report *Rape in America*, issued by the National Victim Center and the Crime Victims Research Center. The report stated that almost half of all rape victims are under eighteen, and of those, two-thirds are between twelve and seventeen. Often the perpetrator is an acquaintance or boyfriend.

Now Jessica says she understands why her parents are always warning her to "never, unless you know the person really well, get into a situation where you can't ask somebody to help you get out of it." She adds, "I don't think I ever will." But in the next breath she denies that their social life had placed her and her friends at greater risk of being in such situations. "I wasn't so drunk past the point that I wouldn't know what I was doing."

After the rape, Jessica began to have bad feelings about the group of boys they socialized with. Then, once when they all were at Rachel's, somebody stole fifteen dollars from Jessica's purse. She was furious and no one wanted to do anything. Everyone sat around and said, "Oh that's messed up. That's messed up." But even though they all knew who did it, nobody cared. Nobody cared because they were all stoned. That night was the first time Jessica smoked marijuana. She says she only had it once more after that, again at Rachel's house. She's really not interested in dope, "because it reminds me of that time in my life." Jessica was so disgusted with the guys that even though she continued to see Rachel, she and Annie started hanging out less and less with the group.

Jessica feels really bad for Rachel. It was horrible to get hurt like that. Whenever Rachel thought she saw Donny, she would burst out crying because she didn't want to face him. Rachel still seems fragile. She asked Jessica, "Just make sure that I don't have sex with anybody that I don't care about a lot." In the event that she does have sex, however, Rachel remains on the pill. Her mom says it is okay, it only costs twenty dollars a month.

If last year was about stretching the limits, now Jessica's instinct is to rein in and pull her friends with her. She sincerely believes that Agape will benefit Annie and Rachel because "this year we are talking about ourselves, and our self-worth." She thinks the teachers are great, especially Father Jim. "He's so real," she says. "He helps you with life without being a holier-than-thou kind of priest."

Jessica loves her friends so much. She thinks back to how she longed for friends when she was younger. She and Rachel and Annie have gone through so much together and it makes them close. This year in high school will be a whole new start.

The girls talk a lot about what made them so wild last year, and have come up with three distinct explanations. It was "that rebellion stage that everyone says they go through," says Rachel. "I think I went through it worse than some people did. It was like the drinking and drugs and everything, it was like, Oh well, it's rebellion time. I screwed up."

Annie, ambitious and hard-driving, thinks that the stress of approaching high school, which can "make or break your life," made her want one last fling. "Last year was like the year that you panic," she says. She felt the stress of deciding what she would do with her life by the time she entered ninth grade. She tried a fast, loose persona for a while to relieve the pressure. "I regret every guy I've ever touched," she says at this time. "That's why right now I would never, ever touch anybody again unless I cared about him a lot. I won't even play spin the bottle."

Jessica swears she just wanted to have some fun. "I was thinking, I'm sure my parents did it when they were younger. This is my time to be young. I wasn't trying to do anything against them. It just happened."

Since many parents like Jessica's are in the dark, never even entertaining what is going on, change has to emanate from the adolescent.

Luckily, Jessica has a strong sense of direction. Jessica and Annie drop out of the scene sooner, start spending more time together going to the movies, seeing other friends. "I think a lot of it was that I realized they weren't friends, and maybe it was a good time and it was fun to get drunk, but it can't be your whole life," says Jessica. "You can do that maybe a couple of times, but things happen that you don't want to happen, like with Rachel. I didn't do it enough times for it to get boring but it probably would have gotten boring."

The girls wish that adults understood that their decisions one way or another have nothing to do with parents, that parents should stop thinking they are the reason for everything their kids do. "I know my parents' being loving and caring about me helps me, but your parents don't make every decision for you," Jessica explains. "You make your own decisions, so even kids with good parents and good homes get into stuff and don't come out. It is really your choice, what you do, your strength."

It would be nice if there were a neat explanation for how Chris ends up being a young boy in eighth grade playing video games and Jessica becomes a party girl when both come from close supportive families, but these days it seems family is not a powerful predictor of adolescent choices. Katy, a friend to both Jessica and Chris, who spent a good deal of her eighth grade partying, once explained the difference between a kid like her who came from a great family and a kid who came from a bad situation: "A good kid will do the bad things less often." What she meant was that she would probably sneak out of the house in the middle of the night fewer times than a "messed up" kid! Regardless of the values held in adult society, in the adolescent community video games, ice skating, partying and drinking are equivalent. Kids feel the choice is up to them. In *Healthy Communities, Healthy Youth*, the Search Institute discovered that "Care and support within the family do not necessarily spill over the family's borders." If a community does not assume responsibility for all of its children through strong supportive institutions and programs for all kids, once a child leaves the family incubator, it is all a crap shoot.

The sex issue looms large for Jessica. Sex and its consequences had already been a big deal for her since her sister got pregnant while still in high school. Rachel's rape added one more concern. So far Jessica thinks she has been lucky with guys who have listened when she turns down their requests for sex. "If I'm going to have sex," she says, "I'm going to have sex because I want to, not because

I'm going to get it out of the way. I'm going to do it because I feel it's right. And it probably won't happen for a while. I want to wait until I'm making love and not having sex. They're two different things for me."

Jessica is not by any means a prude but she has her boundaries. She is always figuring out the rules that work in adolescent society. "Right now the furthest I really let them go is up my shirt because I don't want to get them going," she explains. "I see no point in getting fingered because that does nothing for them and it doesn't do anything for me. I don't see why guys have to finger a girl. They are just like, 'Oh, if you don't want to have sex with me then let me go down your pants.' What's that going to do? That's not going to get him off. I don't want to ever have oral sex. That's gross."

Jessica showcases how seemingly inconsistent behaviors can coexist comfortably within an adolescent. During eighth grade, even as her social life careened in unexpected directions, Jessica maintained her other interests. That's why her parents' uneasiness about her friends never erupted into full-blown suspicion. Her fast-and-loose social life proceeded comfortably alongside her commitment to school, church, family, sports, and whatever else sparked her boundless passion. "Basically it was like two totally separate things. School would come first because I wanted good grades and didn't want anything to mess that up. So when I went to a party it was something separate."

At the end of the summer before high school, Jessica has a clear sense of what matters to her most. Like Chris, when asked she has no trouble coming up with a list of her most deeply felt values. She describes a web of caring supports and inspiration starting with God. "I'm not a total Catholic, but I thank God for all the things he has done for me. I guess that keeps me going—that God always loves me and always forgives me." She likes that priests in the churches she's gone to don't dictate, especially Father Jim, who "was so great through the whole pregnancy thing with Kelly. He didn't judge her and he didn't say that's not right for God."

As she talks, it is obvious her parents have spent a great deal of time talking about the difficult parts of life with sensitivity and candor appropriate for her age. She tells of how her uncle, a homosexual, died of AIDS because he was not just with one person. She thanks God for taking him away from his suffering easily in his sleep. She also speaks of her other uncle's suffering from mental illness and his unfortunate death last year. He had left the hospital and wandered off into the night and stumbled to his death. Jessica knew that her uncle had introduced her parents to each other, and that somehow made her feel especially sad at his death. Hers is a family, Jessica would later say, that has gone through "just about everything. But we handle it with love." She knows this somehow connects with her faith in God—lofty thoughts for a girl just fourteen. She concludes what is most important is "not the religion in church, but the religion in her heart."

After God, she values her parents. "A lot of times I want to get a lot of money so I can take them on a cruise," she says, "and have them happy. I love them so much. I don't know what I would do without them." She admires her mom because her family had eleven children and she took care of all her kid brothers and sisters and she cooked for them.

One of the reasons Jessica strives to do well in school is to make her parents happy. "They deserve it and I owe it to them," she says. Her dad, with his ambition and fortitude, is her role model. He worked since he was twelve and paid his own way through college. She wants to earn a scholarship by getting great grades.

She values her family, her sister and brother and all her relatives. It's not all sweetness and light with her siblings, but she loves them all the same. She asked her sister to be her sponsor for Confirmation last spring. It was a way for each to heal a wound and seal a bond. One of Jessica's treasures is a letter her sister wrote her from a church-sponsored Engaged Encounter weekend which said: "I want to thank you for being a sister for the thirteen years that I haven't. I guess being an older sister made me believe the only way to help you was to be mean and get my point across. Jessica, I apologize for all the times in your life that you thought you could count on me and I wasn't there, but always remember the times I was. I feel honored to be your sponsor and I will be there from here on out. You are a great person and I truly love you and cry out for all those things we missed together. . . . Love always, your big sister Kelly." When Jessica was confirmed, her whole family was there to celebrate, but for Jessica the greatest gift was that she had not lost her sister after all.

There were other milestone celebrations the summer before high school. In July, Kelly and Matt's wedding, with their ten-month-old son in attendance, looked past all the judgments and celebrated a new

union. It was a lesson in hanging in and working things out and unconditional love. Jessica had learned a good life lesson in making the
most of a difficult situation from her family's struggle with an unin-
tended pregnancy. But she wasn't thinking about it. What Jessica
loved most were the beautiful dresses, drinking lots of champagne,
and dancing the night away.

When her grandparents celebrated fifty years of marriage the
month after Kelly's wedding, there was another family gala. Their
ten children plus the grandchild whose dad had died the year before
each placed on a box frame a symbol of the rich life this marriage en-
compassed, and spoke about its meaning. The symbols—house, for
hearth and home; a heart, for their enduring love; a cross, for the life
of the spirit; building blocks, for nurturing the young; a shell, for
family reunions at the beach; and so on—represented the universal
hopes for all children as they reach adulthood. When the speeches
were over, a quilt bearing the same symbols was wrapped around the
grandparents.

Just as that quilt wrapped her grandparents in love, so does the
love of her family and a set of clearly communicated values embrace
Jessica even during life's confusing moments. From the small moments like sitting with her mom at the table after school, to her daily
commute with her dad downtown to her job as a gofer in a law office
during the summer, to baby-sitting for her aunt, to softball games
and church group, the nexuses between Jessica and her family and
other adults give her stability. They cushion life's blows and help her
deal with adversity in a constructive way. She could never stray far
because she wouldn't want to. These people are everything to her.

But Jessica also has an insatiable appetite for exploring life on her
own terms, so that even with deep roots and solid support there is
still lots of room for her to choose values for herself. As important as
God and family are to her, it is the time of her life when top billing
goes to her friends.

The first few months of freshman year are two steps forward and
one step back. Agape turns out to be less than the perfect cure for
what ailed her friends. Rachel and Annie stop coming. Rachel sinks
back into her old ways and Jessica and Annie follow for a while.

As her first Homecoming approaches, Jessica hopes against hope
that one particular boy will ask her. He does. She can't wait for the
dance. Sean is kind of rough, she knows, but he is so nice to her. In

a moment of candor, she also admits: "He has a police record of one count of larceny, one count of breaking and entering, and one count of having a concealed weapon. It was an unloaded gun he stole from a brownie—a military car. It was a military weapon." But he is so cool.

Everything is great until the Saturday night the week before Homecoming. Jessica, Annie, and Rachel have been to a movie and are strolling around Town Center when they sense a big commotion at the end of the street. It is Sean going berserk, so out of his mind that his friends cannot restrain him. The girls are horrified when he ends up being picked up by the police, then hospitalized in a psychiatric facility. Jessica's parents come home early from work the day she finds out he's been sent to a hospital, and help her sort things through. They never once chastise her for her choice in people, or let loose with their relief that she had not gone to the Homecoming dance with Sean.

Jessica miraculously recovers after a few days of great drama and hysterics. She didn't know him *that* well, after all. She decides to go to the dance anyway, date or not. After all, she had her new outfit and was psyched for the occasion. She persuades Annie and Rachel to join her. It is Jessica the social organizer in action again. The girls go to Clyde's for dinner and pick up a couple of guy friends coincidentally eating there too, and drag them to the dance. They stop first at Rachel's house to borrow some clothes from her dad since one of the boys was dressed too casually.

An hour after the dance has begun, the girls make a grand entrance looking absolutely grown-up and glamorous in their black velvet spaghetti-strap dresses, hair piled high, with sexy tendrils around their faces, bright lipstick on their lips. They are definitely noticed.

Jessica dances with everybody, especially with Lou, who holds her close. She says he's nice, just a friend. She never sits down the entire evening. Toward the end of the night, there is one boy in particular she dances with who she thinks she likes. She's thinking maybe he could be a boyfriend. "I'm talking to someone, kind of. Talking to someone is kind of like a step before going out with someone. This guy named Steve. Rachel asked him and he likes me." She's still thinking about it when her dad comes to pick the girls up.

Her parents are careful not to lecture, but they wonder why their bright, engaging daughter seems to gravitate to boys who are not the type they might have chosen. Jessica shrugs and says there's no way she'd be interested in the boys in her gifted and talented classes at school. "I don't like really good boys because they just don't appeal to me. I like the rougher type. I don't like guys that have a police record a mile long who are going to go to jail, I just like guys that aren't afraid of doing stuff on the edge."

Jessica's reasons for her choices reflect the tolerance her sixties parents have taught her. She gravitates to people who are different from her, feeling the differences are what draws them together. "We all have talents that make us different. They may be better looking than I am, or they may be more mature in ways that I am not. But I don't feel superior because I'm better in school. That's not right." As her parents have always told her, "Nobody likes a person who goes around and thinks they're better than everybody else."

But when the time comes, she's thinking maybe twenty-five, she'll marry a family values poster boy. Forget about the tough guys, she wants to find "somebody that's going to love me the way that my father loves my mother, and is always going to be faithful to me." She wants that man to be able to provide a nice home and some money. And especially, "They have to love to dance, and like the ocean a lot, because I do."

In time her life steadies itself, mostly because she and Annie finally break away from Rachel, who pushed them too far. The thing that severed the relationship, however, was not that Rachel was a bad influence—cutting classes all the time, hanging out with kids who were older and more wild—but that she was rude to Jessica, was not a good friend. "Rachel started bossing," explains Jessica. She started acting mean and insulting to Jessica and Annie and they never knew when it was coming. She could be all sweetness and light, then turn on them in a minute. Jessica thought it was offensive and stupid, but she was also intimidated and followed Rachel like "a puppet." She felt diminished and taken advantage of, but Rachel had a hold. By the spring of her freshman year, she'd had enough. The feisty, determined Jessica came through and she told Rachel to leave her and Annie alone. Jessica doesn't want to admit that she was kind of under Rachel's spell. She likes to think she chose to stay involved in Rachel's world. She says simply, "Rachel was like the radical side of all of us."

Jessica and Annie grow closer, aware that they truly share the same values. "We both want to get good grades and go to a good college and everything." Rachel didn't care. She said she did in the fall, but Annie and Jessica know that someone who skips classes all the time is not serious about school. Annie and Jessica love school, "the atmosphere, how everyone is." They especially love drama class and the forensics club. They share a love of acting out emotions and speaking out their ideas. It's a good common ground for friendship. They both come from strong families they appreciate. "Annie," says Jessica, "I love her. She is my best friend and like a sister."

Of course this doesn't mean that life sans Rachel is pristine. Jessica knows how to clear space in her life for things her peers are doing. If there's pot around you might smoke it, for example, "but you're not an addict or anything, you don't crave it." She knows her parents would not approve of her smoking pot, but "they would approve it more so than going out and getting stoned with people I don't know." She is certain if she were a parent she would not want her kid drinking, because "a lot of things can happen." She says, "I think my parents are right, not wanting me to drink. But I think it's only fair that I can drink a couple of times."

When it comes right down to it, Jessica believes, the only thing her parents probably wouldn't approve of is her "continuous flirting." "They wouldn't be like, 'You're flirting, you're grounded.' But they would be like, 'Jessica, don't do that because it gives people the wrong impression.' " That is just too bad, says Jessica. She is not going to stop flirting because "it's not the sixties, and people don't really take it that you're a whore because you flirt with people."

If you are an adolescent, Jessica believes, you've got to do some things. "I'm not a goody-goody, but I'm not horrible. So I think it's okay for me to do those things sometimes."

Talking to Jessica at fourteen is always a wild ride inside the workings of a child restless and caught at the top end of young adolescence in a world where at-risk behaviors start earlier and earlier. She slumps in a chair, her legs over one side, her head tossed back, her long hair hanging. She is alternately wildly animated, in charge, bored, distracted. She says in the same breath how she wishes she were older so she'd be taken more seriously by the upperclassmen because the kids her age are so immature, and how she loves having three classes above her because there are all those cool older kids.

She confides how she has matured since last year and never drinks or does drugs, and then moments later reveals she smokes pot on occasion and loves sharing wine coolers with her friends. She's not exactly lying. She is seeking her own truth on a jagged trail with lots of side trips. It all makes sense to her.

Except for one thing. She sits up, twirls her hair, struggles with the thoughts running through her brain. Then she says, in an absolutely serious tone, that she wishes "kids didn't have to be so hard." She's sick and tired of being fourteen, she explains, because fourteen is too old to have the comfort of being young. "It's like you have to pretend like you're somebody else. You can't be like naive or vulnerable because if you are, you're just going to get trampled all over."

She wishes there were room to talk about the ocean. "There's a kind of peace underneath the water that I get, and nothing else matters. Everybody finds that in something and I guess the ocean is that for me." She dreams of snorkeling in waters like the Caribbean where she could see things really well. But she can't share these things with her friends and she wishes she could.

She doesn't talk to her friends about the summer trips to Newport to her grandparents' place, and going scuba diving with her dad. She wishes she could tell her friends about the coves she and her dad explore, and how the water is freezing in Newport all the time. She can't share with her friends how her dad gets cold easily now that he's lost a lot of weight.

She never shares how she loves her grandfather's slide photo collection. She thinks it is the neatest thing, all arranged chronologically in books. She loves how she can just tell him a time—her baptism, or her dad as a young man—and he gives her a personal slide show. She is crazy about her grandfather. She loves the family stories. "This summer when I went up there I was asking him to tell me stories about his childhood. He told me one story where he saved his little brother's life or something like that. I said, 'Oh, really, did you tell your parents about that? He said, 'Jessica, my parents didn't care where I was, when I got home, unless I was not home for dinner.' He vowed never to do that to his family, so he was a very good father." Her monologue creates for her a tapestry in her mind, woven with a knowledge of where she is from, and her feeling of uniqueness in a family of three kids. But her friends know none of this side of her because she feels compelled to edit herself in the adolescent community.

In the winter of her freshman year, Jessica finds true love. She had liked Jeremy from afar for most of the year. Around January they talked in drama class, and she was instantly infatuated. "He's such a good actor and he can sing, and he's really nice," she gushes.

Their relationship begins around the school production of *Noises Off*. Jeremy keeps a list of all the things talked about in the play and he just goes down the list with her. He says, "Yeah, we talk about sex a lot." She says, "Yeah, I'll bet you I can outtalk you on sex any day." And he says, "No way." That's how they get started.

She finds out he is a virgin like she is. Perfect. It opens up a whole new area of conversation about what their dreamlike first time would be. She tells him she would like to be "on the beach or in a jacuzzi or in front of a fire with no other furniture in the room. That's my dream. Or on a washing machine."

He says he's going to take his date out to dinner—but not something like McDonald's—and to see a play. "He's like, 'I'd take my date out to a nice restaurant and then to the Kennedy Center.' " She is smitten. "I was like, 'Here, why don't you take me out on a date?' I was like, 'You were going to pay for all of this?' " she recalls. He told her, "Yes."

Their romance begins on the Friday night of *Guys and Dolls*, the end of April. Annie invites her to the cast party. Jeremy will be there. The kids are going over to Janice's house. Jessica's dad says she has to be home at 2 A.M. because she had stayed out really late the night before and he was mad. "I was like, 'Dad, I'll get home the same time. I'll just go and spend the night at Annie's.' He said okay, 'but you better call me as soon as you get home to Annie's. It should be like about two-ten.' "

The girls get back to Annie's on time, Jessica calls her dad at 2:10, and then they leave to go to Mike's house. "He had people over, and his parents were out of town, I think," recalls Jessica. "It wasn't anything like with Cal. They had beer there. I don't know if anybody had done marijuana. But I didn't do it. There was one beer for me and Annie so we didn't get drunk or anything." Jeremy didn't drink anything. By the time he dropped his car off, because he was going to spend the night at Mike's, there was no beer left anyway.

They stay there all night. At first, the house is packed with kids, but they start leaving as the morning goes on until there are only a handful left. "We had a lot of fun. We were just talking and stuff." Around 4:30, Annie went to sleep. It was okay because she told her parents she would be home late. "So they expected her home really late," recalls Jessica. The girls figure they just need to be back at Annie's by the time her parents wake up. Before Annie crashes, she tells Jessica to wake her up by 6 A.M.

It is still and quiet in the living room. Jessica and Jeremy, lying together on the couch, start kissing. "We kissed, then we stopped. He was like, 'I don't know if that was such a good idea.' I'm like, 'I'm sorry.' He was like, 'No, it's not your fault, it's just that I'm not sure that's such a good idea,' because he didn't want that to happen again. I was like, 'Okay.' "

They lie embraced, not doing anything for a little while. Both of them are drawn to each other and it is impossible not to kiss. For hours they kiss and talk and kiss again. It is exciting and beautiful. Suddenly, she sits up and exclaims, "Oh God, Annie's going to kill me." Jessica had lost all sense of time and it is 8:30 A.M. She runs upstairs to wake Annie and tells her they really, really have to go now. But there is a problem: they have no ride home.

After several tries, they finally get Nancy, "a girl who was leaving the party and said her mom would take us home." She drops Jessica off first. Jessica takes a deep breath and walks in her front door. Her parents are sitting at the kitchen table having breakfast. "They looked up and said, 'Hi. How are you doing?' " Jessica recalls. "I was like, 'Fine. This other girl spent the night at Annie's house, so she gave me a ride home. I'll just go upstairs now, 'bye.' I was so scared, and I got off."

After the all-nighter, Jessica and Jeremy are a couple. He gives her his senior ring on Friday, May 13th. Her lucky day. "I'm his woman," she says blissfully. "We've been talking on the telephone until like four in the morning."

While Jessica samples these pleasures, she keeps her eye on the prize—those perfect grades. Admittedly her schedule is a bit daffy. To make room for homework, sports, church, family, friends, and now (sigh) Jeremy, she stays up late. "I stay up usually until around eleven-thirty, go to sleep, wake up at two, go to sleep, wake up at four, go to sleep. I wake up to talk to Jeremy and do my homework," she explains. She definitely is tired when she wakes up, she says, but she would be tired anyway if she went to sleep at midnight and got up at six. She always feels okay by the time she gets to school.

The possibility that their youngest daughter has a steady boyfriend is creating some tension about sex in the Jones household. Her parents really like Jeremy but are "going nuts about the sex thing," says Jessica. "My parents say, 'It's not that we don't trust you, it's just that when you get one person vulnerable at one time and another person vulnerable at another time you can keep from having sex, but if both of you are vulnerable at the same time, then it's going to happen.' That's what they don't want to happen to me."

Jessica keeps telling them, "I am not Kelly. I am not Kelly. Me and Jeremy do things. We kiss and we're intimate with each other, I guess, but we haven't talked about having sex." Then her mom suggests that maybe she and Jessica's dad should have a talk with the young couple. Jessica freaks, "I was like, 'No! No, Mom, no. You cannot do that to me.' She can't sit there and treat me like I don't know how to talk about things with my boyfriend. I was like, 'No way, Mom. You're not going to do that. Sorry.' " Jessica thinks her mom believes that a talk would prevent sex from happening. "But she can't do that. That would totally scare him off. I think that would scare any guy off."

Jessica believes her parents have no need to worry. She is convinced she will have sex for the right reasons. "I'm never going to do that," she says, "just have sex for the first time like, 'Oh, we'll have sex really good another time. Let's just do it in the car now, babe.' No, sorry. I'm not going to be downgraded to that. That's just a crock."

She wonders whether fourteen is too young to have sex. "Everybody just has sex, and I don't want to be everybody," she says. "I just don't want to regret it, and I think that will happen if I have sex too early." There is actually a part of her that thinks it would be nice to wait until she is married. It would be nice "to marry a virgin, but I don't think there's going to be any left by the time I get up there."

The relationship with Jeremy is everything Jessica had hoped for. They always have something to talk about, so many common interests, so much fun. "I really think I love him. I really do," she says. "I'd go out with guys and expect to get sick of them, and expect a reason for breaking up with them by like a month or a month and a half. But this one, I can't find anything wrong."

The day of her last softball game, she is stressed and in a bad mood. She'd had lots of homework, a test and a quiz, and then the game after school. When Jeremy meets her between classes, she snaps at him and says, "Don't lean on me, Jeremy." But then she opens her locker and finds a single rose attached to the coat hook, with a note that says, "Good luck with your last game. Love, Jeremy." Jessica cannot believe how wonderful she feels.

The year ends and Jessica fulfills her goals, to be a good friend, to have a Real Boyfriend, and to get straight As. Through many ups and downs, decisions discussed with parents and friends, and secrets that demarcate her home world and the adolescent world, she grows more firmly into her own set of values. The difference between eighth and tenth grade, she says, is huge in terms of becoming her own person. She looks back at all her activities as experiments, trying to see what fit and what didn't—"like socks," she says with a grin.

She's thinking of telling Jeremy how much she loves the ocean.

*Creating My Own Space:*
*The Long Cold Winter*
*and Descent into Darkness*

Brendon loves to paint in the city, lured by the darkness of its soul, the peril. "Everybody's always known that painting in the suburbs is for suckers. It is not dangerous enough." Brendon has gone metropolitan. A favorite location, deep in a railroad tunnel just blocks away from the National Gallery, is the "Smithsonian" of graffiti, "the Hall of Fame." He and his friends scramble down an embankment, walk in at the entrance to a long expanse that is divided in two for trains. One side has tracks that apparently aren't being used anymore. The other side is used by Amtrak.

Inside, it is dark even during the day. Once one's eyes adjust, a dazzling display of piece art is revealed. Huge drawings adorn the sides of both tunnels—elaborate abstract renderings of tags, cartoon figures with bowler hats and flowing scarfs, monsterlike creatures, even a political cartoon. The talent displayed is considerable, especially given the conditions of darkness and risk under which the works were made. It takes special daring to paint on the train side: as a train approaches, its vibrations warn the painter to jump out of the way. To an outsider, the art seems defaced by all the scribbling around the works. It turns out that the scribbling is a part of the communication system where the artists draw and others critique the pieces, integrating a solitary act of drawing into a community effort.

Just as there are two sides to these tunnels, there are two ways of looking at what is housed here: the art and the vandalism, the beauty and the ugliness, the bravura and the stupidity. The tunnel is at least a block long, and as the boys walk, their feet crunch bottles underfoot, steer clear of used hypodermic needles.

The artists coexist with the homeless and other nighttime inhabitants of this subterranean refuge. Everywhere there are signs of the people who call this home: a filthy couch, mattresses, clothing, empty tin cans, ashes from fires. Unlike the public walls in Reston, this is a gallery known only to graffiti artists, the homeless, and whatever detritus of society passes through. Maybe some Amtrak people have noticed, but it would be hard to see much as they speed by. The Reston artists who come here feel the thrill of a secret society.

The hardest part of the trip is getting a ride when you can't drive yet, although there is always the nearby Metro stop. Clearing the time is easy, since parents are rarely consulted. Brendon's friends describe a typical plan: "We were going to come downtown, go to a show at a music club, go down to the Hall of Fame, paint, and spend the night down here somewhere on a bench." They each tell their parents they are staying at the other's house overnight. No problem. His friend says, "I've done it before, and my parents don't check. They're too lazy." For Brendon, it is just another middle-of-the-night adventure. If they come by car, maybe they'll stop on the way and tag some places along Route 66—a risky proposition where they hang precariously from the sound walls along the road to leave their marks. None of them stop to consider what might happen if they were to get hurt, or feel any responsibility to be honest with their parents.

Deep in this tunnel, Brendon finds a home for his impulses—another arena where his anger, acting out, and soulful expression come into play. It is about the power of getting away with something as an antidote to the powerlessness he feels in his life. Of course Brendon's parents would not approve, but they are out of the loop. It appears Brendon and his folks live parallel lives as Brendon's increasingly oppositional behaviors proceed uninterrupted.

As the summer ends, however, the Hall of Fame might as well be a thousand miles away. Brendon sits day after day alone in his house. What his family sees is yet another one of his sulky moods, "teenage stuff." Nobody asks, and he doesn't reveal the magnitude of his pain. This Boy Scout, wrestler, trackman, churchgoer's dark side is beginning to cast a longer shadow. His choices, dancing at the edges of crime, his loneliness, his desire to belong are pulling him deeper into delinquency. Although he only sees it as an unfortunate chain of events, there is trouble all around.

The high of the danger shared with other graffiti artists has come crashing down. The fellowship of his drug pals is shattered. He has alienated every group of his friends and he feels, as usual, that it is not his fault, he is a victim. It is his version of the mind-set he perceives in his parents' capitulation to economic circumstances, and like his parents, he feels stuck and helpless. He has nowhere to go, no one to see. Actually, he is frightened. But he blows it off, playing the tough loner.

Last year after wrestling season, he began to spend more and more time with a drug crowd. A bunch of them got in trouble at the end of the school year for stealing a girl's wallet and using her gas card. Brendon says he told them it was stupid. "It's like robbing a bank in broad daylight. You're not going to be able to get away with it." He went with them anyway. "They were my friends. What the hey. They got busted, and they ended up paying for what they charged, like two hundred fifty-eight dollars on a Mobil card, for food and cigarette lighters and flashlights." The day they did it he sat in the car, he says. When they were caught, there were fines to pay. Brendon was never implicated because the police never found out he was with them. His friends were angry. They wondered why Brendon wasn't caught. He told them he honestly didn't know. But they thought something was fishy. "They were just all over me calling me up all summer with threats, saying they were going to kick my ass for telling on them." In the end, says Brendon, "It's all about who's got the biggest friends, and the way it turns out, I did." They stopped hassling him, but that doesn't ease the worry about how it will be for him in school when he has to pass them in the halls every day.

His original plan was to hang out with Tommy, a drug friend. Except this summer Tommy got arrested in Town Center for possession of alcohol, possession of an illegal substance, being under the influence of marijuana, and possession of a concealed weapon. Brendon thinks it's a bitch that he's now locked up.

The worst is his alienation from his graffiti friends. Tad got caught for possession of stolen paint and for painting. "Everybody's being busted for the art," says Brendon. It isn't the underpass in Reston that got them busted, but the sound wall on the toll road toward

Tysons Corner, which is state property. "It's the visible stuff that got the police mad," says Brendon.

Brendon's name came up. He was pretty scared. The cops came to his house shortly before his trip to Louisiana in July. They didn't say what his friends got busted for. "For some reason, I don't know what the hell I was thinking, I don't know why I was scared of the cops at that time because I'm not usually afraid," says Brendon. "Well, then I slipped out a name, but it wasn't a big deal. They had a bunch of names. They just wanted to know who these people were, who all these writers were. I knew everybody, but I wasn't about to tell them, it was out of respect more or less. What these people can do with a paint can is incredible. I wouldn't want to bring these people down. I figured just to get the cops off my butt I'd spill them one name. It was no big deal, but I feel real guilty about it now." Only his mom knows. "Most of the time if I'm lucky, the police will go to my mom. Me and my mom keep that kind of stuff from my dad because my dad has a bad temper."

The police won't let up on Brendon because they sense that he knows much more than he told them, that he is being "uncooperative." What they've been doing, according to Brendon, is trying to "intimidate all these other big writers, saying that Brendon Lamont said you were this so-and-so person, and it's gotten me in a lot of trouble. Ratting on someone is the equivalent to a death sentence. It brands you. You can get beat up, which is no big deal. The only thing I care about when I fight is that I don't get a black eye. It tells people you got beat up."

In his twisted morality, the person Brendon believes is really to blame for all the trouble is the arresting officer, "an evil woman." "She's just destroying everybody's friendships," says Brendon. "She's telling everybody that other people rat on them to try to get them to confess. She won't lay off. Heads are going to roll."

Tad finally turned himself in under pressure from his mom. Brendon fears that when Tad's case comes to trial, the cops might say that he was the one who spilled the beans and got his friends in trouble. "If they do," says Brendon, "I'd be the first one in court saying no, he's not so and so, even if it's a lie."

Thank goodness for his trip to Louisiana. Brendon recalls with warmth and affection his summer vacation with his relatives. Like an enthusiastic child, he tells of how they went on a swamp tour and visited an alligator farm, how he played with his spirited little cousins, and the ways family activities flowed. He thrived in the comfort of extended family and the rhythms of the Deep South. "It's real different there," Brendon explains. "It's good to see everybody come home and get together; they all live pretty close by. It's good to talk. They are less concerned with money and material goods, more concerned about staying together as a family, having a good time. It's a good example to follow."

It's like he's been yanked away when he comes home. He feels a huge letdown; he's isolated and lonely. The predicament with his friends is torture. However, he is intent on solving the problems himself. "I don't really need anybody else's advice. I want my outcome to be my own fault if it ends up badly. Or my credit. I just want to be left alone. I think that's all that anyone who's ever had any serious trouble wants, just to be left alone by everyone."

As always, he has his art to keep him company. He begins a project in the corner of the laundry room in the basement. On a long wood table flush with the wall, he sets up meticulously, even lovingly.

He goes up and down the two flights of stairs bringing things from his bedroom—his art supplies, everything else that matters—to surround himself in this private space. He begins to shape the area, this cozy nook in the laundry room, the space where his mom is the mom he longs for her to be. The fact that he chooses to be right in his mother's most domestic domain speaks to a longing for a world where he remembers feeling less alone.

Moving into the basement, in the bowels of his home, he also signals an impulse to move deeper into himself. He is creating an environment where he can look at who he is, think about what it means, write and draw about how it feels.

On his desk are all his drawing tools and books, including books by Robert Frost and Richard Brautigan that he has been reading. The wall in front of him is decorated with mementos and a poster that shows an eclipse of the moon and a field of skeletons and reads: "The Darkness That Enlightens." There is an ad cut out of the paper that asks: "Is your child caught in the failure chain?" His own art is everywhere. In a place directly in front of his eyes when he works, there is an image he has painted, cut out, and mounted: a large gloved hand pulling the trigger of a gun. Below it, sitting on the desk itself, is a hand-painted American eagle.

One night, well buzzed by several joints, he begins a journal of himself. First the cover, with his name in bold letters: Brendon

Lamont. The letters are cracked and broken. He writes: "don't shoot me / don't talk to me / don't look at me / don't touch me! / leave me alone." The second page is a Xerox copy of a definition of depression. The quote talks about how loneliness and depression are a normal part of grief that affect everybody to some extent. They will pass, it says. It suggests reaching out to others as an antidote. On the facing page he draws gravestones with two eyeless figures extending a hand to each other.

He is relieved when school begins and nothing awful happens. His sophomore year—a clean slate to make new choices if he wants. He frames some goals for himself: "My goal in wrestling is to be feared as a wrestler. In cross-country, my goal is to get in shape for wrestling, and I think I'm going to accomplish that. My goal as an artist is to express myself so I can make a drawing that I like and I can say expresses the way I'm feeling at the time."

His freshman year seems a million years ago. He thinks he was "a fool." "I sort of liked my style last year, but it was kind of goofy. Last year was just like cutting up and laughing. I think maybe I'll take school a little more seriously this year." Determination and commitment, however, are not part of the picture. He says, "That's a hope."

He enters school of two minds: wanting to join the mainstream and to defy it, be involved and isolate himself, improve and do what he feels like. "I don't see myself being the same sort of outgoing person," he explains, yet he reaches out in a number of ways.

Church and religion remain central to his life. He attends Young Life, a nondenominational Christian youth group—a fun way to get people involved with Jesus, he explains. He also goes to his family's church, and spends more time trying to understand the church's point of view on faith and morality.

But even in Young Life and church, he is ambivalent. In both, he is involved in serious Christian fellowship and respectable fun. He joins in the singing and ice cream socials at Young Life. Yet he also knows some of the members are "drug users and weirdos" like he is. Is it hypocritical? No, he insists, drugs are not the mark of whether a person is good or bad, just something people do.

In his parents' church, he has two main friends. One guy he hangs out with is "awesome." Brendon says: "He's really one of my best friends. He keeps me straight," meaning he exerts some moral pressure. He also likes a guy with whom he has drinking contests. "He's from Tennessee and his parents are really, real Deep South. We just drink until we can't drink anymore. I used to think that the point of getting drunk was to make a story that you could tell these people what would be really funny." He likes both friends, both styles. He especially likes keeping all his options open.

He finds a "real girlfriend" in Carol, a year older, who becomes his lover and good friend. He reaches out to her from his softer side, responding to the obvious fact that she "genuinely cares, will go out of her way for me." He admits he is often difficult in the relationship. He wants someone to penetrate his shell even when he pushes away.

Brendon's two sides—the public and the private, the social animal and the recluse, the vulnerable and the hard—are always in play and one typically threatens the other. The year starts well with track, parties, his girl, and church. But he lacks staying power; his darkness returns the moment things don't go his way. He gives up, gets angry. It takes no time for him to abandon his optimism. Within weeks, his Astros cap no longer is turned around backwards, but faces forward, pulled down low over his eyes, keeping the world out.

It is the same old story: if he gets disciplined or even reprimanded for breaking the rules, he is being attacked. If he screws up an assignment, it isn't his fault. If things don't go his way, then fuck the whole thing. "My opinion of school is that it is hell, and people are a bunch of morons—teachers are morons, hypocrites, and there are too many stupid rules like you can't talk back to the teacher even though most of the time they deserve it." He rails at all authority: "If I am forced by law to go here, why should I take it seriously?" He photocopies a Matt Groening "Life Is Hell" cartoon for his journal that captures his own attitude about school: The teacher asks if the class has any questions. The cartoon character Bongo sits and asks himself why school is run like a jail, has so many stupid rules, is so boring, uncomfortable, pointless, trivial, and so on. He raises his hand to ask if he can sharpen his pencil, and the teacher says no.

No one in school really cares, says Brendon. "The teachers act like, 'I've got to teach this class today, damn.'" So screw them, he won't do their assignments or go to their classes. "None of the teachers really sees you as a person, except in the art department," he says. His thoughts race a thousand miles a minute but his face registers nothing. He comes across as just another sulky kid with attitude.

Brendon is uncomfortable with himself and looks to others for a core. Invariably they fail him. He refuses to accept the standards and expectations for all students, yet he must comply and put in a certain amount of effort, so he is in a state of drift. As always, he sees the problem as outside himself: "Whatever group you're in, people are still trying to fit in," he says. "That's what our school is about, being upset over what you don't have."

What he doesn't have—whether it be money or grades or acceptance—ties him in knots. He becomes increasingly sullen and oppositional. He feels emotionally explosive. He copies another Groening cartoon for his journal. It shows Bongo bound and gagged in a locked chamber. Outside the door, eyes peer through the tiny window and a voice is saying, "Don't be bitter." Brendon sees school as a prison: "The bars of the prison are the requirements for a diploma, my ball and chain is my backpack."

He gravitates toward people he can "appreciate and relate to, and they are the people not going to school." On bad days, he leaves at lunchtime, "most times to do drugs. There's always company." Take this day for example. After third period he leaves school to have a cigarette in the parking lot. A kid comes up and asks if he has any weed. Brendon tells the kid that he doesn't, "but my friend does and he'll smoke you up. He's like, 'Cool, I'll drive.' " They take off to go find the friend but he isn't at home. They drive back to school and he's there. All three leave school again. "Then we go to this guy's house and smoke and talk, and then go back to school for sixth and seventh periods. It kind of pisses you off when you come back to school stoned because you can't enjoy it. You can't sit down and relax." Brendon doesn't think twice about going to school stoned. "We've done it so many times," he says. Even if a teacher caught on, no big deal, "one time out of what, a hundred, two hundred?"

He starts dealing drugs. It is a casual sort of thing at first. Brendon and a couple of his buddies purchase a lot of acid and people start buying from them. He sells it at three dollars a hit "just to break even." It is an "easy sell" and eventually really pays off. He broadens to sell weed too.

Getting involved in the drug trade, explains Brendon, "is all about connections." In any group of kids using drugs, there are always the buyers and the sellers. To sell, all you need to do is go to any person who sells and let him know that you are interested in selling too. They give you what you want and you are in business. It often stays at a low level of buying a little more than you need and selling the excess to cover the cost of your own use. Brendon says the dealing "trickles down and trickles down—everybody is a small dealer. It's all about money."

Adults have it all wrong when they imagine evil dealers luring kids into the trap of a drug-addicted life. The real dealing is among friends. Dealing to strangers is too risky; there are plenty of kids already looking to buy. "You have to know the people," says Brendon, otherwise you may get caught. "When you are a consumer and you consume a lot, it just ends up that you sell to people you smoke out with—like they need bags, who do they get them from? Well, I can get you a bag. Then when a dealer decides he doesn't want to deal anymore, he introduces you to his dealer and that is how you move up."

Doing the exchanges in school is "no problem." Most of his initial clientele are the kids he goes outside for a smoke with. So they just start doing some business out there on the paths or in the woods. A cigarette in one hand, he slips them dope with the other.

He says his parents don't suspect anything. "I keep it pretty much incognito. I'm not an idiot. You don't ever trip during dinner. With all drugs, with everything, you can be in control." His sister knows but keeps it secret. When his mom once found his water pipe she told him to destroy it. He promised her he would, then put it back in its hiding place. "She said, 'It's your marijuana inhaler, isn't it?' I told her yes. She said, 'You're in big trouble.' But she wouldn't tell my dad."

It is no surprise that things begin to go downhill as the semester progresses. He's failing Algebra II, the only subject his dad cares about since it is key to Brendon's decision to do architecture or design when he graduates. He wishes he could communicate better with his dad, but says his dad "doesn't really seem to give a shit about what I think, even if I confront him."

In Brendon's mind, the discipline in his house is lax because of the economic situation. He imagines a deal with the devil, a trade-off in the family. "I guess it's like a two-way street sometimes," he says, "because we are doing a lot of sacrificing right now. We're not that bad, so my parents give us a little leeway with school and grades and stuff." The other half of the equation is that, according to Brendon, his parents "realize like what the hell are they going to do? They can't ground me because I'll just leave. If they try to track me down I won't be there. There's no way they can make me give in." His parents realize he is bitter and angry at the way things have to be. "They're sorry, and they love me," he says, but "sometimes who gives a damn about love? I need some stuff."

The cold, drawn-out winter of his sophomore year feels endless. His mood matches the silent icy grayness of the landscape. More and more, he escapes to his basement room and works into the wee hours of the morning. Sometimes he draws while tripping. Since an LSD trip lasts up to twelve hours, he often stays up the entire night. One picture that he drew tripping is being exhibited at school in the hallway in front of the main office. "It has like a dose on the guy's tongue. It's pretty funny. It was in a show, too."

Although his above-ground life is disordered and messy, Brendon's basement work space is neat because it is important to him. Under his worktable is a large turquoise file set up with labeled hanging folders. In school, if he does his work at all, Brendon can barely hold on to it long enough to hand it in. It disappears in the trash heap inside his locker, or so he says. Here in his file he has carefully stored visual and written materials that strike his fancy. There are pictures from *National Geographic* of interesting-looking faces, warfare, the Statue of Liberty. In a pile on his desk to be filed are photos of his grandma at her wedding reception; a cemetery with a prominent Celtic cross he would like on his grave; an oil refinery at night.

He's put together a collection of all the family pictures he could find. He gives long explanations about them: the fishing pictures, the old school pictures that show childhood friends, family pictures through the years. There are not a lot of them, but they are all important. "If things went to hell in a handbasket," Brendon says, "I'm pretty sure my family would always be there for me. They just piss me off, that's all."

The day the sun comes out after weeks of cold grayness and the snow and ice begin to melt, the streets around Reston are filled with smiling families. There is a warm small-town atmosphere of neighborliness. People walk carrying grocery bags, stopping to chat along the way. There is a collective sigh of relief that the real thaw may at last be on its way, and the kids will go back to school. While all this is happening, Brendon sits at his desk in the basement reading *As I Lay Dying*, by William Faulkner, the dryer is humming as it finishes a load and his Scout uniform is hanging on a line right above his head, waiting for his mom to iron it.

Spring finally comes, and with it some decisions. Brendon gets a job at the dry cleaners with Courtney's help. He gets a conservative haircut, references from his Boy Scout troop leaders, and two from members of his church. He even has decent grades for the winter quarter, so in applying he lists those too. His purpose is to save enough money "so I can fulfill my own needs."

Once again, he slips. The third quarter his grades go down. He says he's trying not to let his drug use interfere with bringing up his grades. "Do your homework before you get high," Brendon explains. "That's the closest to a work ethic I have."

Within a few months, he hates his job, resenting that he has to work at all. He's furious that he has to spend his paycheck on Carol's Junior prom, even though he realizes it is his prom too since he has decided to graduate a year early. He has gotten special permission, if he can pass algebra, to take government and history at the same time in summer school. He thinks it is because South Lakes will be glad to get rid of him.

He and Carol go to the prom, and although he wants to maintain his cynicism, Brendon has a good time. Like most couples, they go out for a long, expensive dinner first, attend the dance for maybe half an hour, then go to their room at the Days Inn. While their parents think they are at the prom breakfast, they are chilling out drinking, doing some dope, being close at the motel. The prom pictures could be their parents' prom pictures—he with his boutonniere, she with her corsage, both looking clean-cut, young, and innocent. Brendon thinks Carol looks beautiful. He likes the evening with her but he has a hard time allowing himself to stay in the role of a loving and lovable young man.

While he's in summer school, his drug dealing really takes off and becomes his most lucrative form of employment. All through his sophomore year his own use had escalated so that he was getting "torn up" most days with acid, pot, codeine, hash, whatever. "I wouldn't say I'm a real junkie or anything," Brendon says defensively. "I've got a job. It's very controlled." Throughout the year, more and more people came to him for weed.

By summer school he has hit the big time. "I'm getting big amounts now," he brags. "I'm one of the biggest dealers in South Lakes, selling a pound of weed a day this summer, little acid here and there, 'shrooms and stuff—all good for me. My outlook is I came into the world and nobody owes me anything. I'm here on my own, I guess I'm going to make it on my own. It pretty much goes from there."

He says, "I knew everybody who was trying to deal and everybody would come to me for weed. You sell in ounces—quarters is the lowest I would go, which is a fourth of an ounce. Forty dollars. A half I would sell for fifty or sixty dollars. An ounce is one hundred dollars, which is a great price—I was probably the cheapest dealer around. I had people coming from McLean, all over. It is just friends of friends of friends."

When he needs a drop he calls "his guy" and tells him what amount he requires. "It is delivered in a big brick. He tells me where to meet him, and he's like, 'Do you have the money that you owe me?' and I'm like, 'Yeah, here,' and he says, 'This is going to be eleven hundred or twelve hundred dollars,' and I say, 'Cool, see you tomorrow.' Then I go and people pay me all day." By the fall, Brendon quits his job at the cleaners so he has the time to collect payments.

Once Brendon has his cash, he makes the connection. "You meet on some road. I pull up. They stop the car. I go out on the road, smoke a couple of cigarettes. He flashes me, I hop in his car. It's, 'What's up?' He says, 'What's up?' We drive around a little bit. Drop me back off and I'm out. It is easy. Or meet like at McDonald's. If somebody sees me so what—they are not going to be able to identify me." The odd thing is that sixteen-year-old Brendon needs to be driven everywhere by a friend. He could have gotten his license during the summer. His parents arranged for private driving lessons but Brendon says it was too much trouble having to get up to meet the instructor. So he depends on his beeper and a network of friends with cars to keep the business afloat.

By his last year, his junior/senior year in high school, Brendon has no illusions. "I have never sat down and said this is going to be a good year because I know how school is. I don't want to be sober in school, I don't want to kiss my teachers' asses because they are all jerks. I'm not going to have good attendance because I shouldn't have to have good attendance. If they are going to force me to go to school, I'm not going to do a good job."

Basically you watch a whole year go by while you are in school, says Brendon, and then at night you come home and do homework. "It's just a big game. I knew what I wanted to do early on and I think

I should have been able to go to a special school or take more art classes. There are classes I shouldn't have had to take—like gym. I got a little out of English and government and history but I have interest in that stuff, and I could learn it on my own. I think I should have been able to draw for three or four periods a day. My parents pay tax money.

"It sucks that if you don't come to classes they call your parents," he goes on. "Getting suspended for smoking cigarettes is totally worthless. There is no respect for students. You feel like cattle when you are in school."

He has no compunction about the criminality of his life. "I don't give a shit about this country or its rules. This country is screwed up," he says. "It could be a great country but it is so backward. This country is all about money and free enterprise. Basically money talks. Everybody is corrupt. If I can make my money illegally, why shouldn't I?" The only aspect that gives him pause is being caught and thrown out of school, "but I am too slick. Because I am not going to be a dealer dealing to fifty people a day. I'm going to be a dealer dealing with three main people or four who sell for me. That is why you don't get caught if you are a big drug dealer." He is convinced he runs a tight ship. "I don't put myself at risk, I am careful about what I do. I sell to people I trust, people I know."

The drug dealing solves his money problems in the short run. "I had an incredible lifestyle for a while. I was putting in my pocket at least two hundred dollars a week." He bought clothes, good dinners, had a ball "hanging out, getting drunk, cooking my friends up." He found however that some people took advantage of his generosity and were not real friends at all.

His parents knew and didn't know, Brendon says. His dad actually found a half-pound bag of weed. He was angry, said to get rid of it, but nothing really happened. His mom wanted to believe that when Brendon said he'd stop, that was sufficient. His sister says their mom would rather not think Brendon's drug use is as bad as it is, "for her own peace of mind. If she allowed herself to really figure out what is going on, she would not be able to function."

Brendon admits to a "split lifestyle" made of assorted parts that never meld into an integrated life. He races from sensation to sensation, sailing high, dipping low, never stable. He says he always feels stressed. "There's just too much going on in my head, something's just stuck in there."

He wants somebody to care, to reach out to his softer side—a teacher, a real friend, his dad—but he is also guarded and angry. "They have their own problems to deal with."

He rolls through groups of friends, never carrying any close connection from one year to another. He talks about his "friends from school, friends who don't go to school, graffiti friends, and drug-dealing friends." But in truth, except for Carol, he does not entirely belong with any of them. Carol is the one who since sophomore year has cared and has loved him. That is why, he says simply, he loves her so much.

He feels there is no place for his private, expressive self in the world, it blossoms deep in the corner of his basement and rarely rises to the surface. "It's just for me, to help myself relax. Do it for yourself, do whatever you need to get by."

There is never any reason to doubt his pain and anger and his rush to escape, as if some haunting cloud hovers and suffuses his existence. But there is nothing like that apparent in his home or even in what he reveals.

Brendon and his sister share the feeling that when Mom went to work, the heart of the house broke. "My mom is an awesome person," Brendon says. "I could totally see myself as a Christian kid growing up in Houston but it is like I am alone all of the time." It is as if he imputes to his mother the link that would have kept him a good Christian boy and he is forever seeking a way back. He never talks about religion in the same disparaging way he speaks of other institutions in society. He believes in his most cynical moments that there might be something there if he could just find it. He admires the faith his mother and sister share. The deep emotional part of him that seeks solace in God, but is denied it, acts out in ways that are callous, materialistic, and criminal. He lacks a moral compass: his mom covers for him, his dad is kept out, the family bargains with the devil, but his religious roots are a source of tension. Ultimately Brendon cannot free himself to be totally amoral. He suffers the stress of conscience.

As he analyzes his life, his dealing, his future, he cautiously dips back into an incredible pocket of pain. It turns out God let him down. "God made me mental I guess. I was sitting back watching people die and it just fucks with your brain. When I was eight, my friend was at a playground at Deepwood and he had a canteen around his neck and it got stuck on the slide and he fell off and he broke his neck."

Brendon was on vacation, and when he came back he found out his friend was dead. It raised questions about God, he says, and maybe made him afraid to get close to people.

Then three years ago, a woman at his church, whom he and his sister sat for, died a torturously slow death from cancer. "She had four kids and it was mind-blowing. She had cancer and then went into remission for a couple of years and then it destroyed her. It was tough seeing somebody that weak with no hair." It also raised fears around who else could die.

These are the things that tear him up inside. Unlike Jessica, whose family has also suffered grave losses, Brendon seems to have no help in putting things in perspective. So he turns to drugs. That is what drugs are, he explains, an escape from feelings. "They don't take away the pain," says Brendon. "They just put it aside."

When these difficult things happened, his parents could not offer the solace that might have helped him cope better. He doesn't blame them. "They try. My mom and dad try, but there's so much other stuff. They get so stressed out. Both working, moving, new place."

"New place"—that was in 1985! Brendon always returns to that original scar that brings back all the "what ifs." He has lived in Reston for a decade and still says, "I think I was a pretty happy kid until we moved here." The "what ifs" that haunt his family become, in this teenager, the "could haves" of his life. He could have been a good student if he had worked harder at it. He could have been a team player in school. He remembers the disillusionment of his freshman year. He really liked working on the Homecoming float, he really liked the potential of high school friendships, but they failed him. He could have had school spirit but it eluded him. He could have been an Eagle Scout but he got tired of the ranks and badges and quit in his sophomore year. He also quit track after his sophomore year, because it "wasn't fun." He could have been a star wrestler if he'd been able to reach his potential, but since he couldn't he remained on the team but "gave up this last year."

He sees in himself "definitely wasted potential." Then he says: "There's a million and one things I'd like to do. It's not really wasted potential. It's still in my brain."

Brendon has drifted and acted out through the years on the outside while he has wrestled with demons inside. He has gotten his way all along with few consequences. He says, it is "a weird thing. I've pretty much proved to myself that I can do whatever I want."

But what he wants is to be a good Christian boy, to be Joe High-school, to belong and to be at peace. As he waits in his house the week before leaving for college, Brendon still hovers between using his talents productively or destructively. He is struggling to balance his anger with some responsibility to his own future. He is candid about how it is not punishment that will curb his impulses but only a decision within himself about what matters.

He is a bright, talented, creative, loved young man in a mythic battle as the forces of darkness and light tear at him. Far from barren, he is a vessel of wide-ranging interests and experiences, many that are positive, many negative. From Scouts and Sunday School to substance abuse, from fly-fishing to drug dealing, from family togetherness to group vandalism, he is made of contradictions. "I know how bad life is; I pretty much realize how good life is." He dreams of being happy, of having a lucrative legitimate job, of being a father to his own son, whom he will love and allow to find his own way.

But in a flash his optimism fades. He always gets back to regrets, to bitterness, to the wound to the heart of the family—the loss of who they could have been. Brendon's life experiences are overlaid by a mental turmoil that drives him deep into the tunnels of his soul.

# *Broken Promises:*
# *Theirs and Ours*

Courtney feels her usual sense of relief that fourth period is over. She packs up her books efficiently and hurries out of the classroom. It's time to split. She meets Allie at the school entrance this cool, breezy April day, and they dash across the road, up the path a short bit, and into Mandy's house. A few of the kids beat them there.

It's the Lunch Bunch. Six to eight kids, and a few occasional others, meet daily in this clubhouse of the nineties, a welcoming townhouse across from school where the back door is always unlocked and the drugs flow freely. The house rules are clear: you bring your own weed; Mandy does not permit anybody to use her mom's supply. Other than that, her mom doesn't mind the use of her house. One of the regulars recalls, "Her mom is hardly home, but her mom told us the first few days we were hanging out there that we couldn't smoke cigarettes in the house because she hated the smell of tobacco. Then she said she didn't mind the smell of pot so we could smoke that."

The regulars take turns providing the marijuana and share with each other. There is invariably a supply because if all else fails, everyone knows Allie carries a bowl with her in her school backpack.

Courtney always finds an invitation difficult to turn down. Even when she is thinking she doesn't really want to go because she has a quiz in a class or has to go to work, when she gets to her fourth period and Allie whispers that she's going to meet Brendon and all them today, Courtney almost always agrees to join her. Courtney is so social, it is hard to resist being with her friends in the middle of a school day. Sometimes she tells herself, I'm not going to do any. "But then I get there. . . ."

Some kids go there after school too, but not Courtney. She just met Mandy through Allie and they only go for lunch. Some kids stay into the afternoon, but Courtney and Allie always go back for fifth period.

At first, Courtney thought it was the scariest thing to go back to school high. "You think everybody knows that you're high, and you can't concentrate." She knows a lot of kids are in school stoned, and she thinks teachers know about it. "But what are they supposed to do? It's not really the teacher's job."

By this quarter, however, she feels more confident about handling school and drugs. She's in the second semester of her sophomore year. She is getting her best grades ever in her fifth-period geometry class—an A, and she hasn't had an A since seventh grade! She is very proud of her ability to handle drugs and be successful in school. She brags how every day during third quarter she was on some sort of drugs and she managed to get the best grades she's gotten all year. What makes her accomplishment so notable is, "if I go to school high it's really hard for me to concentrate, especially in math. Some people say it's really easy for them, but for me, it's harder because I can't pay attention."

She is more concerned about going to her job at the dry cleaners stoned. "You can't be all tired and high and hungry at work," she says. "You have to be waiting on the customers and you don't want to mess up." Once Brendon started working with her, they would try to coordinate. "Yesterday, he and I both worked. I smoked, but he didn't," she reports. He still was with the Lunch Bunch, "but he didn't have any. Sometimes I'll do that"—just have "one or two hits," but still hang out with the group.

Before she developed enough confidence to buy her own weed, she'd share the cost of a bag. She was afraid she would get ripped off so she'd often split a bag with Brendon. She and her friends know they can easily get as much marijuana or other drug as they want. "It would be a lot harder to get a six-pack of beer," says Courtney.

She is thinking about trying LSD again. Brendon swears that having sex when you're on acid is the best. The night he found out she had sex with Nat, he wondered if she had ever had an orgasm when she was tripping. Courtney told him she had only tried half a dose of acid during the winter at a party. Nat's best friend was there and they encouraged her to try it. She told them she had to go home to her mom in half an hour so she only took half and then gave the other half to Allie. She thought it was okay, "but it was only half."

She's a little scared to take a full hit: "I need the perfect circumstances." Since a trip lasts from eight to twelve hours, Courtney says, "I need a full day of no parents. What if I do freak out? I'm asking people to take care of me. Brendon said he'd take care of me and Allie said she'd take care of me. I need people who have done it before who are experienced." She'd certainly never be tripping in school like Brendon has a few times.

She and Dee laugh at their parents' naïveté since finding out about their drug use last year. They have got to be either dumb or in denial to believe they would only try drugs once. The girls think it is funny that their parents probably have some image of the older boys luring them into drugs. Quite the contrary. The girls asked them. "We were the ones who made them go out because we wanted to try it."

Courtney likes doing drugs most in the middle of the night. Until the time they got caught, it worked well. "We weren't scared because you'd go home and you didn't have to talk to anybody, didn't have to face anybody. You'd just go to sleep for about an hour and then you'd get up and go to school. If you miss sleep it doesn't bother you for another few days." The only scary thing is when you leave the house and then come back in, "but that's what makes it so much fun."

The best part of dope for Courtney is that "if you're high, you can just sit there and do nothing, but it's more fun than if you weren't and you just sat there and did nothing." She sometimes questions if she has more fun high because of the drugs, the company, or both. She also wonders if she does drugs "because I can't take my family." But she knows herself and believes, "I would have done them even if everything wasn't bad. So I can't say it's only because of that, because the first time I did drugs was just because I wanted to." Part of her involvement is natural teenage experimentation, she says. However, she adds, "If you have some messed-up family life, you're not going to try to be like this good citizen."

Some people might think Courtney is incorrigible. She apparently was not one bit chastised by her experience at Christian Outward

Bound camp last summer, punishment for her middle-of-the-night lifestyle. Happy-go-lucky and spontaneous to her sister Ann's intensity and rigidity, Courtney is the ultimate "whatever" girl. She thinks her parents are so "irrational" and that they overreacted last year. She's looking to have a good time, to have her way, not to be hassled. She feels that if it doesn't affect her parents, her life is her choice.

Courtney lives somewhat mindlessly from experience to experience, seeking sensations as many kids do, moving through the pathways of what is the new conventional teen life. Her grades are okay, she has a job at the local dry cleaners, she broke up with her boyfriend. She doesn't sneak out too often at night anymore because it got old. "I don't know what will come along now," she says. "But I never saw myself doing that kind of stuff before. I never planned it. It just happens. Opportunities come along."

The beginning of her sophomore year was disrupted by the tension of all the sex stuff with Nat, but this spring, she's got it pretty much under control. She still shudders over the pregnancy scare. It was so dumb. That last time she had sex with Nat, which was the day before Brendon told her Nat was cheating on her, they had sex without any protection. She had always provided the condoms for them, and still had exactly one left. He never had any with him. Anyway, this one time they were careless. When they broke up and she started thinking about what could happen she was freaked. Her period came, thank goodness.

She and Dee still spend hours talking about sex and its ramifications. During one conversation, Courtney rambles on about how she cannot figure out why parents are always saying to "wait until you're older. They never tell us to wait until we're married." She tells Dee how, after the first time she did it, she asked Allie what she thought people meant when they say their kids are too young emotionally to have sex. "What do you think goes into it emotionally? I never really understood the whole emotional part of it. I thought it was really awkward and everything. But what's there to handle? I guess there are feelings, but I really don't quite understand the big deal."

Courtney and Dee agree that maybe it's because it is new at first. "But it's just like when you kiss someone," says Courtney. "Nobody ever says don't kiss someone until you're older. It's just another step."

Courtney wishes parents would talk more about having safe sex using condoms and pills. She wishes they would warn their children about how "it's going to be awkward the first time so they don't think they're the only person in the world who doesn't know what they're doing . . . instead of trying to force them to wait." She thinks that the more parents talk about how kids shouldn't have sex because they "can't handle it now,"the more kids want to see what it is to handle. The girls agree the whole line of thought makes sex ever more tantalizing. "I think they should say be safe instead of wait, wait," says Courtney.

Courtney knows that when she goes out with someone again, she'll probably have sex because she's not scared about it anymore. "If you think about it, it's the same with everything," she says. "The first time you do something it's a big deal, but then it gets more common. The first time you kiss somebody you're like, Whoa, I kissed somebody. After that it is, I just kissed him, it's not a big deal." It becomes like going out in the middle of the night. Forget all the admonitions of her parents, the punishments, the special camp. She never had any attack of conscience about her nighttime forays. "After a while Dee and I thought this is stupid because we'll be tired the next day. This is so dumb, we aren't doing anything, we just drive around and fall asleep." It wasn't exciting anymore.

Now instead of slipping out in the middle of the night, Courtney skips out of school during the day with great regularity. "Allie and I used to leave school every day anyway, whether we had anything to do or not. Just to get out," she says. The problem is, skipping becomes addictive. "If you leave school, it's hard to come back. When you're out of school, you say you'll come back, but then you don't want to," Courtney says. Except she does this year. It turns out her seventh-period teacher moonlights at the local grocery store, so there is no telling when her parents will run into him. "If I didn't have him seventh period, nothing would hold me back, but because he talks to my parents all the time I know he would tell my parents." But there is absolutely no problem skipping first period because "you just come in late and you're like, 'Oops, overslept'; then you go to your second-period class."

Courtney cuts as many classes as possible without getting an automatic F in a class. The school's tough new attendance policy allows only five unexcused absences a quarter. She's figured out that she is much better off cutting random periods than whole days. There is an underlying cautiousness in her daring, so that she pushes the limits but avoids reaching the point of no return. She thinks her parents "kind of knew about it" but never did anything.

Courtney displays no apparent intellectual curiosity, no passionate commitment, no respect for rules in school. Her explanation is, "Kids don't like to do what they have to do. Just like they don't like to obey their parents because they have to."

The one place where she is different is at her job at the dry cleaners. She seems to thrive on the responsibility vested in her and the structure of clear demands. It is grown-up work, not childhood obligations. It is an arena she chose that is separate from her family and teachers. "If I could choose any job I wouldn't say, 'I want this one,' but it's not bad to work here." Unlike her coworker Brendon, she likes her job and is committed to it.

Courtney may zone out in the rest of her life, but at the cleaners she is focused on every detail and is meticulous in doing her work. She gives a monologue on the dry cleaning business that would make her boss proud: "If they bring in shirts to be laundered you have to tag each individual shirt, then put in starch or no starch; if it's due back for a special day you have to put it in a special bin. You have to sort the clothes, then sign the tag, and write it in the book and everything. When the truck delivers all the clothes back, the driver just hangs them up. You have to put them in all the files, write them in, sign it on the little piece of paper; then you have to write those in the book; then you have to put them in alphabetical order like in the file. It's like you never finish." But she does it, unlike anything else in her life, with consistency, responsibility, and reliability. She makes a dollar over minimum wage and saves most of her paychecks.

The job and the money are the keys to her freedom. The job keeps her out of the house—something she wants as much as Ann. Like her sister, Courtney has worked out a life that allows her to avoid seeing her folks. "I don't see my parents too much anymore because they come home from work at five, and I go to work at four, so I'm usually at work. A lot of times I'll go out with my friends. Heidi will pick me up or my parents will drop me off somewhere directly from work. I don't get home until midnight, and then my parents are already asleep. They leave for work in the morning before I wake up, so I don't really see them all that often."

Courtney's days are at least fourteen hours long. She potentially has a break for an hour or so after school, but she ends up just waiting at school because she has no way to get home and then back to work.

The car issue is a big one. Courtney is really mad at how difficult it is for her to get to work, that she has to twiddle her thumbs around the school and then walk to her job. Her parents don't ever do anything to make her life easier. She realizes her mom and stepdad can't take off from their jobs to chauffeur her, but there is an obvious solution. Ann is seventeen. All she needs to do is get a license, but their parents won't let her and for no good reason.

Courtney hopes her paychecks will eventually get her some transportation of her own. "They always say I should save my money. They make me feel bad if I cash two paychecks in a row." Since they won't let Ann get her license, and Courtney won't be sixteen until next December, both girls are stuck. Courtney, always the more assertive of the two, is trying to finesse a deal with her mom using her money as leverage. Courtney tells her mom she will pay for her insurance if her mom will buy her "a cheap used car, like two thousand dollars. You and dad can split the price." Her mom tells her if Courtney keeps her grades up, "We'll see." Courtney promises she will make good grades, they should negotiate now. Her mom says it sounds like they can work out a deal, so Courtney is hoping.

The car is essential to organize her life. It is not that Courtney just wants it to mess around with friends. It's a practical thing. "It's like we have no time," she says, "especially if you have a project to do or something. And like photography, I can only do it on the weekends. Every Saturday I work from nine to six, that's a full day. On Sundays, almost every Sunday, Dee and I go to the mall. If I go to the mall, there's no time."

The only worries Courtney has are about driving and college. "I always worry about whether I'm going to get my license or not. I always worry about whether I'm going to get accepted in college or not. If I have a fight with my friend or something then I'll worry about that, but overall, I just worry about college and driving."

Courtney only recently started paying attention to the requisites for college. She's developing a longer view, and now understands she needs to depend on grades since she has no interest in extracurricular activities. She thinks her job actually helps her grades by getting her to budget her time. "If I wasn't working then I'd just come home from school and do whatever I wanted," she says. "I'd never get around to doing my homework because I'd say, I'll do it later, then I'd be like, I'm too tired. I'd try to do it in the morning, and it would never get done. But with my job, I go from school right to work, then I get off work, come home, eat dinner, do my homework, and then go to bed. So I have a schedule that I have to follow every day."

She feels bad about how she messed up her grades her freshman year. At the time, she didn't care, "because my parents were being so irrational and going so overboard with everything that I felt like there was no way I was ever going to get to do what I wanted and I was always going to be grounded, so I totally gave up trying." Now she realizes that if she ever wants to get out of her house and into a good college, she has to have good grades. She thinks it won't be so hard. "You just have to figure out what kind of teachers your teachers are, what they want from you, and how they grade," says Courtney. "I copy people's homework, but not tests. Most of our teachers separate the desks and everything." Next year, she will continue to work at bringing up her grade point average. She's thinking, "Take easy classes to bring up my grades, or take something pass/fail, like SAT prep."

Courtney has to discover things for herself. Luckily she learns pretty quickly because her parents don't have much influence. When she talks about her life, the only thing reliable is her job. Nowhere in her story is the notion of doing things to please her parents, or anything about love in the family, about rules and roles and structure. Nowhere is there ambition or forgiveness or caring or effort, respect or nurturing, fairness or reciprocity. Nobody acts like they believe in anybody else. There is no mention of hugs, of listening, no invitation to be close, no joy.

There is something not quite right at Courtney and Ann's house. There is an out-of-kilter feeling in a family room not for family, a parents' bedroom that is off-limits to the kids. There is something fake in a lavish Christmas celebration when there are no day-to-day connections, in the ceramic jack-o'-lantern at Halloween when it is impossible to imagine the parents and kids ever carving a real one together, in the untouchable brocade and gold lamé teddy bears that inhabit the living room alongside an abundance of pictures of children from two broken families.

Courtney's total disregard for any obligation to her parents has its roots in other broken promises and secrets that surround her every day. "My home life is different," says Courtney. "If I compare it to

Dee's, her parents are always like, 'Dee, we want to be with you.' My parents are like, 'I don't like you.' " Once when Nat was around and they were in the car with her mom, Courtney teased, "I'm your favorite daughter, right, Mom?" Her mom answered, "No, you're not. I don't like either of you." Maybe it was a joke, says Courtney. "But not exactly. I think she's serious."

Courtney says she doesn't understand her mom. "She's not like a real mom. She's not like the kind of mom that makes you breakfast." She and her sister think that something weird happened to her that she won't talk about. The mystery of her mom is only the beginning of secrets in the house. "Like she was married before she was married to my dad, but she won't tell me about it. My dad told me about it once. Then he said, ask your mom. I thought okay. My mom said, we'll talk about it when you're older. Then my stepfather told me about it a few weeks ago. Then my mom yelled at him so he wouldn't talk to me about it. My mom's like, 'I don't want to talk about it.' So she hides a lot of stuff. There's something messed up in her life. I think something happened to her. So I don't know. Until I'm older I'm not going to be able to know about her life."

Her mom married her stepdad when Courtney was four. Even though he has been around for ten years, Courtney does not think of him as a dad. "He tried to adopt me but I wouldn't let him. He gets really, really mad if I say that he's not my dad. Not that he thinks he is my dad, but he'll hit me if I say he's not my dad. He'll yell at me and say, 'I take the place of your dad.' I say, 'No you don't, no one takes the place of my dad.' "

She remembers how her mom and stepdad used to force Ann and her to call him Dad, "so we used to call him Daddy Bob because we didn't want to call him Dad." Her first memory of him is of the day before they got married, when she couldn't stop crying. "I was four years old. And he brought me up into the hotel room and spanked me." She doesn't really like him. "Sometimes I get along with him and sometimes I don't," says Courtney.

They never do anything as a family, she says, because "We can't. They want to but we can't get along. It all ends up in fights." The compromise is that sometimes her mom and Ann do something, or she and her mom, or Bob and Ann. "But it never ends up as a family thing," says Courtney. "Ann and I won't let it."

The one thing that should be kept a secret is not: her parents' infidelity. Bob cheats on her mom when he travels and Courtney knows.

The reason Courtney knows is that they have discussed it in front of her and Ann. A few years ago, they even brought her into the conversation. Her stepfather asked if she would be mad at him if he cheated on her mom. Courtney said no. Then he asked if Courtney would be mad at her mother if she cheated on him. Courtney said she wouldn't but she wasn't sure she meant it. "I guess I would care," she now admits. "I would care more about my stepfather cheating than my mom. I'm more protective of my mom."

The girls knew it was happening because they could also overhear their parents arguing and when her mom discussed it on the phone with friends. It was harder for Ann, Courtney thinks. She tried to talk to Bob about it. "If she gets in fights with him, she'll yell at him how he cheats on Mom," says Courtney. "It was like a family joke after a while. If he'd be on the phone, Mom would say, 'Is that another one of your girlfriends?' It got crazy."

Recently Courtney was sitting and talking to her mom. Her mom told her not to tie up the phone because she had a lot of phone calls to make. She joked that she had to call her boyfriend. Then she said to Courtney, "That would be the best fantasy, to have a boyfriend and be having an affair." Courtney, a little taken aback, said, "Isn't that kind of like crossing the line of faithful?" Her mom said no, it was a fantasy. But when Courtney asked, "If the chance came along would you go for it?" her mom answered yes. Courtney doesn't know if she is kidding or not. "I don't know if it had an effect on me," says Courtney, "if her bad relationships have an effect on me. She hides a lot."

Courtney holds on to her own fantasy about the kind of man she'd like to marry. "He has to be good-looking, or at least somewhat handsome because I don't want my kids to be really ugly. He has to have a job. I'm not saying he has to be a doctor, but he can't just sit home. He has to feel the same way about raising kids, that's a big thing. And have stuff in common with me, because we're going to be living together. He has to be caring and loving. He's going to have to be a good dad, and he can't have a bad temper because I don't want him to hit the kids or anything. But he can't be one of those people that just sits there. Sometimes you have to fight with people, so when you yell at them they can't just say okay, okay. He has to be opinionated too. He has to love me and show affection. I think it would be cute if he got jealous sometimes, but he can't be threatening."

Courtney's conversation is replete with references to anger, threats, spankings, fighting, and punishments. Then one day she mentions that her stepdad's violence went beyond that spanking when she was four. The last time he hit her, she shares, was the week before, when she got into a fight with him, but "he's traveling now so things are better."

Just like that, like she is discussing her homework assignment in geometry, she discloses the biggest secret of all in her house. "My stepfather is really abusive," Courtney says. "He hits people. He's hit my mom before, but she's hit him before, too. He broke her nose, but she didn't tell anybody. She wouldn't go to the doctor because she hates doctors, so she just let it heal. It's really messed up. And he hits me and hits my sister."

Bob was in the Marines, so he's used to violence, Courtney thinks. "Like if he doesn't have control, then he'll just hit you and he's really strong. He doesn't know how strong he is. So he'll hit me, just like he's hitting someone his own size."

Bob tells the girls that you're allowed to hit your children. But Courtney thinks that "legally he's not allowed to hit me because he's not my legal guardian, he's just a stepfather. I think you should be able to hit your kids, but when you start leaving marks on them, I think that's crossing the line to abuse. I used to start stuff about it, say that I was going to call the police, but they don't care." One time Courtney tried to leave. Her parents wouldn't let her go out the door. They stood in front of it and pushed her away.

Then last summer, the girls found out that Bob had been abused as a child. "Everybody knew that for years and years, but I didn't know that," says Courtney. "I had a lot of hatred toward him since he was so abusive, but now that I found out he was abused, it kind of explains it so it's not quite as bad. But I wish he would have told me that before."

He hit Courtney a few weeks ago and left finger marks on her cheek. Ann came home from sitting, saw the marks on her sister's face, and asked what happened. Courtney said, "What do you think happened? Should I do something about it?" Ann said, "No, no, no. Don't worry about it." Courtney sees her sister as "the kind of person that puts up a front to make everybody think everything's okay. She doesn't let anybody know what's going on."

Courtney admits to being abusive in the past with her sister. "I used to hit her a lot and take out all my anger on my sister. She wouldn't fight back. I could go up and hit her and she wouldn't fight back. It was just easy." She tries not to do it anymore.

When Courtney was in fifth grade she desperately wanted to move in with her dad. When she would visit him, she would refuse to go back to her mom's house. "They had to physically put me on the airplane because I wouldn't want to leave him. I would tell them about it, saying, 'You don't know what happens.' I told him everything. But since my stepmom doesn't want to raise children anymore, my dad's kind of like, 'Don't worry about it.' There's not much he can do. He's also kind of confused about it because it's my side and he doesn't really know."

She remembers how she used to idolize her dad, but after all these years of being trapped with Bob, she's beginning to rethink her feelings about her real father. It's not right that she and Ann go to Florida to visit and tell their dad how "it's really hard to deal with Mom and Bob, they're being crazy about things. And then we ask him, 'How do you feel?' He'll say, 'I agree, they're going overboard.' We say, 'Okay, great. Can you help us out a little bit, maybe talk to her?' He says he doesn't feel it's his place. I say, 'What do you mean, it's not your place? You are my father, aren't you?' "

Last year her stepdad threatened her every day. " 'You're moving in with your dad, you're moving to your dad's.' And he'd throw suitcases in my room and say, 'Pack, pack, you're living with your dad,' and I'd say no. A few weeks ago they were like, 'You're going to move in with your father.' I said okay, whatever. But I could never live with my dad because he doesn't want me to live with him. They'd have to send me to boarding school." It turns out there is no safe place for her to be. She just has to do the best she can under the circumstances. Staying away from home as much as possible is the solution she and Ann have devised.

Since her own dad doesn't do anything to help, she hasn't bothered to open up to any other adults about her problems. Not even when she briefly went to therapy last year. "We went to a social worker for a day and I had a chance to talk but I didn't. My parents were in there saying everything bad about me, so all I was doing was sitting there crying." When she was alone with the therapist and had a chance, "I didn't want to make it all legal because I thought it would make things worse. I think they'd get madder at me if I went to the police. Then they'd be in trouble and I'd end up going to a foster home."

She talks to her friends about the abuse sometimes. Dee can always tell when she gets into a fight. She invites Courtney to come stay with her, but it is not an option unless she runs away. She's thought about it. "I was going to run away last year, but I ran away in fifth grade and that made everything bad," she says. "If I ran away it would make things worse."

Courtney and Ann always say, "The day we turn eighteen we're going to move out." But Courtney is going to graduate from high school and go to college when she's seventeen. She's counting the days.

The failure of all the adults in her life to be there in a reliable, supportive way, the trail of their broken promises to care well for her and her sister, all converge over the issue of driving and a car. Her dad always promised his daughters since they were little that his old car would become theirs. It took hold of the girls' imaginations early on, and they have spent many hours anticipating the freedom it represents.

When Courtney said to him, "Dad, we're older, can we have the car?" he told her he wasn't done with it yet. Then he said he would lend it to them for two years until they went to college. "He's like, 'Okay, this is what we'll do,' " Courtney recalls. " 'You and Ann both get your licenses, you share the car fifty-fifty, and then you guys can use it until you're both in college, and then the car gets returned to me.' I was like, 'Dad, it's eleven years old, it's an old car, I'll buy it from you. I'm like your family. I have eight hundred dollars in the bank.' He's said that he would never sell it to his daughters." Then he was going to drive to Virginia and drop it off in the summer when he came up to visit, but that got changed to maybe sometime in the fall.

Her mom keeps making promises about Courtney getting a license and about helping out with buying the car or insurance. Courtney keeps up her grades as she said she would. Like her dad, her mother doesn't keep her promises.

During the summer, the girls' mother and stepfather go out of town and hire an eighteen-year-old, Sue, to take care of them. When the parents were away a few weeks before, Courtney was supposed to stay at a friend's house but didn't. She spent the weekend at home. It was so good, she recalls, and "I was so happy they were gone. It's not like I really did anything wrong, it's just like it was so much better. It was like you didn't have to deal with your parents about when you're going here, and how you're going there, and when you'll be home. It was so much more carefree."

Courtney is angry about this girl Sue coming. She thinks it sucks that she and Ann can't be alone, but then admits that for two weeks, they probably need someone who can drive. "I'm still kind of mad about it, but I figure it will be easier at least to lie and get away with things with Sue, because she doesn't know anything about me. She doesn't know who I'm friends with. I don't think she's going to be checking up on me, like calling up my friends' houses or anything. That's definitely a plus. I figure she works in the morning and everything, so it will be easier. Unless she's really trying to get me in trouble, she might fall for things later. If I come in late or something, she'll take my excuses better than my parents would."

Courtney and her friend Heidi have decided to go to the beach. They'll both work on Saturday. Heidi will pick her up after work, and they'll go. They plan to spend Saturday night at the beach and then come home on Sunday. Courtney will tell Sue that she is spending the night at Heidi's house. The only catch right now is coming up with a "really good plan" so Heidi's parents will let her have the car overnight. "We were going to say that we were going to Kings Dominion on Sunday, leaving early on Sunday from my house," says Courtney.

Courtney has no compunction about betraying her parents' trust, particularly since it galls her that they don't trust her. "I think they should definitely trust me and have respect for me," she insists, "if I can go through school and get good grades, have a social life, have a part-time job where I work like twenty hours a week, and still find time to do drugs."

Screw them. Whether they notice or not, Courtney will continue to work hard at her job, save her money, get the grades she needs to get into college, and have the social life she wants. If she has to cheat a little to accomplish her goals she will. If she has to break promises to others she will. If it seems selfish and self-centered, so what? After all, these are the lessons she has learned at home.

# Doing High School
# the Old-Fashioned Way

A s the 1993–94 school year approaches, Charles is ready and eager, although it would be hard to guess by looking at his reclining body. He's totally zonked on the couch in front of the television. His father has to stir him. He sits up groggily, rubs his eyes, runs his hand over his shaved head, and pokes out one long limb at a time getting it all together, then rises. He is growing so fast that these naps are not laziness, they're restorative. The Big Growth Spurt finally happened this summer. He has grown five inches and gained nearly forty pounds; there's an unfamiliar feel to his own body. His mom and sister have been on a journey to the South to visit colleges, and the two guys have been bachelors together for a week.

In preparation for their homecoming, Charles and his dad need to clean up the pizza boxes and the dishes piled in the sink. The floor needs to be vacuumed, magazines and newspapers organized, a few groceries purchased. Father and son have had a good time, but they both miss the other half of the family.

There is an awareness that this is the last year all four of them will live together every day. This time next year Nika will be off to college. Behind all the teasing, the exclamations of how nice it will be to take over the space she occupies, or how great it will be to have fewer games to attend, this family works as a unit. They all, even her brother, are a bit sad realizing that the kids are growing up and Nika will be graduating. Her mom's eyes instantly tear at the very mention of it. Her dad is less obvious, but no less emotional inside. Charles, in his more communicative moments, admits he is used to Nika's being around.

Charles's days are just full enough in the summer. He likes being around home doing projects with his dad, playing basketball at school, working out in the weight room, hustling some pool. He goes to lacrosse camp, plays in a summer league and practices as much as he can, already thinking ahead to lacrosse season when he'll be on the varsity team. He and his parents agree it is a good investment of his time and effort. Not only is the sport his passion but it also has the potential to get him a scholarship to college, along with his good grades. His parents see no point in his working a menial job for the summer. They think it is much healthier for him to have some time to regroup and work on honing his game. During the lazy days of summer, Charles gets a reprieve, time to think, and a chance to work on other aspects of himself—even if he doesn't see it that way.

When he is not cradling a ball, Charles, with some friends, has been working on his car. It sits in the driveway in all its splendor, a tangerine 1971 Volkswagen bus that his dad bought for nine dollars the last year Charles played Reston Youth League football. At the time, his dad had some work done on it, and it lasted a few seasons of car pools until it started spitting fire out the back. It would have made sense to junk it, but Charles would not allow his dad to dispose of wheels that could be his. Getting "his car" in shape has become a major pastime for Charles. The first thing he and his buddies did was take out the crummy stereo and put in an upgraded system. Charles spends hours perusing trucker magazines and car books looking for custom parts and wheels, pricing things out. When he got in his hands an authentic 1971 repair manual, he studied it all the time. His dad is helping him, as his grandfather had helped his dad so many years ago.

Charles and his buddies like to go out and sit in the car with the stereo booming and imagine they are driving. They can see themselves sailing along, the girls at their sides, the wind blowing on their faces as the stereo announces their presence to everyone. Charles can picture how he'll be able to hang out wherever he wants, live the high life. He recalls an evening he spent with one of his sister's friends: "We went up to McDonald's, got some food. There were three parties going on. We stopped by each one of them just to see who was there. One party had already ended, another one hadn't begun yet, and another one was real boring so everybody was leaving when we got there. So we just kept going. I figure once I get to drive I'll be able to do stuff like that, just go around and hang out."

For now he is stymied. Only a total nerd would use his bike as transportation for a party, or even to hang out at McDonald's. "It doesn't look good to ride your bike anywhere except for up to school to work out in the weight room." As he works on his car, Charles daydreams. "It seems like everything will change once I get to drive."

He has it all planned. "The first day of lacrosse practice I'll go to practice, tell the coach that I won't be there the next day because I've got to get my license. I've been waiting too long to get my license, I'm getting my license. Since it's during the week, there shouldn't be a long line."

His father has been thinking about lacrosse too, but in connection with the infamous Madison game. "The Incident," as the family refers to it, has preoccupied his dad, who is on a letter-writing campaign, battling the system for justice. The letters never in any way excuse Charles's violent reaction on the field. What they do request is parity in the punishment for the boy who called his son a nigger, setting the chain of events in motion. It is the lack of an apology, or any kind of admission that a racial slur was made, that galls his dad. "At the time that it happened, I was appalled that Charles was beating that boy. Until I knew," he says. "I still say that he shouldn't have reacted to that degree and he should have been punished for it. I like things balanced. I assumed the other boy was punished. The referee tried to reach equilibrium at the time, and he took both boys out of the game, giving them the same amount of penalty time. Then the other boy went back in the game. The referee didn't call him into the game, the coach substituted him. It's been unbalanced ever since." He writes to the principal of Madison High School using extraordinary restraint, keeping his focus not on what was said or not said, but on the behavior of the Madison player immediately following the incident. Giving the player, Ralph Meeks, the benefit of the doubt as to whether or not the initial slash that set Charles off was malicious (i.e., that he simultaneously called Charles a "stupid nigger"), writes his dad, "does not account for his actions after the whistle was blown. Meeks started

off the field with his arms raised high. This posture is normally associated with having achieved some meritable accomplishment, such as
scoring a goal or an assist but certainly not for committing an infrac-
tion of the rules." All the Sutters want is an apology from the player
and the coach for what was said. Until that happens, his son is suffering the double whammy of racial insult and the refusal of anybody
official to deal with it.

Charles's father is frustrated and infuriated by the lack of a gra-
cious response to his carefully restrained statements of outrage at
the unfairness. He demands a viewing of the tape of the game with
the involved parties present. Finally he gets it. The evidence is deemed
inconclusive. "They said they can't prove who said it," he recounts.
"There were three kids in the general area. Charles says he knows
who said it. They're saying they are sticking to it. The boy's parents
are concerned that we're painting their son to be a racist. I said I'm
not trying to indict this young man. I don't want my son hurt. Now
he's been called a nigger, he's been hit, he's been thrown out of the
game that he was in, he's been suspended for the next two games for
retaliating, and you're saying everything's inconclusive. What do I
tell my son? They have no answer."

The thing that kills his dad is that nobody at the other school is
punished. Dave Morgan, the director of student activities at South
Lakes, had Charles write an apology to the young man, the student
body, and the principal. Charles also had to attend a meeting of both
school athletic directors, to apologize to the boy who slashed him.
Charles came home and told his parents that he had done all the talking. His dad is baffled: Charles was being made the fall guy "as if he
had called himself a nigger and then lashed out." Charles is hurt that
in this face-to-face meeting, Ralph still never apologized.

Over the summer, the issue goes round and round, with letters,
calls, and follow-up meetings with the powers that be. What it gets
down to, explains Charles's dad, is this: "All I'm looking for is the de-
cency of an apology." Finally the Madison athletic director says per-
functorily, "Oh, I'm sorry."

Summer ends, and the Sutter family plunges into the frantic pace
of another school year. Schedules go up on the refrigerator, papers
start piling up around the house, everybody goes off in a million directions as usual.

Unlike his dad, who has been obsessed and outwardly agitated,
Charles reacts more quietly to the injustice. He still can't believe that

he was called a nigger in a world he thought was beyond such things, and then to have the kid moved up to varsity the next game rather than being punished for it is too much. When cross-country season begins and Charles is docked the first two meets because of the lacrosse penalty, his own plan gels. He and his lacrosse buddies will get the kid in the spring during the Madison game. They work on the details. "I figure if I have to serve that two-game suspension, then Meeks should have to serve the same thing—either end his lacrosse career, or if he gets hurt and misses two weeks, he'll miss his last game of the regular season and the first game of playoffs. He'll regret what he said."

Charles appreciates his father's efforts on his behalf but thinks that, over the summer, "it became really more his issue. That's what he felt he should do as a father. The one I've argued with is my mom, because she knows what I'm going to try and do to this boy this year. She's like, don't hurt that boy, he'll get his later on." She doesn't understand the male way of handling things. Satisfied with his own plan to resolve the situation, Charles puts the issue aside until next spring.

He has many things to do now that school has started. As president of the sophomore class, he forges new resolve to lead effectively and to bring his class together. He had already had a meeting of the officers before classes started since he and the vice president were cross-country runners and would be pressed for time.

His class this year is smaller by 70 students, down to 420. Sophomore principal Hoy says it is because, of the 60 kids who failed, only 10 went to summer school to bring their grades up. Another 20 were thrown out of school at the end of the year or are not returning. What amazes Charles is that among this group were a bunch of kids that had repeated their freshman class with them, and some of them had even been freshmen a year before that. "Do we really need these people in there?" Charles wonders. "The way I figure it, if they don't want to be there, why are we forcing them to be there?" Also this year the state increased the dropout age from sixteen to eighteen. "They're forcing you to be there and if you don't want to be there, you're just there to cause trouble," says Charles. "The one thing that people don't need is trouble when they're trying to get an education." He hopes that this purging of his class will eliminate the problem of its being referred to as "the Ghetto."

The first order of business on Charles's class agenda is to try and get everything planned for this year's Homecoming float. The theme is the 1970s. The administration has ruled that the floats be built on pickup trucks and the idea has turned away many kids as much less fun. Charles is concerned because building the float is one of the only times a large number of class members come together on anything. "For the car wash it was the officers and maybe three or four other people, and people who ran for office," says Charles. "When it comes to the float, everybody comes together to work on it."

In the days before Homecoming, Charles's leadership is put to the test by the traditional rampages in which each class tries to find where the other classes are building their floats and vandalize them. His class unfortunately does the most damage to all the others. The freshman float is attacked repeatedly. Kids throw rocks and eggs at it and rip things off of it. The float is completely destroyed and Charles later learns it was his class that did it.

While the sophomores protect their float the Friday night before Homecoming, the seniors try to get it. They drive by, throwing eggs. Charles and a few other kids are sentries in the woods, watching to recognize any float bandits. One of the parents helping the sophomores hurls his recycling bin at the car of seniors as it comes past, hitting the car. People start picking up rocks. One of the sophomore boys gets hit with a bottle. The seniors return a second time and throw rocks. One rock goes through the windshield of a parked car, another through the driver's side window, knocking off the rearview mirror. The damage to the car would later be estimated at over three thousand dollars. The sophomores return fire with rocks of their own. Finally the police arrive.

The kids doing the vandalism are not the thugs of the school but the active, involved high achievers. Their parents would probably deny to the end that their children could possibly be involved in such mischief. The worst offender in this incident is a varsity soccer player.

The sophomore class gets off the hook because it was a parent that started the conflagration by throwing the recycling bin. The whole scene is but another example of how all the old high school traditions are fragile, threatened by violence. There have been shootings at football games, class and team pranks that get out of hand, dances ruined by alcohol, deadly car crashes around school events, bomb scares in schools, and drug overdoses even at well-chaperoned events like the Jam for Man concert. Not just in Fairfax County, Virginia, but across the United States, today's adolescence is police patrolled. The emphasis has shifted to control, not fun. The feeling that surrounds kids is that they are always a nanosecond away from something going very wrong.

The weather for Homecoming is horrendous. It pours buckets all day long. More logistical problems confront Charles. The parade isn't canceled, but a number of the traditional convertibles never show. "Our officers gave up the car we would have ridden in the parade to the princesses from our class so they wouldn't get wet, because they were all dressed up," he recalls. "We walked with our float and got soaked. But it was a good way to bring the class together and our class had the most people that showed up." Such things truly matter to Charles. He does not attend the dance that evening with his classmates, even though his sister is a princess. His sleep is more important.

Charles's days are ridiculously full. School starts at 7:30. He has classes all day long and often meetings over class business during lunch. "If it's cross-country season I have maybe a half hour to do whatever I have to do, and then I have to get ready for practice," says Charles. He tries to squeeze in after-school art two to three times a week so he can get official credit on his transcript. He also likes the freedom of creating whatever moves him: "It's my work. It's what you think is right, not what other people think." Art is a welcome relief from all the other things he does, which have outside standards that he tries not only to meet but to exceed.

Cross-country practice starts at 3:30, but if he has to get an ankle taped or his knee iced, he has to get ready by 3:00, because he'll be competing with the football players and players from the other sports to get into the training room to see the trainer. Cross-country practice is over about 5:30 or 6:00. He comes home, eats something, then tries to take an hour's nap, and then does homework, finishing between ten and eleven. If he doesn't have much homework, he might wait until the next day and do it in leadership class. Sometimes he goes to sleep and then gets up at around 3 A.M., does his homework, and goes back to bed again by 5:00, to be up by 6:15.

One of his goals for high school is to try to see every school sport at least once. So often Charles will be found after practice or on weekends watching one of the South Lakes teams. On weekends, he plays fall league lacrosse or Reston League basketball, and when he can, he helps his dad coach and referee.

What is remarkable is that Charles's involvement is not primarily for "building a résumé," as kids in school now coldheartedly refer to their activities to get into college. He knows what he does will help him for college, but he is really involved for the love of it all. He lives and breathes school spirit in the old-fashioned sense of loyalty and a sense of belonging. It builds his character, is fun, and makes a major contribution to his school. He is a refreshing anachronism in a time when school activities are on the wane and are pursued without much heart.

He thinks his classes are pretty good. He especially likes biology, English, and math because he finds them challenging. He appreciates teachers who keep him thinking and working. He would actually prefer to get a lower grade from a demanding teacher than an easy A from a boring one. Most of his classmates would find such ideas blasphemous.

The class that drives him nuts is Leadership. Charles relishes being a leader and is eager to hone his skills. He is one of two underclassmen in the whole class. But he finds the class frustrating. "I had all these expectations of doing a lot of different things in class, and it turned out to be just a tutorial that we're getting a credit for," he says. "I never expected to be sitting around doing homework. It's like study hall. Or you just sit around and go to sleep, or talk with your friends." The core conflict, which eventually hits the school newspaper, is a difference in philosophy between the teacher and his students. The teacher wants to focus on developing leadership skills through self-disclosure in journal writings and running classroom meetings using parliamentary procedure, while the students want action. The kids are interested in community service projects and more activities in school. They try to do things over the year. For example, they tried to push through a dance planned with the freshman and sophomore classes for the beginning of February, since other than sports, the only school occasion for the underclassmen is Homecoming. The idea, says Charles, was shot down.

This year the administrators in the school are trying to toughen up all around. The expulsion policy is more exacting, rules are implemented more rigorously. School security is tighter, enforced by a full-time police officer in the school. But Charles has a feeling the students aren't being kept informed about the full range of problems. Some-times when he sees Officer Hodges walk out the door with a student, he says, "something's happened and they don't tell the students about it." Charles thinks that the police officer knows more than they do, and rumor has it he wears a bullet-proof vest. Although the school does not have a lot of outright violence, the students notice how tense the adult staff is. Charles understands the problem. If they criticize a kid in class, he says, teachers never know what might happen any-more. "If a teacher pushes the wrong student, they don't know if they're going to have to check their car when they leave school to make sure it wasn't messed with, like their brakes. A lot of the kids who are troublemakers take auto shop, wood shop, things that could teach them how to make weapons."

The strangest thing to Charles is that "people who don't do any-thing can get in trouble just as bad as if they had been troublemakers." If a fight breaks out, for example, "you're not allowed to watch any-more. All you're doing is sitting there watching, and someone else is fighting. Then after it's done, you leave. Now you can get in trouble for just sitting there watching them."

The way he sees it, "They're putting more and more restrictions not on the troublemakers, but on the leaders of the class." The people who play sports, for example. On game days last year, Charles ex-plains, you'd be able to go to your first four periods or your last four periods and leave, check out with a legitimate excuse, and still be able to play in your game that night. "You wanted to save your energy for the game. Now you can't do that. You have to be in all seven of your classes."

Most controversial is a new county policy that requires all high school students involved in extracurricular activities to sign a pledge not to drink, smoke, or use drugs at any time. Previously, only athletic programs in the school required such a pledge. By signing, which is mandatory for participation, students agree that they can be sus-pended from their activities if they are caught breaking the rules—even on weekends. Students argue it is an invasion of their privacy that turns their parents, teachers, advisers, and administrators into police. They say it targets the best and most involved students for punishment for the behaviors that are commonplace among all adolescents, even though they acknowledge they are illegal. "I think what they want to do is keep the people that are drinking and stuff at

parties from doing it by telling them no, don't do this, don't do that,"
says Charles. "And a high school student just doesn't want to be bothered with that."

The rule is enforced big time on the South Lakes choir trip the beginning of April. Three or four kids on the trip were drinking. They
had bought the beer on the trip. Everybody in the class knew about
it. And the people who drank got in trouble. The people who were in
the room but didn't drink got in trouble; those who had been in the
room and had left the room got in trouble. The punishment was five
days' suspension and a thirty-day activity suspension. "But the
thing is, if they wanted to suspend people for the knowledge of alcohol, they should have suspended the whole choir, not just the people
who were in the room," says Charles.

The irony is that it makes a kid like Charles, who is as straight as
they come, very nervous. "It makes me have to double-check what's
going to happen at a party, or what people are doing around me,
make sure that I don't get in trouble for what they do." At the same
time, it does nothing to stop the large number of top students, athletes, and other active kids and leaders of the school from doing exactly as they wish on weekends. The rule is difficult to enforce, and
the kids know it's unlikely that anybody is checking.

One of the things class officers and student government are de-
bating is a faculty suggestion to change the Homecoming parade to
Friday night in an attempt to minimize the float vandalism. "Kids
have school Friday morning, so how are they supposed to build on
Thursday night?" Charles asks. "They're talking about moving all the
Homecoming activities to Friday. I've made a valid point that Homecoming is for the returning college students. That's who it's really
for."

Charles looks at things from the point of view of what is more
fun, what satisfies the purposes of kids, while most of the adults involved are trying to figure out ways of damage control. The adult
agenda is not about what might work better for adolescents. It's all
about let's control the kids, keep them in check. That is the attitude
that turns kids away.

Charles thinks the blanket of repression is what keeps the preponderance of students from being interested in school-related activities.
Most adults take a far more negative tack, believing that kids stay
away from school activities because they can't drink and do dope.

The year goes by at breakneck speed. Charles's sixteenth birthday comes and goes in March with no time even to get a learner's permit. Lacrosse season begins and he is happy. The fall and winter leagues keep his skills up but there is nothing like being on varsity.

Before he knows it, it's May and class elections. He's always planned on running but is exhausted. A campaign is just one more thing on his packed schedule. "Right before the campaign started I thought, I don't have time for this now, I've got too much homework, I have to study for two tests," says Charles. "I had to work on all these different things plus my campaign. Then one day I had a lacrosse game and I had to study for a test the next day, had to work on my campaign, and I had to do tons of math homework. I thought just let me have a half hour nap, and I fell asleep and didn't wake up all night." He finally got it together and drew a few quick posters based on his campaign slogan: "Go with the Fro."

Charles's shaved head of last summer has now sprouted an Afro about six inches high all around. The Afro has created a bit of a stir at home even though his father used to wear the very same hairstyle in the sixties. "My dad says I have to go through this phase," Charles says. "My mom keeps pressuring me to cut my hair, and I'm like, 'I don't want to cut my hair. I want to get braids or twists and just let it grow.' My mom says if I do that, I have to get it cut by my senior picture day. I really don't want to put my senior picture in as how my parents want me to look rather than as how I look."

The day of the class assembly, Charles arrives dressed in blue shirt, tie, black slacks—the complete politician. When it is his turn, he speaks about how well the class is doing, how his administration has made a lot of money for the class, how they did really well with their Homecoming float despite the rain. He tells his classmates how they really need to maintain some of the same officers. "Why change? Just keep the same," he says. "Why change? Just go with the Fro."

When the votes are counted, Charles learns that he lost the election by a small margin. What bothers him is that one of the people running for president did it more as a joke than a serious commitment. The kid just wanted to see if he could win, and he split the vote. "I could understand if he had run sophomore or freshman year because we don't do anything those years," says Charles, "but next year is not the year to do it. We have to plan Mr. Seahawk, Prom, Seahawk Surge, and all the various activities that the junior class puts on for the seniors. We need really strong leaders to be able to get those things accomplished. We don't need someone who just did it as a joke." Luckily, the girl who became class president is somebody Charles thinks will do a great job. "I'll run again next year and try to be senior class president," says Charles, "and just go on with my life."

He insists his graciousness and ability to bounce back have to do with lacrosse. "I found out right before I went to lacrosse, so I went and took it out on the lacrosse field. I think it's lacrosse that keeps me balanced. It's a good way to let out frustrations—against other teams. You figure you're not going to see them ever again, unless you see them in the playoffs. By the time that comes around, they probably forgot what happened. You know the other person can't get hurt. It really takes a burden off your conscience that if you hit somebody with your stick that it's not going to hurt them. If you hit somebody in the street you know they might get mad and upset and want to come back and fight you, or you might hurt them. With lacrosse, you can hit somebody and not get in trouble for doing it."

Finally the Big Day arrives: the long-awaited rematch between the Madison Warhawks and the South Lakes Seahawks at South Lakes. The team is psyched and Charles's mom is a nervous wreck. There is electricity in the air, as if people know something's going to happen. There are more fans in the stands than usual from both schools. Rumors about retribution have been floating around, and everybody loves a good fight whether they admit it or not—especially on the athletic field.

On the field, both teams sit on the same side. Madison outnumbers South Lakes in players nearly two to one. In the stands, the parents from both teams also sit side by side, separated by an aisle, Ralph Meeks's dad looking as tense as Charles's mom.

Charles and his team have been unofficially putting the plans in place for a long time, including arrangements with a classmate in the stands to videotape the game. The beauty of the scheme is that Charles will do nothing violent. One of his friends on the team is going to conveniently trip into the side of Ralph's knee—usually a career-ending injury in any sport. "I'm going to make sure that he's looking right at me," says Charles. "I'll go over and say, 'Do you want some help?' And then, 'Oh, wait. You don't want a nigger to help you. Never mind.' " It is such a perfect plan.

The starting lineups are announced. The game begins. It is a warm spring night, darkening softly as the sun sets over the bleachers. Two geese fly overhead in the fading light. The ball boys, lacrosse wanna-bees, toss balls back and forth to each other just outside the action. The bright field lights come on.

Lacrosse is always a rough game, but this time every check, every push, every foul holds the potential for escalating trouble, so every-body worries. The air is electric, and the worst tension is when Charles and Ralph are both on the field. Charles's mom is yelling "Watch out, Charles!" every time a Madison player comes up be-hind him. His dad, announcing from the pressbox, is more comfort-able. He figures Charles is not going to be the perpetrator, and however the teams play it out is going to make for a good game. Keeping up a constant entertaining banter, he not only announces the game but also wishes one of the players a happy sixteenth birth-day, congratulates a girl in the stands for being the star of tonight's softball game, calls for a hand for the boy who made a goal in the ju-nior varsity lacrosse game, and so on. He even extends a personal greeting to the "soon to be great Seahawk goalie, Chris Hughes," who is in the stands watching his mentor Charles on the field, dreaming of when he'll be the varsity goalie.

In the first half, underdog South Lakes holds its own, taking a 2–1 lead. It is almost as if there are two games being played—the one on the scoreboard and the game of revenge. In the second half, Madison takes over, decisively winning 8–2. That is it. No fighting, no retalia-tion. Charles's parents are clearly relieved when they meet their son after the game. And somehow, Charles is relieved too and lets the in-cident go. Not everything in adolescence is melodrama. The support of his family and team and his own sense of self won through successes in many activities give Charles a strong inner core that will not be broken by an unjust racial attack. It would have been nice to get back, but Charles doesn't have time to waste on the incident anymore.

The year ends with his sister's graduation, a joyful rite of passage celebrated with the whole extended family. As he greets the visitors to his house during his sister's graduation party, the awkward, loose-limbed boy now moves with greater grace and confidence. It's as if you can see the man emerging from the boy, and you can pick up right away what a winner he's going to be in life. He's very serious and very dedicated, but he has a real sense of fun that is displayed in his repartee with relatives and friends.

When the festivities are over, and summer vacation begins, the family gathers up all the unwanted papers from all over the house and tosses them into a huge garbage bag. One of the piles evacuated from the kitchen is Nika's college catalogs. She's going to the University of Virginia and after all the reading, thinking, filling out applications over two years, that pile can now be cleared to make a space for the catalogs and applications her brother will soon be considering. There is a special poignancy to these moments.

During the summer Charles hopes to get that learner's permit so he can get his driver's license. That is, if he can find the time between his lacrosse camps and games. He is moving toward a lacrosse scholarship to college. That's what he wants and there is little reason to doubt that he will be able to achieve it with continued hard work and commitment.

His Volkswagen bus sits awaiting his attention in the driveway. He hopes to get it ready by the time he gets his license. All it needs is a new fan belt, and he and his dad will work on it together.

CHAPTER

20

# *It's My Prom, My Life*

Ann smiles and waves at her friends as she turns onto her walk after school. Her sister, who is who-knows-where, left the front door unlocked again. The smile fades, her school persona vanishes. She sighs and enters the house to the wildly yapping dog awaiting her.

The minute she closes the front door the feeling engulfs her. The emptiness, the loneliness, like homesickness for a family she doesn't have. Like a robot, she releases the dog from its captivity behind a gate in the laundry room, lets her outside and in again, gives her fresh water, walks over to the phone and calls her mom—the daily ritual. She's home, is going to be sitting, will be back around nine. It would be nice if just once her mom would ask about her day.

Awakening to her hunger, Ann goes to the refrigerator. She takes out the leftover Chinese food and sits down at the table. She glances at the clock and sees she has only fifteen minutes to get over to her sitting job. As she gathers her things to take with her, she bursts into tears.

It is the fall of her junior year. She doesn't know how she can stand another two years of this now that Ron is back in Reston, something that should be a purely happy event. Her parents are always suspicious. "You'd think after two years they'd say all right, maybe this relationship is something we should look at, maybe rethink." After all, they have accepted with open arms Courtney's beau Nat, who has been in and out of mental hospitals. Ron is hardworking, considerate, ambitious, drug-free. It's so unfair!

Earlier this year, Ann had flirted with the idea of going to Home-coming with Ron, but it got too complicated. She considered sneak-ing behind their back, then decided, No, I can't. What she hates most is that she is pretty much incapable of deception. Now that is ludi-crous in a family like hers. Hell, she lives in a family of cheaters and liars, and all Ann wants is to live out her own relationship honestly, but she is denied that right.

The damnedest thing is that she still cares what her parents think. Ann does not know how to prove herself to them. She's been trying to figure it out for years. "If I knew what they wanted, I would gladly give it to them," she says. "If I make the honor roll then they have absolutely nothing more from me that they could possibly want." Sometimes she wonders if she maintains mediocre grades to avoid that ultimate moment when she might find that nothing deliv-ered their love. Not even the honor roll. That would be the ultimate risk and the most devastating loss.

She's a good girl and gets nothing. It just isn't fair, especially in light of the way they treat her sister. "Courtney's done everything wrong she can possibly do, and look what she gets. She gets to go out on the weekends, and she stays out until all hours and nothing is ever said about it," Ann complains. Her stepfather once told Ann, "We think you're worth saving. Courtney's already a lost cause." That attitude infuriates Ann. "Why don't you try and save her? I'm fine," she says. "I've raised myself for the past seventeen years. I can do without this."

She's tried talking to her stepfather. "You don't even respect me, how am I supposed to respect you?" she challenged him. He replied, "I don't respect you. You're the child. I don't have to." Discussion closed.

She ended up capitulating on Homecoming. She went with her dear friend Alan. They always have a good time but that is not the point. There is no way she'll sacrifice her junior prom. For all her toughness, her stoicism, she really, really wants to go to her prom and dance in the arms of her boyfriend for all to see. "I'm going to go to the prom, and hopefully with him. It's my prom." She didn't get to go to his senior prom last year. Her parents said no way, so he went with a friend. "I feel I missed out on that and I'd like to get it back." This May, she'll get dressed in a beautiful gown, Ron will greet her at the door. They will drift out into the night. Nobody will stop them. She will confront her parents, saying, "Too bad if you can't deal with it, now you're going to. It's my prom, and I'll go if I want." Or, she adds tentatively, "I may just not even tell them I'm going."

All she wants is one of the adults in her life to acknowledge her relationship with Ron. She talks to her dad about him and he listens but concludes he doesn't like the relationship because Ron's black. At least he admits his prejudice. " 'You're known by the company you keep.' That's the only explanation he gave. I was getting very defensive, so I just let it go. I was getting defensive because anything anyone has ever said to me has always been negative. Nobody in my family has ever been positive."

Why can't she just come home to people who are happy to see her, who she can share her dreams with, her happiness, her love? She can't give up her fantasies of how nice it would be to come into the kitchen and show the dozen roses her boyfriend sent her, and have her mom share her joy. Dream on.

As the year progresses, Ann gets worn down just thinking about the complications of her relationship. "If you asked me last year and if you ask me now, if you're going to date someone outside of your own race, I'd ask you, are you ready to give up everything you have right now and just drop it for this guy or girl? If you answer no, don't do it." If she had to do it all over again, she thinks she'd still do it because she really loves Ron, but sometimes she is not sure. "I have given up everything," she says. "My friends haven't ditched me or anything like that. My parents have."

Her parents try to control Ann like a marionette. The past two years, for example, she hasn't been allowed to do cross-country because of her parents. Her sophomore year they pulled her out midseason and said she couldn't do it anymore, even when the coach asked them to let her stay. The year before she had to keep begging to stay with the team on a daily basis. It was because her grades weren't perfect, "Like I'd get a C on my interims." While her sister fights them every step of the way by flagrant acting out, Ann is the ultimate complier. "It's easier. I don't want to deal with the conflict."

Her parents always put her down. "They'll say, 'You're never going to get your grades up. If you're going to work at Kmart you ought to start filling out that Kmart application.' And they do it in front of the neighbors, too." Ann considers that plain bad manners.

They don't let up: "You're going to the community college, and we're not paying for you to go to Old Dominion or Radford." She tells them, "I didn't ask you to pay for my college. I'll pay my own way through college. If it means taking five years off, working at Kmart, and then going to college, I'll pay for it myself."

They razz her but never help her. They just expect the girls to get everything done because they are supposed to and the logistics are their responsibility. "If I've got a report, I need to go to the library," says Ann. Her mom tells her to find her own ride even if she is at home with the car. "I have to rely on somebody else to take me to the library. I have to rely on somebody else to help me. If I don't get it myself, I can't go ask them, because they're certainly not going to help me, so I'm kind of screwed. We don't even have a set of encyclopedias in my house. I'm totally stuck." It makes everything a million times harder, and it is even worse since Ann is being denied the right to get her driver's license. "I wish I could explain to colleges and people and teachers, 'I'm trying the best I can. Just give me a little slack.' "

People in school are always shocked to find out that Ann doesn't get top grades all the time. She seems so intelligent and involved in her classes. She is happy to be there; it helps her forget her misery for a while. When she does poorly on tests, her friends are surprised. But homework has come to symbolize everything that is wrong in her home life—the lack of support, the sheer logistical difficulty, the aloneness she feels in her studies. She can't shake off the feelings of defeat. Her sister blows off everything with attitude. It is as if she has given herself permission not to give a damn. Ann just feels wounded and desperate and is ashamed to let anybody know. "It's kind of like my private life," Ann says. "I don't want anybody else to know that everything's not okay."

She had the dream again last night. It is always the same. She is watching the whales swim in a huge tank like at Sea World, one of her very favorite places. She walks around the pool to find a better viewing spot and the floor opens up and drops her in the water. She is helpless as the whales swim toward her. "I fall in, and it's like the worst horrible thing that is going to come get me and kill me."

She wakes up in a cold sweat, her heart pounding. It's the stress of everything. She knows it. Her eyes dart around her room, a bright cheery retreat decorated with her pewter collection of whales and dolphins and other animals, a picture of Ron, her books and magazines. Her room is her haven away from the family she wants to separate from, where she spends most of her time. It is here that she has had a few stolen moments of intimacy with Ron. It is here where she shares her most happy and intimate moments, talking for hours to her friend Linda about her life. "We go to my room and I sit on one end of the bed and she sits on the other, and we just talk about guys and grades and my family and coping. It's great," says Ann of her best friend.

Linda sees what goes on in Ann's house. Even her mother noticed. A couple of years ago, four kids were at Ann's working on a group project for school. Linda's mom arrived at almost the same time the other parents came. The phone was ringing, the dog was going nuts with all the people. It was kind of wild, Linda recalls, and "Ann's mother was sitting on the stairs, not answering the phone, not answering the door. Ann, meanwhile, is running around answering the phone, answering the door, dealing with the dog, while her mother just sat there. My mom is like, 'That's the rudest thing to do, because you have guests in the house."

When the family is home, there is mostly separation and yelling. The minute her mom walks in the house after work, Ann says, she begins giving orders: "Do the dishwasher, Ann, do the trash, pick up your clothes, whose book bag is this?" Sometimes Ann asks, "Mom, how was your day?" "Work is work," her mom snaps. Courtney concurs. "When we come home from school, they can't understand that we've worked hard. If we come home and fall asleep or something, it's like, 'Why are you sleepy?' You didn't have to do anything. They get all mad at us. Or if you didn't feel that good and you just come home and sit in a chair, they start yelling at you. 'Bring this upstairs, do this, do that.' And if you're really tired or you had a bad day, you just don't want to be bothered."

Christmas vacation the girls go to their dad's house in Florida. For most of their lives, the girls have idealized their absentee dad. Ann sees her father as a refuge, a role model, and his home as a welcome relief. Ann says she can sense how her dad and stepmother love each other, that it creates "a nice environment to be in." Ann feels her father's love. "He likes me for who I am. He doesn't try and change me. He's not always telling me my priorities are screwed up."

Ann opens up with her dad and stepmom, responding to their interest. She has so much to talk about, especially college. "When I ask them, how was your day? my dad says, 'Work's work. What did you do today?' They're interested in what I do. They actually make me feel like a person, like I'm important. They talk to me and they don't yell at me. They ask me my opinion. When I talk to them, they don't ignore me and tell me to be quiet because they're listening to the TV."

The relationship with her dad and stepmom was not always easy but they have worked it out over the years. Her stepmom used to get very jealous of the two girls "because for the whole summer we would take away my dad's affection and his time and all of that. She would have to cook dinner for all of us, and she couldn't go out and do her own things which she had been used to doing." The girls thought she was mad all the time and they didn't know why. But the girls noticed that their stepmom also drove with their dad every few months from Massachusetts (where they used to live) to Reston to visit for the weekend. "If you can imagine, they aren't your kids," recalls Ann, "why should she have to drive ten hours each way to go see her husband's kids?" But she did. "A little kid doesn't put two and two together," Ann explains. When they got older they understood better how complicated stepfamilies are.

After the holidays, back in Reston, Ann's trouble continues. In early January, she has a sitting job and is seized by one of the miserable migraine headaches that have hounded her since the first grade. She doesn't want to cancel on the family because they are going to a special concert. Knowing that the only way to beat the headache is to sleep it off, Ann pleads with her mom to help her, to take over for a few hours. She hopes her mom will be compassionate since she used to get migraines too. Instead her mom gets mad, and refuses. In desperation, Ann asks a friend's mom to help.

While Mrs. Ross is agreeing to fill in, Ann's own mom is yelling at her to just cancel. She tells Ann that when the people come to pick her up, she'll go to the door and tell them she can't go. Ann is appalled. "I'm like, 'Mom, I have a baby-sitting job. I already committed myself to that, I can't just cancel. It's not fair to them. Then they're going to come back and say, I can't count on her, I'll never ask her again.' "

Ann likes to do things right. Dependable Ann. Growing up in a home where she can never count on her mom makes her live her life in a way that everybody can count on her. She won't let people down.

On the heels of the baby-sitting incident, there is the job fiasco.

When Courtney gets the job at the cleaners, her parents think it is great. Ann gets a job offer at Claire's Boutique at Tysons Corner Shopping Center, which is six miles from Reston. It is the store where she buys all her hair ornaments, and she'd love to work there. Her parents say she can't because she doesn't have transportation to Tysons. Ann shoots back, she can take the bus. They counter that she's never ridden the bus before. It is so absurd. She is seventeen years old!

The real issue is that she should have her driver's license and they refuse to let her get it. It's a power thing with her mom, Ann says. "You complain every time you have to drive me somewhere," Ann tells her mom. "Well, if you let me get my license we won't have that problem, yet I can't drive your car because it's too precious. You won't invest in another used one." It is the issue that makes her sister apoplectic too, and there seems to be no compromise. Courtney keeps her job because she can walk. Ann turns down the job at Claire's and continues to baby-sit in Reston.

Meanwhile, the problems around Ron continue. Ann, so worn down over all the other issues in her life, breaks up with him during the winter. "I just don't have the time or the desire for a commitment right now. I'm tired of it," she says. She tells Ron as much and he understands, saying, "That's a hard thing to ask somebody to do—keep fighting it and fighting it and fighting it." She still loves him. She just feels whipped. But since they had not been able to go out anyway, this change is more psychological than real. They continue to talk on the telephone daily.

The tension with her parents heats up during the long, icy winter. They argue night after night about Ron, life in general, Ann's attitude. They keep on needling her about her friends, about who she can or can't date, about school. They are relentless and she is getting wound tighter and tighter inside. One day Ann breaks. She screams, "What's your problem? I've finally come to the conclusion that I don't need to deal with this! I have many, many other things to do and I just don't need to deal with this!"

She jumps up, goes to the phone, and calls her dad to ask if she can go live with him. She promises she would be no problem. "I can do things myself. Give me a driver's license. If I need to go to the store, I'll go to the store. I won't ask them for money. All I want is a place to stay. And I don't want conflict, I don't need conflict. I don't need anybody telling me what to do. I've done it myself this long, why can't I keep doing it myself? I haven't gone and gotten myself killed yet."

There is a silence while he tells her stepmom what is going on. Her stepmom hedges, saying, "The only thing we're worried about is your social adjustment, because there aren't really any people down here for you to meet." She tells Ann that "senior year is supposed to be the best year of your life." Ann retorts that maybe it is, but if she can't do anything or go anywhere, then why does it matter where she is? They talk some more, then tell her she is welcome to come. At last Ann has that option. "So I'm thinking about it."

A few weeks later, on one of the snow days off from school, Linda, Alan, and Ann decide to go to the movies. Ann calls her mom and tells her the plans to go to the Worldgate theaters, who she is going with, and when. Her mom says fine. When Ann comes into the house after the show, her mom demands to know who drove her home. Ann tells her Alan. Her mom accuses her of being with Ron, not Alan. Ann goes ballistic and says she refuses to continue the discussion. She leaves the room and goes downstairs. Her stepfather calls her back. He wants to know why she was with Ron, says he knows it was Ron's car in their driveway. Ann loses it. She shrieks it was Alan, and curses him out.

For nights after that, the arguing continues. The more her parents won't believe her, the angrier Ann gets. It's like they are on some perverse rampage to get her. They keep on bringing up Ron, and she's not even dating him. They tell her she can't move to her dad's. She feels they are verbally battering her.

One day it explodes. She and her stepfather are arguing about something and the phone rings. While she is speaking to Linda, he keeps going. Finally, Ann tells him to shut up, and he is obviously offended. "I sat there and said, 'Does that make you feel bad? That's how I feel when you do this to me,' " Ann recalls. She asks why it should be any different than when he says that to her. He answers, "Because you're a punk kid."

Ann stands up and says, "You know, I don't need to be here. If that's the way I'm treated, I don't need to be here anymore. I'm done. I'm finished. I don't care anymore." She leaves the room and goes upstairs. Her stepdad follows right behind calling her names. "He was standing in my doorway, and I pushed him for him to leave, and he slapped me. I was like, 'That's it. That's it. That's the last,' " Ann recalls.

She reluctantly admits that this was not the first time she'd been hit. But, unlike Courtney, who was willing to come forward with the information when it was relevant to her story, Ann finds it extremely tortuous to talk about. "Maybe I have the syndrome, If I ignore it long enough it will go away," she says. "I do kind of have that problem, and a lot of people say that." Then she begins to open up. "When I was little, I got spanked a lot. I can recount a lot of occasions. I was always spanked with a leather belt. I was still getting spanked in fourth or fifth grade." She partially excuses her stepdad, just as her sister does, because she has learned that he was abused as a child. "So I can kind of understand that and overlook it," Ann says, "but yet, I don't know."

Her sister has gotten hit, Ann thinks, because she does things and she mouths off. "But my sister thinks she never does anything wrong. She has my mother's self-righteous attitude, and she gets hit for stuff that's well-deserving of a slap across the face." Courtney also hits back. "She'll haul off and smack you. I have scars from where my sister has hit me and scratched me and stabbed me. When I was a little kid, my stepdad would say 'I'm going to tie your necks together and stuff you in a room.' They didn't stop us at home."

That's not all. Their mom is free with a slap to the face. "I still flinch," says Ann, "because she hit me so much when I was a little kid. She backhanded us all the time. When she raises her hand during a conversation, and I'm standing right near her, I still flinch and bend down. You learn, you do something, you just get down and you cover your face because you know you're going to get backhanded bad." She still gets swatted by her mom on occasion. "The provocations are petty things. That's what bothers me."

Most of her life, she has not mentioned the violence to anybody. Ann thinks that "if you grow up with it, it doesn't really seem out of the ordinary until someone brings it to your attention and says that's a little weird." Besides, she says, if she really looked at it and analyzed it, "I don't think I could deal with it. I don't think I could face it and really deal with what it made me, how it made me feel. Some day I will, maybe. Maybe I never will. I don't know." Ann always thinks there's somebody out there who has it worse than she does. "Therefore, I can't classify that this is abuse because there's always somebody who's got it worse and that's really abuse and this isn't."

She has made some meager attempts to get help. She brought her parents in for a conference freshman year with her counselor. His conclusion: "You guys need to work things out." Right. Like that did any good. "They came home and made fun of me," Ann says.

When she was under "house arrest" for seeing Ron, she was so upset her friend Jill insisted she talk to somebody. Ann went to Mr. Perez, her science teacher. He was so nice, she recalls. She cried telling him what it was like in her house, how horrible her parents made her feel. He was very sympathetic and said that he couldn't help her, but he knew somebody who could. "So I got a peer helper, and that helped because I could just talk to somebody other than my friends," Ann says. "Sophomore year I got a peer helper too. They told me, 'You're okay. It's your parents, it's not you. You haven't done anything wrong.' I just needed somebody to tell me I was okay."

This is the first year she does not have a peer helper because she thinks she can handle things herself, and besides, "eventually I'm going to have to learn to do it by myself anyway." Ann says she doesn't get hit that often by her stepdad. "It's like very rarely. Once every three months maybe."

The bottom line is that if she looked her situation squarely in the eye, called it for what it is, she'd have to leave. "I'd have a really good reason, and it would be justified, and I could get a lawyer and go to court and say I want out. Plain and simple, I want out and I don't want to ever go back. I think I have a justifiable case." What stops her is that it would "hurt too many people."

She says the person she would hurt the most would be her dad. Her dad knows, but she doesn't think "he knows to what extent it happens because I don't talk about it." It's just not something that is discussed. "I think he would feel really guilty that he never saw it, or that he never said anything if he did see it. I don't like to hurt anybody."

The person she is protecting the most is herself. "If I realize it and think about it then I'm going to get upset. I'm going to say, 'You know, you did this to me, and you all should pay for it. You treated me like shit my seventeen years. You didn't ever care. You didn't do anything for me. I don't ask you for anything because I don't get anything when I do ask. It's not worth my effort. I'll do it myself.' " She doesn't want to open a Pandora's box. "I don't want anybody to know. I don't want people feeling sorry for me. I'm okay. You don't need to feel sorry for me. I've done okay until now. It's almost to save face. It's almost like something's wrong with me."

A few weeks later she has yet another argument with her stepfather. He tries to tell her that she cannot go live with her dad. He tells her she is going to get messed up academically, and on and on. Then he gets around to his real agenda: Ann is hurting her mother.

Ann is incredulous. She's tried to make her mom happy. "I'm done. I stopped caring," Ann says. "If she's hurt, then good for her. I'm really sorry about that, but I've been hurt for the past two and a half years and no one's cared. Why should I care now whether or not you're upset? You dug your own grave." Her plan is to go to her dad's for spring break and not come back.

While she struggles to extricate herself from the mess in her house, Ann is also looking into colleges. In the school newspaper office she finds out about a potential scholarship Discover is giving out for students who have over a 2.7 grade point average. Ann decides to go for it but it is only four days until the deadline, and the application requires five personal essays. She works late into every night while her mom sits and tells her she'll never get it. Ann refuses to be discouraged. She finishes the application the afternoon of the day before it is due. She calls her mom at her office to tell her she's done, and could they please go over to the Federal Express office that night in Reston. They can mail it up to 9 P.M. Her mom says no. Ann has to find a friend to help.

Ann is strangely torn about whether she should go to Florida. A part of her wishes she could work things out with her mom, but Ann says, "It would be nice if fairy angels could drop down, and say, 'Oh, Joanne, you really need to work things out with your daughter because otherwise it's going to get bad, you're going to be hurt, and Ann's going to say you made your own mistake, it's not her problem.' "

Ann feels like she is upset and bitchy all the time. She can't help it. Her friend Phil, who has seen her mother at her best and her worst, says, "I know totally why you are the way you are." He says it no longer bothers him because he knows "that's just the way your parents make you."

Other people, who have no idea what it is like in her home, label Ann uptight and rigid. Like her friend Sam, who is always telling her to loosen up. She wants to tell him, "If you only knew," but she can't. "When I get out of high school," Ann says, "I want to show people, look, this is the hell that I went through. You thought I was fine and I was a bright person and I was the smartest kid in the class, and blah, blah. Look what really went on. There are reasons that people are the way they are. There are very good reasons for it. Your saying 'You need to loosen up,' or 'You're so uptight,' or 'You're so anal,' doesn't help."

As winter wanes and the first weak signs of spring appear, Ann comes to the conclusion that she's "an okay person and life's going to go on whether or not I move to Florida, and if I have to repeat my senior year because of my grades getting messed up, then I guess I do. I'm going to be fine."

She won't let the enormity of her pain swallow her up. "For some reason I'm above water. I don't know why. I can't explain that. But if I wasn't, I would have been long since gone by my own hand." The people who keep her afloat are first and foremost her dad, who is there saying, "You're okay and I care about you." And her friends, especially Linda, who's been with her through thick and thin. She's always said, "You're okay. You're not the problem, it's your parents." Over the years, Ann has also encircled herself with a number of caring adults, teachers, friends' parents, and the families she sits for. She says, "I go over there and have conversations with them that I should be having at home." These adults counter the angry, demeaning voices in her own house by telling her, "You're doing such a great job, and you're so wonderful."

Both sisters have worked out ways to protect and nurture themselves, whether through drugs, in Courtney's case, or books, in Ann's. "If you read books like I do," says Ann, "you come up with these coping strategies. Sometimes it's denial, sometimes it's like split personalities. It all depends on how much stress there is, and everyone has their way. When it's done then you get over it and you move on. These coping abilities kind of recede until you need them again."

Ann gets through the winter somehow. April finds her shopping for a prom dress and applying for an editorship on the school paper next year. She decides she can stay at her dad's after the school year ends if things get horrible again. But then she and Ron get back together and she puts the option to move on the back burner. Ann is thinking maybe it is time to have sex, and she's considering getting pills.

She decides to try one last time talking to her mom about Ron and going to the prom. Last night she sat her mom down and tried to explain how she and Ron "really do care about each other. I'm like can't we all be adults about this." No response. "It's just a prom, not a wedding," Ann implores. "It's like that's all I'm asking, one evening." Her mom won't discuss it.

She calls her dad to enlist his support. He says he will talk to her mom about the prom, and then he decides he doesn't think it is a good idea. He tells his daughter, "It would be like pouring boiling water over a scab or something." This incident is but another in an unfolding realization that as much as Ann adores her dad, he has not come through for her. Ever. "I would cry on the phone and he never said anything. He was like, 'Well, I feel really bad for you.' Well, a hell of a lot of good that does me. What are you going to do about it? He never offered for me to come and live down there, I had to ask. Then he was like, well, okay. He didn't call my mother and say look, lay off. He never did anything. I never thought about it, but it's true. I've always been sticking up for him, and I love him more than anyone else in my family, but I didn't get anything."

April becomes May and the prom is getting closer. Ann has come to the realization that it doesn't matter what her parents think anymore. "Every time I go out I get twenty questions. 'Is Ron going to be there?' So now I say no."

Like her sister, Ann senses a mystery that surrounds her mom. "Somebody must have done something to her. She's not a nice person. She just doesn't have any care or love in her. If only I could find out what it is and make her happy."

Only a week to go, Ann has a dress and a date who wants to be with her, but now it is an issue of will. "I desperately want to go to the prom," says Ann, but it is clear she is not quite resolved. Linda's boyfriend tells her he could stop by, pretend to be her date, and then deliver her into the arms of Ron. Or maybe she will just defy everybody and march out the door in that fabulous dress, arm in arm with the boy she loves. What would her parents do? "I have no idea. The locks would be changed when I got home. Either that or they'd call the cops."

The psychological wrangling only intensifies as the day of the prom approaches. Ann is bone tired. After a year of plotting, planning, dreaming, hoping, struggling with her family, she decides she can't do it. "I'm not going to the prom," she says simply. "I don't like conflict, and I was going to lose anyway." She spends the night baby-sitting.

But there is always next year. "I'll be eighteen so I'm going. They can't stop me. Then I can finally tell them, do whatever you want. Call the cops."

# Resignation:
# Adolescence Is Sometimes
# a Life-or-Death Issue

The first morning of school her senior year, as on every school morning since seventh grade, Joan comes into the building and sits up against the wall of the bustling locker area. Later in the day she will finish some last-minute homework. Sometimes she laughs and chats with friends, sometimes she just people-watches. Actually, it is one of her little tests, a barometer of her popularity. Will somebody come join her on the floor? "It's like choosing teams in PE," she says, "that scary feeling that you might not get picked." She sees lots of friends before they see her, but she never calls out to them to join her. Some people pass by and wave. She nods, her heart aching. The minutes tick by, and soon it will be time for class. Every second feels like an eternity of rejection. The bell rings. The area begins to clear. She drags herself up, lost in the old familiar loneliness.

Every hurt, real or imagined, is amplified a thousandfold in her mind. She is too sensitive—for God's sake, she cries over the evening news! She knows this about herself, but self-knowledge provides no protection from the isolation she feels. It is hard to put her finger on the cause, but since she walked in the doors of school this year, she "felt left out for some reason." All the old feelings of being unimportant and invisible are stirred up inside her.

Sooner or later everything in Joan's life becomes glazed with her own sense of meaninglessness. Take the school newspaper, which was always the highlight of her days. Things got off on the wrong foot in the spring when she developed conflicts with the new staff. First, she was made the art editor—a position she was not crazy about. "They tell me what to take pictures of and I tell the photographers. I'm like the in-between person that doesn't really need to be there."

This issue she is assigned a story where she runs into problems arranging a meeting with her source. The editors accuse her of dragging her feet on the assignment. She tells them, "I can't just make up a story. I'll do it even if I have to sit and type it the day of deadline." The editors accuse her of slacking. "They just started saying things to me that they had no need to say," Joan recalls, "like 'You are a bee-loving, tree-hugging type—why don't you stop doing all that Greenpeace stuff?' They were getting on my case about things that had nothing to do with the newspaper, which shows me they didn't like me anyway. So I got really angry." Joan says it had been a long time since she cussed out anybody in public, maybe three years, but she blew up. "I was standing there and I was just going, 'Fuck you! Don't you come here talking to me that way!'" The editors have never heard Joan like this and are stunned silent.

Joan complains to paper sponsor Larry Ward about how she is being treated. She asks if he can intercede with the editors on her behalf. She tells him that if she is going to be treated like this, she will leave the newspaper, switch out of his class. He tells her she cannot leave, and he does talk to the editors.

The editors apologize, yet Joan is left feeling alienated. "They treat me as if I'm not anything. I just have a name," she says. "I'm not asking to be a star, I just wish they would ask my opinion on the artwork or photos once in a while."

Joan's hypersensitivity casts a shadow everywhere. Take her relationship with Andy, Jonathan's best friend. Her junior year, Joan had watched Andy all the time in after-school art class. She really liked him because he was friendly, a nice person, and totally into nature. Her insecurity with guys made her afraid to let him know how she felt. "Then it started to be a downfall thing because I would feel bad about not being able to tell him I liked him. I would keep on assuming that he wouldn't like me anyway." So she never said anything and she became depressed about her failure.

Eventually Joan and Andy became friends, Joan being very careful not to let him know that she *really* liked him. It made her happy that by the end of last school year they often talked and ate lunch together. This year they continue their shared lunchtime, but Joan is having a hard time being natural with him. She is always monitoring her every move, their every conversation, and analyzing his responses to her. The emotional pressure of her inner tumult makes her upset, then angry and hostile toward the unsuspecting Andy. She begins to feel "weird" about him, their conversations "don't feel normal," and what once made her happy takes on a negative cast. As if an invisible miasma were creeping across her life, everything gets vaguely changed. "I am feeling like I am getting bad vibes from Andy for some reason," Joan says.

It builds and builds, distorting her perceptions. One morning Joan and her friends are sitting together in the locker area before school, and she decides Andy likes a particular girl because he always talks to her. Joan tells herself she doesn't care. But sitting there among her companions, Joan sees everybody "completely ignoring me"—sitting with her and not talking to her. First she feels bad, then "stupid," and finally, she feels angry. "That was the day all hell broke loose," she recalls, "and I was angry for the whole week. I was like, Screw you, don't talk to me!"

Joan says nothing. Her anger doesn't show. She crams it all inside and sits quiet and withdrawn. People around her have no idea what turbulence racks her insides. When she gave up that angry, aggressive pose a few years ago and transformed herself into the gentle flower child of today, her anger got stuck inside in a self-flagellating fury.

The more oppressive Joan's life feels, the more she wishes she could escape it. "I wish I could be a bird," she says. "I could fly anywhere in the world at any time that I wanted to. I could go anywhere and be anybody." She could flee the tension of her life and not deal with people who hurt her. "I don't want to answer to anyone," she says.

If she could fly away, she could avoid having people leave her. A massive fear of rejection is at the core of her problems at the school paper, with friends, with life. When her mother abandoned her as a child, it left a scar so deep that she feels she will never recover. Joan thinks she will spend her every moment on earth fearful that people she cares about will leave her. And the worst damage is that Joan always blames herself. "I'm always worried if I do something stupid or something wrong, people will hate me," she says.

On the outside Joan is a hippie, a friend of the earth, a gentle soul who writes poetry and loves humanity, but her insides are ravaged by rejection both real and imagined. Things that others might brush off, discuss, or work through echo incessantly within her own negative self-judgments. Her days are lived out on very shaky ground. It's a good day, she hiked with Lisa. It's a bad day, everyone talked past her at lunch. A good day can be turned around in an instant by a look, a gesture, a thought. This year, bright moments are rare.

The tension at home is unrelenting. Dependent upon her remaining parent for love, Joan never speaks up, never draws the line defining her own needs. She is imprisoned by her responsibilities and the never-ending demands of family that tie her up as surely as rope. Her charges are not only her twelve-year-old brother but also her six-year-old half-sister. Her mother, who has maintained a friendship with Joan's father, daily drops off the daughter she had with her present husband. Joan takes good care of her sister, never addressing how it feels to care for the little girl who lives with the mother she desperately wants.

Joan is being crushed in the trap of her life. "I want to get out of here. I want to move out," she complains. "If I don't go to college, I still want to be on my own."

She feels oppressed by always having to worry about somebody else. She is constantly concerned about whether the kids are okay, what they are doing outside, who they are playing with, if they are where they are supposed to be. "It gets to the point where I get tension headaches," says Joan. "I'm like, oh my God, where are the kids?"

Joan senses she is sinking. Sometimes she wishes she could spill her soul to an adult, but she is wary. She says she needs somebody to talk to who "won't tell." "You want to talk to somebody who's not really going to get into your business, someone who's going to say, 'Maybe you should do this' or 'I suggest this,' but not someone who says, 'I'm calling right now to get you help.' " Joan needs somebody who understands the complexity of her situation, who will not jump to conclusions. "If I were to say, 'My dad's beating me (which he is not), don't take him to jail because of my brother and sister,' they would ask, 'Why are you taking care of your brother and sister? You're too young.' They would find this and that and it would be the destruction of my family right away."

That's why she is so careful about opening up to an adult. She doesn't want to deal with somebody who's going to jump on the phone to the Child Abuse Hotline and then call Social Services or Child Welfare because they think her dad's "not supposed to have us. Yes, he used to throw things. He tried to hit me once, but I hit him back and he never hit me again. He yells, but *he is there*," says Joan. "Whatever it is they think, the authorities don't really understand the situation because they haven't lived it. I mean, my dad lives with us because my mom abandoned us. I've heard people say, 'Your mom is your mom, she had you, you're supposed to be with her.' They say, 'She has a house and more money than your dad does.' " Joan says that is not the point. She looks at the fact that her mother left her brother and her, and it was her dad who wanted to stay and take care of them. "I don't look at who has more money, who has a bigger house. I look at who loves me more."

Her father has made a good home in many ways. Those high-and-mighty authorities should see what a warm, comfortable home her dad created for them. He may make little consistent income as a house painter, but his handiness and sense of color shine everywhere. He built and refinished furniture so it looks like it comes from the best stores. There are a tablecloth and flowers on the dining room table, art and plants to brighten the living room. This modest man with the broad, rough-hewn hands of a laborer has a graceful artistic sensibility, a warm smile, and a loving manner when he is not blowing up. He treasures his children. For all the things wrong with him, things for which others might judge him harshly, Joan says, "He's my mom and dad."

Not that her mom is totally out of the picture. "I call her a friend," Joan says. "I'll talk to her about things like 'It's a nice day,' or 'It was a good movie.' But I don't talk to her about personal things. I just don't feel like she's my mom."

The problem is that as defensive as she is about her situation, she longs for how "it should be," a mom and dad at home who are the parents to their child. "I get the impression that they kind of forgot about my childhood," says Joan. "Like they think it's over, it's gone, forget it. I've already grown up, I guess. They tell me that all the time, like I've passed that age and I don't need a childhood."

Joan pores over the family photo albums. There she is with her mom and dad at Christmas. Her mom is on her knees, too pregnant to sit, snuggling close to her husband and Joan, who sit on the floor. Another Christmas, her dad as Santa with his arms around his wife and Joan, her baby brother on the mom's lap. All four of them standing together at a family celebration, the young children leaning on their parents, a parent's hand on each one's shoulder. Then suddenly that is it. The rest of the family pictures show only Joan and her brother with their dad. Her mom pops up in an occasional photo, but she is the visitor, not the mom of the house anymore.

Joan knows, always has known, that forced to play grown-up at ten, she has never been mothered herself. It is a loss that creates a hole inside her. It is an emptiness she stuffs and stuffs with food to make it go away. But then, overweight and no happier, she turns the wrath on herself. She's needed help for a long time but gets it only piecemeal from her pastor in church, who speaks to her in biblical quotes; from her counselors, to whom she can't tell everything. She would like to get solace from her friends, but even in the midst of a good friendship she feels lonely—a bone-wearying, stomach-cramping loneliness that swallows her up as surely as a monster in some dark fairy tale. "You think your life is in high school," says Joan. "It feels like you are going to be thirty and in the same situation because it feels never ending." Birds flying away become increasingly the endpoint of Joan's despair.

When things are bad, Joan always spirals downward into the morass of her memories, the worst being the beatings. These memories haunt her and don't square with the confusing fact that her father has been the parent there for her, the villain becoming the savior. "I remember it so well. When I see somebody hitting somebody, it comes back. It's awful." The fights took place right in front of her. She can still hear her mother's screams. "I can remember her going, 'Help me!' but I was small. I was afraid of him too," Joan says. "I felt like maybe it was my fault because I didn't help her when he was hitting her and I couldn't do anything about it."

The violence gave her mom reason to leave. But Joan is left with the fact that her mother also was having an affair with her dad's best friend and got pregnant. The two years her mom vanished with no word were an eternity for ten-year-old Joan. "Those were the years when I needed a mother. It was really hard because my dad didn't talk to us that much. He'd work, come home, and I would have to have dinner for him, and do things, like clean the house. I was afraid that if I didn't do things right he would hit me like my mother."

She can't make the memories go away. When she is unhappy, they all come swirling around her, all the years of hurt and pain and she cannot escape. One month into this school year, it just gets to be too much. "Everything was going wrong all week," she recalls. "Then one night there was a family argument. I don't even remember what it was, but I got cussed out by my father. I felt, Okay, this is it. I got so mad." She raced out of the room crying and went upstairs to her room.

Joan is mad and frustrated about her dad, the school paper, her friends. She ruminates over all the things wrong in her life and finally gets down to her mom. It always gets down to her mom. "My mother doesn't even know that I am alive. It's like, Who's Joan?"

She lies on her bed weeping, beating her pillow with her fist. "I lost it. I totally lost it," Joan recalls. "I had the feeling I was going to lose it any second for a long time. I just hadn't told anybody. If I had been walking on a bridge, I would have jumped." Sometimes when she feels like this, she goes outside in her yard and smokes a joint or two to defuse her anguish. But not this time. "I didn't have anything to smoke so I figured, Well, I'll suffocate myself," she recalls. "It was just something I thought I'd do then. It wasn't like, 'I'll show them!' It was more like, 'I don't want it anymore. I don't want to feel this way, so I want to die.' I really wanted to die." She feels, "If I die, there's no difference. No difference in the world. No difference anywhere. It doesn't matter."

She gets up from her bed, walks across the room to her closet, and unloops the sash from one of her favorite dresses and takes it back to the bed. She pushes aside her beloved stuffed animals. She sits down on her comforter and takes the pillow and puts it across her face, securing it tightly by wrapping the sash around and around and knotting it. "Then I just sat there and waited for death," Joan says.

At first it feels like she is getting high, pretty cool. But the whole time she is sitting there in the pitch-black of having a pillow on her face, she is thinking of other ways to get out of the mess of her life, such as going away. But it is unrealistic to think that might work. She thinks: I can't just leave it all here, leave it behind. I can't just say, Look, I don't want to do this anymore.

The next thing she knows, it is morning. Her dad had come into her room late at night on one of those uneasy feelings parents sometimes get. He found her passed out. He immediately untied the pillow and began shaking her and talking to her. "He said I woke up when he untied it, but I don't remember," says Joan. "I guess I was sleeping."

The day after her suicide attempt, her dad hovers around her, alternately scared and angry. "He didn't know how to deal with it," Joan recalls. "He tried to talk to me but I wouldn't talk to him about it. I was afraid he would get more angry."

Joan is angry at herself for failing at her attempt. "I was thinking, I can't even do this right."

Her best friend Lisa insists she talk to somebody at school. "She made me go to the counselor but I never wanted to tell anyone. I don't want people in my business." Sure enough, as soon as she hears what happened, the counselor says she has to talk to Joan's dad. Joan explains that he knows, but the counselor says they have to have a conference. Joan ends up with an appointment with a psychiatrist, whom she obediently visits a few times. "I liked the guy but nobody was going to change my mind," Joan says. She has a plan; she is just waiting for "the perfect moment."

She actually feels a little better having made her decision, more in control. She decides to resign from *The South Lakes Sentinel*. Her troubles with the editors have not diminished as far as she is concerned. Mr. Ward tries to dissuade her but she is determined. On a late October night she writes her letter of resignation. "I didn't want rumors to start. I didn't want people to say I couldn't handle it. I didn't want people to think I didn't want the responsibility," Joan explains. "I care what people think about me and I didn't want them thinking the wrong thing so I wrote the letter to tell them once and for all how I feel."

The next day she comes to class looking terrific. She has dressed carefully and wears brightly colored beads. Her hair, newly styled, has been rinsed a brilliant black and she is even wearing makeup. Mr. Ward tells the class how sorry he is that Joan is resigning, how much she has contributed over the years, and how he will miss having her in his class. Joan gets up before her classmates and reads her letter in a strong voice:

> I am writing this letter to inform you of my decision to resign from my position as art/photo editor and as a writer for your newspaper. The main reason for my decision is that I do not agree with certain values the *Sentinel* appears to stand for. There seems to be no respect for the writer's efforts and abilities, there also seems to be no consideration for the writer's intelligence in general. I personally have heard rude and unprofessional techniques used to communicate with staff members, and it really annoys me to witness such condescending behavior. We are all equally responsible for the

outcome of this newspaper, therefore we are all equal in status, i.e., let us treat others as we would like to be treated. I refuse to be part of this any longer. I am not for treating fellow humans in such a manner nor do I want to be treated in such a manner.

It is difficult for me to leave because I enjoy writing very much. This is a decision that has been well thought out, and it has come to be the best decision.

Thank you, Mr. Ward, for being very understanding and supportive in this situation and for every other time you have helped me since I arrived at South Lakes. You are greatly appreciated although sometimes it may not be apparent.

Thanks to you, the staff, for giving up some of your time to hear me out. If I have offended anyone in any form, forgive me, but this is the way I feel. Here is a suggestion: Do not focus on having the grade-A perfect newspaper all the time, but take some time to focus on the human spirit of the newspaper—the writers—because they are the true soul of the *Sentinel.*

The students are moved. When she finishes, they almost all come forward to praise her courage for taking a stand, to say they will miss her and to wish her well. Her letter is so authoritative, her delivery so convincing that nobody tries to change her mind.

The editors, somewhat embarrassed knowing they have some culpability for her decision, ask her to join them in an idea meeting for stories after school. She stays and they all end up sparring verbally. One of the editors gets angry and tells her everything she said in her letter was bullshit, and that whatever she says in this meeting is irrelevant. Ward tries to intervene and keep the peace. It doesn't work.

Everything goes downhill from there. Someone inadvertently offends Joan in after-school art. She goes home and she gets into a tussle with her dad and brother. They both end up yelling at her, then they just walk out to go to a Little League game.

Sitting alone in her house, she is determined this time to end her life. She activates her plan. The psychiatrist has her on the antidepressant Zoloft, and there are many other medications around the house that warn: "Do not take if you are taking antidepressants." She gathers up every medication she can find, her own and anybody else's. She lines them up in a double row on her dresser. She goes to the bathroom and gets a big glass of water, and then she begins. She takes them by twos because she can't swallow medication that well, so it takes a while. She does enough to begin to feel woozy, like she is going to lose consciousness, then tops them all off with an asthma inhaler. Just as she feels she is drifting off, the phone rings. It is her mother.

The next thing Joan remembers is waking up in the ambulance racing to the hospital. She is furious to be alive and remembers screaming at the attendant, "What the fuck is wrong? Why didn't I die?"

A fortuitous combination of circumstances set Joan on a journey back to life. First, it was a miracle that the drugs didn't kill her outright. Second, there was serendipity in her mother's calling Joan moments before she lost consciousness; her mom discerned a problem and called for help. Finally, following the call, her father's confusion about how to handle Joan's psychological problems put her mom squarely in charge. Joan's mom finally stepped forward as a mother to her.

In the safe environment of the psychiatric ward of the hospital, Joan begins to receive the support she has needed all along.

It turns out that Joan has a long history of childhood depression and several suicide attempts. She cannot remember a time when she was not depressed, and her first suicide attempt was in seventh grade. "I took pills or something," Joan recalls. "I always tried cheesy stuff because I didn't know how to do it. I considered hanging myself in ninth grade. I made the noose but I didn't try it." Then the two attempts this year. She captures the depth of her pain in a poem she writes right after entering the hospital:

> *Depression is my companion forever*
> *        until I die;*
> *Oh won't you come and eat with me*
> *        the fruit of bitterness.*
> *But when you leave,*
> *        don't ask me to come with you.*
> *Here is where I live.*
>
> *My body is my tomb,*
> *        and my tears are my killer.*
> *I have no home except my room*
> *        There are dead flowers all around.*

*I was not born to laugh*
*I was the girl who was born to be alone.*
*Alone to cry, alone to think,*
*Alone to scream, alone to dream,*
*Alone to die, alone to fly.*

Joan is lucky to have survived to get help. In the cocoon of the hospital, all the players in her life are paying attention, surrounding her in the presence of professionals who know what to do. Her mom at her side, her friends coming in a steady stream, begin to make a dent in Joan's feelings of rejection. "It's taken me a long time to realize that people care about me," she admits. "It's hard for me to believe." In group sessions her isolation is lessened by discovering she is not the only one with problems, and that some people's problems are even worse than hers. Joan begins to understand little by little that maybe she belongs in the world a lot more than she thought.

After a few days of a love fest with her parents, the true nature of her family difficulties begins to surface. Things start unraveling when Joan is expected to go home to her mother's. The morning she is supposed to leave, her mom comes in, sits Joan down, and says, "I want to get some things straight with you before I take you home, because I don't want your type of person in my house." She then delivers a long list of things about Joan that essentially attack who Joan is. Joan snaps. She yells at her mother that there is no way she is going home with her, that she is not leaving until her father comes to pick her up. Her mom says, "Fine," and walks out.

The staff descend on Joan. Joan finds out that while her mom "told the truth that my dad beat her and my dad is the rage master and everything, she never said that she left the house. She never said that she's never been there for us. She never said that she called my house coincidentally the night I tried to kill myself, so they were unaware of it and they had never asked me. They made her look like the sainted one and my dad look like the bad guy."

Joan insists that she is going home with her dad. If she does, a staff member tells her, "we're going to throw child protection on you." "I don't get beat up," Joan replies. "He calls me a bitch sometimes, but hey, he's there." The staff finally compromise and tell Joan they will release her to her dad if he comes in to talk, and she promises to tell him how she feels. For the first time, Joan explains calmly to her dad that he makes her feel bad when he says certain things and how she doesn't like the way he deals with her sometimes.

After a few weeks at home she says: "It hasn't been a bed of roses but it is okay. If he does go off on temper tantrums, I just tell him to stop." But she wonders if part of the blame in their relationship is hers. "I was sitting there taking all the crap. I thought it was evil to tell my dad to leave me alone." Now, she says, she is learning to speak up. "I'm seventeen now, not a little kid."

Her mom, free of the responsibility of having to keep Joan, continues to reach out. She calls Joan every day. They go out for dinner and shopping. They work together on developing a relationship. "I honestly think she wants to make up for not being here," says Joan. "All of a sudden her daughter is trying to commit suicide and she realizes that she hasn't talked to her in the six years since she left. She's been really trying hard now. I like it and I don't feel it is too late. I just feel, Why didn't this happen before?"

The day she has to return to school, Joan is scared about facing people. Jonathan comes by to pick her up. He has been supportive all through this, Joan says. He called her when she was in the hospital and made a point of offering to bring her to school this day.

"I always wanted to be Jonathan's friend," says Joan. "He's like one of those people that you try to be friends with all the time and I think that sometimes I get on his nerves, but I don't mean harm." She finally gets the courage to confront the issue directly, something she never would have done before the hospital and therapy. She tells Jonathan, "I value your friendship. I think you're cool." She goes on to tell him how she feels about him, his insights, and his compassion. "I didn't feel weird at all doing it. It just happened. It was easy because it wasn't like saying 'I love you.' I really admire and respect him a lot. I think he's a great person." And of course, after she said all that, she hoped she hadn't scared him.

A few days later, Joan and Jonathan are walking back to his car after school when Joan sees one of her old teachers. They stop and talk. The teacher asks Jonathan, "Oh, is this your friend?" Joan nervously intercedes and says, "He's *my* friend." Jonathan looks at Joan, and she thinks, Oh no, maybe he doesn't think I'm his friend. She can see Jonathan is thinking. Finally he says, "Well, I take care of her and she takes care of me." Joan thinks this is the nicest thing anybody's ever said. She is reassured that taking the emotional chance she did with Jonathan paid off. She's willing to trust him. "I don't think Jonathan would ever say something he didn't mean," Joan says. "Everything he says is genuine."

Christmas at Joan's house is special this year. Joan cooks the meal of chili and empanadas, rice, salad, and some pastries for dessert for her family, including her mom's husband and daughter. Her dad gives her duck boots, a wilderness T-shirt, and "awesome" hiking pants with legs you can zip off to make shorts. Her mom gets her clothes, a makeup box, and a new Pooh bear. Joan cries when she sees the bear.

Joan loves Pooh bear and the Pooh stories. She thinks if you read them seriously, and reflect about what the characters say and do, they are like a guide to life. Her favorite story is about when Eeyore's house blows down and he sets out to rebuild it from the pieces. Pooh and friends come by and can't find Eeyore's house and conclude that he is homeless. So they go and find a big pile of sticks to build him a new one. Meanwhile, Eeyore goes back to his project and discovers his sticks are gone. It turns out that Pooh and Piglet have used them to build a new house for Eeyore on the other side of the tree so the wind won't blow it down anymore. "That is the best story," laughs Joan. "What could be more wonderful than building your friend a house with love."

That is how she feels about this Christmas. Her family is together, her mom and dad are working to be better parents, and "the presents they gave were me," says Joan.

The first of the year, Joan attends a church retreat in Virginia Beach about teenage life. It is focused on what lessons the Bible has to teach, in a convocation of two thousand teenagers and "lots of cool music." Joan is impressed by the lack of didacticism: the retreat isn't about "You must do this and that" or "You are bad teenagers and must repent."

Joan is touched in many ways, but the key lesson comes from a session on forgiveness. She realizes that she has not forgiven her mother and a lot of the things her dad has done. She thinks about how she buries everything so deep inside to avoid thinking about it. When the group leader speaks about parents who have molested their children, parents where the father beats the mother, or parents who abandon their children, Joan becomes aware of how she has not forgiven and how she holds "a big grudge and resentment against society" because of things she has gone through. "I just kept saying that people are so evil and I was always trying to isolate myself." Somehow, the session opens her heart and she feels the forgiveness flow in to fill some of the empty spaces.

Joan returns from the retreat with a new resolve to take power over her life and to reach outside of herself to others. "I'm one of those people who have to do it to believe it," she says. "I don't want to just sit here and say that life is worth living. I want to go out and live."

Within a few weeks, she is assisting the English as a Second Language teacher and working in the main office in the school. She is beginning to transform her Hispanic background into an asset. And she is having fun. She finds life far more interesting the more she puts herself in the flow of it. In the school office, she sees a whole new side of adults. "I like it," she says. "I get to see the other side of the teachers and administrators. It's funny. They are not bad guys and they are not holy people either. It's funny to see how they act without kids around, like they bust loose." The people in the office take Joan under their wing.

In February, she has a breakthrough with her dad. He had never given her anything for Valentine's Day, but this year he gives her a Whitman Sampler. The true gift is an accompanying handwritten note that wishes her a happy Valentine's Day with love. For most people this would be nice but no big deal. For Joan and her dad it is a grand gesture of love that she will hold forever. Her father has never written anything before in English. That is how much he wants his daughter to know he loves her.

A short time after, her dad is sitting on the couch watching television. Joan walks in as she has a thousand times and sits across from him to watch too. He gets up, turns off the television, and returns to the couch. He looks her squarely in the eye and says: "If I have ever offended you before, or hurt you in any way by saying things, I didn't really mean to hurt you. I'm really sorry and I want you to forgive me. I want to be your friend and I want you to be able to talk to me." Satisfied that he said what he had to, he gets up, walks over to the television, and flips it back on.

"First I sat there and thought, What the hell is going on," recalls Joan. Then her dad gets up and turns off the television again and asks, "So what do you think?" She says, "Okay." But she is thinking, with an inner smile that lights up her entire being, He is just saying he is sorry.

Working things out with her parents is an ongoing process. Her dad occasionally lapses into verbal abuse, but he's much more aware. Harder to change are the biases in Hispanic culture, like the idea that the boy in the family is more important than the girl. "It is so evident that my brother can get away with so much more than I can," says Joan, "and when things happen it is never his fault, always mine."

Her mom, who is much more Americanized, has intervened in her life in ways that ease the confines of her dad's world. For example, Joan lived at her mom's house briefly during exams so as not to be distracted by housework. Her mom has also talked to her dad about allowing Joan to partake more in the social life of an American teenager.

When Joan looks back at the year, she describes it as a deep dark forest. "I feel like I'm walking through it, that there are sunny spots every now and then, and eventually I'll come to the end." She says she always pictures the end in her mind as a sunny meadow filled with flowers. But the dark forest remains at the edge of that field, and Joan believes that sometimes "you forget something and you have to go back into the forest, but it is your decision to stay there or leave." She still has good days and bad, but the good days are increasing. Therapy helps her learn that there are many ways she can remain in charge of her life without having to be a bird and fly away.

One of her great victories centers around her senior prom. She has a date briefly but it falls through. She sits around and mopes, dredging up all the other times her social life has failed her. Then one day she says to herself, Why am I being so cheesy about this, I'm being harder on myself than anyone else, Prince Charming is not going to knock on my door and say, "Let's go to the prom."

Joan takes matters in her own hands and invites three of her closest girlfriends to share the evening. They have a ball. Their limo picks them up at their homes and drives them to an Irish pub in Old Town Alexandria for dinner. They eat and sit around singing Irish drinking songs until 10:30. They make a grand entrance when they pull up to the Hyatt Regency in Reston for the dance. "When we got to the prom it was weird," recalls Joan. "Everyone sits at the door watching to see who is with whom. So they see our limo drive up and I'm waving out the window, knowing everybody is wondering who is beside me." She knows people expect her to be with the guy who originally asked her. "They were expecting him and then they see these four girls come out of the car." They were freaking out and Joan loved the surprise of it all.

Standing patiently at the edge of the gawking crowd is Joan's mother. She has been waiting for Joan to arrive to take pictures of the occasion, not wanting to miss this milestone in her daughter's life. Joan and her friends greet her and pose for several shots. Then mother and daughter embrace, and Joan and her friends go laughing into the celebration.

# The Great Unknown Lies Ahead:
## To the Wilderness
## or to College

The balmy March wind has been beckoning all day. Jonathan hears it in his head as he sits restlessly through his classes. At lunchtime, he rushes outside and imbibes the freshness of the oncoming spring. If he were a different kid he might skip, but that is not his style. "I've just skipped once or twice. All my friends have skipped all along. I've just never done it. I was scared to. I didn't want to get caught. The other thing is I don't want my teachers to think I don't like them. I don't want to disrespect my teachers. But people skip because they can't take it, and the more you skip, the less you can take it." He forces himself to "take it," not necessarily by focusing on his classes, but by carrying on a running critique of school in his head and by imagining and planning what he will do out of school.

The winter has seemed endless, and in some ways the Bahamas trip made it even worse. It tantalized him with the tropical heat, with the vibrant clear colors of any season but winter. By engaging him in a superlative learning experience, it made school even duller by comparison. The long winter coupled with senior slump left Jonathan feeling like he was jumping out of his skin. He retreated into himself during the cold, dark months and now feels himself awakening like the brilliant green shoots of plants emerging for a new season.

At last, seventh period is over, and Jonathan flees the confines of South Lakes. He meets Andy outside. They stop at each of their houses to pick up their kayaks, their gear—spray jackets, helmets, and flotation vests—and they are off to the river.

Jonathan is brimming with enthusiasm for this sport. Turned on last year by a video clip he saw on television, he knew he had to learn how to kayak. He feels it is a total body-mind connection: when you are good, the kayak becomes an extension of the body and the confidence and euphoria from the experience stays with you. That's why he passionately seeks converts. "The greatest gift I think I could give to someone is to teach them how to kayak," says Jonathan. And that's what he did this year with his best friend. Andy was a quick study. He learned the Eskimo roll, how to turn yourself over when upside down, in no time. Jonathan shared everything he knew. "From there it's up to him," says Jonathan. "We're both competent paddlers right now. I'm no better than him, he's no better than me. We're just both good paddlers."

Only twenty minutes away from his doorstep, suburbia runs into the wild. He and Andy drive into Great Falls Park, a dramatic rocky gorge of the Potomac River with panoramic views and sweeping currents. They park the car, unload their gear, and make the difficult descent down the rocks. Their destination is a relatively tranquil cove away from the often wild waters so they can get in without being banged up. They put their boats into the water and are on their way. For the next several hours they ride down the river, joyfully "play boating," experimenting with the currents, the rapids, and the four-foot standing waves under the falls. "You just have to focus and fight your way through whatever's coming at you," says Jonathan. It is exhilarating, like surfing, says Andy. "You feel at one with nature like a fish."

There is nothing like the feeling when they drag their boats from the water and collapse on the shore, pleased with their time well spent. There is a camaraderie that is as close to love as boys like to admit about their feelings for each other. It opens them up to conversations that are intense, connected, and real. Jonathan confides to his friend how he perceives things more clearly out on the river: "All of the society I've been introduced to creates doubts for me, and most of the doubts are about myself. When I go out on the river, I see the doubts shouldn't really be about myself but about the society we're being raised in."

Jonathan worries about everything. He tells Andy about Tom

Brown Jr.'s latest book, *The Quest*, which claims that the end of civilization is coming soon. "I don't know whether to believe that. I keep on thinking, Is everything this messed up?" says Jonathan. "Is everything landsliding downhill? Or is everything just moving over a bit this way to make things better? That gets me really upset because if everything is messed up then my chief concern is my parents are messed up; my secondary concern is I'm messed up, but I know how to alleviate that—just leave civilization. But if everything is messed up then I have to get my parents and move aside and do something else. I'm not really sure. Do you think there are people out there who are pretty content with what they are doing—lawyers or whoever they are?"

That is what Jonathan is trying to figure out. Should he feel as bad about everything as he does when he feels bad? "I know that life is a struggle that can't always be up or down," he says. "But I don't think it's right to feel so desperate and then so good. I think it should be more balanced. If you are backpacking or kayaking, it all seems to work right, to move right."

Andy can relate. He too perceives the shallowness of society and the truth in nature, the immediacy of fulfillment from backpacking or kayaking. The two have shared their passion for the outdoors for over four years now, from the camping trips when their parents used to drop them off and pick them up to these grown-up adventures of their own.

Jonathan tells his friend about his concern that "when I'm in these really down moods, it seems like I look ahead and it's like, God, is everything going to be this bad? Is everything going to be filled with doubts and things like that? It's really a horrible feeling. What is there to look forward to if everything's just going to be filled with doubts?"

That's the kind of year it's been—a year of decisions, of facing the unknown, of closings and yet-to-be-defined openings. School, which sometimes felt like a prison, now feels like a stop on the way to some unknown destination. When Jonathan started the school year, his goals were "not to let this place get me down, try not to let people push me around, just stick up for what I believe in, what I'm trying to do." As second semester moves on toward graduation, his goals are loftier and more urgent, to "try to figure out where I'm going, which I don't know yet, and what I'm doing with my life so far."

One of the big things going on since the middle of the icy winter is that Jonathan and Andy have been scheming how they are going to move off to the woods and live subsistence for three or four years. Then try to go to school.

This is not about dropping out or goofing off, but about seeking life's meaning. One of Jonathan's inspirations is a picture of one of Andy's uncles who lives on a farm. Jonathan sees "a look in his eye, it's that feeling of something that's real." It reminds Jonathan of the last line in *A River Runs Through It*, where the surviving brother, now an old man, says, "I'm haunted by waters." We're not touching that feeling in school, says Jonathan. "That's a big thing about moving off to the woods. You can actually live your life."

The more he considers it, says Jonathan, the more it seems like the right thing to do. "Out there you'd be living day to day, and struggling for your survival. You're struggling for your life, and you start to appreciate your life more because you're struggling for it. I get the impression that we're just a bunch of bratty kids. I see it in myself a lot. People are starving to death, and we're complaining about the school. We've never touched anything real." If he goes to college, it would be a continuation of high school. "It's so sheltered. It's just another box. It's almost like you never want to deal with anything tough."

But there is another consideration for Jonathan. Andy keeps on saying they can go to college after they live in the woods, but Jonathan has concerns about time. Jonathan wants his mom to be able to retire as soon as she wants to, and she's basically waiting for him to get out of college. So if she has to wait another two or three years while he's in the woods, then another four years in college, "I'm holding back her life. I can't do that." So maybe he'll go to Virginia Tech, the University of Montana, or the University of Oregon instead of the wilderness.

At one level, Jonathan resents college. "I really think we've made things too complicated, the whole way that humans live. I don't see why you have to take twenty years of your life to learn a profession." If he goes to college and finds it stultifying, he'll just leave it. Then he would not be able to be a teacher, but he might drop out and do something else. "Maybe I'll go study how to be a wilderness first aid person, or a wilderness emergency medical technician, something like that," Jonathan speculates. "But farther on down the line, you really can't feed your children as a wilderness EMT."

Two big trails. Two totally different life paths. Jonathan can hardly think of anything else. It is like he must decide the direction of his life. He tries to convince himself there is nothing irreversible but he can't shake the feeling that this is momentous. He talks to all of his friends about it, trying to consider each perspective.

Nature has such a hold on Jonathan. It would be difficult to untangle the strands of the outdoors and its relationship to times in his life that were less complicated, when his family was one unit, when life opened fresh and new before him. Now, at the old age of eighteen, he is deep into a search to integrate his fractured school experience, his separated parents, his yearning for a life that makes sense and has the clarity that Jonathan has always found in the wilderness.

The outdoors is synonymous with all the best times in his life: camping with parents and friends, fishing with his dad, skiing with his mom, sitting alone in touch with himself. Nature represents harmony, balance, freedom from the need for words, life.

Most of all it is the arena where he feels whole and at peace. Thank goodness for the temperate weather so he can get out. When he is in a bad place, like a few weeks ago, camping always helps. He went to Difficult Run, out on the rocks along the river and spent the night. Right after the sun went down, a flock of geese flew overhead in formation, then landed. "It's the first time I've ever seen them land. They changed their call as they got closer and closer to the river. Then they landed. Later on, two more geese came from the same direction and landed there, so I figured that must be a meeting spot. It was really cool, I'm sitting out here on the cliff looking over the Potomac, and here I'm seeing this meeting spot for these geese and they're communicating." Observing the geese uplifted his spirit. "There's nothing artificial in nature," says Jonathan. "It's all by need, and it all works. Things die but it's all the natural process, and it seems like in our society so much is fake and too much time is spent worrying about this and that and the other thing."

Another day, on a hike after school, Jonathan and Andy argue about whether they have any obligation to come back. Jonathan refers again to Tom Brown Jr.'s book *The Quest*, which is all about why you should come back from the wilderness. "That's a consideration. If people that care about nature and unity and wholeness all leave, then how is anybody else going to learn?" says Jonathan. The trick is to establish a rhythm: you come back to civilization as long as you can stand it, and then you return to the wilderness. It's like "go-ing back to the well to get another bucket of water. Every time any-body gets some goodwill, they come back and spread it around as much as they can. People who are feeling good are nice to people; people who are feeling bad are mean to people."

The big difference Jonathan sees between him and Andy is that Jonathan feels if he goes out there, "I'd have to come back and share what I've learned and try to help out. Andy's like, 'Hey man, I'm go-ing. Sorry.' "

They respect each other's point of view. They agree that the pre-mier reason for going to live in the wilderness is just to have done it. Jonathan, always mentally grabbing for the quote that pinpoints his feelings, paraphrases Thoreau: "This is one of the lives I wanted to live, and the reason I left is I felt I had several other lives to live."

The idea evolves. Jonathan has spent the requisite time looking at colleges but even then nature beckoned and was the highlight of the tour. He and his mom traveled to several schools, camping along the way. He liked James Madison but his grades might be a hindrance. Virginia Tech was okay but not inspiring, with its huge, businesslike campus. From Tech, they went to the University of Asheville, and that was too small. Then Jonathan went kayaking for several days with a group from the Nantahala Outdoor Center in the Great Smoky Mountains near Asheville. He met wonderful people who were open and free and connected and loving.

While he was on the river his mom visited a friend in Asheville. In the midst of his college tour, the time he spent kayaking taught him something. Originally he thought he ought to go to school some-where near his parents, so he could keep the parts of his life con-nected. "Then when I was on NOC and I didn't see my parents for four days it didn't really bother me because I was around a lot of people that I was getting along with really well. So I figured if I go to a college, even though you care about your parents you need to move toward your own life." Jonathan began to understand how he would always be a part of their life, but he felt free to look at places beyond the borders of his home area.

This whole year Jonathan has been thinking a lot about his par-ents. The Vision Quest jolted him into the realization of passing time. He's not ashamed of how he feels, and he is in touch with his sense of yearning and responsibility to do right by them. He was impressed by the nurse who addressed his history class last year about her experiences in the Vietnam War, telling them how the last thing that the soldiers would say before they died was, "I want my mommy." Jonathan understands. "I don't think you ever can grow out of your parents. They're the only people that you can always trust to love you, for whatever you do. If you don't have someone like that, then that messes you up, I think. You need to have that triangle of love."

As he tries to forge the next link on his pathway to the rest of his life, Jonathan can't rid himself of the feeling of gates closing behind him, of childhood ending and adulthood beginning. It reminds him of that feeling he had returning from his Vision Quest when he felt between two worlds.

All year long every activity has an overlay of great meaning. Like the skiing trip with his mom at White Tail during the winter. They both love to cross-country ski, but once on the trails his fantasy of mother and son gliding across the new-fallen snow was compromised. The reason was simple: she was out of shape. But Jonathan turned that into a metaphysical problem. "I didn't know exactly what to do. I tried to go back and help her out, but it didn't seem like she really wanted help," he recalls. "So I'd go off on my own and then feel bad, and come back." Rather than consider their age and activity differences, Jonathan feared they were out of sync.

He thinks about Andy and the synchrony when they are together on the trails or in the water. Even though he and Andy are different, says Jonathan, "we're both headed in the same direction, that's why it works. With me and my mom, I'm trying to move fifty miles an hour and she's trying to move two. We just can't ski together. I think because of the lifestyle she's living, she's not in as good shape as she should be." Jonathan doesn't carry the thought to its logical conclusion that he's growing up, and as much as he loves his mom, the time is here to move out in his own direction at his own pace.

The trip gives him two "ambititious goals" for his last semester at school: "to get my mom in shape and get my parents back together." He's going to try to walk around the lake with her a couple of times a week, especially in the spring, when the sun comes up earlier.

Then there is the business of his parents' separation. The year before when he was not liking school so much, he thought he ought to get his parents back together and move to Alaska. It has always bothered him that he lives with his mother while his father "seems like he's sort of alone."

It's more than that. Even though they have not lived as man and wife for over a decade, their separation still breaks Jonathan's heart. "I looked at pictures of myself when I was really young, and then there's a drop-off point where there's a strange sad look in my eyes." There are tons of photos of a busy, active child skiing, playing out front, then there's the "drop-off." It is right there in the face of a little boy who used to have mommy and daddy living together with him, a happy family, and then it ended.

He remembers how in fourth grade the teacher asked the class to draw something they liked. He drew a picture of a log cabin like the one he remembered from when his family lived together. Then the teacher wrote down the words "I wish." Jonathan responded by writing, "That my dog Daffer didn't die, and that my parents had me when they were younger, and that my parents would not be divorced." He remembers: "These are the three things that in my brain were most important to me to fix. Not fix the earth, I didn't even know about that. It was those three things."

When they moved from Alaska back to Reston, Jonathan explains, his dad stayed because his son was here. "That's one of the main reasons my mom may have never formally divorced my father. Because she wanted to make sure he stuck around for me." What concerns Jonathan is that his dad can't move on because he can't get a divorce. "He's half her husband, half my father, but on the other half, he's stuck," Jonathan says. "I don't think he'd sue her for divorce. So he's stuck in between starting another life and being a part of this life."

Jonathan sees hope because he knows his dad doesn't have to come over every night like he does. He does it because he wants to. "That's the thing. He loves my mom, and he loves me. But he's only half there. So I guess if we broke down that one barrier right there then the whole thing would work." Jonathan truly believes their marriage is "just a little bit broken and it can be fixed without changing it that much. If he would give her some freedom and she would give him some freedom."

Jonathan hatches a plan. "I'm going to be really devious and sneaky. If I do better in terms of the basic things that really bother my mom, like if I clean my room, clean the kitchen, it will make her a little bit happier. If I'm doing everything I'm supposed to be doing then it will take some pressure off. So that will maybe just open her up a little bit. I'm planning a trip with my dad to either New York or Maine for a week-long canoe trip, and I'm trying to think whether I should invite my mom along or not. It could go either way." What Jonathan would really like is to take them kayaking.

There is an urgency about resolving this before he leaves. He feels that once he leaves, there will be no mediator.

It feels as though Jonathan is carrying around a mental checklist of the seminal relationships and events in his life, "like this lost section behind me where things have already gone by."

Two years ago he fell in love with Angie, and, he says "that was one of the things that changed my life more than anything." He met her in creative writing one day when she stole his seat. She was beautiful, with a smile that practically made him tremble. When she realized what she had done she said, "I'm sorry, was this your seat?" Jonathan told her it was okay, she could have it. "Then she wrote about this picture and I read it, and we just had this communication that I'd never had before with a person. It was this understanding."

Jonathan was much too shy to talk to her until the day he and Andy decided they wanted to try marijuana. Andy talked to Angie and she did it with them the first time. "I think that's one of the reasons why I think it's a good thing," says Jonathan. "We did it with her, and she talked about it as being part of the earth and as a peaceful thing." In other words, it was not merely "Let's do dope," but rather "Let's connect with the earth."

After that, they both knew that they cared about each other. One night out on a canoe on Lake Anne, they admitted their feelings for each other and Jonathan read her some things he'd written about her. But the sad thing was that she was a graduating senior and in a month was going away to tour with the Grateful Dead around the country before going to college. Loving her was beautiful and terrible simultaneously because he knew from the beginning he would lose her.

For a long time Jonathan didn't know whether he wanted to try to be interested in a different girl because he still loved Angie. The relationship never actually ended, Jonathan explains. "We were in love and she vanished, and then she came back for a little time and we were in love, and she vanished. The last time she came back it was pretty strange because she said she thought about me a lot, but I saw her once and then I could tell that things weren't working right."

Last summer he went to a Bob Dylan concert. The final song

Dylan played was "Shooting Star." Jonathan says he felt Angie's presence in the song, so close and warm. Dylan sang, "Seen a shooting star tonight/And I thought of you./ . . . I always kind of wondered/ If you ever made it through./ . . . If I ever became what you wanted me to be./" Jonathan thought about how being with Angie coaxed him into being more open to things and helped him to see things that he'd never seen or experienced before. "But now it's gone, it's back there, it can't come back," he says sadly.

Yet he still feels her spirit in him. On the way back from his ski trip this winter he was thinking about her. The next day he was poking around on his dresser and he opened this box and one of her blond locks was inside. He picked it up and held it in his hand and he could sense her and what she was to him. He holds on to those memories even as Angie is in Reston, temporarily out of college, because he knows she's changed and he's changed, and things can never be the same as they were. Jonathan says he will always love her and remember how special that time of his life was.

"I'm really lucky that it happened to me," says Jonathan of Angie, "but it's behind me. I try to think whether I should be thinking about how so much is over."

Jonathan thinks maybe the difference between the valedictorian, straight-A student going to the University of Virginia and him is that maybe that student is happier, "but I'm feeling real things that are touching me deep inside. I'm feeling loss and gain and I'm really feeling things, whereas a lot of people that are becoming great doctors or whatever are never feeling anything."

The spring explodes into one glorious day after another. There are days to hike, to kayak, long days of sunshine that stretch each day a minute or two longer. Jonathan thinks his parents see him as pretty irresponsible, and they are right. His grades are so-so, he's been getting home late and not putting enough effort into things, tending to say "Mom wanted me to do this, but I've got to get kayaking" or "I've got this project due, but the river's at four feet eight inches."

His spring fever is also affecting his plans with Andy. They were supposed to go to the Department of Agriculture last week, then this week, then next week, to find out what kind of wilderness land, if any, is available. They are supposed to write Canada and see what is available there, although it seems too far away. If they choose to live in the woods, they need to figure out which woods.

Jonathan says he's made the decision about ten times, it's just been a different decision each time. His parents get grumpy about this whole wilderness notion, but he's not surprised. "When I originally thought about this, I thought my parents would be upset at first but later on they'd see it was better," says Jonathan, "because if I'm happier it's going to make them happier." He hopes they respect the thought that is going into his decision.

Plans keep changing between the boys too. This week Andy's thinking about going to the University of Oregon. That's cool as far as Jonathan is concerned. So they decide they are going to move to Oregon and live off the land for a year, then they will go to the University of Oregon. "But we decide something new that sounds completely wonderful every other week," says Jonathan.

As his senior year winds down, Jonathan thinks about things he regrets, things he might change if he had his adolescence to replay. He wishes he had been part of a sport in high school; he likes the idea of playing your heart out on a team. He used to be a good soccer player when he was a little kid; maybe if he'd kept it up he would have been able to play on varsity. He already plays the harmonica but he'd intended to learn to play the jazz harmonica for the band. He'd hoped to do more for the Environmental Club, like the great canoe trip that fizzled. He regrets not communicating better with people. During the winter when he was feeling down, he stopped talking to a lot of his friends. "What I didn't realize is that everybody feels uncomfortable sometimes and everybody feels bad sometimes. So instead of me being reclusive and this person being reclusive, we should all have been talking about it." He feels he should be putting more effort into being nice and just talking to other people instead of being withdrawn. "I've learned it so many times, but I don't put it into practice. So it's becoming a bad, bad habit that I'm trying to break."

All the things Jonathan regrets are related to plans not kept that would have brought him closer to a group—a team, a band, a club, his friends. They are regrets about missed connections.

More than anything, Jonathan does not want to regret the way he lives his life. He wants to live fully and vitally. He does not want to get caught in half a life like his dad or wait too long to make time for what he loves like his uncle who waits impatiently for his one week hunting trip a year. He remembers something his uncle said the last time they parted: 'Once you do it, nobody can take it away.' " Jonathan knew exactly what he meant. The best and most real moments he has had in his life—with his parents, with Angie, with his friends, in the water, on the top of a mountain—are his, forever. They are a part of him. That's what he wants for his future: a life full of authentic living that nobody can take away.

As the May 1 deadline draws near, it is getting down to Virginia Tech. He is still confused as to whether he wants to go to college at all. He's beginning to think it may be the best thing to do. But he's not sure. Maybe he should still go off into the wild. He can't decide.

He wonders if he and Andy are chickening out. They know in their hearts that they should go to the woods. "The question is, is it the right thing to do. You know what I'm saying? If we think about it enough, we know we're going to want to do it, but we're trying to push ourselves to go to college," says Jonathan. You don't know what's going to happen down the road. If you go out to live in the woods a couple of years like Thoreau, Jonathan speculates, "what if you bump into a woman and you have children? Then what do you do? You're kind of on the edge. But I think maybe that's part of life, being on the edge like that."

He worries whether his fear is getting in the way. It is, he believes, his worst trait. He ticks off his failures that happened because he was afraid: "I didn't talk to the girl in the Bahamas, I couldn't give Angie what she needed, I couldn't give my parents what they wanted." He worries that his fear keeps him from being fully himself.

This whole senior year, Jonathan has paused repeatedly to evaluate where he is and who he is. Some kids may rush forward into the stream of sensations, others into a deliberate life plan for success. For Jonathan, it is always a spiritual struggle of grand proportions as he seeks meaning and value in a world that often disappoints him. He is qualifiedly optimistic, believing that if he remains in touch with the earth, he will find a life of significance. He is never a marginal person but is deeply involved in the flow of life. He revealed this ongoing process in an essay for one of his college applications: "Over the years I have learned so much about the things going on around me. I've tried a lot of new things—playing the guitar, identifying trees, wood carving, sailing, photography, writing—but just about anything you catch me doing involves the self, nature, or children. I don't like cars, and I don't like parties. I love to sit and talk with good friends, wander through forests, fish along old green rivers with my father, glide through cold snowy forests on free-heeled skis with my mother. When I think about my life, it is round like our planet, jagged like rock faces, narrow and deep like canyons, long as the mesa, and full of sparkling, crystal lights like the stars of night."

The end of April, he and Andy send in their acceptances to Virginia Tech. They request each other as roommates and make plans to go camping across the country before school begins.

# E P I L O G U E

## *A Warm Embrace*

I t is a steamy June evening in 1994, right after a sudden violent thunderstorm. The setting sun ignites the dense black clouds in a brilliant blaze of orange light. I go to pick up Joan. She greets me wearing a soft, feminine pastel floral dress of lilac, yellow, and green, her Doc Martens visible below the graceful hemline. We're going to the senior dinner and talent show. Joan is cheerful and happy, and I am grateful each time I see her that she is alive.

As we drive to the school she tells me about how the senior prank went awry. There's always a senior prank, usually something like festooning an administrator's office with toilet paper or turning office furniture upside down. This year the plan was to remove chairs from the building and arrange them in the parking lot. But something went terribly wrong, and instead, a group of kids went on a rampage in the school that resulted in several thousand dollars' worth of damage. There was a swath of destruction that included cracked windows, broken ceiling panels, motor oil spilled in hallways, and obscenities spray-painted across walls. The scuttlebutt is that kids came in drunk, annoyed that they were not included in the "Prank Committee." They hadn't planned such mayhem, but the event developed its own momentum. The group started moving things around, for example, then decided, Hell, why not throw the stuff through the window? One teacher's room was especially hard hit, and she was devastated not just by the tremendous damage, but also because she had been targeted and didn't know why. Some wondered if it had to do with her being one of the advisers to the Honor Society, which had some contentiousness this year between students and teachers. In fact, it became known later that many top students were among the 150 perpetrators.

Earlier in the day the whole class was hauled into a special assembly. The class sponsor, Wynn Thompson, was crying. "I want you to know I've worked until 8:00 every night for the last year, and then when I get home I do more work," she sniffled. "And I don't deserve this." The scolding continued. The administrators immediately canceled the class picnic to pay for the damage.

Joan listened and felt really bad. She wanted to do something so graduation wasn't ruined. She knew her dad had the cleaning equipment to do the job, so she offered their services to clean up. To her it was "my way of thanking a lot of the teachers and people who were really nice to me during my depression and my problems." By 10 A.M., her dad arrived with a power washer and cleaning solutions. Father and daughter worked side by side until 4 P.M. with the help of several students. Joan and her dad were heroes. She says they were glad to help; it was "no big deal."

She was being modest. The headline of *The Reston Times* would later scream: "Seniors Vandalize South Lakes High," then below it, "Father, Daughter, Aid Clean Up." "The cost of the damage would have been greater," the article said, "if Eduardo Garcia and his daughter Joan, a senior, hadn't offered to help clean up."

As we drive, she tells me how her dad was invited to the talent show and dinner this evening, but he declined because he "has to take care of the kids." Joan and I know it is something more. He is a part-time painter who speaks little English, and while he is thrilled to have his children grow up Americans, he is still uncomfortable in their world.

We reach the school and walk in; I greet many kids that I know. It is no longer a strange land to me. I have spent so many hours here that I feel part of the place as "the lady who is writing the book about us." The hallways and classrooms, the cafeterias and the athletic fields are alive with stories. What once seemed like a mind-spinning blur of activity now has come into focus as one of the stages where individual dramas of adolescence are played out. As the kids say, it is so "unboring."

In my own journey into the adolescent community, the hours

have turned to years, and now I often feel out-of-place among the adults. It's not that I feel like one of the kids, but rather that I have experienced the reality of adolescent lives in a way that most people haven't, and it has changed me. I have shared so much, have seen the invisible, heard the secrets, penetrated the darkness, and witnessed the spellbinding inconsistencies of who they are.

My problem was clear at that buffet dinner. In a formal school situation like that, I was expected to sit with the grown-ups, in this case, the teachers, counselors, and administrators. I liked them fine but the truth was, I preferred listening to the conversations of the kids.

I couldn't help but notice that night how natural and lighthearted the kids were in this structured setting that had been arranged by their graduation committee in partnership with adults. They relished being here with each other. This was not a typical night where a school event was a place to drop by on the way to the real destination of a night in a hotel or a party in an empty house. This dinner and show were the destination, and the kids slipped comfortably into the occasion. The graduating seniors felt like seventeen- and eighteen-year-olds we re-member, not the mysterious, hardened, blasé stereotypes to which we've become accustomed.

The seniors, most of whom have been in the same schools from at least seventh grade, greet each other like long-lost friends, with hugs and exclamations of joy. Such is not the customary school posturing. Joan thinks it is because they are leaving and don't have to worry anymore about pretenses of being cool and associated with the "right" group.

It is perfectly consistent in today's adolescent community that the very same kids who maliciously damaged their school less than twenty-four hours ago are now flush with school spirit and warm feelings about their fellow students and the faculty. The adults, not wanting to ruin the occasion, accept the inconsistency. Last night more than a quarter of the class wreaked havoc. Earlier today the school staff were so furious they considered bringing charges. This evening it feels like the incident is forgotten or ignored, and everybody hugs. Such inconsistencies are normal in the adolescent community. To the kids, both sides are real.

After dinner, the class appreciation begins. First a slide presenta-tion. With Simon and Garfunkel's "Kodachrome" blasting in the back-ground, the class is treated to a race through time with pictures sent in by parents and kids. *Click:* a baby in a blanket; *click:* a toddler blowing bubbles; *click:* a birthday party for a five-year-old; *click:* day camp; *click:* a ballet recital; *click:* three ten-year-olds swimming; *click:* the eighth-grade dance; *click:* freshman Homecoming; *click:* the prom. The kids squeal and clap in recognition of years past, of friend-ships that span a decade, of that toddler face looking so much like the young man or woman of today. It is a reminder to adults and kids of how quickly time passes.

Then the class gifts. The mood is ebullient. The class representa-tive stands to call up Mrs. Thompson, the class sponsor. He begins by crediting her with "no more fourth-place finishes in spirit competi-tions," a reference to the fact that during the two years she has been sponsor, their class won first place during the Homecoming pep ral-lies. The kids go nuts screaming their approval, as if this were of ma-jor importance to them, when any other time they would consider it a joke. Mrs. Thompson comes to the stage looking like a human pen-nant, decked out in school colors, a green suit with a royal-blue shell. She opens her gift, a watch inscribed with a pun on her first name: "You are the Wynn beneath our wings." She cries, thanks them, tells them she is already planning their class reunion. "I got the paper-work last week about it! You've reached a mountaintop—enjoy your view." She tactfully makes no mention of the Valley of the Vandals last night.

There are several more gifts, and then the entertainment, put on by the seniors. For the next several hours, the class displays a vast range of talent, in a dynamic mix of rock, reggae, rap, even classical. There is a scene from a play, a wrestling exhibition, a song simulta-neously sung and signed. The mixture of acts in that talent show and the enthusiasm with which the audience receives it demonstrate what a multicultural, multifaceted group of kids this generation can be when provided an appropriate forum. Their blended community is the future of this nation and they are working out the details in their styles, their friendships, their social lives even as they struggle with legacies of prejudice.

When it is Joan's turn to perform, the master of ceremonies says he wishes he had known her before, because now she's "a great friend. She also is very dedicated to this class in two ways: one, she showed up for every single rehearsal I had, and two, she donated a lot of time and effort and machinery to clean up the spray paint that was done last night. I now introduce Joan."

The spotlight shines on her as she walks onstage to an explosion of cheers. She has never done anything like this before. Her dad taught her how to play the guitar, but it was a pastime she enjoyed in the privacy of her bedroom, the same bedroom where she tried to take her own life. People chant, "Joan, Joan." She stands in the spotlight looking a bit stunned.

When the audience quiets down she speaks. "Several months ago a friend of mine dedicated this song to me." Her voice quivers. "I was going through a hard time and a lot of trouble. Every time that I feel sad or I feel lonely, I think of this song. I'd like to dedicate this song to all of you in the class who've helped me in my time of need." There is total silence in the room. Her voice trembles as she thanks a handful of people by name: her counselors, Mrs. Knapp, a special adult from the main office, two friends including Jonathan Tompkins, and me.

When she mentions me by name in this auditorium, my eyes fill with tears. In many ways, moving inside adolescence was a lonely, challenging task for me. Her recognition in that place validated my work, my journey with them. It was a moment that captured why this book has been so much more than reporting. The kids in this book, like Joan, opened wide the windows of their lives and it was impossible to look in untouched.

Joan starts playing her guitar, softly singing an Indigo Girls song from their *Rites of Passage* album. She's a bit timid in her delivery but doing fine until she gets to the refrain: "And I say, love will come to you, Hoping just because I spoke the words that they are true. As if I had a crystal ball to look through. And where there is now one there will be two." She stops singing abruptly. Her body quakes and she breaks downs and cries.

The audience wraps its arms around her with its applause. Everyone stands clapping as she struggles to get her composure. It is an amazing scene: This lonely girl onstage, so locked in herself, so utterly alone and desolate that she sought twice to end her own life only months ago, is now embraced by cheering compassionate peers who seek to hold her up, not beat her down, who have been touched and brought inside her honest love. Joan smiles her beautiful warm smile that crinkles her eyes and lights her face and says simply, "Sorry about that." The audience keeps clapping and chanting her name. Joan laughs and they laugh with her. She tells them, "I'll finish the song now."

She starts where she left off, but now her voice is strong, clear, full and resonant as if some previously suppressed part of her is released in the alchemy of the moment. She plays an interlude of solo guitar, then winds up the song, which has such significance to her life. "And I wish you insight to battle love's blindness. Strength from the milk of human kindness. A safe place for all the pieces that scatter. And learn to pretend that there's more than love that matters."

She bows to thunderous applause.

The evening ends, and Joan leaves with me after a warm reception from her classmates, lots of hugs and kisses, the positive stroking she never got during most of high school but which in the end seems to work its magic. On the way to my car, a male friend asks her out on a date. It has been glorious.

She admits on the way home that she "was afraid that instead of what happened tonight it was going to be completely opposite. People were going to take my feelings and just reject them. That was my worst fear. I can't really express the way I feel about that moment. Tonight was the best spiritual experience I've ever had. It's like people were crying, people were yelling. I felt like I was able to take my spirit, my emotions and have them feel how I felt. And in a way, have them understand me."

This is but one more transformation Joan has gone through during her adolescent journey. From lost child to tough girl to born-again hippie and friend of the earth. Hers is a dramatic metamorphosis. After all, she almost died before she could reach this moment of publicly reaching out, declaring she exists and is unique and valuable. If I had dropped in on her life and stayed a shorter time, her image at any particular moment would have belied the trapped and tormented soul inside. Judgments might have been made, a helping hand not extended, a conversation never heard. It would have been a loss to her potential and to pathways yet to come.

This anecdote could stand as an explanation of why this book has taken so many years. As a parent, I know how frustrating a child's "stage" can be, and how never-ending it sometimes seems. The responsibilities of parenthood and the pressures of day-to-day life often make it difficult to take the long view. But even as a mother, I am forever the journalist. Over the years, as each of my own three kids in adolescence has sometimes frustrated me, enraged me, frightened me, surprised me, thrilled me, made me prouder and angrier and happier and sadder than I've ever been, my journalistic self kept on saying, "Wow! What a tale." As an author, I could get inside the story. I knew I could explore with other people's kids how growing up *is*, the process and the evolution involved. I would have the opportunity to observe kids *in the process*, utilizing time, my full attention, and great patience, all of which can be elusive for a parent in the heat of a moment.

That night I told Joan that she displayed tremendous courage in opening her heart like that in a room full of teenagers and adults who have spent most of their lives trying to be anything other than open and emotional. It's not that they don't feel anything. They simply can't take the risk of becoming emotionally vulnerable. I pointed out to her how far she had come—from that tough wamma who fought with her fists for her place in the world to the talented young woman who triumphed with her heart and mind.

Graduation is a few days later. Dressed in royal-blue robes and mortarboards, 424 graduating seniors march in to "Pomp and Circumstance." It is a ceremony like every graduation for all time with all the formality, the speeches, and the platitudes. The seniors are exhorted to "plug away," told that "the more you put into life the more you get out of it," and on and on. The proud families cry and smile as they sit fanning themselves with programs, the younger members squirming out of boredom. The only break in the solemnity is a brightly colored beach ball that appears and is bounced around the heads of the graduates, to be confiscated by a teacher, yet always appearing again. Finally, the names are called, each youngster marching across the stage, shaking hands, and hugging the administrators while flashbulbs pop and camcorders whir. I'm taking pictures too. Joan reaches out to greet her parents. I snap the picture of her smiling broadly between her mom and dad. Jonathan, looking pensive, walks his hunched thoughtful walk right past me until I tap him on the shoulder and he gives me a quick grin. Nika Sutter, Charles's sister, nods at me, looking radiant and self-composed as usual, smiling happily, ready to take on the next challenge of her life. The tassels have been turned, the hats have been tossed, and 424 teenagers have marked an end and a beginning.

That night, the all-night graduation party in the Reston Community Center is attended by virtually every member of the class. A large number of parents also participate in this marathon evening of wholesome celebration. It is the culmination of a no-holds-barred outpouring of manpower, cash, and in-kind contributions, the realization of an idea that has taken hold all across the country to capture the graduates in an alcohol-free celebration of graduation. The concept of the event, which was hatched a decade or so ago, shows the power of parents coming up with creative alternatives to make the world safer for their kids and to give them a good time in the process. Although the impetus for the all-night party was that too many youngsters got hurt or killed in accidents on graduation night, the celebration has long since taken off as so much more than a trick to keep kids off the streets. It is a must-do, must-go, totally cool event. The Reston Community Center is filled with entertainment such as carnival games, fortune-telling, caricature-making, manicures and tattoos, a casino, and swimming, and donated food and prizes. Parents and members of the community have been working on it most of the year and it is splendid down to the smallest details. The majority of participants spend the whole night, and parents actually volunteer on a weeknight to do shifts like from two until five in the morning.

Jonathan, Joan, and their friends have a ball. They romp through the different activities. Their favorite is making a video they will no doubt show their own children and grandchildren someday. Jonathan cuts loose, wearing a cowboy hat and a Roy Rogers shirt and strumming a guitar. His buddy Bill, who has taken to wearing kilts to school this year and island shirts, is wearing a sundress with corduroys under it. Andy stars in the movie wearing a wild orange wig, a Superfly seventies jacket, and weird glasses. "He just looks like a cheesy seventies guy," says Joan. She wears her tie-dyed shirt topped by a glittered red cape, a genie turban, and a sword selected from a pile of props. For an hour, these seniors suspend their worries about the future and do something Chris Hughes felt he had to give up by eighth grade: they *play*, giggling and laughing until they think they will drop.

During the singular week of graduation, the community is together, all the parents with their kids. It feels like a Norman Rockwell painting or a simple, sweet, and comfortably old-fashioned episode of *The Wonder Years*. But of course it is not. The final event cannot neutralize years of neglect, not necessarily on the part of individual parents but of a society that does not pay enough attention in a comprehensive, consistent way to the needs of developing adolescents.

Starting in middle school, the school culture is weak. Not enough kids participate in school activities. Not enough parents participate either. These are documentable truths, as Nicholas Zill and Christine Winquist Nord's previously mentioned study indicates. About half of parents and youth are uninvolved in school activities. A more ominous survey released in the fall of 1995 by the National Center for Juvenile Justice demonstrates that the peak hours for juvenile crime are between 3 P.M. and 6 P.M. Are we surprised? As kids and parents drift away from the anchor of school activities, as extracurricular activities are gutted and canceled by budget cuts and the lack of involved adults, as communities become ghost towns day after day, and parents return stressed and frazzled from their jobs, kids wander freely, figuring out their own forms of entertainment. The activities might be benign like television or video games. They might be positive like homework, a job, or community service. They might be dangerous and criminal. Or maybe the kids will learn as Courtney did that doing nothing on drugs makes it "more fun."

The all-night party and the prom breakfast, marvelous events without a doubt, perpetuate an illusion that things are better than they are. Like a gorgeous shooting star that flashes across the horizon and vanishes, the events around graduation create the mirage of support and involvement when there has been little. How utterly ironic that the one mega school event is right before the kids walk out the door and scatter for good.

Graduation itself obscures the fact that adolescence is a million ends and beginnings that go unnoticed and yet are at the heart and soul of what makes every one of those graduates' pathways to this shared moment unique. History teacher David Roush, the teacher chosen by the Class of 1994 to address them, said: "Each of us must find out our own answer. No one can give it to you. You must find it yourself. Good luck on your quest."

Every one of the adolescents in this book is on his or her own quest, and I have been privileged to share their journeys. They reveal in their stories across time that the key to understanding adolescence today is to focus less on the milestone markers and more on the routes taken. As the stories I have shared so vividly illustrate, kids may get the grades, go to sports practice, have a job, and graduate, but by pathways often far too difficult and dangerous than we would wish for them. My conversations with them convinced me that we fool ourselves thinking we can look from the outside at markers and know how our kids are doing. "We draw the wrong conclusion when we say they look like they are not getting arrested or pregnant or drunk, or they seem happy," says social historian Sarah Larson, "and then conclude the tribe is fine and only those kids arrested, pregnant and drunk are in trouble." Over a decade, adolescents themselves have rewritten the map of their journey to adulthood in infinite variations and we need to study the new geography.

The lives of the kids in this book illustrate in subtle and not so subtle ways the need for adult presence to help them learn the new lessons of growing up. Kids need adults who bear witness to the details of their lives and count them as something. They require the watchful eyes and the community standards that provide greater stability. They need appreciation for who they are. It may be as simple as it is for Chris and Charles, who find succor and encouragement in their homes and in sports. It may be as complicated as it was for Ann, who developed ways to be nurtured in the homes of others when her own failed her. The kids in the book who do best are those who have a strong interactive family and a web of relationships and activities that surround them consistently.

Writing this book has always been a partnership. The kids always knew I needed them or my book could not exist, and in the end they needed me. I was an extra adult for them, or sometimes the only one, always available and there to listen. We became comfortable with each other. They were great at filling in blanks. They sometimes would call out of the blue just to talk, or stop by my house. Jonathan was a frequent visitor, and I was always happy to see him. I remember one afternoon when he came by to chat. He came in, followed me into my office, folded his lanky body into the cozy easy chair while I went and got our customary glasses of ice water. We went on, as usual, for hours. Before he left, he lifted himself up to get out of the chair then sat down again. His face was set in that thoughtful look I had often seen just before he said something of special importance. "Talking to you has helped me tremendously," he said. "Nobody has a chance to really talk to anybody about what they are thinking." He wondered if I'd ever heard Pink Floyd's *The Wall* or seen the movie. "The whole movie is the wall between all these different people. You need to break down those walls. People need to feel all right about feeling good or feeling bad. They don't need to be pretending like they are happy," Jonathan said. "People need to talk to people, and they need to talk to people that aren't trying to figure out what is wrong with them." Actually, I had seen the movie. My oldest son as a young adolescent loved it because it conveys powerfully the alienation adolescents feel.

Every adolescent needs a mentor, not just the "deprived" children of the inner city. Kids need adults to listen to them and serve as role models. Grown-ups who, by their availability and presence, convey a sense of safety and control. They need teachers like Larry Ward in journalism, Steve Lundy in eighth-grade civics, Mary Ann Brown, who took Jonathan's class to the Bahamas. They need a parent like Charles's who shares a son's new sport; parents who listen and provide support and options like Charles's, Chris's, and Jessica's, or parents like Jonathan's, who have strong family traditions even though separated. Kids need a community that rallies round as it did for Joan; or other adults, like the manager of the dry cleaners where Courtney worked, or other kids' parents, like the ones Ann found. Even Brendon's parents, with all their difficulties, gave their son rich exposure to church, Scouts, art, and family ties that may have been out of step with him but in the end saved him. What kids need from adults is not just rides, pizza, chaperones, and discipline. They need the telling of stories, the close ongoing contact so that they can learn and be accepted. If nobody is there to talk to, it is difficult to get the lessons of your own life so that you are adequately prepared to do the next thing. Without a link across generations, kids will only hear from peers. The Carnegie Council on Adolescent Development report *A Matter of Time* found: "Young adolescents do not want to be left to their own devices. In national surveys and focus groups, America's youth have given voice to serious longing. They want more regular contact with adults who care about and respect them."

We need to look at the journey as much as the destinations. It is hard and, as my work shows, it is a long-term, intense, time-consuming task. It took three years to get at the heart of who Brendon is. It took two years to discover the abuse in Courtney and Ann's house. It took a year to find out the pressures in middle school for Chris. It took five minutes for Jessica to reveal her eighth-grade social life, but much longer for her to make sense of it. It took hours and hours over months, even years, to explore any of the issues raised by the kids in this book. Their process is the story, especially since they mature day by day and are constantly able to bring new insights to their own growing up. They displayed enormous courage every time they spoke to me. They tossed out in words, like a handful of rough gemstones, the raw materials of their lives. Doing so allowed both them and me to examine the pieces, turn them over, hold them up to the light to see the surfaces from many angles. We then cracked them open, looking for the gems of insight, the essence of who each one is.

But it doesn't take writing a book to establish these relationships. I was trying to get inside the lives of many adolescents. For most people, one adult to one kid would do just fine. The issue is friendship: adolescents are interesting folks to know even when you are not getting to the core. And for every moment spent with them, they are learning, just as you will.

It is a popular notion that adolescents careen out of control, are hypnotized by peer pressure or manipulated by demons for six years or so, and then if they don't get messed up or hurt or killed, they become sensible adults. That's ridiculous. The youngsters I have spoken to are trying the best they can in the present world to do what is right for them. Many of the things that adults judge as mindless acts or immoral acts are actually based on careful consideration, even if the rationale turns out to be wrong. An eighth grader explains: "We're kind of like adults. We've learned how to run our own lives, think for ourselves, make decisions for ourselves."

These years can be characterized by the symbols of doors and passages. When the door of the middle school opens for them, a process begins where it seems they are invited into a new world (they see it that way and it becomes a self-fulfilling prophecy) and parents feel they are increasingly shut out. Other doors open and shut—the front door, the bedroom door, the car door. In a community of adolescents where for hours each day most kids inhabit empty houses, doors previously controlled by adults are in the charge of kids. The world of this book is surprisingly not one of doors slammed in the face of parents, because that particular gesture of defiance is not always necessary and in fact seldom represents the major struggle. The turbulence of adolescence today comes not so much from rebellion as from the loss of communication between adults and kids, and from the lack of a realistic, honest understanding of what the kids' world really looks like. The bottom line: we can lecture kids to our heart's content but if they don't care what we think, or there is no relationship between us that matters to them, or they think we are ignorant of the reality of their lives, they will not listen.

When I began this book, the statistics bandied about were from the Carnegie report quoted in the introduction. As I finish the book more than five years later, the latest study, *Great Transitions: Preparing Adolescents for a New Century*, released by the Carnegie Council on Adolescent Development in late 1995 in a torrent of publicity, concludes that things are absolutely no better, and in some areas are worse: "By age 17," it reports, "about a quarter of all adolescents have engaged in behaviors that are harmful or dangerous to themselves or others: getting pregnant, using drugs, taking part in antisocial activity, and failing at school. Nearly half of American adolescents are at high or moderate risk of seriously damaging their life chances. The damage may be near term and vivid, or it may be delayed by a time bomb set in youth." The statistics are staggering and the behaviors are being tracked in younger and younger children. The "Monitoring the Future" study for 1996 showed marijuana, tobacco and alcohol use "still rising" among eighth and tenth graders. The Josephson Institute of Ethics in the 1996 *Report Card on American Integrity* finds that since its original 1992 report, "the hole in the moral ozone is getting bigger still." Statistics can easily be piled up to make a case against our adolescents.

Nothing has changed, and wave after wave of children are growing up in this world of adolescence that surrounds them with risk—even the "regular" kids. They take this world for granted, as their stories have displayed. It is just the way the adolescent community lives. The developmental tasks of adolescence are consistent, but the context is remarkably changed. Denying the truth does not help. Even the very best kids are often in danger. Adolescence is rife with drugs, alcohol, cigarettes, sex, lying, violence, unstable and broken families, and so on. This is the mainstream of adolescence today.

Kids growing up know no other reality. Adults do. Maybe it is time to decide that the amount of risk to the nation's teens is unacceptable. We don't need another study four years from now to remind us again. Concerned adults always act like the solutions are too complex to imagine. That's why all the studies. Maybe some of the answers are as simple as an all-night party that has made a significant dent in teenage fatalities on graduation night, that at its core is just one way for adults to be involved in the lives of adolescents. It is an occasion where adults are part of the fun, not just monitors to keep order like they were at the mosh pit. Kids always know the difference.

Luckily, the exuberance of adolescence is not easily extinguished.

A few months after Joan and Jonathan's graduation, Chris and his best friend Brad are inside South Lakes High School picking up their football uniforms. They have been practicing for several days and Chris is elated. He is now actually on the high school field he has stared at longingly for years. The two boys lunge up the stairs from the locker room two steps at a time, carrying their South Lakes laundry bags full of pads, pants, and jerseys. Each is wearing his South Lakes High School football hat. They laugh and joke as they wander up and down the main hall in the school looking inside their gymnasium, their cafeterias, their school. The words of their head coach Bob Grauman dance in their heads: "You're not in hamsterville anymore, you're in the Big Leagues now." And they couldn't be happier.

The years between seventh and twelfth grades are so intense they are often compared to the years between birth and two; only this time the youngster is aware of the rapid changes. What do kids take away from their experiences? Jonathan, as we have come to expect, waxes philosophical. "I go through huge struggles and I come to realizations. Then I go through huge struggles and realizations and it's kind of like I'm climbing these mountains. One of my biggest fears is that there's so much behind me. I've had so many wonderful times behind me that it's kind of scary. I don't want to spend my whole life thinking about what's behind."

He tells me about a song the folk singer sings at the Old Brogue, where he and his dad have dinner once a week. It's "Souvenirs," by John Prine. He writes out the lyrics for me and circles this verse:

> *Memories that can't be bought,*
> *Can't be won at carnivals for free;*
> *Well, it took me years to get these souvenirs*
> *And I don't know how they*
> *Slipped away from me.*

Joan says, "The funny thing about high school is that when you get there it seems you'll take forever to be an upperclassman and when you reach June of your senior year you wonder where it went." Senior year starts with celebrating one foot out the door, and ends with sentimentality as the graduates hold on to each other and their youth. Chris stepping into high school and Jonathan and Joan leaving it span a rich spectrum of growth and development.

Before I finished writing in the spring of 1997, I asked each of the kids to update me on where they are now because their stories continue to evolve.

Jonathan dropped out of Virginia Tech after his first semester. He has considered many options since. "I feel like I really slipped off my track and I am trying to find the pieces to put myself back." He thinks he made the wrong decision to go to college. He has attended several sessions of Tom Brown's wilderness school hoping to feel certain about which direction to travel. He has made some tentative forays into the wilderness, taken some classes at the community college where he and Joan played Ping-Pong every day after classes, but so far he has not been able to commit himself to his next pathway. He reads, he thinks, he writes, and in time he will find his route.

Joan completed two years at Trinity College, majoring in communication and art history before having to take a year off to earn more money for tuition. She came back to Reston, attended the local community college for a year while working full time, also participating in a northern soul band, starting a 'zine, writing, and being a good friend to many people. This year she will return to Trinity and expects to pick up where she left off—being active in the environmental club, singing and playing guitar in coffeehouses, belonging to a feminist group, and writing for the school's literary magazine. She can't wait to get back to Washington, D.C., and school, where she feels so alive, energized by the richness and variety of people in the city, the rich options available to her. She thinks she wants to be a journalist writing about music of all varieties. Her relationship with her parents is in a much better place now that she has the distance to lead her own life, she says. She wants readers to know: "People change constantly and I don't regret anything that I did, I was, or who I am now. I don't want to be conceited but I am proud of myself. I've been lucky to go through a lot of things and learn from them."

Ann graduated in 1995 and moved in with her dad and her stepmother in Florida. She flourished in that environment, maintaining a B+ average in college and a busy social life. She is presently out of school, working full-time as a receptionist in a doctor's office and living with her boyfriend in a house they rent. She met him in Florida. She and Ron never made it to the senior prom; their relationship ended in her senior year although they remained friends. She says she wants readers of this book to know that "kids are very resilient. They can do just about anything they want."

Charles graduated in June 1996, and went to Rensselaer Polytechnic Institute in Troy, New York, on a lacrosse scholarship; he is working hard in his studies toward becoming an architect. It was tough acclimating to living in the North and being away from his family. Especially hard was not playing lacrosse, a sacrifice he made this first year because his studies were too demanding. During the summer, he will work at the National Traffic Safety Board in Washington, D.C., doing graphics troubleshooting for their computer system. Before leaving South Lakes, he maintained his deep involvement in sports, leadership, and school activities right through his senior year. His connection to the school was more comprehensive, and gave him more satisfaction, than that of any other kid I interviewed. He says: "I just figured it is supposed to be one of the best experiences of your life and I was going to make the best out of it."

Courtney also graduated in June 1996, and after being accepted at several schools, decided to join her sister in Florida. Both sisters clearly needed to spend some time in proximity to their dad. She ended up only staying a few weeks; Ann's boyfriend was too uptight for her. Her dad finally gave her the car he promised so long ago. She brought the car back to Reston and lived with her boyfriend for six months. She now lives back at home, attending the local community college to study business administration. Annoyed that her parents want her to pay rent, she plans to move in with her former manager at the dry cleaners, the young woman who has served as a mentor and older friend to her for so many years. Before we hung up the phone, Courtney thanked me for our conversations, saying, "It's good to talk. It always helps when someone asks about your life because it helps you to see things differently."

Brendon, sitting on the deck of his parents' new townhouse in an exclusive part of Reston, is happy his dad finally made it. He is quick to let me know, "My dad proved everybody wrong, especially me." Brendon has successfully finished his second year at Virginia Commonwealth University. He's not being an angel, but he says he's "pretty motivated" by goals he has set for himself. "I couldn't live down failure to everybody; I couldn't let that happen to myself." He's working hard to get into a prestigious specialized graphics design/business–oriented program at school. He didn't make it on his first attempt but he's determined and is motivated to keep trying—a huge change from how he was in high school. His relationship with his parents is less strained, he says; they are happy that he is doing pretty decently on the track he's on—and that he's on a "track" at all. He likes college better than high school because, "I'm in charge of everything and if I mess up, which I am not going to, my parents don't get called." He says he has not been dealing drugs; in fact, he is nursing a rash on his hands and arms from spending thirty hours a week at his dishwashing job, a position he has held since beginning school. He will go back as a prep cook, preparing things for the chefs. In response to my surprise that a big-time drug dealer has chosen this route, he tells me how he's decided to "hang in there" (school and job). "I'm on my own and making good choices for myself. I have to work; that's a reality. I have to get used to it if I have to have a job for the rest of my life." When asked if he regrets his past, he is adamant: "Everything I did, I felt I had to do; I don't regret anything. I felt I had to provide for myself and I did. Maybe it was a bit of excess, but whatever I did, I kept my act together. I managed things smartly. I gained a lot of respect in that illegal community for being a smart guy." He still grumbles but he also laughs more and it is clear he is going to be okay. He's liked our conversations because "What artists live for is to share and to communicate."

Jessica graduated and will attend the College of William and Mary. She did not achieve honor student status but did have a 3.8 or 3.9 average at graduation. She remained involved in drama all through high school, and Annie remains her dearest friend. Her romance with Jeremy broke up the spring of her junior year. She says, "I still love him and I always will." They shared a wonderful relationship with many firsts, including sex. She says she doesn't regret doing it, "but I do feel sorry that now I can never give that gift to the person I marry." She still cares about social life, but is focused on having "a life of substance." She plans to become a doctor and to work in Third World countries. Through family trips to Cancún, she developed a love for Mexico as her "second home," spending time visiting friends there, especially a special young man. She remains very close to her parents and thinks she will miss them desperately in college. She has told them they will be "shocked" to read some of the things in this book. Their relationship remains strong and loving because, she says, "No matter what happens there will always be that unconditional love in my family. No one can take it away." Her sister Kelly and her husband had a second child last year, and Kelly is going to college studying to be a nurse-midwife.

Chris has thrived in high school, with good grades, good friends, and a positive experience. This coming year he will be a senior so he is beginning to look into colleges. He's been the varsity lacrosse goalie since his sophomore year, and is hoping for a lacrosse scholarship to a top school because his grades are also good. His junior year he broke the school and the district record on saves and was also invited into the National Honor Society. Lacrosse is his passion and he plays in leagues all year round. After a year's hiatus because of an injury, he will play football again his senior year. The high school life, and especially the sports, have made these years memorable and happy. He is no longer afraid or timid about being his own person. As he prepares for his senior year, he is removing everything from his walls and repainting his room. He doesn't need to be surrounded by heroes. He is himself.

These kids have given me memories too: of days in the classroom, of rendezvous at all hours about all kinds of secrets. I have memories of walking the same trail Jonathan journeyed on his Vision Quest, sitting on top of the same mountain imagining what it was like for him. I have memories of sitting in the hospital with Joan after her suicide attempt and the exquisite joy of her triumph at graduation. In the "Hall of Fame" I have both admired the sensational graffiti and trembled thinking of Brendon and his friends there in the middle of the night. I have sat alongside Brendon in his private nook in the basement, honored to be let inside his most honest place. I shared the trauma of the lacrosse incident with Charles and his family, and sat nervously with his mom during the planned retaliation game. I have shared the excitement of the school newspaper with Ann, spent time with her and Ron, and over many cups of coffee heard the sad story of her struggle with her home life. My ears have been talked off by the exuberant chatter of Jessica and Courtney, who spared no detail in describing every nanosecond of their adventures and then how they dealt with them. I've also had the privilege of hearing their serious insights as they come to terms and make decisions about their lives. I have been to sports and arcades with Chris, who has been my guide into all the codes of boys and their passions, communicating to me less in words than actions in his well-ordered, well-disciplined, delightful life. These memories and more are engraved in my mind forever. I wonder and worry and rejoice with these kids right along with my own.

It is hard for me to let go. I feel excitement that this book will get their stories out, that I can illuminate their world previously hidden in the shadows of the adolescent community, but sadness that minute by minute my involvement is coming to a close.

After years out there among them, particularly as I write this book from my home office, alone with their voices and their lives, I miss being in school, out and about talking to the kids. I love it when I run into an adolescent I know and we stop and talk. I still make dates to keep in touch with the kids in my book when they are around. My world is amplified and made more vital by incorporating adolescents into it. When I go to school events with my youngest son, I look around and see hundreds of youngsters making up the kaleidoscope of adolescence and I feel a sadness that I don't know them and their stories. When I run in the morning past the school buses, I peer inside and wonder. The difference is that I have experienced the tremendous vitality beyond the pale, a rich and vibrant tapestry of lives that hold promise for our nation's future. I don't know the kids but they no longer seem distant and foreign.

We have to reconnect the adolescent community to ours. It is not so hard. We just need to reach out and embrace them and take the time to get to know them—one by one, as individuals, not a tribe.

# POSTSCRIPT

*E*ven when the last words of a book are written, the book is far from finished. There are edits, layout tasks, and production requirements that take months. So in early 1997, I had to tell myself it was time to put the final touches on my manuscript and let it go to the next step. The decision was not an easy one. Because the lives of the kids were always moving, I found it difficult to resist the urge to add one more update, to capture one more moment of significance in their evolution. With this group of youngsters, I will never be able to mindlessly carry on a conversation. Their words have such significance to me, I feel naked without a tape recorder; it is impossible for me to listen without wanting to quote them to somebody.

So it becomes even more difficult for me to tell you that since that time when I thought my work was done, the unthinkable happened. Jonathan committed suicide. There is no way to make this less than the shockingly brutal, heartbreaking reality that it is.

The Jonathan I knew had been devoured by schizophrenia that had begun that first semester in college. The disease characteristically strikes in late adolescence, and in this case, month by month I helplessly watched the gentle, sensitive, and wise soul that is captured in these pages vanish, trapped in a tormented mind. At first it hadn't been clear what was wrong, the roots of his indecision and unhappiness at college. But over time, the demons overtook him and crushed his spirit, filling his conversations with paranoid thoughts and confused logic. Of course, he was helped. With medical attention and medication, for a time he seemed improved. He even went back to the local community college in the fall of 1996 and spoke to me with measured optimism about getting back on track again in his life. In October we had gone rowing on Lake Anne, round and round the Reston landmark for hours, talking and greeting people who lived in homes along the shoreline. Jonathan was warm and friendly, chatty like I remembered him before the illness silenced and terrified him for so many months. We had a good time and promised each other we'd get together soon.

Time passed and we talked some on the phone. But schizophrenia is often a daunting disease, hard to contain, subject to relapses. And one day I got the heart-stopping call. Jonathan was dead.

On March 4, 1997, Jonathan Tompkins returned to the wilderness he so loved, parked his Volkswagen in the parking lot, and hiked to a place that felt right. We don't know exactly what happened next, what he was thinking, but he placed the butt of his hunting rifle into the ground, leaned over and shot himself in the heart. He died instantly. His mother cried that she could not imagine a life without her son in it.

I visited his home as soon as I heard. I slipped away from the people calling and went upstairs to his room. His bed was neatly made, his kindergarten mobile swung in a breeze, his drums were on the floor, and papers were as he left them. In the bathroom, his toothbrush and razor were on the sink. I went downstairs, and only his mom and I remained. We shared a cup of tea in the kitchen in mugs she and Jonathan had bought less than a month before on a cross-country ski trip they took together.

How fleeting and fragile is life. The images in this book are static and unchanging; seven of the eight characters have moved on and are doing fine. But for all of them it has been to some degree that long, dark, and winding tunnel eluded to at the beginning of the book. There is so little time for adults to know and embrace the younger generation, to guide them with understanding and to share the moments of their lives. This is not a Hallmark advertisement but a tough reality. The moments of adolescence are as precious as every other moment in the life of a child. We should savor them. If

*Jonathan's life and death have a message, it is that we never know the future. His life graced these pages and all are fortunate to have the opportunity to be touched by him. I know I have.*

*In memory of*
*Caleb Purdy Topping*
*December 24, 1975–March 4, 1997*

# ACKNOWLEDGMENTS

*A Tribe Apart*, which took over six years from research to publication, has gathered a virtual troop of supporters. It would be impossible for me to name every person who stimulated a new idea, shaped my thinking, or pointed me to a new source, but I am indebted to each encounter that added to the texture of the work. I depended on the people listed here in an ongoing way.

When I arrived in the lives of R. Edgar Thacker, principal of Langston Hughes Middle School, and Diana Schmelzer, principal of South Lakes High School, in early 1992, it was the worst of times for Fairfax County schools. Budget cuts had weakened morale and they faced many new challenges— yet they invited me inside their schools with warmth and a belief in what I was doing, and took time out of their exhausting schedules to listen and make suggestions. No matter what was going on, they always took time to talk to me. When I had trouble cutting through the county education bureaucracy, Diana hand-carried my request to Robert Spillane, the Superintendent of Schools, who embraced my quest and allowed the doors of the schools to open freely to me. At Forest Edge Elementary School, Principal Frank Bensinger's enthusiasm and openness illuminated the transition from sixth to seventh grades. These four educators took a chance with me because they care about kids, and they had a hunch my work could make a difference. I am grateful for their support.

Many teachers, counselors, and administrators at South Lakes and Hughes gave generously of their time to talk to me, answer my questions, and allow me to sit in their classes. Thanks to: Mary Ann Brown, Diane Bruce, Nancy Burke, John Butterfield, Marianne Cordyack, Jeff Davis, Joyce Dotterweich, Ellen Fay, Bob Grauman, Kent Harris, Linda Hayward, Peggy Hoover, Jim Hoy, Theresa Larsen, Kay Lawson, Steve and Mary Lundy, Mary Francis Musgrave, Beverly Nance, Barb Roberts, Ernie Sepulski, Judy Skirbunt, Emmanuel Slade, Patty Warstler, and Cynthia Yobs.

Sally Comerford and Larry Ward, of the South Lakes English department, deserve special accolades. Teachers of the finest caliber, they not only headed the two classes I attended the most (creative writing and the school newspaper, respectively), but they also served as sounding boards for my observations and ideas, provided a place for me to go to decompress, and for the duration of the project have always been there for me. More than sources, they have become friends, and I want to single them out for their contribution to the young lives they touch and for their unflagging commitment to my work.

Thanks also go to a number of other adults whose insights were valuable: Tom Ahart, Margaret Boyd, Susan Gerstein, Tom Gatewood, John Hawley, Doug and Joey Johnson, Robert Simon, and David and Olivia Toatley.

The greatest contribution to this work is from the kids themselves, who took time out of their lives to get this grownup on track about what it is truly like to be an adolescent these days. To them I owe my most profound thanks. In some ways, every adolescent I came in contact with added something to my understanding. I couldn't begin to name all the kids I spoke to over the years, but once I tuned into them, they all were my teachers. Special thanks to the following: Anna Adams, Britt Ahart, Joeller Bartoe, Jonathan Bates, Jessica Bates, Mike Beale, Katy Beale, Brad Bowden, Marc Brewer, Melissa Brewer, Alli Bruce, Nakesa Burke, Amber Busch, Pam Chambliss, Cheric Chambliss, Bobby Chambliss, Sami Cuccini, Ian Dapot, Patricia Droguett, Steven Edge, Joseph Facen, Brian Falls, Jeff Faucheux, Jeanne Faucheux, Hassan Freeman, Adam Gerstein, Tepper Gill, Alfred Head, Ryan Hoedt, Nick Jester, Charmaine Johnson, Jennifer Johnson, Nate Keysor, Amoz Leeb, Laurie Marhoffer, Carolene Mayers, Amy McClung, Melanie Myers, Maritza Ortiz, Brendon O'Fallon, Derrick Paige, Brendon Roy, Alyssa Rubenstein, Mike Sass, Jaime Schmidt, Nicole Schmidt, Andrew Schwab, Meg Searing, Fred Shank, Anika Smith, Jay Smith, Rebecca Stauber, Barika Toatley, Coulter Toatley, Caleb Topping, Jenny Weinberg, and Leigh Wells.

And for the eight of you whose lives comprise this book, and to your parents who allowed you to talk to me, you are precious to me. You are brave, articulate representatives of your generation. Your individual lives blast apart all stereotypes of teens, making you trailblazers. You *are* the book. I was merely the scribe.

The book would not have happened at all had it not been for my agent and friend Anne Edelstein, who patiently waited by my side for the book in me to emerge, never once doubting me and always urging me on. My editor at Ballantine, Joanne Wyckoff, who years ago called me out of the blue because of an article of mine she read, has been everything I always imagined a fine editor to be. Tough and demanding the best of me, she has honed my creativity and has made me a better writer. These two are my dream team, bringing intelligence, literary flair, sensitivity, and sharp, critical eyes to my work. Janet Fletcher did an exquisite job of copyediting. Irina Reyn, Joanne's assistant, has been wonderful at shepherding the manuscript through the ranks at Ballantine.

Marcia Thurmond, transcriber extraordinaire, brought her skills as mother and professional to my interview tapes. Her ability to understand the recordings and to always spend some time chatting about them penetrated the loneliness I sometimes felt with all my information.

Sarah Larson, another carpooling mom I met at lacrosse practice two years ago, dropped into my life like an angel. Not only did she do an amazing job helping me round up volunteer parents for the concession stand at games, she also became an outstanding editor and critic for the first draft of my book. Her incisive mind, pointed questions, abilities to make connections to issues, and her sensitivity regarding her own adolescent children made my second draft soar. She gave me exactly the challenges and discussions I needed to help clarify my own thinking. She made revising fun. Our children no longer play lacrosse together, but she and I remain fast friends.

A first book is always the culmination of a dream and many people who influence it. My mentors over the years bolstered my confidence as I forged ahead, building the career I wanted for myself. The years I worked with Joel Swerdlow were invaluable in teaching the craft of writing books. The gentle tenacity of Elliot Liebow, his humanity and heart, which he never sacrificed in his work, was inspiration for the author I wanted to be. Liebow's classic, *Tally's Corner*, provided the model for how a simple location and a handful of human beings could shed light on a complex problem. I am grateful to George Beschner, formerly of the National Institutes of Mental Health, for giving me the opportunity to put Liebow's model to the test when he hired me to do my first ethnographic study of the lifestyles of streetkids on Larkin Street in San Francisco and in Times Square, New York. Michael Clatts, who guided me through the streets, tunnels, and the shadows of New York where streetkids exist, opened new worlds for me that changed my life forever. Rich Simon, my editor at *Family Therapy Networker*, provided me the opportunity to explore many of my ideas on adolescence in articles for his magazine and always challenges my thinking. Mary Wylie, senior editor at *Networker*, has graced my writing at the magazine with her skillful pen, and also did me the favor of a penetrating critique of my first draft. Wray Herbert gave me my first big break when he was editor at *Psychology Today*, and as friend and mentor has always encouraged me to write with the passion I feel. A devoted father and a topnotch writer himself, he has been involved for years in the issues and the unfolding of my book. Mike Arons instilled in me the wisdom and self-knowledge to make the quest.

Writing a book is a lonely endeavor. I am fortunate to have a most wonderful circle of friends who accompanied me on this creative journey, surrounding me with their love and support: Dacy Bellingham, who sent me to her kitchen to work when my house got too crazy and supplied me with Wheat Thins galore, and who shared her knowledge of grammar and punctuation and cried tears of joy when I succeeded; Sharon Canner, my longtime running partner, confidant, and cheerleader, who for thousands of miles on pathways over the years has nudged me to be the professional I always wanted to be; Bonnie Egertson, who shares my passion for books, who paid me the honor of enthusiastically reading my book not once but twice, and who, with her husband, Joel, listened for years to my expostulations on adolescents, adding to my thinking with their responses; Jim Levine, my cousin, who has given me not only invaluable advice on this project but the emotional support only another writer can provide. Finally, Ralph and Gwen Bates, who are extended family, kin of the heart, who have traveled with me through all of life's passages. Their confidence and moral support, and hugs and conversation (not to mention great meals), are always treasured.

To my parents, the late Priscilla and Lawrence LeKashman, a debt of gratitude for always making sure I had the books I loved to read, and encouraging my passion for the written word. They would be so proud.

My father-in-law, the late Bernard Hersch, deserves special recognition. A true believer in my dream of becoming an author, it was his pleasure to make it financially possible for me to build a writing career in the direction I wanted without fear of fiscal limitations in the shortrun. I'm sorry he is not here to see the fruition of his generosity.

My children—all three young men now—are the true inspiration of this book. Michael, thanks for telling me the Real Truth about your adolescence as I began this book and we were both old enough for me to hear it. You taught me how little we know when our kids go out into the world. The week we spent at the farm together, me writing my proposal, you writing your music, was a testament to the togetherness and individualization we dream of for our children. Jamie, your willingness to let your mom actually come to class with you during your senior year in high school, and inviting your friends to help guide my research, was above and beyond the call of duty. You made me feel less alone those first weeks in school. And Eric, poor Eric, you got the worst and the best of it—your mom going along for the whole ride, sixth through twelfth grade with you. You are such an incredibly good sport. It has been my privilege and delight to be so involved in your world, but I also apologize for any infringement on your space. All three boys taught me how precious and interesting the adolescent years are and how quickly they pass. The vast differences between the world of Michael's adolescence in the eighties and Eric's in the nineties are the Ground Zero for *A Tribe Apart*.

To Jay, my husband, whose love, belief in me, gentle nudges when I slow down, my calming influence when I flare up, whose knowledge of how I work and superb editorial advice help me flourish. The years on this first book showed your mettle as much as any in our marriage. You weathered my storms and shared my excitement. You always listened and tried to help. You knew when it was time for us to go to the farm, whose serenity and space stoke my creativity, you never wavered in your belief that I would succeed when I doubted myself, and you always encouraged me to speak with my own voice. Our synergy makes me better at all I do.

# INDEX

A former contributing editor to *Psychology Today*, Patricia Hersch has been published in *The Washington Post, McCall's, Family Therapy Networker, The Baltimore Sun, New Age Journal,* and other newspapers and magazines. She was the editor of the "Women in Development" newsletter for the United Nations and conducted an ethnographic study of homeless adolescents in San Francisco and New York for the National Institute of Drug Abuse and Georgetown University Child Development Center. Ms. Hersch lives in Reston, Virginia, with her husband and has three sons.